Destination Australia

Professor Eric Richards is a member of
the Department of History at Flinders
University in Adelaide. He publishes widely
on British history, most recently *Debating the
Highland Clearances* (2007). He is author and
editor of a range of books on migration
history, notably his very broad survey
*Britannia's Children: Emigration from England,
Scotland, Wales and Ireland since 1600* (2004).

ERIC RICHARDS

Destination
Australia

MIGRATION TO AUSTRALIA SINCE 1901

To the Neurology Department and the
Comprehensive Epilepsy Program of the
Austin Hospital, Heidelberg, Melbourne

A UNSW Press book
© Eric Richards 2008
First published 2008

Simultaneously published in

Australia and New Zealand and their dependent
territories, Papua New Guinea and Fiji by

University of New South Wales Press Ltd
University of New South Wales
Sydney NSW 2052
AUSTRALIA
www.unswpress.com.au

National Library of Australia
Cataloguing-in-Publication entry

Author: Richards, Eric, 1940–
Title: Destination Australia: migration to Australia
    since 1901/Eric Richards.
ISBN: 978 1 921410 57 4 (pbk.)
Subjects: Immigrants – Australia – History.
    Multiculturalism – Australia – History.
    Australia – Emigration and immigration
    – History.
Dewey Number: 994.0086912

Design Di Quick
Printer Ligare
Text paper 70gsm Enso
Coverboard 265gsm Candesce

The rest of the world by

Manchester University Press
Oxford Road
Manchester M13 9NR
UNITED KINGDOM
www.manchesteruniversitypress.co.uk

and Room 400, 175 Fifth Avenue
New York, NY 10010, USA

Distributed in the United States exclusively by Palgrave
Macmillan, 175 Fifth Avenue
New York, NY 10010, USA

Distributed in Canada exclusively by
UBC Press, University of British Columbia
2029 West Mall, Vancouver, BC
V6T 1Z2 Canada

British Library Cataloguing-in-Publication Data
A catalogue record for this book is available from
the British Library

Library of Congress Cataloguing-in-Publication Data
applied for

ISBN 978 0 7190 8037 1   paperback

Contents

Preface   ix

1   The new century: 1900 and 2000   1

2   The slow awakening: 1900–14   28

3   Migrants and the Great War: 1914–18   58

4   White British Australia resuscitated: the 1920s   80

5   Malaise, recrimination and demographic   113
    pessimism: the 1930s

6   Race, refugees, war and the future: 1939–45   141

7   Arthur Calwell and the new Australia: 1945–51   166

8   The great diversification: the 1950s and 1960s   204

9   White Australia dismantled: the 1970s   244

10   The end of the heroic days: the 1980s   269

11   Whither immigrant Australia?   297

12   The new century   321

13   Retrospect   350

     Statistics   385

     Notes   392

     Select bibliography   420

     Index   424

Preface

I first arrived in Australia in 1963 at an interesting historical moment. It was the final decade of the great British peopling of this continent which had begun with convicts in 1788. Coming from North Wales and Shropshire by way of Nottingham, I was one of the assisted immigrants (the 'ten pound Poms'); many, like me, expected to stay for a few years before returning to Britain. Many of us did, but then became re-returners. I settled in Adelaide, thereafter moving back and forth to the United Kingdom much more frequently than I had ever expected.

'Settler' was the old word for the Australian immigrant, but it became anachronistic in a society which is one of the most mobile in the world. Now the movement of people into and out of Australia, and also within the country, is so vigorous that it is extremely difficult to keep track of their movements. Even counting the migrants is now more complicated than ever; all migration statistics are subject to errors and controversy which bedevil the entire story. My own story is mundane compared with so many others contained in the oscillating narrative of Australian immigration of the 20th century. British immigrants were always the most numerous of the people coming to

Australia, and they were far from homogeneous and uninteresting. But the non-British migrants were often more colourful, literally and metaphorically, and this is a central theme in this account.

This effort to tell the story of modern Australian immigration has taken too long to write. It began at the suggestion of Dr John Nieuwenhuysen on behalf of the old Bureau of Immigration, Multicultural and Population Research (itself a creature of its times, and abolished in August 1996, a decisive action of the new Howard government). Between its conception and its delivery the book has turned into a different beast. The original idea was a short synoptic survey of 20th century Australian immigration to accompany a parallel volume of illustrations.[1] As it turned out I was incapable of forcing the story into such a jacket; I became entangled with all the interwoven issues that make the subject so absorbing and controversial.

Immigration has been the great conductor of change, tension and growth in the modern Australian experience; it has been critical to its political maturity, to its demography, its economic development, its social cohesion and its relations with the rest of the world, and also to its very self-understanding and identity.

Imposing a single narrative and structure upon this story is a challenge, partly because it comprises millions of different migrant trajectories, and partly because its impact on Australia has always been exceedingly difficult to assay and reduce to a single verdict about the consequences of immigration. Nevertheless this account gives centre stage to two seismic changes which worked as social revolutions in the otherwise relative calm of modern Australian history. In brief, the story begins with the reaffirmation and prolongation of White British Australia to about 1947; this was the continuing commitment to British exclusivity inherited from the 19th century, which had made Australia more British, and indeed whiter, than Britain itself. This was the transplanted world of the British Isles set down in the South Pacific and mirrored in New Zealand too.

The first great shift in the foundations of Australia was its Europeanisation, accomplished between 1947 and 1972. This shift entailed the end of the exclusive dependence on immigrants from the British Isles, and the quite sudden recruitment of very large numbers of non-British migrants from Europe. It altered the composition and culture, if not the complexion, of the Australian population in the third quarter of the 20th century. But Australia remained defiantly white, and this commitment continued to define Australia's identity beyond its shores late into the 20th century.

The third phase of the story followed the dissolution of White Australia and the marked differentiation in the origins of its migrants after 1975. In this phase Australian immigration became more complicated and variegated, more divisive in its effects, generating problems of assimilation, population growth and political cohesion. Australia became more interesting and also more similar to other industrialised countries of the West.

These transitions, as we shall see, possessed large implications for questions such as Australia's relationship with Britain, its attitudes to race and alien cultures and religions, the size and composition of its population, its connections with its region and the rest of the world, as well as its obligations to the international community.

Behind these transitions, Australia has remained one the greatest immigrant nations. Its immigrants have been conduits for changing currents from the rest of the world including war, genocide, famine and population displacement; their individual stories brought vibrations of these distant worlds directly into an otherwise insulated Australia. What Australia made of them and their alien baggage is a central issue in the story, as also is the fate of the immigrants themselves.

~ ~ ~

My debts have accumulated, not least to those who originally commissioned this account, and I am grateful for their forbearance. I owe intellectual thanks to other scholars in the field of 20th century Australian immigration studies upon whose work I have drawn copiously: notably Reg Appleyard, Sean Brawley, Stephen Castles, Jim Hammerton, Graeme Hugo, James Jupp, John Lack, Michele Langfield, David Pope, Michael Roe, Geoffrey Sherington and Gwenda Tavan. I have benefited from the special stimulation of participants in the series of seminars held since 1990 at the History Program of the Research School of Social Sciences in the Australian National University under the rubric of 'Visible Immigrants'. David Hilliard has been the source of much material on ethnic elements and religion too. I have received a great deal of expert research assistance from Dr Robert Fitzsimons. Over many years I have received help from many people including Karen Agutter, Richard De Angelis, Michael Ekin Smyth, Christine Finnimore of the Migration Museum in Adelaide, Gerald Fischer, Robin Haines, Ann Herraman, Barry Higman, Bob Holton, James Jupp, Margrette Kleinig, Ngaire Naffine, Erik Olssen, Sue Richardson, Ralph Shlomowitz and Kate Walsh, and earlier from Marie Boland and Robert Thornton. I have benefited greatly from visiting positions at the Australian National University in the 1990s, at the Menzies Australian Studies Centre in King's College, University of London, at Cardiff University, at Case Western Reserve University in Ohio, and at the University of Edinburgh. I am grateful to archivists who look after the records of Australian migrants in many repositories in Australia and in the British Isles. And I am always grateful to Flinders University Library, which has provided very good services over many years. I remain responsible for all surviving error. I should also mention that the title of this volume is an echo of a similar study by Maldwyn A Jones, *Destination America* (1976).

~~~

As this book was being finished, I found myself in a place which seemed to encapsulate some of the essence of modern Australia and also gave me a personal measure of the impact of its immigration experience over the past half century. In November 2007 my daughter was treated for her long-time epilepsy at the Department of Neurology and the Epilepsy Centre at the Austin Hospital in Melbourne. Her medical team was led by a distinguished epileptologist of evidently middle European roots, whose expertise was recognised as a Fellow of the Royal Society. Her surgical team was led by a renowned neurosurgeon whose father was a well-known Hungarian immigrant who had escaped fascism in 1939. Before her operations, of extreme audacity and delicacy, my daughter was tended in the hospital by nurses, male and female, 24 hours a day. Some were from the Pacific Islands (one of whom might have been a rugby player); others were Greek in origin; one was clearly Japanese, another Chinese from Hong Kong; one was an Indonesian Muslim in traditional dress. There was a homesick nurse from Lusaka in Zambia, another from Nigeria; they were supported by a technician from Sheffield and a legion of doctors from various parts of Asia. The medical teams were orchestrated by a Highland Scot and a person of rather obvious Irish connections. And my middle daughter came from Ireland to help out and my youngest from New Zealand.

All this astonishing and professional attention was lavished on my eldest daughter, a true hero. She had almost been prevented entry into Australia when her family re-migrated to Adelaide in 1971 – at that time Australia was resistant not only to non-whites but also to people with certain medical conditions (and especially epilepsy). She was able to overcome the hurdles of the Immigration Department because she had actually been born in Adelaide five years before, the child of 'ten pound Poms' who were now re-returning to Australia. Her fellow patients in the Austin Hospital included some 'old Australians' from country towns, a Maori New Zealand immigrant with a large family and a German lady who had arrived in 1949, as well as an Italian couple from two different waves of migration.

And thus the Austin Hospital in November 2007 had assembled a full cast of multicultural modern Australia, a remarkable interacting convergence of the elements of the new Australia, here vividly working to a better future. It was also a scene which was, in virtually every respect, totally inconceivable in 1901 and a demonstration of the change that had been wrought upon this continent during the intervening century, the subject of this book.

1 The new century: 1900 and 2000

Old migrant Australia

Modern Australia was effectively possessed by people who origi-
nated on the other side of the planet. It is a story of intercontinental
expropriation at the far end of the earth. And the story began,
infamously, in 1788, with outcasts from the British penal system.
The convicts, together with the free British emigrants who followed them, gave Australia a distinctive complexion. It was a grand
exercise in very long-distance white colonisation. This fact alone
greatly affected the way in which Australia was perceived by the
outside world, then and since.

Until 1901 Australia remained a loose collection of British colonies, robustly independent of each other, yet far from secure in
their separation. They were still disconnected in vital ways – their
trains ran on different and incompatible gauges; they enacted different law systems; they pursued rival and opposite trade policies;
and (apart from the unifying force of cricket) they adhered passionately to different sporting codes. The colonies competed with

each other, even for their immigrants. But, for all that, they were linked by their common and resolutely British origins, and by their unquestioned loyalty to the Empire and to the 'British Race'. This was a term employed without embarrassment throughout the colonies. Australia, after all, lived under the protection of the British flag and the British navy, though the last British soldier had left as long ago as 1870. In 1900 British coins and banknotes were still in circulation in the Australian colonies.

At the opening of the new century the Australian colonies galvanised themselves into a federation, a new nation on the outer edge of the Western world. It was now a united continent, jubilant in its independent maturity. Nevertheless, Australia remained in a close clinch with Britain, its motherland. In 1900 virtually all its immigrant people had come from Britain and Ireland, apart from small residual minorities of Germans, Chinese and Pacific Islanders.[1] Australia, in reality, was more homogenous than the homeland. In recent decades Britain had received great numbers of people from Europe especially. It was a polyglot population, a country of immigrants and emigrants, as it had been since 1600.[2] By contrast, very few migrants of any sort had entered Australia during the previous dozen years. And so an increasing proportion of Australia's small population (less than 4 million in 1900) was home grown. They were now mainly second- or third-generation products of earlier migrants from the British Isles, during more expansive earlier decades.

The 1850s stood out as the great years of immigration when the high costs of the Australian passage and the old convict taint were counteracted by the greedy lure of gold. Tens of thousands of British immigrants (and many other nationals too) paid their own passage during the gold rushes. This anarchy of immigration reigned for a decade. But soon the rushes subsided and the colonies generally reverted to their intermittent heavy subsidisation of immigrants. They were essentially white and British, and this was by design. But by 1900 any first-generation immigrants from 'the old country', from 'Home', were getting older and fewer. They were not being replenished. The Australian economy was flat and depressed during most of the 1890s, a decade in which immigrants were generally unwelcome.

None of this augured well for the new century. Nevertheless, British immigrants, old and new, maintained the pattern of migration established from the start of the Victorian Age. Some of the realities of immigrant Australia are captured in individual lives.

Late Victorian migrants

William Clayton was a survivor from the first age of Australian mass immigration – the age of sail. Born in Manchester in 1833, before the reign of Victoria and just after the first Reform Bill, Clayton was the son of a Catholic hand-sawyer from Yorkshire (possibly Irish in origin) and a Protestant mother. These were working people of the early Industrial Revolution, already mobile and highly urbanised. William began work at 7 years of age as an errand boy to a fishmonger at one shilling a week together with his dinners. He then assisted a pastry cook before employment in a dye works at two shillings a week. His father died when he was eleven and William became apprenticed, beginning at 2s 6d for a 12-hour day, 6 days a week and rising to 25 shillings as a skilled tradesman at 21 years of age. He remembered a strike in 1847 and the appearance of Chartists in Manchester in the same decade. In 1854 he married Mary, 20 years of age, employed as a cotton-winder in a Manchester factory. The cotton trade was disrupted in the Crimean War, and thus the newlyweds obtained an assisted passage to Melbourne. Somehow they missed the ship but nevertheless, in a terrible hurry, gained berths on another, the *Grand Trianon* heading for Port Adelaide, which they reached in less than 100 days. Mrs Clayton gave birth to twins during the voyage. Clayton embarked with only an Irish halfpenny, but earned £2 as a steward during the voyage. In the great age of migration, mid-century, massive sailing ships, some crowded with more than 900 immigrants, poured into the Australian ports.

Clayton led a peripatetic life as a sawyer in the colony, re-currently unemployed, but saved enough to return with his family (now four children) to England in 1864. This was an unfortunate homecoming: Clayton could not find work in his old trade as a casemaker. At a great family reunion at Selby in Yorkshire, relations fell apart and all was soured, apparently because of a dispute over a parrot he brought from Australia. In reaction the Claytons thought to return to Australia and, astonishingly, the Emigration Commissioners sanctioned their second assisted passages in 1866 – with the severe proviso that it could never be repeated. Back in South Australia, Clayton was again sawyering at Victoria Creek (Williamstown), sometimes working on his own account but still tramping for employment, at one time working for the poet Adam Lindsay Gordon. Clayton never accumulated much savings, but penned a remarkable semi-literate memoir and lived on for another 21 years. He died of chronic bronchitis at the age of 100, still renowned for his recollections of the Chartist riots.[3]

Clayton outlasted Queen Victoria and lived through the first 30 years of the new Federation. He was the product of industrial England, whose needs interlocked with the Australian colonies which grew so rapidly that they used public revenues to subsidise the importation of labour from across the globe. A system of recruitment had been devised in the early 1830s to appeal to prospective working migrants such as the Claytons. It was a rough and ready scheme that attracted many mobile elements in the home population. The population at large generally resisted these Antipodean blandishments – and Australia therefore recruited in Ireland and parts of Scotland to a disproportionate degree. It was often a random process, well symbolised in Clayton's own career – he was hardly tailor-made for Australian needs yet he was twice recruited, and on arrival was temporarily surplus to labour requirements in Adelaide. Yet he and his family persevered, and they were part of the British demographic exchange which extended through the coming century. Clayton and his sort were the bone and sinew of Australia's first century. His ostensibly disorderly migrations were borne along by the colonial urge to determine the composition of its population.

But at the end of the old century, in the 1890s, Australia had exhausted its appetite for immigrants. The economy was now in the doldrums and labour in excess supply. Virtually the only exception was the demand for female domestic servants, which was never satisfied, even in depressed times. In 1898 the SS *Cornwall* headed for Western Australia with a small party of young women, specially recruited for service in the colony. The *Cornwall* was half empty and therefore unusually comfortable, the recruits all nominated immigrants, paid for by the colonial government to be employed on arrival as domestic workers. Of the 46 women, 10 were from Ireland, which matched their usual prevalence among assisted immigrants to Australia.

The surgeon's diary of the *Cornwall*'s voyage describes the examination of the women before departure. The procedures had changed little since mid-century. Since the inception of the assistance schemes 70 years before, the migrants were, in the words of the ship's surgeon, 'subjected to a more or less close scrutiny'. Only two were rejected. These young women were cheerful and in good health, in the charge of a matron who had already made the journey six times. During the voyage, as always, many of the passengers were seasick and several became very ill, and even the surgeon succumbed at one point. Brandy was dispensed to the sick. One woman became seriously melancholic, but they all mustered well. They were referred to as 'emigrants', a mildly derogatory term by which contemporaries distinguished them from private self-funding 'settlers'. Nevertheless the 'emigrants' were encouraged to participate in the ship's concert. Their health and well-being were closely monitored, and when nits were discovered in the women's hair it was severely cut and treated with perchloride of mercury. They were given another close inspection at Fremantle and on their arrival were properly welcomed to Australia by the Immigration Officer.

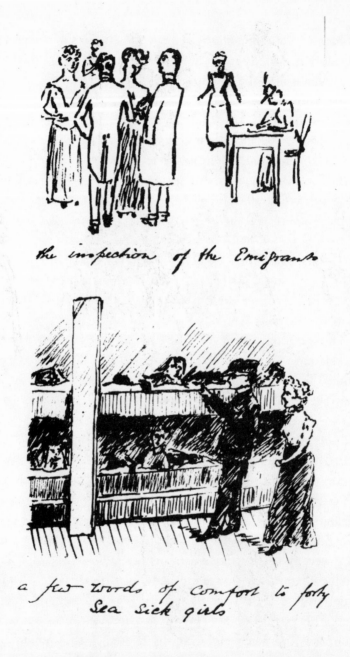

the inspection of the Emigrants

*a few words of comfort to forty
Sea sick girls*

The end of the Victorian Age: assisted female immigrants from Britain aboard the SS *Cornwall*, 1898; inspected, paraded and comforted, *MS2327 Sketched by Douglas Darbyshire, surgeon-in-charge. National Library of Australia.*

they filed past in answer to their names

At this point some of the emigrants burst into tears because they were sorry to leave the ship, and the captain was also in tears at the quayside: 'Most of the girls wept, the Irish contingent howled'. The women were accommodated at the immigration depot until they found a job or a husband.[4]

The voyage of the *Cornwall* was part of a system of immigration, mainly in abeyance at the end of the century, which firmly controlled the flow of working people into Australia. The colonies selected assisted immigrants and determined who should come. Distance and subsidisation of passages gave Australia an almost unique power to regulate its immigrant intake and this made it distinctive among the immigrant-seeking countries in both the old and the new centuries.

Australian immigration had been devised to connect the needs of the colonies with availability of selected mobile people from the homeland. British immigrants came from the most industrialised nation and were often highly urbanised folk, though many of the Irish migrants from a profoundly rural society were better equipped to fit colonial requirements. By the 1890s the flow of people from the British Isles to Australia was reduced to a trickle, and in some years the net flow was actually reversed.

1900 and 2000

AD Hope, one of Australia's most forthright and acerbic poets, famously described the southern continent as populated by 'second-hand Europeans' who 'pullulate timidly on the edge of alien shores'. In 1900 Australia was not pullulating but sleeping. Eventually it awoke in fright about its future. This became a recurrent anxiety over the entire 20th century.

Yet the achievement of colonisation was striking, both in the hugely expanded productivity of the land and in the growth of metropolitan cities. A vital new European society had been created at a vast distance from its source. As a social anthropologist has remarked, 'Australia is by far the driest, smallest, flattest, most infertile, climatically most unpredictable, and biologically most impoverished continent'. It was also the last to be occupied by Europeans; its Aboriginal populations had been effectively disconnected from the rest of the world for at least 40 000 years. In 1788 there was a population of perhaps 300 000 Aborigines, which fell to about 60 000 by the early 20th century. The British, with their imported technology, their diseases, their new crops and domesticated and feral animals, pushed the indigenous peoples out to the most marginal lands. The extent of violence in this great displacement is still debated, but the last massacre was in 1929 in Alice Springs, when 31 Aborigines died. By then the British takeover was virtually complete and Australia had long been Europeanised.[5]

In 1900 Australia was an idiosyncratic version of Britain in the Antipodes; most of its institutions were re-creations of those of Britain, including its laws, its parliamentary system, its language, its food, its education and its churches. There were interesting local variations, in accent, sport, manners, living standards, architecture, but there was no masking Australia's highly specific and exclusively British origins. Australia was overwhelmingly British and Irish in composition and was about to become a federated nation across its wide and mainly arid continent. The new Australian democracy was explicitly, frankly and indeed self-righteously committed to the concept of 'White Australia' which, for foreign observers, became its single most identifying trait during most of the following century.

The timid pullulation of the British in Australia had achieved, in 1900, a total population of 3.7 million. A century later, in 2001, the population was approaching 20 million, of whom Aborigines constituted perhaps 400 000 (depending on definition). Since 1945 Australia, in proportional terms, has ranked at the top of the league table of immigrant-receiving countries. But this was achieved only by a radical augmentation of its demographic sources from continental Europe. By 2000 Australia had become emphatically less British in orientation, though it had remained resolutely 'White' until the 1970s. In the final quarter of the 20th century the White British monopoly of immigration changed significantly and immigrants became much more variegated in origin. By 1980 Australia's immigration policies were avowedly non-racial and non-discriminatory. Across the 20th century immigration was a great variable element in the Australian experience. Like the climate, immigration was subject to deluge and drought; it was never the orderly augmentation of the population planned by the governments of the day, it rarely flowed consistently with demographers' predictions, and the immigration question always threatened to erupt into political turmoil.

The years between 1900 and 2000 were, therefore, the second century of mainly European occupation of the continent. In the changes wrought between those benchmark years, immigration was a central force, most of all in the evolution of the new post-British Australia which is at the core of this story.

This book chronicles the way in which this small distant nation planned its incoming population and coped with the anxieties that attended its fluctuating need for immigrants. Australia has a selective historical consciousness: it forgets that migration has been a universal factor in the life of almost all modern communities. It is strangely introverted about its intimate connection with the currents of the outside world that have shaped its own immigrations.

Australia in 1900

The population first passed 3 million in 1889, but during the following decade Australia was unable to attract enough immigrants to compensate for those departing. The birth rate was falling (the influential colonial statistician Timothy A Coghlan said it was an issue that should 'command the serious consideration of all thoughtful people') and the economy in 1900 was suffering from probably the worst drought in Australia's white history. Apart from the small colony of Western Australia, which was in the throes of a gold rush, Australia, on the brink of Federation, was still depressed. Capital had ceased to flow and unemployment was a clear enemy of immigration, even from Britain.[6]

Until the 1890s the colonies had generally prospered despite their unpropitious beginnings in 1788. Australians were still the butt of jokes about their forbears – who, it was said, had been carefully selected for the penal colonies by some of Britain's best judges. When the 7th Earl Beauchamp arrived as the new Governor of New South Wales in 1899 his opening message was to remind colonists of 'your birthstain', which they had commendably 'turned to good'.[7] This bout of badly judged condescension was howled down at the time. Yet the convicts were indeed the foundation population of British Australia; 160 000 were transported and few of them returned. Moreover they had mainly thrived in Australia and reproduced vigorously, and grew tall and strong. But the main flows of convicts were staunched in the 1840s, replaced by free immigrants who, by 1900, accounted for ten times the original convict flows. The boom of the 1880s, which had produced 'Marvellous Melbourne', was followed by severe contraction. Immigration from Britain dwindled to a small rivulet by the mid 1890s and then virtually dried up for a decade or so. Australia was a much further and more expensive destination for migrants than North America, and half of all its immigrants were conveyed by generously subsidised passages. For more than a century Australia had regularly channelled a very high proportion of its State revenues into the recruitment of immigrants, and this gave it almost unique control over their selection. Nevertheless almost half of all immigrants in the 19th century had paid their own way.

The Australian colonies were outposts of the Pax Britannica, their populations concentrated mainly along the southeast seaboard, with the vast inland in many parts uninhabited, scarcely even explored by Europeans, as the 20th century started. Australia had developed an unusual economic structure heavily entangled with the international economy. Its growth and prosperity were based on export markets: wheat, wool and minerals (gold being important in the 1890s as other sectors faced adverse conditions internally and abroad). The colonies imported many of their consumption products and drew copiously on the London capital market to finance their further economic development. During phases of expansion, especially in the 1850s and the 1880s, Australia sought large transfusions of imported capital and immigrant labour. It was a classic primary-producing economy 'of recent settlement' connected, umbilically, with the mother country by trade, demography and sentiment.

Distance and control had made the Australian colonies more homogeneously British than anywhere else in the British diaspora. In 1891 it is calculated that 87 per cent of the population was 'Anglo-Celtic' in origin; 6 per cent from northern Europe and less than 1 per cent from southern and eastern Europe; 1.9 per cent Asian and 3.4 per cent Aboriginal. In the following 60 years the ethnic base became even narrower — testimony to the effects of a rigorously patrolled White Australia policy and 'its widely accepted legitimacy of racial discrimination'.[8]

There were two surprising aspects of this dependent status. First, the average standard of living was one of the highest in the measurable world. Australians were better fed, better housed, lived longer and grew taller and healthier than, for instance, most contemporary Europeans.[9] According to Angus Maddison's figures, Australia had a per capita GDP of $4000 in 1898, which was about the same as the United States and higher than most other countries.[10] Australia's prevailing living standards were high, but in 1900 they remained decidedly depressed. The maintenance of the economic differential between Australia and its immigrant suppliers was always the vital prerequisite for the continuing flow of migrants. This was the essential propellant of international migration, particularly for the very distant Australia. In 1900 the old British reservoir supplying

Australian immigration had not run dry: Britons continued to flow straight across the Atlantic. Since at least 1890, however, Australia had lost its appetite for immigrants and the essential differential was much diminished.

The second distinctive characteristic of Australian life was its degree of urbanisation. So large a proportion of its people lived in the cities of the seaboard that they began increasingly to look like 'city states', especially as the rural population declined in proportion (and then in aggregate) in the next century. Already by the 1860s British immigrants were commonly urban people emigrating to a mainly urban destination, though this was not widely recognised or accepted by contemporaries. Despite its enduring and powerful 'outback' image, Australia was already one of the most urbanised of countries. Melbourne and Sydney each possessed half a million people. By 1861 urbanisation in Australia was greater than in the United States. Partly it was a consequence of the entrepot functions of Sydney and Melbourne, Brisbane and Adelaide, each servicing its hinterland and performing the needs of trade. Each city witnessed a spontaneous growth of industries and service functions and a concentration of population. They became surprisingly sophisticated urban economies with a widening range of industries attached, fuelling further growth. These industries were substantial – but mainly tied to local markets and limited in scale. Australia remained mainly pre-industrial and did not experience self-sustaining industrialisation for several decades, even as late as 1939 (and the timing of this is in dispute). Consequently Australia was a paradox, a prosperous primary producer, affluent but not industrialised, distinctively rural but heavily urbanised.

In 1900 there was a sinister reminder of pre-industrial conditions. Bubonic plague was reported in Adelaide and then in Sydney: the epidemic eventually killed 155 people in that year alone, leading ultimately to 452 fatalities in the first decade of the century. Special rat-catchers were employed in The Rocks in Sydney and there were frenetic clearances to cleanse the district. The more familiar, though no less elemental, hazard of bushfires erupted in Victoria, and severe weather caused terrible disruption in New South Wales in July. Despite such setbacks there were 9.5 million acres under crop in the first decade of the new century.[11]

General health was relatively good and improving. Life expectancy increased from about 45 mid-century to 55 at the end, one of the highest in the world at that time (though close to 10 per cent died in infancy).[12] The birth rate was high but had fallen from more than 40 per thousand in the 1850s to 26.8 in 1899: married women were having far fewer children. Death rates were lower than in most countries, but there could be no disguising the fact that Australia was thinly populated and its population had risen only slowly, and had been stagnant for ten years. In the 1880s immigration added 373 754 to the Australian population. In the 1890s the corresponding figure was a mere 9185: Western Australia had increased by 117 505, while most colonies had actually lost population by migration (Victoria lost 111 814). Few people were arriving from overseas and more were leaving. Assisted immigration, which had begun in 1832, had been suspended since 1888.

By the 1890s the colonies were no longer raw immigrant societies. Native-born Australians began to outnumber immigrants in the 1860s, though it was not until 1911 that there were more native-born people than immigrants over the age of 40.[13] Reduced immigration, and the consequences of earlier planned immigration schemes, had finally produced a balance of the sexes. The original male bias had evaporated, helped by nature's own balancing act in a stabilising population. Moreover the ratio of Australian-born, 46 per cent in 1861, had increased substantially in the past decade and was 85 per cent by 1900. But in a demographic sense Australia was marking time, though social change continued. Thus between 1860 and 1900 the proportion of the population able to read and write increased from 57 per cent to 80 per cent, partly in response to better teaching and partly to the immigration of increasingly literate people from the United Kingdom. The reading habits and book consumption were very high by any current standards.[14] But literacy did not diminish crime and there were 115 prisons with 4251 prisoners, which was 11.2 per 10000 of the population; detection was improved when finger-printing was introduced in 1902. And other innovations were beckoning: in 1900 there were nearly 1.7 million horses in Australia (and a considerable horse export trade), but in that year the first motor car was imported, a French model. Immigrants tended always to gravitate towards the cities, allegedly exacerbating the unhealthy tendency of the nation at large.[15] As the cities grew they were increasingly regarded as dangerous to the nation's health. There was no comfort in urbanisation, and this would be another recurrent lament during the coming century.

In 1900 Australia was at war: several contingents of troops went to the Boer War, which eventually engaged 16314 Australians of whom 1400 died. Australia was also supporting the British in China in the Boxer Rebellion, with the dispatch of a gunboat. These were rehearsals for a much greater participation in the First World War, when recent immigrants found themselves quickly returned to Europe to support the Empire.

Federation

Federation signified unification and independence but Australia remained markedly Anglophile and was not stretching and straining for separation. Moreover even the simple question of 'independence' was less than total because Australian courts remained directly subject to the Privy Council in London. The British monarch continued to appoint the governors-general and governors of Australia. Foreign policy was still effectively conducted by Britain (but by 1919 Australia had an independent seat at the Peace Conference at Versailles). Reliance on British foreign policy and capital was undiminished. Nevertheless within Australia there were new currents: the first Labor government in the world achieved power in Queensland in December

1899. There was even a move to separate the Kalgoorlie goldfields from the rest of the colony, an evident counterpoint to the federal movements of the time. Questions relating to labour legislation caused friction throughout negotiations between the colonies. Australia was deeply embroiled in discussion with the Colonial Office in London to design and finalise the constitution for the new Commonwealth. The thorny issue of internal free trade monopolised much of the energy invested in the movement for federation, and New Zealand simply opted out. Nevertheless, despite the rifts and tensions surrounding federation, the continent was joined together in direct and practical ways, for instance by means of postal communications, improved integration of the railways and widening use of the telephone and telegraph systems.

This was a society which was politically advanced by Western standards: it was 'an adult Anglo-Saxon democracy', declared the visiting Fabian, Sidney Webb.[16] Australia had pioneered votes for women, though not for Aborigines. A new Labor Party was emerging and Australia had already introduced manhood suffrage, and the secret ballot. But, for a small country, the political apparatus was extraordinarily complicated. Australia, counting the new Commonwealth, possessed 14 houses of parliament. Each took initiatives – thus early closing legislation was passed in South Australia and New South Wales, giving a half-day to shop workers. Although the country seemed to have become stuck in recession, modest social progress was clear. Thus in South Australia the first kindergarten training school had been founded, the Art Gallery was begun, together with the first electric light and a new conservatorium. Australia was producing novels and plays, though it was still largely dependent on England and Scotland for its artistic culture. It was a great importer of pianos. There were only four universities, in Adelaide, Melbourne, Sydney and Hobart, with 42 professors and 147 other academic staff teaching 2598 students, of whom less than 300 were female. The plutocracy continued to send its sons to England for final education, a sort of finishing process. Australia was

resolutely monocultural: in the 1890s it had missed out on the spectacular diversification of immigration experienced in North America. Australia was adamant in its determination to remain a uniform
and pure British population.

Federation was the achievement of the 1890s and the colonies
surrendered their sovereignty, which all but Western Australia had
enjoyed since the 1850s. The outcome was described by Alfred
Deakin as 'something of a miracle', and Edmund Barton, the first
prime minister, famously called it a 'nation for a continent and continent for a nation'. This was a crucial time for Australian nationalism, when Australia explored its cultural identity in the visual arts,
literature and social reform. But Australian Federation was not precipitated by any dramatic contingency which demanded national
unification. John Bannon points out that there was no 'war and revolution or civil violence ... no great innovation or technology: no
spirit of republicanism', nor any rupturing independence from the
imperial mother country. As Helen Irving says, 'To form a nation
without external pressure or crisis, without a common religious or
ethnic imperative, in time of peace and ready to begin on the first
day of a new century – to *write* a nation by agreement – represents,
if not a utopian undertaking, at least an act of profound optimism
and concentrated imagination'.[17]

There was no public criticism of Australia's reliance on Britain, which provided almost 90 per cent of its imports in 1886.
Despite increasing imports from Germany and the United States,
Australia in 1914 still derived 70 per cent of its imports from the
motherland. It was increasingly financing its own capital formation but did not object to the idea of imperial economic unity:
closer economic ties were favoured by everyone.[18] But there also
existed pressures for the protection of young industries, which
was the source of heated contention, especially between New
South Wales and Victoria. Protection from competition was generally favoured by manufacturing interests. The labour movement,
strong in Australia, was unanimously opposed to cheap imports of

labour and this carried powerful implications for immigration initiatives. As long ago as 1840 James Stephen in the Colonial Office had warned that European society in New South Wales was in danger if Asian coolies replaced convict labour.[19] The origins of White Australia were inextricably entangled with the question of economic protection simply because the greatest danger to wage rates seemed to be posed by any kind of coloured labour, coerced, contracted or otherwise. At all times the labour movement was suspicious of immigration and was vehemently opposed to low-wage migrants. Restriction was central to the newly united Commonwealth of Australia.[20]

Federation was a unifying event in its own right and the idea basked in popular bipartisan enthusiasm. But it was based on exclusion, restricting the roles of workers, of indigenous people, of Asians, of non-English speaking Europeans.[21] Aborigines were thought to be dying out as a race, their fate interpreted according to the lights of Malthusianism and Social Darwinism. It was a time of eugenics, frankly racialist and white supremacist. As the historian Geoffrey Blainey remarked:

> Dispossessed, landless, declining in numbers, the
> Aboriginals, it was said as late as 1914, were destined
> to vanish from the face of the earth. Charles Darwin
> cited the fate of the Aboriginals as an instance of
> what he imagined to be the iron law of nature: the fit
> races survived, the unfit vanished.[22]

Timothy Coghlan at the time said clearly that 'The unanimity with which the Australian states have passed laws restricting the immigration of Chinese may be taken as some evidence of the undesirability of that race as colonists'.[23] The number of such immigrants since 1880, in any case, had been insignificant. The policy was part of a more general rejection of non-whites – the 'Prevention of the influx of Coloured Races' – designed to exclude coloured races from Asia, Africa and the islands of the Pacific and Indian Oceans, irrespective of their British status. A dictation test (borrowed from Natal) was introduced for this precise purpose. The trade unions fully supported restriction on economic and racial grounds: the test was designed not to determine skill or education but to keep out coloured people.

Racism and liberalism coexisted in White Australia. Thus, for instance, Australia possessed some of the most 'innovative and advanced industrial laws and working conditions' in the world. Racism and cultural supremacy were alloyed with economic considerations at all times in Australian immigration history, as in

> the well-founded belief that non-European labour
> would be exploited, employed as *de facto* slaves, and
> ultimately degrade working conditions for all; or
> fears of religious and cultural animosities and ethnic
> mix in a pre-multicultural age.[24]

Australia in 1901 established a national consensus which came to be consolidated into what was later termed the Australian Settlement, a set of national values and understandings which guided that nation for most of the 20th century. It included, therefore, White Australia, industry protection, wage arbitration, State paternalism and Imperial benevolence.[25] Most of all, Federation was designed to guarantee the British/Australian monopoly of the continent – under Federation it would be better coordinated, economically stronger, better defended, exclusively white and British too.

Sealing off the entire continent from non-whites was a challenge to its gatekeepers. Australia has an extremely long coastline. On the other hand it is also an island and not easily approached by unofficial intruders and therefore, until much later, was relatively easily patrolled at its main points of entry. In 1901, more problematic were the relatively small numbers of non-whites already resident. There were, for example, small numbers of Japanese families who had lived in Australia for generations passing with little notice. There was always a sprinkling of merchants from Japan. The Muramatsu family, for example, had opened a shop selling Asian goods in Cossack, Western Australia in the 1890s; their son Jiro later became owner of a large pearling fleet. In 1921, when their extension of stay expired, the youngest son of the family was asked to leave Australia. Other Japanese families stayed through to 1939, when most were interned or repatriated.[26]

Most of the non-white population lived in northern Australia: its European settlement was sparse and many believed that it was geographically and climatically unsuitable for Europeans. The population was in 1900 about 200 000 – half of them Europeans in four Queensland towns. In the Northern Territory there were a mere 4500 Europeans, probably 10 per cent of the total. There were several groups of people from outside the usual orbit of British Australia, including South Sea Islanders in Mackay, Chinese in Cairns and Darwin, Filipinos, Malays and Japanese in Thursday Island and in Broome. Together with the Aborigines, they were 'the northern multiculture'. Even before 1900 about 10 000 Aboriginal people had been drawn into the white economy, into the goldfields and the cattle stations and also to the coastal settlements. By the turn of the century seriously negative attitudes were aroused against the Pacific Islanders and Asians in the north, even though they had been crucial in the trade and development of the Torres Strait. Thus Japanese lugger captains who were opening up the pearling industry were deeply unpopular and regarded as a menace to white society and security. Pacific Islanders were being deported and Chinese migrants subjected to humiliating restrictions. White Australia was being cleansed of its multiracialism and all thought of a vibrant heterogeneous community was outlawed.[27]

The new states of the Federation continued to administer their own immigration policies, but the Commonwealth gradually began to assume responsibility. Between 1901 and 1914 the population of Australia at last passed 4 million. From 1900 to 1905 no assistance was given to immigrants; in 1906 a mere 680 were assisted. The Immigration Restriction Act which instituted the dictation test as a fig leaf for white protectionism was the first legislation passed by the new parliament.

Lurking on the horizon in 1900 were fears of a more directly strategic sort. Japan had just defeated a European power (Russia) and Germany loomed in the region also. There was fear of demographic decline, fear of racial pollution, fear of invasion and fear of racial decline. Australians agreed with current British ideology that

TA Coghlan (1855–1926): influential statistician and chronicler of the nation's progress. At the time of Federation he was deeply concerned about falling birth rates and the low rate of population growth. *National Library of Australia, an24079663*

imperial unity depended on keeping England a great power: 'One head, one heart, one language, one policy ... the Commonwealth must be strong by land as well as by sea'.[28]

One hundred years later

In the following hundred years the greatest single change in Australia was the quintupling of its population. The continent in 2001 not only accommodated vastly more people than at any previous time but supported them at a living standard beyond any expectation in 1900. The role of migrants, as cause and effect of this vital achievement, is the central question throughout this narrative.

At the start of the 21st century Australia had become a mature and experienced democracy, and was also more self-conscious as a nation. It was politically stable and among the most predictable of Western-style democracies. It was now surrounded in Asia and the Pacific by independent republics of differing degrees of stability and danger. Australia was capable of regularly switching governments without violence or even much serious conflict. Yet it had still not finally detached itself from Britain and seemed less than enthusiastic to become a republic. Its population was approaching 20 million, now with rather more women than men. Australia in 2000 was a thoroughly modern economy which had passed through rapid industrialisation several decades earlier. Its economic evolution, by most standards, had been unusual because it had attained a degree of affluence, of relatively 'high mass consumption', before the clear onset of industrial development (the so-called 'take-off' in the 1940s). It was a curious case in world economic development history, not easy to categorise.[29]

Whatever its timing, by the end of the 20th century the economy had not only industrialised into a manufacturing system but had also evolved towards a reliance on service and technology industries. It possessed large banking, education and finance sectors and was increasingly committed to the international economy. The latter was not new except in scale and in kind. In 1900 Australia, of course, had been already a supplier of primary products and a capital importer. In 2000 Australia's exports still reflected a high dependence on primary production, but it had widened the base greatly, and its international educational services had become as great as its wheat exports. Trade with Asia had risen to 40 per cent of Australia's total: there had been a massive reorientation, partly because Australia had embarked on a long-term program of reduced protectionism.[30]

In 2000 Australia counted itself among the OECD countries, the wealthier and most economically sophisticated countries, which group it had joined in 1971.[31] Its economy was a little larger than the Netherlands, smaller than Canada, a quarter of that of Germany, less than a sixth of Japan's, 1.9 per cent of the total OECD. Its per capita income was above the OECD average and very similar to that of many European countries, and still a little higher than the United Kingdom, New Zealand and Sweden; its growth rate was one of the highest, and its net saving rate relatively low. Australia's aid to overseas countries was above the OECD average at 0.26 per cent of the GDP per annum, which was lower than Canada, Denmark and Norway, and higher than the United States. In education its spending was lower per capita than the average and its ratio of teachers to students was generally worse.

Australia possessed more of virtually everything by 2000; Australians had achieved, one way or another, a greater command over resources at home and abroad. Some of this was a qualitative change – better communications, better houses, better food, better leisure. Australians worked shorter hours and played more; they travelled more and they were better educated. The higher standards of living were now associated with greater longevity and more holidays. The whole economy was in many ways more efficient – Australians ploughed fewer hectares but produced far more food; they reared more cattle and also produced far more beef per animal; they worked in factories which were phenomenally more efficient than those of their great-grandparents. Some things were diminished – most notably horses, and travel by train and ship. Road accident fatalities were 6 per 100 000 – higher than the United Kingdom, lower than the United States, and falling. The taxation rate was relatively low, but Australia was a very great emitter of sulphur oxides and nitrogen oxides, one of the several costs of its economic growth.[32]

Mobility in 2000 was astonishing, though this was not new. Even before industrialisation, populations have been on the move: a great turnover of communities, people moving on in astonishing proportions, shifting, migrating, marrying out, working away from their birthplaces. Every five years more than 7 million people were changing their places of residence – more than 43 per cent of the population. Almost a quarter of the population had been born overseas.[33]

Australia in the new century spent a rising percentage of its GDP on its health, which was marginally better than in most OECD countries. But its birth rate had declined further in the 1980s and 1990s, and this affected general psychology in a way reminiscent of the debates about the birth rate in 1900. There was continuing biological fear for the future reproductive capacity of the nation. By contrast no one now questioned the future of the Aboriginal population: the main question was how much of the land should be returned to them and how might the shameful deprivation and high mortality rates in certain Aboriginal populations be radically and swiftly reduced.

Of all other countries, Canada remained the most similar in many respects, especially its high level of overseas-born citizens and its effort to cultivate 'multiculturalism', a term which Australia had borrowed from Canada. The intensity of immigration in the third quarter of the 20th century had left both countries with a much higher level of diversity than ever before. Much of Australia's energy was devoted to an accommodation to this fact; consequently immigration remained high in the political agenda, still able to raise community and political tensions very quickly.

In 1999 23 per cent of Australia's population was foreign born, which was higher than Canada at 17 per cent, the United States at 10 per cent, the United Kingdom at 4 per cent, Switzerland at 19 per cent and Germany at 9 per cent. A substantial proportion of immigrants were now from Asia and other non-European sources. This was a change which, a century earlier, had been utterly inconceivable. Until the mid 20th century Australia received very few immigrants who could be regarded as refugees except at some remove (there were some Jews who had removed themselves from Russia and came to Australia by way of Britain). By 2000 Australia had become a full member of the international community and recognised its obligation to receive considerable numbers of refugees each year, but was determined to maintain an orderly process in its intakes. The size and composition of its immigration continued to be a source of controversy. Premier Bob Carr of New South Wales wanted the immigrants to spread themselves into the countryside and away from the cities. Geoffrey Blainey advocated more tropical cities in Australia, presumably to create a presence along the northern perimeter. Immigrants were no longer regarded as potential defenders of the country nor as occupiers of otherwise empty terrain nor even as guarantors of racial homogeneity. Consequently the expectations of immigrants in 2000 were radically different from those of 1900.

Plus ça change

In other ways Australia had changed little since 1900. For instance, the five main cities still dominated, now more than ever. The primary sector of the economy was still very large, though declining in terms of relative and absolute employment. To a person from, say, China the population would not have looked much different from that of 1900: the dominance of Europeans would not have seemed much less than that of the British a century earlier; the non-Europeans were small in proportion and most of Australia was more thinly populated than ever as a consequence of the retreat of rural settlement. By 2000 the population was more concentrated than ever and there was a vocal school of thought claiming that its level was already too high for the welfare of the environment and of future generations.

Colonial Australia had seen a surprising degree of planning and control by its governments. Much of the infrastructure of the economy was established by government agencies which set the terms of capital formation. Then its immigration schemes had created a population designed to meet the country's economic and racial requirements. Few populations in the world could match the deliberation with which the colonial population had been constructed by government policies. The colonies created a tradition of control that continued into the new century. Australia was one of the most planned of societies, and the flows and composition of its immigrations was one of its central levers.

In 1900 Australia had mobilised itself into a unity and determined a clear-sighted future. There was an almost perfect unanimity about its priorities – to remain British, to develop its natural resources, to grow and defend itself, and to remain racially and culturally separate and unmixed. Between the expectations of 1900 and the realities of 2000 was a century of unpredicted change which one American historian summarised as the 'chaos, the rich ambiguity of historical moments, life's bafflements, the accidents and contingencies ... [all of which ... must be retained if history is to be a true account of human experience'.[34] For Australia these had included the great sea change of industrialisation, the effects of world war and regional conflicts (including Vietnam, Timor and, later, Iraq) and the radically changed mobility of the world. Most of all it eventually changed the philosophy and practice of immigration, though Australia retained its determination to control the process.

In the long perspective Australian immigration was a remarkable project which conveyed more than 10 million people across the face of the globe to one of the most distant destinations in the history of international migration. From the beginning in the late 18th century they were intended to create a new and homogeneous society, ideally without much damage to the thin communities of Aborigines who had been there for at least 50 millennia. These indigenous peoples had very small means of resisting or even negotiating with the incoming peoples from the British Isles. Eventually this transplantation created a special version of European colonisation which was, given the distance involved, astonishingly homogenous. This became the badge of Australia, its declaration of intent. It was the way the outside world looked upon Australia – eventually it became a matter of change and indeed of social revolution.

So this is the story of how a very peripheral Europe outpost, in the mid 20th century, changed its spots and adjusted to a changed world. It carries its own dramas, large and small.

2 The slow awakening: 1900–14

Migrants of the new century

Dave Morris was born in 1899 in Charters Towers in Queensland. In the next year his family decided to emigrate to England. They were part of the reverse migration of the time, returning to the district whence they had originally come. The extent of return migration increased greatly during the long depression of the 1890s. Once returned 'home' the Morris family soon found that wages and living standards were much lower than they had expected. As Dave Morris later recalled, 'It naturally did not take my parents long to decide to return to Australia as soon as possible but it was a few years before they were able to save and ultimately borrow sufficient money to render this possible'.[1] Thus the Morrises were also re-migrants when Australian immigration revived, part of the circular movement which grew over the coming century as travel became easier.

By 1908 the long drought of immigration was over, and eventually a flood of immigrants reached Australia and reconnected it with the rest of the migrant world. But, unlike the seething diversity of peoples famous in the North American melting pots, Australian immigration reverted to its traditional dependence on Britain.

Typical in the great Edwardian flush of migration was the Duckles family, who arrived in Australia in late 1912: they were farming people from rural Yorkshire, a diminishing category in the British population and increasingly difficult to recruit. Annie Duckles filled an exercise book with an account of the journey, which began with ten hours by train to Tilbury Docks, where they boarded the *Orsova*. Annie reported: 'We were not alone. There were old people and young ones, and babys galore, some look only a few weeks old'. The passengers with children were required to stand in a shed where a doctor inspected the children's eyes for signs of infectious disease.

The family occupied a cabin 'about the size of the wardrobe in your spare bedroom'. Annie reported, 'I have not felt nervous so far, we are a long way up above the water, if only we were not going so far'. They experienced the inevitable seasickness in the Bay of Biscay – a common denominator of emigration before the airplane. The Duckles travelled in superior class and spoke critically of the 700 passengers overcrowded in the third-class accommodation: there was a mere 94 feet of deck space for them, and coal fumes and dust were troublesome. Chickenpox broke out and there were three deaths during the voyage. The migrants arrived in Australia by way of Colombo into windswept Fremantle, which Annie Duckles described as 'a nice little place, all English, and we enjoyed a good walk and a cup of tea'.

The Duckles travelled in comfort and were smoothly absorbed into a place which was more like England than they had ever expected. Their emigration was hardly a tortured wrenching of roots. They were British people moving in a British world.[2]

Kennedy Burnside was also an emblematic prewar emigrant. He left Northern Ireland in 1901, at 18, and spent 5 years in the United States, then in Scotland, and New Zealand, a 'sojourner' who accumulated capital to invest in a farm in Western Australia. By 1914 he held 1000 acres which, helped by the state bank, grew threefold by

Migrants from rural Yorkshire: George Duckles (husband of Annie), with daughter Florence and brother Fred, in England, in 1950. *National Library of Australia, Canberra, MS 8546. Courtesy of Mr Kevin Kubank.*

the end of the 1920s, with an annual income of £500. He returned to Northern Ireland to collect his brother's widow and her seven children. Burnside was a highly successful model of the desirable skilled and energetic rural immigrant.

Another was Frank Manning, born in 1902 in County Clare, the source of many Australian 'chain migrants' from Ireland in the previous century. His family was sponsored by relatives who had themselves been assisted by other family members. It was a complicated and hazardous way of financing this great migration, and the plan succeeded. Frank's father was a tailor and miner, and they emigrated in 1912 to settle in Kurri Kurri in the Hunter Valley. Frank was one of a family of six and his mother already had two sisters in Australia who themselves had been sponsored by relatives. His father preceded them in order to pay for the passages of the remainder of the family. Manning much later recollected that 'mother could not read or write, but she had a wonderful memory … she was very shrewd and very alert. No one would ever know she could not read or write'. She was alert enough to get her family to Sydney. But she remained nostalgic for County Clare: 'She always used to say "I'd love to go back and walk down the street once more"'. Frank Manning himself left school at 14 and went into mining. In the coming century Irish emigration to Australia fell into sharp decline.

The Duckles, Kennedy Burnside, Frank Manning and Dave Morris were part of the prewar renewal of immigration which eventually overcame the forces of inertia characteristic of the first years of the new federation.

The international context of migration

When Australia was unified in 1901 its unambiguous priority was to control who should enter its ample territories.[3] The new nation stridently asserted its territorial autonomy. In reality there was no threat to the composition of the population: immigration had been stagnant for 20 years and the nation was acutely aware that its reproductive energy had significantly waned. Nevertheless federated Australia was determined to stay white and British.

The colonial immigration programs had been mothballed for two decades and the engine of economic and demographic development had run down. Immigration was low on the national agenda: the great debates on Federation in the 1890s centred on interconnected questions of whiteness and the protection of labour rather than a renewal of immigration.

In the great age of imperialism Australia was one of the 'countries of recent settlement', all immigrant-receiving societies including the United States, Canada, South Africa, Brazil, Cuba, Argentina and Brazil. Australia was a substantial player in the international system of migration but its remoteness created special difficulties: to counteract these it had devised effective but expensive ways of subsiding its immigrant inflows. Since it paid for a large proportion of its immigrants it naturally believed that it possessed an almost unique capacity to determine the course and composition of its own peopling. This was the ultimate source of recurring political tension within and beyond its shores.

In the mid 19th century European emigration had been dominated by the west, by the British Isles and Germany. Most emigrants went to the United States – though, surprisingly, 1.6 million were channelled in Australia's direction over the course of the century. But Australia depended almost exclusively on British migrants even when the main supply shifted to other parts of Europe in the 1880s. There had been a structural shift in the great flows of people out of Europe. Emigrants from Russia, Italy and Spain (followed by the more easterly Mediterranean countries) quickly joined the great migrations and soon outnumbered the older sources. These new mass migrants were flooding into the United States, always the greatest destination, from as early as the 1870s. Australia conspicuously failed to engage in this movement and set its face against it for three-quarters of a century. Australia, in effect, subsidised emigrants exclusively from Britain and only the smallest trickle of eastern and southern Europeans reached Australia. The White Australia policy did not initiate this bias but certainly reinforced the outcome in the new century.

There was a further massive expansion in the flows of oceanic migration from Europe in the years from 1900 to 1914, sometimes regarded as the last expression of the 19th century world of the Pax Britannica and true laissez-faire. The scale of the outflows, in retrospect, seemed to suggest that the people of Europe were fleeing from the approaching First World War.[4] The impact on North America was astonishing – the United States became a seething cauldron of new immigrants. Many of the widely famed American names of the 20th century were the descendants of these great waves of immigrants, including a high proportion the artists of the new movie industry and American music: thus Igor Stravinsky and the Marx Brothers, Benny Goodman, Artie Shaw and Oscar Hammerstein spring to mind. It was symptomatic of Australia's disengagement from these migratory flows that few of their equivalents ever reached Australia. European (including British) emigration rose to a crescendo by 1913, demonstrating the mercurial character of the surges and declines in international migration.[5] But until 1907/08 Australia responded very lugubriously – its immigration system had fallen into desuetude and even the British had almost stopped thinking much about Australia as an active destination.

The British diaspora was also changing amid this migratory turmoil and underwent a significant re-channelling. In the years 1900–14 British (though not Irish) emigrants became distinctly more Empire-oriented than ever before. For the first time they began to divert from the United States: increasingly they proceeded to Canada and also, to a lesser degree, to the other Dominions. The Empire at last began to overtake the United States as the main destination of British emigrants. This set the direction for much subsequent British emigration. Yet, even within the world of the British diaspora, Australia had lost its attraction: its share of British emigration had fallen in almost every decade since the gold rushes, down from 28 per cent in the 1850s to a mere 8 per cent by the 1910s. The 1890s had been the dullest, most depressed decade since Australia had been colonised, marked by net emigration.[6]

If the health of Australia was to be measured by its population growth, then this was a sick continent. There was little wonder that Australia felt that it had lost its vigour – losing its place in the British world and becoming isolated from the European centre. Australia began the new century in a dour inward-looking condition with a diminishing proportion of the population having been born outside Australia.

Demographic pessimism was heightened by anxiety caused by the decline of reproductive vitality: in the 1830s the colonies had been renowned for their very high birth rates, sometimes attributed to the climate or the high living standards.[7] But between 1860 and 1900 the Australian birth rate had declined by 40 per cent and the annual population growth had fallen from more than 3 per cent in the 1870s and 1880s to only 1.7 per cent in 1903. As Neville Hicks says, the doctors, clergymen, politicians, publicists, and editors 'feared for the future of the Anglo-Saxon race in Australia'.[8] A Royal Commission on the Decline of the Birth Rate was appointed in 1903. The general view was that there was a prevailing moral degeneracy which was the harbinger of national decay, which some attributed to the growth of education for women. The decline of the birth rate was not confined to Australia, which in reality was following similar tendencies in England, France and elsewhere: nevertheless there was talk of race suicide and the eugenics movement gained ground and began to advocate maternity pay and selective breeding. In the Commonwealth Parliament one MP, recommending maternity allowances, spoke of 'women doing their duty to Australia by bringing the unclothed immigrants into the world'.[9] The Royal Commission came to the view that Australian women were controlling their own fertility – a conclusion which encouraged much moralising about the 'selfishness of women'.[10]

TA Coghlan, the Commonwealth Statistician, declared that failing fertility was an 'extremely serious matter' for public policy. It was a demographic disaster, the consequence of women 'Gratifying their selfish desires'. It gave no hope of 'a teeming population springing from Australian parents'. Most of all it made clear that White Australia could not be maintained with such poor birth rates. Moreover there was a sinister corollary: the 'sterility which is blighting these States does not go unnoticed among the cramped-up but still prolific myriads of Japanese and Chinese'.[11]

Coghlan noted how the outbreak of bubonic plague in Sydney and elsewhere in late 1899 'militated against immigration and doubtless assisted to augment the total of emigrants'. Rats, plague and women's education were not, of course, the only enemies of immigration.

The enemies of immigration

Australia was traditionally opposed to cheap labour entering its labour markets, especially in times of high unemployment. Almost all immigrants came under scrutiny, though discrimination against non-white labour was the keystone of the system. Economic recession was the main enemy of immigration and when unemployment rose, organised labour and its supporters invariably resisted additions to the labour force. It was a fact of political life which recurred in all countries.[12] Moreover, throughout the first century and a half of Australia's European history, there was unwavering opposition to any kind of immigration which departed from the traditional reliance on British supplies.

Labour unions were the main instigators of opposition. As early as 1843 the Mutual Protection Association was formed to oppose the renewal of convict transportation and also the importation of 'coolie' labour. Thus the protectionist economic argument was combined with the race issue and they remained entangled until the late 20th century.[13] The same combination fed Australian national feeling as Federation approached. The utopian socialist William Lane declared that Chinese labour was a threat to economic standards in Australia and also 'to the social life and moral standards of the people'. He painted the horrors of the opium dens and 'the insidious attraction of the fan-tan with its peculiar orientalism'. Lane's powerful journalism of bigotry purveyed the dangers of 'Squalor and Disease'. The Chinese in Australia roused him to a high peak of indignation:

> It angered me to see these men so smooth-faced and
> plump and contented, their placid natures nurtured
> by the drug that kills the passionate white man, and
> to think that in this smoky, stifling, stinking den these
> Mongolians were as much at home as if it were in distant
> China, and that all this was in Brisbane, in the capital of
> the colony that we hope to make a great white state.

Racial discrimination was buttressed by the belief that employers and governments were perfectly prepared to 'sell the country's birth right for cheap labour'.[14] These ideas of racial purity were increasingly reinforced by the advocates of the new eugenics movement, who argued that Australia should become 'a paradise of physical perfection' and, with proper biological planning, create 'new standards of health for the entire population'.[15] This would depend on a thorough control of immigration. Racism and economic insecurity fed on each other in such times.

The extent and depth of these attitudes ranged from extreme racism to mild anxiety. CWE Bean became famous as the much respected chronicler of Australia's experience of world war. He epitomised decency, 'the able and gentle scholar ... [who] never lost his love or respect for humanity' and was 'pained ever to write ill of any'. He was the champion of Australian values and also an emblematic product of his times: of Empire and also a British education. In 1907 Bean contributed a defence of White Australia to the *Spectator* in which he declared that white and oriental races could not live together in Australia. There was a growing probability of an oriental invasion, either peaceful or warlike. He pointed out that the resolve of Australians to keep their country white was of 'an intensity undreamed of in England'. Moreover Australians believed that a 'fierce racial war' was inevitable and they would fight it 'at any cost', even if England disapproved. They also believed that Britain would eventually support them despite her imperial misgivings.[16]

The 1890s were a dismal time for the Australian labour market and the labour movement was suspicious of ideas of immigration, despite the fact that the entire continent had a population still substantially less than 4 million. Immigration always depended on a positive differential of wages and incomes, which indeed prevailed throughout most of the 19th century. Organised labour opposed cheap imported labour despite the national priority to populate the continent which, therefore, required a degree of compromise in its practice. Immigrants to Australia, regardless of origins, were rarely greeted with unrestrained enthusiasm or unqualified welcome. The White Australia policy emerged as the working compromise for immigration policy. As AM Taylor says, 'Australia allowed entrance only to a group of potential migrants with real wage levels only just below their own'. The British worker fitted the bill; non-white immigrants definitely did not do so. Thus White Australia propped up Australian wages and also limited the growth of its population and necessarily acted as a brake on economic development.[17]

Federation itself gave centre stage to the White Australia issue as the means to protect labour from cheap immigration, which was consistent with the long tradition of protectionism since mid-century. Even liberal spokesmen, like John Langdon (later Sir John) Bonython, accepted this construction of the national priority. The *Bulletin* always gave the question inflamed expression but the racial and protectionist elements were mutually reinforcing in most people's minds. At the time of Federation the immediate concern related to Pacific Island indentured labour in the Queensland sugar industry. It was recognised that the elimination of indenturing would impede the development of Queensland. Australians were evidently 'prepared to make this sacrifice rather than endure the evils of a mixed race or create in the North a repetition of those Southern difficulties which nearly severed the United States'.[18] Thus the twin pillars of White Australia were erected, founded on the fear of depressed living standards and the fear of racial dilution and conflict. A third pillar was the sheer distaste for anything non-British.

Hostility to non-British immigrants was ever ready to erupt publicly. In 1906 an Australian Labor Party spokesman demanded that the language test be applied to Italian immigrants to cause their deportation. The Labor politician King O'Malley objected to any resumption of immigration because it would result in 'men fighting for jobs like dogs for a bone'. As late as 1914 the *Round Table* said that 'For the political student it is sufficient to note that capital as a rule favours, and labour discourages, effective measures of immigration'.[19]

Suspicion of immigrants did not entirely exclude the British. There was a longstanding belief that Britain was prepared to off-load its social and economic problems on Australia unless Australians were perfectly vigilant. When the illustrious General William Booth of the Salvation Army raised money to settle 5000 British families on Australian land, meeting every criterion of agrarian white Britishness, he was rebuffed and disillusioned.

Thus the resistance to immigration was diverse and powerful: it meant that Australia's participation in the upsurge of world migration at the turn of the century was exceedingly slow. In 1904 Deakin admitted that 'In the matter of immigration Australia is stagnant'. It was in part because there had been a terrible drought since Federation. But at least the Commonwealth had gained control of immigration.[20] In 1905 Deakin raised the matter of migration in the Imperial Conference – advocating the diversion of streams from the United States to the dominions, which had been a recurrent theme of Empire thinking since 1776. But opposition continued even as late as September 1905 when an MP remarked that no immigration should be contemplated 'until we have taken the steps necessary to provide work and food for those who have been born here'. Immigration was overshadowed by another long-standing political question, namely 'unlocking the land', which meant breaking the landed monopoly of the great pastoralists and releasing it to small producers. Some regarded this as a precondition for any renewal of immigration.

The administration of immigration in every decade after Federation was punctuated by test cases which provided a running commentary on the definitions of acceptability and exclusion. In 1902 there was the curious case of the 'six hatters', an almost surreal episode concerning a group of highly skilled tradesmen from London who had been organised to work under a form of contract. Trade union opposition was aroused on the principle that the hatters constituted indentured labour and should be prohibited under the same terms as exclusion of Kanaka labour to Queensland. The

Hatters Case aroused heated controversy and caused great ill will and confusion in Britain, and gave the impression that Australia was hostile to all immigration.[21] Two years later there followed the Hans Max Stelling case in which a person of mixed German and Egyptian origin was subjected to the dictation test, applied on the grounds of colour, and subsequently was deported. This established the rigour of Australia's racial policy in unambiguous terms. Then in 1904 at Kalgoorlie, a frontier town in the West, maltreatment of Greeks by the local population sounded another warning about the limits of popular tolerance of difference and the realties of assimilation. Two more episodes hardened the edge of restriction: in 1908 a Lancastrian with a Jamaican mother, WH Massey, was denied entry even though he was a highly skilled mason, a unionist and had been guaranteed employment. Then in 1913, in another defining test case, Lieutenant-Colonel Dantra, a Eurasian doctor married to an English woman with two sons and wanting to retire to Tasmania was refused entry, again reaffirming the limits of Australia's flexibility.

The argument that the White Australia policy was essentially designed to protect the country from cheap labour clearly did not apply in these cases, all of which concerned skilled bourgeois people who posed no threat to employment nor any real taint of indenture.

The scramble for migrants

The Federation Constitution empowered the Commonwealth to make loans for immigration but the old apparatus had become rusty from disuse. Australia had fallen far behind in the recruitment of migrants. At last, in 1904–05, there were signs of a reawakening, though some regarded it as almost too late. The alarming findings of the Birth Rate Commission was one precipitant: it was calculated that, at its prevailing level of reproduction, Australia would need

600 years to reach the current United States population level.[22] In a single year, 1903, the United States received more immigrants than Australia had attracted in the entire period since 1860. Moreover in the 4 years since 1900 Australia had lost 867 by net migration, but the United States received more than 2 million immigrants.[23] Comparison with the United States was an absurd vanity, but the exercise helped to concentrate minds in Australia.[24]

Between 1905 and 1909 Australia came to the view that it desperately needed immigrants, yet it stuck to the assumption that its supply would come exclusively from the good yeoman stock of Britain. The idea was to 'settle ... the lands of our vast interior' and to sustain 'the very existence as a free Commonwealth under the British flag'. Australia wanted 'agriculturists or yeomen of the British stamp'. The *Trustees and Investors' Review* said, 'If we wish to hold Australia for white races, it must by peopled by white races'. The colonies 'would be at once feeding places of the Motherland ... and self-supporting Imperial garrisons, themselves unconquerable'. Nothing could arrest 'the indefinite and magnificent expansion of the English [sic] Empire'.

TA Coghlan pointed out that Canada had achieved great success by employing modern advertising methods, offering every male over 18 years free grants of land of 160 acres, and was favoured by lower passage costs. In the face of this sort of competition Coghlan advocated Italian immigration, which had also proved successful in Argentina. Meanwhile in London early in 1905 the Queensland Agent-General, Sir Horace Tozer, wrote that Australia was regarded as unfriendly to emigration:

> No one but a resident here, feeling the pulse of the
> emigrating classes, can have the faintest conception
> of the prejudice now existing against Australian
> emigration, principally owing to this restriction
> clause ... All that is bad about us is magnified by
> distance and multiplied by ignorance.[25]

Any campaign to revive immigration therefore faced formidable psychological resistance at home and in Britain itself. Conditions in the United Kingdom were bad, especially in the unemployment crisis of 1907–08: in Glasgow alone 7000 people were dependent on special relief funds by Christmas 1907, and nine months later more than 16 000 in Govan alone were 'on the verge of starvation'.[26] In some respects, therefore, Britain was ripe for emigration.

Some of the first persuasion was initiated by the grandly styled Immigration League of Australia, set up in Sydney in 1905, which urged energetic steps to increase the population, and reinstatement of the long-abandoned policy of State-aided immigration. It declared that 'A vast increase in our population is an absolute necessity if we wish to continue as a free and self-governed Anglo-Saxon community. Let us not delay until it is too late'.[27] There was a strategic urgency. The League pointed out in September 1907 that the Asian context had shifted menacingly: Japan was a great new nation of 40 million people and only 16 days steaming from Australia's coasts — 'it is on a par in naval and military strength with the great military powers'. Nearer still were China with an estimated 400 millions and Java with some 30 millions, on the northern doorstep: 'The population of the Asiatic countries is overflowing and should by the fortunes of war, the protecting power of Great Britain be withdrawn, even for a brief period, Australia will offer itself as a point of least resistance'. It was imperative therefore that Australia develop swiftly a 'great and continuous stream of immigrants of British blood and sentiment'.

But Australia did not want urban people. At the heart of the new push was the idea that the immigrants were destined for the land: the 19th century rural imperative was reasserted. Immigration was entwined with the political demand for closer settlement and the dissolution of the so-called land monopoly. Immigrants would expand rural population and also help channel 'city people on the soil' including 'drafting lads out of the city to country employment'. The Agent-General for New South Wales issued a pamphlet saying that millions of acres of fine wheat lands were awaiting the settler – and though the land was not actually free the conditions of access were 'so liberal as to induce rapid settlement'. The *Bulletin* insisted that the cities were 'huge cancers' which sapped the energy and strength of reproductivity.[28]

As soon as enthusiasm for immigration revived, trade union opposition was reignited. Thus the *Worker* lambasted the Immigration League as 'merely an agency for the importation of cheap labour from abroad' and pointed out that immigration would not be confined to rural settlers.[29] Indeed the realities of 20th century British emigration were incompatible with Australia's obsession with rural migrants. Britain was running out of rural people to send abroad or even to serve its own rural sectors.[30]

Australia found itself in a quandary. It wanted British immigrants, but not Britain's 'dross'.[31] A pamphlet of the time said that 'We do not want to flood this country of ours with crowds of European outcasts'. Australia most of all wanted farmers with 'a little money, and plenty of pluck and muscle', like the Duckles. But this coexisted with anti-immigration sentiment and fear of recruiting the submerged tenth of the British population. There was some basis for this view, since unemployment continued at 6 per cent even in the years 1910–14.

Australia quickly realised that there was a great clamour for migrants, and that renewing the flow would require extraordinary efforts. The new Commonwealth government accepted responsibility and in 1906 Deakin remarked, 'We are faced by the necessity of preparing for a wisely generous encouragement of the vigorous and enterprising people of our own race'. Deakin took a central role in the regeneration of immigration, which entailed reactivating older schemes and agencies in Britain and making new arrangements with shipping lines including White Star, Aberdeen, Shaw-Saville, Orient, P & O and Anderson. Advertising and bonuses for recruiters were introduced together with subsidies for passages. Nomination schemes were given special priority, which proved the most effective means of recruitment.[32] Each state was separately touting for immigrants and the revival of assistance began in New South Wales in 1906, Victoria in 1907, South Australia in 1911 and Tasmania in 1912. In the light of the huge international surge in migration it is clear that Australia was very late in the competition for migrants and had indeed set its face against the main flows out of southern and eastern Europe.

There was resistance to Australian recruiting in Great Britain, some of which was attributed to an improvement in labour conditions and keener competition from other dominions. Parts of the Irish press simply refused to publish Australian advertising and Scandinavian newspapers warned about Australian blandishments. The notion that Americans could be lured to Australia was disappointed. Meanwhile specific labour shortages in Australia persuaded employers to initiate their own recruitment plans. There were great shortages of factory operatives and domestic servants in Sydney in 1911. A special delegation went to England to recruit 1140 artisans and 1100 female operatives, sometimes offering full passage to be repaid out of subsequent wages.[33]

There was opposition in England from factory employers: one recruiter, Margaret Cuthbertson, was called the Lady Poacher in the local press. Queensland looked for 500 railway navvies in 1911, and generated 1500 applications from the Birmingham district alone – which may suggest a greater receptivity in the British labour market.[34] An agent for Western Australia was sent to India in 1911 to secure retiring army men (white only); South Australia began its campaign when there were good harvests in 1910–11. Some of the Australian agencies in Britain developed links with local associations such as the Kent Colonisation Society and the Central Emigration Board, and the Central (Unemployed) Body for London eventually provided assistance to 7500 emigrants.

The states were reluctant to offer full assistance and tried to set tight requirements. Victoria, for instance, wanted farmers with

£200 capital; labourers and domestics were offered only £5 subsidy towards the £17 fare. Recruitment failed to meet targets and special agents were sent to Scotland in 1910–11 and also to Italy and California in search of irrigationists to meet particular needs in Victoria. Charities were activated and many philanthropic organisations sponsored juvenile migrants including city boys who were destined for rural employment. Prominent in this work were the Salvation Army, the Boy Scouts, the Immigration League of Australia and the Child Emigration Society (later the Fairbridge Society). Unusual was the 'Dreadnought scheme', which diverted funds into immigration when £81,321 earmarked for a battleship fund was left unspent. In 1914 insufficient adult migrants came forth and vacant berths were filled by young recruits of this sort.[35]

There were also several exotic recruitments, erratics from the wider world of international migration including some reshuffling from within the older British diaspora. These included groups of Welsh and Spanish migrants out of Patagonia, some of them second-stage migrants from the original Argentinian ventures of the 1870s: 400 had already arrived before 1914. There were smaller parties of Maltese too, a group of 50 arriving in late 1912 and refused settlement on racial grounds. Group migrations of self-funding cooperatives were also among the immigrants before war broke out.[36]

Australia insisted on close medical vetting of its recruits, which was partly a response to the popularity of eugenicist thinking as well as the increasing insistence on racial homogeneity. None of this addressed the problem of populating the north, which gave rise to new debates about the adaptability of Anglo-Saxons to the tropical climate. North Queensland, full of economic potential, posed unsolved questions about Australia's racial future. Some opinion, including even that of Rudyard Kipling and Richard Arthur, suggested a mild degree of interbreeding as an option, but such ideas were anathema to the true believers in White Australia.[37]

The outcome

Ostensibly the campaign to revitalise immigration was a success and migrant numbers rose rapidly after 1905. Between 1906 and 1914 official records show that 393,048 immigrants arrived in Australia of whom 184605 were assisted in one way or another. Immigration between 1907 and 1912 exceeded all previous records, rising to a crescendo in 1912 with 91891 migrants, which was the greatest intake until 1949.[38] The growth was impressive but the extravagant expectations of the time were disappointed. Australia was not able to rival its North American competitors in the race for migrants even in the British supply, and this led to recrimination among the states; there was poor coordination and no uniformity of administration. This was most obvious in the case of the Irish who had contributed so prolifically to the colonial migration schemes. In the migration boom before the First World War only 2 per cent of Irish emigrants chose Australia while 86 per cent went to America. Throughout the rest of the 20th century the Irish component in Australian immigration continued to decline.

The population of Australia doubled between 1890 and 1920 (from 2.25 to 5 million), but only 12 per cent was attributable to net immigration. The nomination system was the most important vehicle and this tended to reinforce the urban orientation of the recruitment. Half the immigrants were self-financed and were not well recorded after arrival. The proportion of farm workers and domestic servants was disappointing to the recruiters and most of the immigrants were town bound: the 1921 census showed that 42 per cent of Australian-born males and 36 per cent of females lived in rural areas, but of the immigrants only 34 per cent of males and 25 per cent of the females lived in the rural areas. Even before 1914 the immigration program had shifted decisively towards urban migrants – a transformation which was not recognised for another two decades either in Britain or Australia. The idea of rural settlement was mainly unfulfilled – of the 7052 immigrants arriving in Victoria in

Australian government advertising for immigrants to the United Kingdom c1912; new methods of publicity included film. *Australian Parliamentary Papers, 1913*

1911 only 201 went on to the land and 183 of these were domestic servants.[39]

By 1913 the immigration boom was over, though the great advertising campaign continued: £50000 was spent in cinemas, the press and on spectacular posters, reinforced by lecturers, and even a film unit. But the Australian High Commission in London warned that migrants were becoming scarcer: agents' commissions were increased and some success was registered in Glasgow.[40] Better labour conditions in the United Kingdom militated against emigration and so did the cost of fares, which increased from £12 to £14 in early 1913. Rider Haggard, one of the Dominions Royal Commissioners, was warning that Britain could not afford to lose its rural labour. Australia's rigorous medical requirements also put off prospective immigrants.[41]

Exclusions from the sleeping nation

While Australia scrambled for immigrants it simultaneously excluded anyone in the wrong categories, determined on a racial basis. Whether race was the primary and motivating force is a matter of minor historical dispute.[42] Most public discussion avoided overt racial vilification and employed economic and cultural reasons to justify the policy, though the term 'White Australia' appeared to most to express its essential priority. In part it stemmed from inaccurate and exaggerated notions of how many coloured aliens there were in Australia in 1901 – Deakin thought that there were 80000 but the new census showed 57656.[43] The implementation of the White Australia policy required a more vigilant and rigorous watch on the gates.

The exclusion of non-European immigrants and the repatriation of the Pacific Islanders engendered widespread support 'by the large majority of politicians and the Australian general public'. Most of them would have 'preferred the naked candour of legislating to keep out all Asians, Africans and Melanesians', but the British government urged a more diplomatic formulation of the policy to minimise insult and offence, particularly to Japanese and Indian sensibilities.[44] This was the so-called 'Natal solution', a dictation test which could be applied arbitrarily to immigrants. The first prime minister, Edmund Barton, who was relatively mild in his attitude to race, believed that 'the English-speaking peoples of the world represented the pinnacle of human achievement' and recommended a 50 word English dictation test to be required of all foreigners. Eventually a more flexible test was devised which could be any European language – 'Rejection would then be due not to the colour of the applicant's skin, but to his or her lamentable ignorance of Swedish or Serbo-Croat'.[45] It was realised that many non-white people were actually proficient in English. It was pointed out that 'Heterogeneous races [are] to be found in Cairo ... [together with] large numbers of Hindoos ... [and] ... in the West Indies again there are hordes of coloured men, half-castes and others, who would be able to pass any ordinary Test such as proposed'. In Hong Kong there were tens of thousands who could pass an English test.

Distance and expense was always the main excluder of potential migrants to Australia but the mechanism of the 'dictation test' gave new teeth to the policy of exclusion. The 1901 legislation provided for exclusion of any immigrant who 'when asked to do so by an officer fails to write out at dictation and sign in the presence of an officer a passage of fifty words in a European language directed by the officer'.

There had been a dictation test in Victoria in 1899, in Western Australia in 1897, and in New South Wales in 1899. The Commonwealth government gave it universal implementation across all Australia. The reason for the test being administered in any European language was that King O'Malley was worried that negroes in the United States would be perfectly able to pass a test in English. Conversely Billy Hughes was worried that the

Welsh would fail because as many as 20 per cent of them spoke no English. Consequently the system allowed discretion as to which European language would be invoked to test the immigrant. It was devised to be failed: a Chinese was tested in Norwegian and a black Jamaican in Russian. After 1909 nobody passed the dictation test though some came close. It was a supremely effective policy and remained in use until 1958; it kept out non-Europeans but it was also employed to exclude specified Europeans at the discretion of the immigration authorities. For six decades this simple mechanism gave Australia extraordinary control over the composition of its immigration. The price it paid was in its much reduced ability to recruit immigrants and also in its international reputation.

Excluding unwanted aliens was only one side of the equation for White Australia. There was the question of un-whiteness already within the gates. Unlike, say, South Africa, Australia had a relatively small non-white population and its Aborigines were, in the minds of the rest of the nation, almost beyond civil society, merely a primitive remnant which, in all probability, would expire in any case. The Aboriginal exception to the ideal of White Australia was expected to solve itself. The position of other non-whites in Australia was more debatable. These included descendants of black convicts and seamen, of Afghan camel drivers, of the Chinese immigrants of the mid-century who had spread thinly across the colonies and had been effectively excluded for several decades: their numbers were in decline from death and out-migration and there had never been much family migration in any case.

A different matter was the Pacific Islanders engaged mainly in the sugar industry. Between 1863 and 1904 62 000 'Kanakas' had been engaged by contracts under the Masters and Servants Act, supplying the primary labour force in Queensland's substantial sugar industry. The trade began with kidnapping and deception but later became a regular recruitment among the Melanesians, who evinced a growing desire for European goods and betterment. Many served for terms of three years, then returning to homes in New Caledonia, Vanuatu, the Solomons, Kiribati, Tuvalu and parts of New Guinea. Much of the trade was regarded as little better than slavery though there is debate about the degree of volition and exploitation that accompanied the system.

In 1901 there were about 10 000 islanders in Queensland and New South Wales and they continued to enter Australia, 1678 of them in 1901 alone. For White Australia to succeed the elimination of the Pacific Islanders was essential. The instrument of this expurgation was the Pacific Islands Labourers Act of 1901, which was designed to deport the main bulk of the labourers currently working in the northerly region by the end of 1906. Eventually 7068 were repatriated in 1904–08 and a further 194 before 1914. This was an exercise in population cleansing; as Clive Moore says, the federal government regarded them as 'a primitive people from the South Seas, able to be written out of Australian history, like indigenous Aborigines'. The sugar producers were given time and protection to adjust to the policy which they had strenuously resisted; they were allowed to recruit under licence to progressive reduction until the inflow entirely ceased.[46]

Many of the Pacific Islanders were repatriated, often in extremely unhappy circumstances. The depth of the human tragedy was given voice in the eloquent letter written to the authorities in broken English by Peter Janky in June 1907. He was frightened to go home to the Solomon Islands for fear of punishment for old offences:

> I might get kill because they are waiting for me all
> the time[.] [T]he best for me to stop with my brother
> Dick Assie and Tom Sulla. Dear Mr Brennan you will
> let me stop in Queensland because I will get kill[.]
> [T]hat is all I ask you ... I remain your truly son,
> Peter Janky, Malaita.

Even sadder was the letter of an islander named Louie who had been working in the lower Burdekin district. His marriage to Rosie had not been recognised, and he wrote to her in October 1906 from The Manse, Ayr:

> Dear Rosie ... I got your letter. I glad you got
> money. I sorry that I can't come see you before I go
> home. Government he hurry up along we fellow.
> We go away along Monday – no matter you stop.
> Might I come back to see you. I take money to go
> home £29. Tell Herbert I can't see him no more.
> Suppose I go home if I alright I come back. Suppose
> I no see you any more along this ground we meet
> in heaven ... I been ask Government along you, but
> you no stop aloong side me ... I sorry I no see my
> Missus any more Mable Rae, good bye, now I no
> say any more. Good by Rosie and plenty of kisses.
> Xxxxxxxxxxxx ... This last letter. You no more
> send letter to Burdekin ... Your loving Louie.

In this letter he anticipated Rosie marrying someone else – one 'of your Countrymen alright' and seemed to be accepting that fate.[47]

Smaller in number and less publicised were the divers who worked in the pearl shell and bêche-de-mer industries of Thursday Island in northern Australia who were mainly Japanese in origin and indentured. They were the backbone of the industry and regarded as the best pearl-shell divers in the world, virtually indispensable and indeed excluded from the ban. There were 1000 Japanese on Thursday Island in 1897 and they continued to serve for another 50 years, with their own boarding houses, public baths, stores and a brothel.[48] Similar non-European populations in other parts of the Northern Territory also became de facto exceptions to the strictest provision of the exclusion policies.

Strategic considerations

Coghlan, in 1905, spoke of immigration as 'firstly an insurance against aggression' and 'secondly as a way of adding to the country more producers, more consumers, more taxpayers'.[49] Australia was determined to keep out certain categories of immigrants, but its defence required not only vigilance but also more immigrants of the right sort.

The basic attitude was captured in the words of Billy Hughes, the populist prime minister, himself a Welsh immigrant. He declared that the world's population was increasing unevenly, notably in Japan:

> ... 80 million of people [are] confined within an
> area less than one twentieth of that of Australia.
> Saturation point has been reached ... The
> alternative to the migration of these surplus millions
> is starvation. Where can they find a country as
> inviting and as vulnerable as Australia. And if they
> come here, what shall we do? To whom shall we
> turn to for help?' [Hughes believed that Australians]
> must recognise our duty to populate and develop
> this great heritage of ours. We must build up our
> defences. Press forward with a vigorous policy
> of immigration of people that can be assimilated
> into the Australian community and by raising the
> birthrate to a healthy level satisfy the world of our
> fitness to remain in control of this great country.[50]

These fears had partly grown out of a perennial optical illusion: Australia always looked far bigger and emptier than it actually was in any habitable sense. Only in the 1930s did the illusion begin to dissolve and by the 1980s the demographic capacity of Australia became a central political question. But at the start of the century it was a pervasive assumption that gave credence to the fear that Asian populations were likely to invade and inundate the southern continent.

Barton had shouldered the task of guiding the original legislation: he had to concede that Asiatic immigration was not presently likely to 'overflow and throng our marts, our fields, and all places of our industry'. Non-white immigration was evidently not an imminent danger. But its restriction was essential for the future: the fear was that one day Australia would repent not having checked the immigration of 'certain Asiatic influxes'. Commentators were bemused by the implications of Australia's immigration policies. The Australian politician BR Wise predicted that Australia would be 'the ultimate heir of Java, Sumatra, and the Celebes in the event of the absorption of Holland by Germany'. This was a Realpolitic reversal of the common formulation of Australia's position vis-à-vis its neighbours, namely the shudders of anxiety registered by the successive concerns about Russians in the Pacific, Germany threatening the north. When the great blood transfusion from the British Isles appeared to falter at the turn of the century questions about the vulnerability of the Australian continent multiplied. Wise described Australia as England's 'outlying frontier'. It was also full of potential in every way. He declared that 'English sentiment towards Australia is suffering from a cold fit. People are a little "tired" of her. She no longer attracts immigrants, and her stocks and enterprises have become unpopular'. Australia had been misrepresented by journalists and politicians.[51]

The British were disappointed in the recent progress of Australia. Prime Minister Arthur Balfour was concerned with questions of imperial defence and sceptical about the value and achievements of the self-governing ex-colonies. Lord Northcote, a future governor-general of Australia, declared in 1903: 'the best service [Australia] can render to the Empire is by developing her population and resources'. He said that at present, in her half-developed state, Australia 'was a positive source of weakness to the Empire'. This was the brutal truth, and imperial unity was utterly vital.[52]

Thus the recurring assumption was that Australia was an increasing temptation to the 'overcrowded and earth hungry nations of Europe and Asia'. The imperial rhetoric was infectious and, combined with the agrarian myth, made immigration from Britain its highest priority. It was a doctrine which was caught in the words of the journalist WT Goodge:

> this huge island continent with fewer people in it
> than are in London, and close beside the almost
> empty land of milk and honey are the crowded
> earth-hungry teeming millions of Asia. A man of
> ordinary horse-sense needs to be no profit [sic] at
> this stage of our history to see that Australia must
> have more white men, or must someday cease to be a
> white man's country.[53]

Immigrants

In the event, the numbers of immigrants attracted to Australia by 1912 were unprecedented though they did not satisfy the country's revived appetite for newcomers. As we have seen, most of them were urban folk from British cities and many of them already had friends or relatives in Australia. The inflows were not so homogeneous as they had been in the previous century and not as British as Australia had generally expected. Indeed they reflected the variegated composition of the British population itself by 1900, some of them people who had migrated to Britain previously from Europe. They introduced a trace of continental flavour to Australia.

Some of these pre-1914 immigrants were interviewed 50 years after their arrival.[54] James Castrission was born in 1902 in the Greek island of Kythera and came to Australia in 1914 with his father, who was a chef at Aroney's fish shop in Circular Quay in Sydney. He was one of the small number of southern Europeans who reached Australia long ahead of the main flows (after 1945) and circumvented the biases of the immigration system. His father had already been to America three times but joined relatives in Sydney and brought his seven sons who became a chain of migration connecting Kythera to Australia, a distant outreach in the great Greek diaspora.

Flora Rossen was born in Stirling, Scotland, in 1894 and arrived in Australia in 1912. Her Jewish family, named Gold, had fled Russia to avoid army conscription. Her father, a tailor, suffered from bronchial asthma and migrated to Sydney ahead of his family. Their migration was an extension of a much wider European movement of people which added annually to the numbers of Australian Jewry. It was also part of a wide category of therapeutic migration to Australia – of people searching for a better environment for their health. Some of these Jewish migrants became so anglicised that they hardly felt simpatico towards the later entrants – especially among the Jews.

Esther Davis was born in 1896 in Shildon in the north of England and emigrated to Australia with the family of six in 1910. Her father was a working miner but they were not badly off and he was able to pay £100 for their passages. Their emigration, as so often, was precipitated by friends in Australia endlessly advocating emigration, 'and they were always on about the beautiful peaches' and the sunshine. The Australian realities were less rosy – her father's wages were ten shillings a day in England and rose only to eleven in Australia. Esther became a domestic servant until she married, in 1919, a Welshman who had emigrated in 1913.

Among the British emigrants to Australia, even before the First World War, were examples of other Diasporas which gently helped to leaven the mass. They were distant echoes from the much larger migration outflows of the time which mostly headed to the United States. Some of them carried their memories to the end of the 20th century, people prized by oral historians.

When in 1906 HG Wells visited Ellis Island, the great entry

point for immigrants in New York, he was astounded and perturbed by the extraordinary mixture of races flowing into the United States. Wells thought it boded unhealthily for the unity and social integrity of the country – America was likely to burst apart with so many differences and tensions among such heterogeneous people. At the same time Canada was also becoming much more varied in its immigrants.[55]

Had HG Wells witnessed the quaysides in Sydney or Melbourne in 1906 he would have seen a totally different scene: Australia's immigrants were even more monocultural and monolingual than before. They were more English and Scottish than ever; the Irish now less represented than previously. British Australia was decisively consolidated, its Britishness reconfirmed. This was the outcome of the prewar era when Australia belatedly joined in the final surge of the great age of international migration. It did not entertain the great polyglot diversification of its immigrant population that was so striking in the other great immigrant countries at this time. As Robin Gollan says, 'In the first ten years of the Commonwealth, governments were occupied erecting a wall against the outside world behind which the white Australian people could develop their wealth and productivity'.[5]

3 Migrants and the Great War: 1914–18

Immigrants and the war

Amid the flood of immigrants who arrived in Australia in the few years before 1914 many were young men who quickly found themselves returning to Europe to serve in the Australian Infantry Forces in the tragic conflagration that engulfed the old continent in August of that year. It was a seminal moment for the Australian nation; it was also indelible in the lives of the immigrants. There was a 'rush of enlistment', as the celebrated historian of the war, CEW Bean remarked, and it included

> hundreds of those newly-arrived younger men who
> knew the old country as the land of their childhood,
> English and Scottish immigrants to whom their
> 'home' was calling; Irishmen with a generous semi-
> religious hatred of the German horrors in Belgium;
> all the romantic, quixotic, adventurous flotsam
> that eddied on the surface of the Australian people

concentrated itself within those first few weeks upon
the recruitment offices of the AIF.[1]

The war itself revealed the surprising diversity within the population. Recruitment into the forces involved many 'non-British Australians' – John Monash was of Jewish origin, a civil engineer who
became commander-in-chief of the Australian Corps in France in
1918. There were small numbers of French men in Australia who
returned to France to serve in French Army. The largest subset of
the Australian population coerced by the war were the Germans
– many of them second- and third-generation immigrants – who
were interned unceremoniously in holding camps in various parts
of Australia. Individual aliens became visible in the war: one was a
Danish immigrant, born in 1890 of middle-class family with good
prospects, who had been inspired by an article on sunny Australia
and went to Western Australia in 1912. For two years he followed
the perfect adventurer career in pearling, fencing, prospecting and
kangaroo shooting. At the start of the war he was not allowed to
enlist since he was not a British citizen, though he eventually succeeded and served three years until he was wounded: he had served,
he remembered, 'for a fine people and a democratic country worth
fighting for'.[2]

Fifty years after the war a group of British-born 'Diggers' were
interviewed about their experiences.[3] They reflected the stories of
their original migrations and also the shock of war. A Londoner,
born in 1896, came from the comfortable lower middle class, son
of a building contractor affluent enough to send his son to private
school. He had strong memories of the coronation of Edward VII
and the patriotic songs of the Boer War, and the jingoism of his day.
Given a conventional upbringing, he imbibed as a faith 'our Glori-
ous British Empire, on which the sun never set, and the map of the
world with so much of it coloured in red'. Remembering his dissatisfaction with suburban life in London, 'quite early I decided I would
travel beyond the limits of the Thames Embankment and Hamp-

stead Heath'. He looked to the British Navy as 'a way of escape and a uniform', but he was rejected as too short. As an 18 year old in 1914 he opted for the next best alternative – and 'turned my attention to emigration'. Australia offered him easy terms, £3 down and a balance of £7 on arrival – and a farm job, 'So in March 1914 I sailed for Australia with a small wooden box and about 10/- pocket money'. He was at that point fighting against the forces of shortness and suburbia, seeking escape. He arrived in Sydney in mid-1914 and went out to a mixed farm in the Riverina, which greatly appealed to his 'romantic feelings'. He contrasted 'the cold, sleaty, fog-ridden scenes of London' with the exhilarating freedom of 'the wide open spaces and the sunshine, the horses and cows, the smell of bark'. He may have regarded himself as a romantic but lurking in his mind were ideas of 'spike helmeted Germans in England shooting Englishmen', images drawn from his childhood. When the call for volunteers was raised he responded promptly: 'I made up my mind I was going to the war', again driven by romance rather than any actual knowledge of realities. Now he overcame his lack of height by presenting himself as 'a Bugler' and thus gained entry into the army in Sydney, which was his passport to Gallipoli in August 1915. He never regretted joining the AIF: 'I learned what 'mateship' meant, and what is now called the digger spirit'.[4]

There was a larrikin spirit among these immigrant diggers, few of whom were the oppressed victims of Edwardian slums. One of them had spent his youth in Cambridgeshire, 'Hunting, Shooting and Horsebreaking'. He had migrated to Australia before the war for similar rural activities – which turned out to be scrub felling, sugar-cane cutting and driving mail coaches. But in Australia when 'things looked bad for the Old Country', he simply came to its aid and served in the AIF until wounded in 1917. Drawn from the thousands of otherwise anonymous immigrants such men spoke with an insouciance, rekindling the bravado of their wartime excitement. There were special opportunities: empire and emigration were channels for the exercise of that sense of romantic footlooseness together with the urgency for escape and adventure which reached its climax with war itself.

Another digger had reached Australia from England by way of Vancouver, working his passage on a shipment of hay in 1914, having originally planned to join the Canadian Navy. His enlistment in Bathurst in 1916 soon took him back to Europe in a full circle. Another Englishman recollected that he had emigrated to a well-paid position in the Rockhampton Meat Works in 1913 at the age of 21. He prospered but began to feel 'inner promptings' and enlisted in the army. Similarly an immigrant employed at the Government Painting Station in Parafield felt the need to defend Australia and the Empire, and so enlisted. Another had left England for Jamaica in 1908 at the age of 15, returned to England in 1913, and then emigrated to Townsville to work for the Colonial Sugar Refinery in a well-paid job. He was a self-confessed adventurer and joined up, despite initial medical rejection.

A Glaswegian man, born in 1896, had arrived in Australia with his parents in 1910 with seven brothers and three sisters, he being the eldest. His father, an opponent of the war, refused to sign his enlistment papers and he was forced to wait till he was 21 (in 1917); he suffered 'itchy feet' in the interim, during which time he trained in the Citizens Forces, and eventually served in France. Another Londoner, born in 1894, had lost both parents and, from the age of 5 to 14, lived in orphanages. He remembered reading adventure stories about Canada with his brother: 'We were very poor and the £5 needed for the assisted passage was beyond us'. But Western Australia offered a more accessible scheme and the brothers emigrated there in 1910, working on farms south of Perth. They soon saved money to make a deposit on 80 acres in 1912; they were nevertheless fired with patriotism and joined the forces — a path which had taken them from industrial England to rural Australia and then back to the battlefields of Europe.

Among the immigrant recruits there was a recurrent feeling of escape from Edwardian England. A Bicester youth recollected that 'I loved the Farm life, but detested the cold winters and having read an article on Australia in June 1914 decided to write to Australia House for details'. He was gripped by 'the spirit of Adventure': his parents had objected but eventually relented. His farming experience stood him in good stead in Australia: 'I arrived at 1 pm and had a job in Hamilton at 10/- a week and keep by 2.30 pm!' He threw himself into the work, and moved on to new jobs with a feeling of great fulfilment. But when he turned 18 he enlisted in the forces, and in October 1916 embarked at Port Melbourne. Another rural youth, born in 1898 in rural Suffolk, son of a farmer on the estate of Lord Rendlesham, and educated at the National School until 1911, had been visited by an uncle from Streaky Bay in the far west of South Australia. The nephew was regaled with stories of Aborigines which captured his imagination and he returned with his uncle on a German liner. At Streaky Bay he became a store assistant, apprenticed as a compositor with a good salary. But while on holiday in Adelaide in 1915 he too suddenly enlisted: 'I think that 5/- a day and the chance of seeing the world was the main reason', he remembered.

Many of the immigrant diggers had lived prewar lives of extraordinary mobility, many reaching Australia by circuitous paths and then continuing their peripatetic lives within Australia – the war itself became an extension of that mobility. One British immigrant, in no way unusual, arrived in Sydney in 1911 via Vancouver; he took employment as a boundary rider, then as a stenographer in Sydney, followed by work in Queensland before joining the war about which, as it turned out, he felt abiding bitterness.

The immigrant recruits were more immediately conscious of the 'German menace' than the home-grown Australian contemporaries. One of the immigrants, born in York in 1887 and educated at Grantham, had emigrated first to New Zealand at 18, and then on to Australia at 21. He recollected that 'As a boy I was passionately fond of horses and spent most of my school holidays hunting in Leicestershire with various packs of hounds'. Even at 80 he had vivid memories of the Cottesmore and Belvoir hounds. He worked with horses in New Zealand and Australia, and developed as a bush craftsman with special skills which served him well with the Light Horse Regiment until 1920. In contrast was the Durham man drawn from a classic industrial revolution background: he could not forget the black smoke and the blacker coal dust in the coal mines in which he worked from the age of 14; he had worked 11-hour shifts from Monday to Friday, with 7 hours on a Saturday. He remembered many strikes also, and emigrated out of poverty, at a time when there was 'not enough to eat'. This kind of deprivation had been 'the cause of my father deciding to get out to the Old Dart, and start a new life in the colonies'. They arrived in Australia in July 1913 to take work in a mine which was better in every way: the family earning wages enough for a home eventually, enjoying the surf, the sun, the beach. But when war intervened the young son persuaded his parents that he should join the forces.

Such glimpses of life in Britain prior to emigration were rare. Another testimony came from a man born in Rochdale in 1898, from a family of nine, who had arrived in Australia in 1910. His father was a gas stoker, fond of his beer 'which made it very hard on family regards good food etc'. He had sold newspapers before school and this did not help his schoolwork: 'I must have been too tired and breakfast consisted mainly of bread soaked in tea and sugar. Still, we were pretty tough and had no sickness'. At eleven he became a half-timer in a local cotton mill, working from 6 am to 12.30 pm and attending school in the afternoons and earning 5 shillings per week. He was nominated by a relative for assistance to New South Wales in 1910. After poor experiences in Newcastle he was eventually able to send money home to his mother, taking on different jobs, growing up into accelerated manhood in the navvy camps. He tried to enlist in the AIF but was at first fobbed off, and was very pleased when eventually he was accepted into the army.

The immigrant diggers were not, of course, a representative sample of the British in Australia: by definition the sample excluded those who did not enlist, those who did not return, those too old and too young, and all the women also. Nevertheless the oral record gave voice to the prewar ethos of the immigrants, most of whom were adventurous, urban and young. The war itself focused on the immigrants as soldiers.

Anzacs and immigrants

Immigration from Britain had already slackened after the great peak of 1912, and was certainly subsiding well before the war was declared in August 1914. The prewar period of 'dormancy' coincided with rising shipping costs and economic contraction; advertising was soon abandoned, and the immigration offices were closed down in London. The war blocked most immigration; a few domestic servants, nominated passengers and juveniles still managed to reach Australia.[5] Domestic service was the category least likely to be staunched by cyclical or external declines in international migration. After the outbreak of war the movement of troops confused the migration data, but the net movements suggest negative outflows in 1914–17 and then a reversal in 1918–20.

The war was a critical test for Australia as a nation, for its soldiery and its defences, and for imperial solidarity. The composition of the armed forces, including the role of the immigrants, was an issue which later became embroiled in wider controversies about the meaning of the war for the Australian psyche. It was an ordeal by fire: 58 000 Australians died or were killed and this represented one-tenth of the male age group, 18–45; 156 000 were wounded, accounting for three-tenths of the same age group. In terms of participation 331 781 embarked in the AIF and of these 77.75 per cent were Australian born and 22.25 per cent were from overseas (overwhelmingly British immigrants, of course). Since the overseas born constituted only 15.87 per cent of the male population aged 15–64 they were significantly over-represented in the recruitments.[6]

Of the first battalions of AIF, which were mainly from urban

Temporary reverse migration from Australia in World War I: munition workers (over age or unfit for military service) in the general service shed at Andover aerodrome, Hampshire 1918. *Australian War Museum*

New South Wales, more than one-third of them were overseas born. The most recently arrived entered the service of Australia and the Empire with greatest alacrity. This highlighted the special value of immigrants, in peace but even more so in war. They were young, fit and able-bodied, and disproportionately male too. The most famous of the digger heroes was John 'Simpson' Kirkpatrick who rescued many wounded men with his donkey at Gallipoli until killed in 1915: he was born in South Shields in County Durham.[7] Therefore, given imperial expectations and the obligations felt by Australia towards Britain, the great recruitments of migrants before 1914 paid a large and prompt dividend to the nation. It was a reaffirmation of imperial ties and the priority of the defence of Australia.[8] Moreover some of the recently arrived British were unable to get commissions in the AIF because they were under the prescribed age limit of 23, and they paid their own way back to Britain to enlist in the British Army, eventually numbering between 8000 and 10 000 in total.[9]

The presence of so many immigrants and urban recruits among the Anzacs has caused some controversy among those who have clung to 'the Bush Digger Legend', eloquently propagated by the historian Charles Bean, himself a British immigrant.[10] Such a stance also cast implicit aspersions on the status of the immigrant in Australian society, more questioned retrospectively than at the time. The war brought the relationship between Britain and Australia into sharp focus, not least because many Australian-born troops visited Britain for the first time. Some responded very positively to the 'home country', but there was also an increasingly critical strain in the reaction. Nevertheless, by December 1918, Australian soldiers were 'marrying English women at the rate of 150 a week'. At the end of the war there were 5626 war brides, and a total of 15 386 children, wives and fiancées returned to Australia with the AIF in 1919. They effectively constituted an ancillary immigration attributable to the war itself. Less positively, wartime statistics suggest that Australian troops contracted venereal disease at much higher rates than among United Kingdom and New Zealand troops. Some said that Britain had become less like 'home' than before.[11]

Other elements in the enlistments also fitted uncomfortably with the Anzac image. Thus, although Aborigines were not counted as citizens, they were able to enlist and were certainly numbered among those killed. The White Australia policy also left its mark on recruitment, so that when the Chinese-Australian, Hedley Tong Woy and his brother Samuel, tried to enlist in the AIF they were rejected as non-Europeans, even though they were citizens. But when China entered the war they were accepted and served in the Signal Corps in France, and indeed survived the great conflict.[12]

Opposition and exclusions

One of the ways that Australia girded itself for the conflict was to stir up xenophobia. Suspicion of aliens rose to great heights and any hint of German or Turkish origins became anathema. Thus many people of German descent were summarily condemned to internment. The grim treatment to German-Australians in the First World War makes an unhappy story.[13] Surviving photographs of the internees show the humiliation which was visited upon these people, many of whom were second- and even third-generation Australians, merely saddled with German names. They included some of the most distinguished members of the community, people of unblemished character and loyalty. The self-conscious preservation of German identity and the *Deutschtum* in some German communities (notably in South Australia) may have played an unwitting role in this tragedy. During the war 14 per cent of Australia's 33 000 German-born residents were interned as 'enemy aliens', as well as a substantial number of Austro-Hungarians.[14] Families were left without breadwinners; 5000 Germans departed the country voluntarily. Government policy caused a rush for naturalisation applications. An Anti-German League was formed and in 1917 it became an offence to anglicise a name – that is, to mask one's alien origins. Wartime xenophobia generated several communal disturbances: in Broken Hill some local Afghans were attacked because they were regarded as Turks; and there was anti-Greek action in Kalgoorlie. In 1918 there were still 1000 Germans interned at Torrens Island near Adelaide, an especially crude and basic facility. At the end of the war more than 4000 were deported.[15]

During the conscription debate it was alleged that compulsory service would give rise to an inflow of cheap immigrants to replace the troops. JT (Jack) Lang, a future premier of New South Wales, circulated the 'rumour' that 'conscription was intended as a cloak for the breaking down of the White Australia policy by the introduction of large numbers of Asiatic or other cheap labour'. This line angered

Prime Minister Hughes.[16] Catholic Archbishop Daniel Mannix of Melbourne argued that Australia must always come before Empire. He said this was already enshrined in policy which he evidently supported – such as the tariff against British manufactures: it was simple patriotism. He also supported the colour bar:

> we, a handful of whites in a huge continent, insist
> on a White Australia policy. Our coloured fellow-
> citizens of the Empire ask for entry. But no, not
> even for the Empire's sake do we lift the embargo ...
> Australia is first and the Empire, with its coloured
> people, and its allies, has to fall into a second place.[17]

The opponents of conscription prevailed and recruitment remained voluntary throughout the war.

Suspicion of foreigners extended to small groups of new immigrants who arrived in Australia during the war years. The arrival of would-be immigrants from Malta in 1916 immediately aroused public debate.[18] A party of 98 self-financed Maltese arrived aboard the *Arabia* in September 1916 (they were part of 307 Maltese immigrants in that year). In the face of union opposition, even though the Maltese were British subjects, they were denied entry. They were subjected to a dictation test in Dutch, which they inevitably failed, and Billy Hughes ensured their diversion to New Caledonia. The Maltese were regarded as racially suspect and likely to undermine wage regimes in Australia. Hughes protested to Britain, asking that no further passports be issued in Malta to single men. This was too late to stop another 200 arriving on a French ship, the *Gange*. Frantic efforts were made to stop them landing and the captain was forced to take them to New Caledonia: they were not wanted there or in New Zealand or Canada or South Africa; they rejected Samoa as a destination and most of them returned to Malta.[19]

Another group of unusual immigrants similarly generated public

The demographic bonus of war: British brides of Australian troops embarking from Plymouth at the end of the war. *From Patsy Adam-Smith,* The Anzacs, *Thomas Nelson, Melbourne, 1978*

consternation. In the 1870s an idealistic Welsh colony had been established in the Chubut Valley in Patagonia; then, in 1913, a group of 220 from Chubut sought to leave for Australia. It was an eccentric twist connecting two distant outreaches of the British diaspora. They were regarded as desirable immigrants and the Commonwealth government made arrangements for their migration. When the party arrived in 1915 it was discovered that only 28 were Welsh; 113 were Spaniards, 45 were Russians, 30 were Italians, one French, one Serb and one Greek. They were an embarrassment but managed to settle, mainly in Queensland and Victoria.[20]

Towards the end of the war a large number of young Italian men in Australia were controversially called up for service in the Italian Army. The Italian government asked the Australian government for assistance with the return for war service of Italian citizens, mostly located in cane gangs in Queensland. But only 500 out of 4000 returned and Italy accused Australia of a lack of cooperation because it wanted to retain their labour for the sugar industry.[21] It is clear that some of the Italians had been coerced to return to war service and were subsequently refused assistance to return to Australia at the end of the war.

War and Empire

War gave a powerful fillip to the idea of Australian nationality but it also enhanced apprehensions about the imperial nexus within Australia and also in London. The war demonstrated definitively that imperial solidarity was imperative and best secured in future by continuing emigration from Britain to the Empire. It was an idea already developed before the war. Indeed the prewar period had reaped some success with the diversion of an increased proportion of British emigrants to Empire destinations. During the war Britain began to think of ways of further channelling emigration to the Empire and established the Dominions Royal Commission. This reflected the influence of empire ideologues and enthusiasts who set up a chorus of support for energetic emigration. An emblematic figure in this imperial enterprise, and one whose influence stretched into Australia itself, was Rider Haggard, the apostle of rural reform and imperial destiny. Haggard, celebrated author of *She* and *King Solomon's Mines*, represented the old England, the purebred Norfolk squire, the rural paternalist, the racial purist, imperial man par excellence. The answer to the survival of England and Empire, he declared, was to spread the race across the agrarian lands of Empire. Australia fitted his advocacy and Australians generally accepted his version of imperial reciprocity and complementarity.

Haggard also pursued the 'back to the land' philosophy as a means to rescue the urban destitute. He believed that far too many people were trapped in industrial cities which were detrimental to health, morality, national efficiency and welfare. His passionate opposition to industrialisation was the reciprocal of his ideas for the regeneration by the land. These precepts fed his unstoppable enthusiasm for emigration. His favourite description of the Empire was 'the great house with the empty rooms'. He spoke to Theodore Roosevelt of the 'glutted, fouled, menacing cities, the gorgeous few, the countless miserables'.[22] Prime Minister Wilfrid Laurier in Ottawa was in accord and offered 240 000 acres of virgin Canadian land as a gift for the settlement of British immigrants. One of Haggard's priorities was to relieve social problems in England along the lines of the Salvation Army colonies in the United States, and his gaze turned to Australia. Haggard had equally aroused public fears of the 'Yellow Peril' and he asked audiences to

> Imagine these 400,000,000 of stolid, strong, patient,
> untiring, land-bred men having no where to live,
> having not earth upon which to stand, and seeking a
> home. And imagine them casting their eyes around
> for worlds to conquer and seeing an island continent
> half-vacant ... Imagine them saying ... we will seek
> the earth, we will take the earth, we will keep the
> earth.

He predicted invasion: 'Is that a bogey – a mere dream of the night? I tell you it is nothing of the sort. It is the thing which will happen within one hundred years unless ... the people are moved from the cities back to the land'. The decline of the birth rate was an urban blight both in Britain and the colonies and it 'presaged the decline of the Anglo-Saxon race'. Inducing men back on the land and into labour colonies in the dominions was Haggard's answer.[23]

This colourful rhetoric chimed with thinking in 'White Australia'. Haggard was enormously popular in Australia when he visited before and during the Great War. Joining together the issues of rural settlement, immigration and defence, Haggard spoke directly to Australian fears – namely the revulsion from the urban blight, the fall in the birth rate, national weakness, the danger of the other races and the emptiness of the colonies. In 1911 Haggard told Roosevelt of his great pessimism. He believed that the future would be witness to

> the practical destruction of the white peoples and
> that within measurable time, say, two or three
> centuries ... Look at Australia. If there were no
> British Fleet, how long would it be before it received
> a considerable number of immigrants of the Mongol
> type?

In early 1913 Haggard, travelling to Australia, wrote to a friend in Norfolk: 'Australia is a fearful way off':

> You steam day after day over a positively empty sea.
> It's like travelling to the planet Mars – everything
> one knows seems to fade away behind – till at last
> one evening, hid in a red glow, Mars, or rather,
> Australia, appears. It is a beautiful, a wonderful
> land and vast, vast. You could chuck Norfolk down
> anywhere and never find it again: it would be like a
> lost sixpence.

When he reached Australia he noted that the numbers of people engaged in primary production were falling, and he was continually amazed at the emptiness of the land. He told the Adelaide *Advertiser*:

'My own idea is to import families from the towns in England ...
Bring them out and place them in settlements under the charge of
some charitable institution such as the Salvation Army'. It would
then produce children.

In March 1915 Haggard was appointed to the Dominions
Royal Commission on the question of emigration and he under-
took another tour of the dominions on behalf of the Royal Colonial Institute. He reported that he could imagine 'that fifty million
white people might well find a home in Australia ... The great need
of the Empire today is population'. But in Sydney he faced a hostile response from the state government, reporting that 'the Labour
Party and all the six Australian governments do not favor British
emigration – especially the Minister for Lands was dead against me'.
Nevertheless he was extremely popular with the general public. He
dreamt of a 'global British nation' to stem the tides threatened by
the Yellow and Jewish Perils. His anti-Semitism was unrestrained
despite his own Jewish origins.[24]

In Brisbane Haggard met the acting Labor Premier, Ted Theodore, the most truculent and sceptical face of the independent Australia:

> He is a Roman Catholic of alien blood, Roumanian
> it is said, and a very tough proposition to tackle, the
> toughest indeed that I have met in Australia. Being
> alien he is not to be easily influenced by arguments
> about patriotism and being labour immigration does
> not particularly appeal to him. Naturally therefore
> he made much of the money difficulties.

Despite Theodore's attitude, the Queenslanders seemed to fall in
with Haggard's philosophy – and offered a million acres 'of dairy
and agricultural land for soldier settlement, if they can raise the
funds to build railways and develop settlements'. They also insisted
on control over selection of settlers. Each of the Australian states

somewhat reluctantly entered the broad plans suggested by Haggard. He twisted the arm of WA Holman, Premier of New South Wales, for 1000 irrigated farms in the Yarroo district, 'subject to selection'. Haggard commented that 'These Labour governments are not easy to deal with'. But he received better support in Western Australia and Victoria and was eventually well pleased with his success in Australia. His mission had been to draw up plans for Imperial migration and land settlement.[25]

Australia's reaction to Haggard and to the school of migrationists was clearly mixed. There was also a tension in Britain between the zealots in the Royal Colonial Institute and the sceptics and conservatives in the Colonial Office and the Treasury. It was part of the intra-imperial dialogue during the war and the planning for the postwar period. Within Australia there were private initiatives. For instance, Samuel W Copley who owned extensive areas of pastoral land in Western Australia suggested that Lord Kitchener, Britain's Secretary of State for War, be given 100 000 acres to settle experienced men with the help of loans. Haggard himself claimed that he had converted a hostile Australia to the idea of mass assisted immigration, but there is some doubt about the actual extent of his influence. Enthusiasm for immigration programs was variable. In 1915 some state premiers were enthusiastic with offers of land for returning soldiers: Tasmania had offered 300 acres of orchards; Queensland said 1 million acres would be made available. But Holman put his finger on the essence of the problem: 'Britain would not want to lose farmers to Australia, and urbanites were incapable of pioneering'.[26]

Prime Minister Billy Hughes, however, was a true believer and in 1916–17 he took up the immigration issue with energy, seeking loan funds to resettle British and Australian soldiers on the land. For all of the imperial rhetoric, funding became the critical issue. The Royal Commission of March 1917 was keen about the idea of settlement 'under the British flag' and recommended a new committee as well as promoting the idea with ex-servicemen from Britain. Yet these positive ideas tended to arouse predictable responses: Australia desired 'only those agricultural labourers whom the mother country herself much needed'; even more clearly Australia did not want unemployed industrial workers from the mother country. It was now evident that the focus was going to be on joint funding of migration by both donor and recipient countries – which required a radical shift of assumptions, by Britain especially. The emigration equation was being rewritten.

Hughes himself was irritated with the lukewarm response in both Britain and Australia to the idea of mass migration facilitated and funded by both countries. He wanted to prepare a great new migration system, ready to spring into life at the end of the war and designed to solve metropolitan and colonial problems at the same time. He sent a secret cable to his deputy in November 1918:

> demobilisation of British Army will offer unique
> opportunity of securing right type of immigrant.
> The glorious exploits of our soldiers have given
> Australia magnificent and priceless advertisement.
> Tens of thousands of men in prime of life, who
> would make most desirable settlers on soil, and who
> will be disinclined to remain in Britain, will soon
> be released from army ... If we want to get men we
> must bestir ourselves immediately ... unified control
> this end, proper handling by States in Australia, and
> shipping facilities.[27]

But there was always a local stream of resistance and at the end of the war strident demands were voiced that jobs should be reserved for returning troops, and resistance to immigration was redoubled.

Billy Hughes's advocacy of vigorous British immigration was paralleled by his loud warnings about the rising danger from Japan. He focused national attention on the Japanese threat, which he pursued with a sort of monomania for several decades, thereby reinforcing all the elements in the White Australia policy. He vehemently opposed immigration from Japan though the likelihood of significant Japanese immigration was remote. For Hughes the issue was not race as such but cultural difference – the Japanese simply could not be absorbed by Australia 'and therefore any immigrants would become a source of provocation and a potential fifth column'.

In 1917 Hughes declared, 'We have lifted up in our top most minaret the badge of white Australia' – and this would have to be defended because 'we are ... a drop in a coloured ocean ringed around with a thousand million of the coloured races'. 'How are we to be saved?' he asked. Hughes's biographer, LF Fitzhardinge, refers to this as 'the Japanese bogey' – the notion that the Japanese were 'pressing for the right of free entry into Australia'. But Hughes also opposed the Japanese attempt to insert a racial equality clause in the covenant of the League of Nations because he saw this as a direct threat to White Australia. As Fitzhardinge says, he simply did not believe that 'a man in Central Africa was created equal to a European'. Relations with Japan were thus focused on the matter of race itself: Hughes held out on the principle and was so tenacious that he caused substantial diplomatic embarrassment. Prime Minister Jan Smuts of South Africa described him to British Prime Minister David Lloyd George as 'pig-headed'. And an Indian diplomat observed of Hughes in 1922 that he seemed 'obsessed with the fear of Japan'.[28]

Planning for peace

Empire enthusiasts in both Britain and Australia planned for a resumption of immigration when peace returned. Wartime immigration had been negligible and the prospects of British emigration were much reduced. The United Kingdom suffered the loss of 610 000 men attributable to the First World War (of which 3 per cent were Irish). About 7 per cent of British males in the age group 13–24 were lost. The demographic consequences were therefore considerable, though the economic historian Rosalind Mitchison has argued that the likely effects were substantially less in net terms, precisely because emigration had ceased in the war. Normally, she estimated, 750 000 left Britain every 10 years (this was the number lost by net emigration in 1901–10). For Australia the reciprocal and opposite argument applied – that is, to the loss of Australian men in the war should be added the emigrants who hypothetically would have arrived had the war not intervened. It is easy to confuse the demographic effects of the war. Similarly, though some marriages were delayed by war service, the average number of marriages did not decline much at all.[29]

The war heightened consciousness about Australia's demographic future as well as the shape of its economy and its defence capacities. In June 1919 the statistician GH Knibbs registered the population as 5 million and projected the current growth to the year 2000 to be only 18 824 000; 'He stressed that this should alarm all those who cared at all for Australia's destiny'.[30] The 1921 census showed an excess of females over males – which had been exacerbated by the war. In Melbourne in 1919 there were 20 000 more unmarried women than unmarried men.

There was clear awareness of these realities during the last stages of the war. State premiers began planning for the recruitment of ex-servicemen, their ideas always predicated on land settlement and large numbers. There was a general belief that the cities had grown too much, partly as a consequence of the decline of goldmining, but also because of restrictions on access to land and the closure of local industries. On the other side of the balance was an acknowledgement that the cities offered higher wages, more diversity and entertainment, and an escape from the common monotony of rural life. Yet the rural argument prevailed: in 1918 Hughes said, 'We must get men [of] the right type and get them in the land and not into the great cities'.[31] Hughes was urgent to

Wartime internment of aliens, 1915: the Torrens Island Camp in South Australia. *History Trust of South Australia*

secure the best immigrants from the British Army: 'Are we going to try and get fair proportion of these or let Canada have all?' he asked. He believed that the Commonwealth should intervene and set up a first-class organisation to set it all in motion.[32]

The enthusiasm for a new scale of immigration did nothing to diminish the commitment to White Australia. Immigration would undoubtedly remain highly selective and exclusive – White Australia had been reinforced, and at the end of the war there was much antagonism to the idea of ex-enemy immigration. Germans, Austrians, Turks, Bulgarians, Hungarians were prohibited altogether; there was also a new fear of Bolshevism to add to the agenda of watchfulness; and there was an antagonism towards Sinn Fein which did not auger well for any revival of mass migration from Catholic Ireland. As for Britain there was the prospect of a sea change in official attitudes to emigration. In 1911 Lord Lucas, Under-Secretary for the Colonies, had declared that 'it was not the [British] government's policy, nor had the Dominions requested, that emigration should be subsidised ... by the state'. But by 1917 the Dominions Royal Commission contemplated a new imperial agenda which entertained the notion that Britain would actually pay its own citizens to leave the country for Empire destinations. This was a genuine turning point in the shifting of a principle which had been sacrosanct since the start of colonisation in 1788.[33]

4 White British Australia resuscitated: the 1920s

Postwar migrants

Among the victors at the end of the war, Australia was surprisingly vocal in the Peace Treaty at Versailles and notable in its opposition to the proposal for an international prohibition of racial discrimination. This was particularly offensive to Japan. Australia also wanted to resume its prewar immigration on the same scale and exclusivity it had achieved before 1914. Immigration was a priority of imperial diplomacy – to work with Britain in their mutual interest for the redistribution of British people to the dominions. But it was no less a matter of money and recruitment – that is, who should pay for the migrants' passages, how were they to be selected, and how would emigrants be attracted to Australia? At the end of the war immigrants seemed to be more welcome in Australia than some of the maimed and limbless soldiers returning from the battlefields of Europe; many of the latter were angry with their reception.[1]

The catch cry at the end of the war in the United States was 'the return to normalcy'. This mainly meant a resumption of investment and expansion, consumption and comfort. Australia adopted a similar psychology, a return to prewar certitudes of Empire and security, and expansion. But there were critical differences between the United States and Australia in the following decades, especially in terms of demography and immigration. In the United States the shutters were drawn down on the great Age of Migration. A series of quotas was cleverly designed not only to restrict immigration but also to discriminate in favour of Anglo-Saxon and west European immigrants. There was blatant racism in government circles: President Calvin Coolidge, for instance, abhorred intermarriage between Nordics and other groups because he believed it produced inferior offspring.[2] The idea of the 'melting pot' was in retreat and defenders of the White Australia policy took comfort from the changes in North American political psychology.

Its vulnerability finally demonstrated in the Great War, Australia adopted the opposite policy and moved positively to fund immigration as never before. During the 'roaring twenties' Australia experienced a measure of nascent industrial growth and rising consumption and revived its vigorous program of immigration. Indeed the British diaspora in the 1920s continued in its redirection away from the United States and towards the Empire in which Australia was an active and continuing partner. Britain itself laboured under serious structural problems in its old industries and regarded emigration as an important tool of social amelioration. Australia tried to recreate and enhance the exact character and scale of its prewar program of British immigration. 'Normalcy' became an extrapolation of the old 'Edwardian' world, now federalised and more fully planned than before. CH Wickens, the Commonwealth Statistician and master of metaphor, remarked in 1925:

> this collection of people which makes up the population
> of Australia is not a mere heap of heterogeneous
> material shot on a dump in the Western Pacific, but
> it is rather a more or less delicately organised piece

of mechanism which is capable of great things if due
attention is paid to appropriate balance of its parts,
but which may be thrown seriously out of gear by any
dislocation of its regular action.[3]

But part of Australia's intention was to coax and cajole the British
government into carrying some of the financial burden of assisting emigration. As the British economy fell into decline and heavy
unemployment in the 1920s, the case for British contributions
strengthened.

Eventually Australia probably gained as many as 300000
migrants during the 1920s, considerably below expectations entertained at the end of the war even though assistance was generously
available to prospective migrants. In the 1920s the fare from Britain to Australia was about £33, of which £11 was funded for suitably nominated immigrants; children under 12 were free; teenagers
paid half price for the passage. Assistance was not available to ex-
enemies or to Russians and Maltese, and it was not available to New
Zealanders. Italians, however, were able to enter under the terms of
a wartime Anglo-Italian agreement which extended automatically
to the dominions (and became a matter of contention in Australia
by the late 1920s). In some states the assistance was restricted to
'nominators ... [who were] engaged in rural industry, and ... their
nominees [who] intend to engage in [the same] industry'.[4] Without
assistance far fewer would have arrived, though, surprisingly, more
that a third of the immigrants financed themselves.

Many British men had responded enthusiastically to Australia's
call for rural migrants, strengthened by their own bucolic dream-
ings and the poor economic prospects at home in postwar Britain.
In 1919 the immigration posters in London and across the United
Kingdom showed horseback riders in the outback proclaiming 'Australia for the British boy'. The Land, journal of the New South Wales
Farmers and Settlers' Association, said in November 1919 that 'A
vigorous policy of immigration, with preference to agricultural and

farm labour, is ... advocated, as if the wealth of Australia is to be increased through primary production a sufficiency of rural workers will have to be guaranteed'.[5] This rural fixation was the source of much subsequent disappointment among the British migrants.

Some of the individual migrant voices of the 1920s have survived. One was Arthur Hackett of Darlington in northern England, who recorded his story in 1960 when he was 93 years old. He recollected 'trying to get to Australia in 1922 – like hundreds of working men'. Married in 1917, Hackett served in the forces and met a fellow serviceman from Townsville who planted the idea of emigrating. Hackett gathered the details and pamphlets but he could not raise the passage expense of £96 for his wife and three children. Though guaranteed work in Australia he had to give up his dream: 'Many a time I have regretted the lost opportunity'.[6] He had been a prospective migrant blocked by the cost and lack of sufficient assistance.

Edward Miles had a different story which cast Australia in a harsh light. Thirty-five years after the event, Miles remembered his emigration in 1924 at the age of 20. He said that 'British boys went because they wanted to see the world, wanted to do better for themselves' than in depressed postwar England. They went to farms and many were severely disappointed: 'We worked hard, an 8 hour day, 8 hours before midday, dinner and 8 hours after – 16 in all ... Our wages 11/- a week and keep and a "doss" to lie on'. Sometimes the pay fell to 15/- a week and keep, and when conditions worsened work became harder still and all they got was their keep 'or tucker as Australians call it'. Miles remembered these times sourly:

> We did not think very highly of the average
> Australian, the 'cocky' or Australian farmer treated
> us as badly as the South African is said to treat
> his black employees. When war came in 1939 and
> Australia stood in danger of invasion some of us
> hoped that the Japs would land and make life hard
> for the Australian. A lash across the face with a whip

Back to normal: renewed immigration, 1921; migrants disembarking.
Department of Immigration and Multicultural Affairs, no. 21/4A/1

would not be too harsh treatment, for the way many
Aussie farmers treated pommies ... I received very
little kindness from Australians.[7]

Miles was a thoroughly embittered returned migrant – a rare voice
in the story – a man caught in the depressed times of Australian
agriculture. He was lucky to leave before agricultural conditions
deteriorated further at the end of the 1920s.

Alexander Forest served an apprenticeship in the Clydeside
shipyards but suffered bouts of unemployment before he headed

for Australia, 'to try his luck'. His brother recollected that 'At first, he found the going pretty tough, clearing scrub by himself in the solitude of the bush after the noise and bustle of Glasgow, but he stuck it out and later worked in Melbourne, Sydney, Townsville, New Guinea and Rum Jungle'.

Robert Keen, younger son of a well-off Oxfordshire farmer, wrote a series of letters from Australia in the 1920s. Keen was unlucky to arrive in Western Australia just a few months before the economy plummeted into an appalling agricultural depression in 1928. He had left England in May 1928 and noted in his log that there were at least twenty other 'public school boys' on board his ship – which gave him some comfort. He arrived in Perth in June and soon found work on a wheat and sheep farm at Culham, 75 miles from Perth. His employer was a 60-year-old Yorkshireman, Thackray, a 'great churchman' and a good employer, who paid Keen £1 a week and keep; Keen was soon engaged in ploughing, which he regarded as the pioneering life, initially sending back good reports about the extraordinary cheapness of land. It is clear that he had been helped by his own farming family back in England and he began to talk of getting land on his own account, with more financial help from his father. He reported home in 1928: 'I don't think I have thanked you for letting me come out here and all the rest but will do so now. I love it here but shall look forward to a trip home in a year or two'. Australia was a great country and ready for rapid expansion – in contrast with the family back home in Berkshire where an outbreak of swine fever had produced much gloom.[8] Keen's subsequent career is followed in the next chapter.

Rudyard Kipling, like Haggard, was a great advocate of emigration and he conducted a correspondence with an Australian farmer in Cumindi in October 1911, remarking on the recent expansion of emigration to Australia:

> I am more glad than I can say to tell that Australia
> is getting a move on in the way of attracting

immigrants. I was in the country twenty odd years
ago and all the set of public opinion was against
anything of the sort.

Writing from his Sussex home, Kipling observed that from 12 to 17
people from his own immediate district were departing for Australia
in the autumn – mainly to Western Australia. He remarked, 'They
are the best and they leave the weaker type behind for the State
(i.e. the common or garden taxpayer) to look after. However that
doesn't matter in comparison with getting the good men out'.[9]

After the war Kipling was the voice of the imperial centre,
keenly promoting emigration to colonies for the imperial good.
From his small country estate, he discovered that one of his own
gardeners – a young man on good wages and a rent-free house –
thought to 'better himself' by going to Australia. Kipling agreed to
help with his passage. But six months later the gardener returned
to Sussex begging Kipling to reinstate him. In Australia he had
been required to 'ride the boundaries', to work day or night and
to sleep in the open, and to lead 'an uncivilised life'. Kipling was
caustically critical and enjoyed telling the story, and clearly took
pleasure in turning the man away from his door – 'so poor a speci-
men of an Englishman'.[10]

From beyond the Anglophile world in the 1920s came a slowly
increasing number of other immigrants, mainly Italians. One was
Sam Contarino, who emigrated from Sicily to Queensland in March
1922 on the *Omar* with 35 others from the same place. Most of
them headed for the sugar industry at Mourilyan. Contarino cut
cane throughout the interwar years and spoke vividly of that heavy
work:

This cane cuttin', oh, it's something incredible.
When you cut the sugar cane, we had to cut it
green. All this burn-out and machines came out after
the (Second War). In the early days, we had to do it

all by hand … The cane, it cuts you, cuts your skin like a razor… The first week you feel all broken but then you've got to cut five, six ton of sugar cane. At the time the price was 7/6 a ton. You had to cut it, load it, move the rail, portable rail … Oh, we worked from four o'clock sometime, in the morning. Almost from daylight to dawn. All the time.[11]

The changing status of Italian immigrants in Australia from the time of Contarino's arrival through to the 1950s is a central theme in the longer story.[12]

Imperial relations

The war had 'depleted the British reservoir of migrants' but the general situation favoured a strong revival of emigration to Australia. The essential differential of income and prospects was widened by the dismal condition of Britain's economy in a decade in which Australia experienced some of the first fruits of higher mass consumption. In the 1920s the average weekly earning in Australia was 94s 4d; in the United Kingdom it was 60 shillings.[13] This was the decade of the motor car, the cinema and radio, which Australians tasted sooner than the British. Australia was committed to increased immigration and now British governments, against tradition, were reluctantly persuaded that the needs of Empire solidarity, as well as the relief of structural unemployment, justified official British subsidies to emigrants. In this new context Australian negotiators were able to bargain for more favourable terms for cooperation in migration. The traditional dialogue between Britain and Australia was changing tune.

There were two main arguments. The first was immediate: in March 1919 Britain faced the prospect of 300 000 war veterans on unemployment benefits and Lloyd George became enthusiastic for schemes of free emigration passages.[14] Australia was equally committed to the prompt resumption of migration. Prime Minister Hughes, in November 1918, was all urgency and secrecy and cabled home: 'If we are to hold Australia and develop its tremendous resources we must have numerous population'. Hughes thought that the demobilisation of the British Army offered a 'unique opportunity of securing the right type of immigrant'. He said that there were tens of thousands of 'men in the prime of life, who would make most desirable settlers on soil, and who will be disinclined to remain in Britain'. Australia must bestir itself. He activated Australia House and a conference of premiers was arranged for January 1919. This was disrupted by the Spanish influenza epidemic and some of the head of steam was lost.[15]

The second argument was essentially the old imperial dream now revisited as 'an organic system, harmoniously balanced between industrial metropole and agricultural periphery'. But a new reality had intruded, because the dominions had begun to expand their industrial bases while also exerting their independent national interests. The idea of Empire remained in the balance and required great faith.

The first migration scheme was directed to returned servicemen, who were offered special assistance with passages and settlement in the dominions in the years 1919–22. It was remarkably popular and the number of applicants easily outran the limits of the scheme. Only a third of the applicants were accepted, which suggests that the propensity for emigration in Britain was high and mainly blocked by the costs. Nevertheless the British government supported the emigration of 82 196 families – of which a quarter went to Australia, 17 000 families, a total of 35 000 people.

Australia meanwhile was slowly edging towards a national policy on immigration. In 1921 Commonwealth and state governments clarified their respective responsibilities. A broad national consensus evolved on development, overseas markets and closer settlement, which led to the promotion of immigration in conjunction with ambitious and costly land settlement schemes.[16] Under the famous slogan 'men, money and markets', land development became the key to national prosperity. This was not difficult to connect with grander notions of imperial reciprocation. Halford Mackinder, the former Director of the London School of Economics and founder of academic geography in Britain, had remarked that 'Those regions [West Africa] ought to be treated as assets of the Empire. If we keep the *Pax Britannica* throughout vast areas of the world ... then we are entitled to treat those regions as imperial estates'.[17] The challenge was to connect this vision with the practical politics of migration: Australia was suggestible and cooperated, though increasingly on its own terms. HS Gullett, the Commonwealth Superintendent of Immigration, said that Australia was 'a whole continent brimming with golden opportunities for capital and labour, and ideal home-making possibilities'. This supreme optimism propelled the emigration schemes of the 1920s. In 1924 British Prime Minister Stanley Baldwin declared that 'The Australians are the Young of the British', and he recommended increased emigration together with a reconsideration of the whole question of Anglo-Australian tariff cooperation.[18]

There were also strategic considerations about Australia's security, enhanced by the war itself, by the 'Red Menace of Communism' too which was inextricable among imperial assumptions. In 1921 Rider Haggard read a piece in *The Times* by Keith Murdoch entitled 'Will Britain, if needs be, fight for a white Australia?' He thought, 'Britain probably would fight to prevent Australia being invaded and captured by the yellow races to whom her empty lands are a great temptation. But to prevent immigrants of that blood from landing on her shores ... well I am not sure'. Haggard regretted that his settlement scheme of 1916 had been wasted: 'Are we waiting for a fight for an empty Australia?' was the real question. He thought the Northern Territory (with a non-indigenous population of some 3500) could support 30 million.[19] Haggard believed that Britain had become degenerate and advocated national regeneration through agriculture at home and across the Empire. British cities were over-crowded with thousands of children 'utterly without prospects, except such as are afforded by the hospital, the poorhouse and the gaol.' They would become 'healthy, happy and prosperous' in the dominions and at little cost to the Mother Country.[20]

Haggard and other imperial enthusiasts were frustrated by the politicking associated with their efforts to arouse grand new emi-gration and development schemes, and they faced scepticism even from within their own literary circles. Thus, for instance, HG Wells believed that imperialism was finished and that the British Empire should follow German and Russian empires onto the 'dust heap' of history. But the advocates of emigration kept alive the idea of an Empire Settlement Bill, led in Britain by Leo Amery, Under-Secretary for the Colonies, despite repeated delays and resistance from Treasury. Amery was the complete visionary:

> If the United States have grown in the last century
> from five millions to a hundred millions, there is
> no reason why, in the coming century, we should
> not grow to a population of two hundred or three
> hundred millions of white people in the Empire.[21]

Amery told the British Cabinet that policy should aim to redis-tribute the Empire's population so as 'best to promote develop-ment, stability and defence'. Land settlement was vital otherwise the Dominions might 'reach the limit of their powers to absorb our unemployed or other classes'.[22]

This brand of Empire ideology was infectious and sometimes effective. By 1922 several ambitious settlement schemes were being considered. Western Australia was especially enthusias-tic, opening up lands on a grand scale, facilitated further by new railways and irrigation schemes. Group farming was a popular notion though there was always Australian suspicion that Britain still wanted to 'shovel out its paupers'. In 1923 the Prime Minister's Department expressed its anxiety about workhouse inmates coming to Australia.[23]

The politics of migration were becoming clearer and harder. Thus if emigration was an imperial question then London had a responsibility which was unavoidably financial. Prime Minister Stanley Bruce, the greatest of Anglophiles and firmest advocate of 'men, money and markets', gave a blunt assessment of the Anglo-Australian relationship. In 1923 he told a meeting of the Conservative Women's Reform Association in England:

> Before the war, Britain never spent a farthing to
> assist the migration of people under her own flag.
> Australia cannot absorb the unemployed of Britain.
> Australia is prepared to take all the people she can,
> compatible with her rate of development. She is not
> prepared to have people poured into the country
> without any idea of what is to be done with them. It
> is no use Australia pretending she can give people
> chances unless she has markets for her produce.[24]

Negotiations between Britain and Australia descended into increasingly irritable and cynical horse dealing. In the outcome, by the mid 1920s, Australia emerged with unprecedented financial cooperation from Britain which entailed large subsidised immigration and heavy capital outlays on favourable terms from London. Ambitious capital works were announced to synchronise with the closer settlement of the land. Australia flexed its muscles in these negotiations and induced Britain to provide long-term funding in the form of conditional loans at preferential rates. The agreement was finally articulated in 1924 with the Loan Plan: over the following 10 years Britain would release £34 million to state governments to increase immigration on to the land.

Bruce made it clear that 'the provision of money at nominal rates of interest to the states to carry our developmental works would increase Australia's power to absorb migrants'.[25] The grand plan was designed to prime the immigration pump by subsidised passages, greater access to land and the creation of large-scale rural infrastructure on easy terms. It was an exceedingly bold Anglo-Australian scheme which envisaged 450 000 immigrants and great rural expansion over a period of 10 years. It was a dream based on assumptions about the stability and growth of the primary sector and therefore of the buoyancy of international commodity markets. The money was used to assist immigrants and to create new reciprocating markets for both Britain and Australia. It was a grand articulated imperial plan to be manifested in roads and bridges, electricity and water conservation, railways, sugar mills, butter factories, all assisting in the process of absorbing migrants.[26]

Herbert (later Sir Herbert) Gepp, Chairman of the Development and Migration Commission, responsible for much of the administration of the plan, believed that the scheme was designed to fill up the 'the vast empty spaces' of Australia with British migrant settlers.[27] He pointed out that Australia had lost 60 000 of its best and most energetic brains in the Great War and the purpose of the £34 million scheme was to draw 'to its shores the worthiest elements from the Motherland'. He was explicit that 'The conception of mass migration as a governmental method of alleviating economic difficulties has long been abandoned both in Great Britain and overseas'. As late as March 1929 Gepp was claiming that the scheme had already produced a great increase in the infrastructure for development and that there were 3500 new farms in Western Australia, 600 in New South Wales. The policy had been to create opportunities for emigrants in primary and secondary industries.[28]

These ambitious plans were the products of the imperial imagination. They were not stringently tested for market requirements, and the criteria of investment were speculative and extremely optimistic. Most notably, the 'rural myth' was reinstated and this was the ultimate source of a great deal of the subsequent suffering for many of the migrants involved. Only after 1928 was there a 'sober realization that the large-scale land settlement scheme had been over-ambitious and extremely costly'.[29] Much of the impetus within Australia came from a group of latter day immigrationists who were especially anxious about the continuing fall in the Australian birth rate. Frederic (later Sir Frederic) Eggleston was a distinguished leader of the immigration push involved in the coterie of the Round Table, 'a small band of believers in British civilization'; CH Wickens gave it statistical impetus, having predicted on the 1924–33 growth rate that the Australian population would take at least 48 years to double.[30]

In the outcome government policies helped to reinforce the revival of Australian immigration in the 1920s and were associated with capital inflows augmented by public and private investment. Thus was the demand for labour expanded which then generated further incentives to migrants. Australia became a more attractive destination for migrants and the flow was effectively boosted by the greater subsidisation of passages. Immigration increased the demand for houses and helped the expansion of the building sector even though the primary producing sector was the central focus of national policy.[31]

In Britain emigration was regarded as an instrument of social engineering but it failed to capture a central place in British political thinking. Support sagged in the late 1920s and Leo Amery registered this disillusion in his diary entry in November 1928 when he complained:

the attitude of many of my colleagues [members of the Migration Committee at the House of Commons] about the whole migration business has been rather unreasonable and very anti-Dominion. They ... persist in treating migration as a scheme for dealing with our unemployment which the Dominions ought to be grateful to help us with. Got quite annoyed at the end and gave them a piece of my mind which won't help things.[32]

In Australia itself, as we shall see, the dream eventually turned into a nightmare in 1929.

Conditions for recruitment

In the 1920s Australia recruited its immigrants in a new context. The greatest traditional destination for emigrants, the United States, had already moved to close its doors to indiscriminate immigration by way of quotas. Any possible diversion of European immigrants to Australia was controlled by its own restrictions – except in the case of Italians, who were favoured by the Anglo-Italian agreement. Australia wanted British people who, despite unfavourable economic conditions at home, displayed a diminishing inclination to emigrate; there was also increased competition from Canada. Consequently Australia stepped up its advertising campaign. Gullett, Commonwealth Superintendent of Immigration, was not embarrassed to say that the 'whole continent [is] brimming with golden opportunities for capital and labour, and ideal home-making possibilities'.[33] The advertising campaigns became so rapturous that some politicians were beginning to express reservations – notably when a film about Group Settlement in Western Australia described the climate 'as mild as a mother's kiss' and the soil as 'kindly as God's love'. Films with titles such as *Sons of the Surf* and *Sanctuary of the Untamed* were propagated for prospective migrants, among much other more sober propaganda.[34] But Australians were urged to expurgate from their vocabularies such words as 'drought', 'strike', 'rabbits', 'taxes' and 'politics'.[35]

Competition with Canada for emigrants dated back to the 1880s when New Zealand, Queensland and New South Wales began offering bonuses and commissions to their recruiting agents. In 1921 a Canadian migrant agent claimed that 'We have no difficulty in getting far more people than we can absorb. Our difficulty is not to make Canada better known in the Mother Country, but rather to make an intelligent selection of those who are anxious to emigrate'. But by 1925 the Canadian press was saying Australia and New Zealand were indeed skimming 'the cream of the British agricultural population'.[36] The Australian recruiters were now using the services of 2000 employment exchanges and 30 special agencies across the country, equipped with special advertising allowances and 30 shillings per migrant as a commission.

An extraordinary raft of special schemes was hatched to stimulate the flow to Australia. Tasmania, for instance, opened its scheme to non-British persons of white race, under certain restrictions. Like other states, Tasmania also initiated a child-migration scheme by which it recruited 'boy farm learners' of 14–16 years of age who were selected by the Commonwealth Office in London. They were required to work for a given period, till the passage was paid off (it was an echo of 18th century colonial indenture schemes). In 1924, 71 children arrived in Hobart, but they were not happy migrants. It was reported that 'Most of the boys came from urban areas and many had been out of work for some time'. Most Tasmanian immigrants of the period were 'nominated', commonly by close relatives among recent immigrants, usually within 12 months of the first arrival. This was, in effect, chain migration reinforced by the State with its subsidies, and a very high proportion of the people nominated were obviously urban people with industrial occupations, or were domestics, a trend that had been clear even before the war. Tasmania was a small player in the immigration schemes of the period but was keen to attract farming settlers with capital, who were encouraged with a special loan scheme for those possessing more than £3000.[37]

Yet the results in general were below expectations and led to vociferous complaint in Australia. The Melbourne *Argus* in July 1924 claimed that Australian expenditure on immigration since the war had been 'upon an unprecedented colossal scale', yet the outcome was bitterly disappointing, especially compared with the prewar successes and despite that fact that conditions in the United

The rural dream, 1925. *Mitchell Library, State Library of New South Wales*

Kingdom were worse than in the prewar period. The immigration policy was condemned as 'utterly inadequate'.[38] It is true that shipping costs rose rapidly in the postwar years but this did not account for the relatively poor response since Australia increased its generous subsidies to counteract the trend.

For Australia at large, despite its great investment, immigration targets in the 1920s were not fulfilled, though it managed to attract a higher percentage of British emigrants than before.[39] In total, therefore, about 323 000 immigrants came to Australia between 1921 and 1929, 66 per cent of them assisted in some way. Net immigration accounted for 22 per cent of the growth of the Australian population and the great majority went to urban locations. Nomination by friends and relatives in Australia probably accounted for two-thirds of the assisted immigrants, augmented by those assisted by charities and churches, notably organisations such as the YMCA, the Church of England and the Salvation Army.

Who were the British immigrants in the 1920s? A Royal Commission on National Insurance in 1927 confirmed that the majority came from industrial centres and declared that 'if these are to be encouraged as immigrants it will be necessary to foster secondary industries, otherwise many will swell the ranks of the unemployed in this country'. Immigrants tended to leave for the cities even if they first went to the countryside.[40]

The migrants were not well documented, though perhaps 20 per cent were rural people, which suggests a degree of effective recruitment in this difficult category: agricultural workers were rapidly vanishing from the British economy at this time. Australia's own rural population grew very slowly in the 1920s. Although 82 000 new British immigrants went into rural areas (39 per cent assisted, 29 per cent of net immigration) many of them soon left. And immigrants were therefore insufficient in number to replace the 170 000 who drifted from the land in this period. The *Argus* complained that British immigrants were not prepared to do farm work even though that was how they had been recruited. There were too many 'townies' and many of the women expected 'to take up shorthand and typing'.[41] Behind these complaints was the fact that in both Australia and Britain (and all other modernising economies) the populations of the rural sector were in the process of continuous decline, which in Australia was neither understood nor welcomed.[42]

One-third of the immigrants were deemed to be 'skilled', and they contributed strongly to the growth of the manufacturing labour force. There was some special industrial recruitment: thus the Victorian textile industry grew with substantial reinforcement derived from imported British labour. In New South Wales coalminers were particularly good nominators.[43] Even more successful were a group of Scottish masons who were specially recruited in 1926 for construction work on the Sydney Harbour Bridge: trade unions helped to arrange 5-year passages paid under contract by the bridge builders, Dorman and Long of Middlesborough: they sailed in two parties from Liverpool to work in quarries at Moruya, New South Wales.[44] Two-thirds of all the immigrants arrived in Melbourne and Sydney, and certainly helped to boost the urban workforce. Up to a quarter of the immigrants were domestic servants or housewives. Domestic servants were regarded as vital, yet their numbers were falling in the 1920s even though special training centres were established in England, notably at Market Harborough, in an attempt to activate a supply for Australia at a time when they were becoming less and less likely to be available in the United Kingdom.[45] Most prospective female migrants from Britain in the 1920s were urban factory and office girls, categories regarded as unsuited for Australian needs.

In the halcyon 4 years before 1914 British immigrants had accounted for 35 per cent of Australia's population increase; between 1920 and 1930 it was less than 25 per cent. Nevertheless 10.8 per cent of the Australian population in 1933 was British-born. Most of them went to the most urbanised regions in Victoria and New South Wales, from 'the great cities of Great Britain'. Of their urban orientation in Australian, David Pope remarked, 'These locations most closely approximated their traditional home environments and it may be added that the nomination system reinforced this geographic and urban slant. For the nominators were themselves city dwellers'. There were many complaints that immigrants declared untruthfully that they were farm labourers (another echo from the previous century) – they were 'general labourers, fishermen, maltmen, window cleaners, soldiers, seamen, bakers, clerks, cotton operatives', and ' few had backgrounds even vaguely related to the rural life'.[46]

Another change in the context of Australian recruitment in the 1920s was Ireland. Ireland in the 19th century had provided up to a third of all the immigrants (particularly among those assisted), and filled many of its crucial labouring needs. When the new agreement for British emigration to Australia was drawn up in 1921 some of its provisions were specifically denied to Ireland, or at least as far as their children were concerned. Eire was not eligible under the Empire Settlement Act. The new Irish government was invited to join a parallel scheme but declined,[47] though certain rebates for nominated immigrants still applied, being £11 per adult.[48] Northern Ireland remained within the prime area of recruitment and there were particular opportunities among the disbanded men of the Royal Irish Constabulary – a force of 10 000 officers who, with the 'Black and Tans', had roughly maintained law and order through the years of conflict. After 1921 they were stranded, many of them ostracised, and faced a very poor future in Republican Ireland. Some settled in Ulster; a few were welcomed into the British police forces; some went to Palestine. Australia was asked to take some of them and 433 eventually arrived despite some controversy about their acceptability. Those who went to Perth found work hard to get: they wasted their pensions; one of them remarked that 'some of us are thinking of going back to Ireland, as we might as well be shot there as die here'.[49]

There were other initiatives for intra-imperial migration to Australia. For instance, projects to lure British personnel from other colonies were revived, but as Pope notes, 'the reservoir of white British nationals in India and Ceylon, the Straits Settlements and Hong Kong was exceedingly shallow ... The Victorian government did attempt to tap India, but succeeded only in attracting a score of white ex-India regiment officers'. When Prime Minister Bruce was asked about non-European Indian immigration he said he had no objection to colour as such, but used the classic argument that such immigration would tend to undermine work standards.[50]

The least visible component of the intake was the unassisted immigrants, who constituted a third of the total and who left little if any trace in the official data. They were evidently able and prepared to foot the entire bill for the passages – in the long tradition of private migration which had accounted for about the same proportion in the previous century. The real problem was the lack of synchronisation between the British and the Australia economies. Britain's workforce was overwhelmingly urban and industrial and was suffering structural decline; Australia was only on the brink of industrialisation in the 1920s. It is likely that the urban immigrants of that decade aided the growth of Australian industry; equally clear, in retrospect, is the fact that rural migration had little future at either end of the relationship.

Australian immigration in the 1920s was imprisoned in the anachronistic philosophy of 'an organic Empire' in which 'Australia might become ever richer through supplying primary produce to the United Kingdom'. The migrants were meant to be the 'ideal yeoman type'; in reality they were predominantly townspeople who gravitated inexorably to the cities of suburban Australia. In the end industrialisation was the only basis for the much increased population that Australia so warmly craved.[51]

Trouble on the land

The grandiose settlement schemes were based on the assumption that the British had a surplus of labour and capital, and that Australia was thirsty for both. The states, partly driven by rivalry, each promoted closer settlement schemes on the land. Thus Victoria began with notions of settling 10 000 immigrant families on the land – each expected to bring £1000 in capital which then entitled each of them to a loan of £1500. Some of the advertising was absurdly optimistic and misleading – some promised the settlers a profit of £400 per annum. By the mid 1920s these promises were scaled back. By then 814 settlers had arrived, three-quarters of whom were ex-servicemen, but 455 did not stay. In New South Wales the scale of the program was smaller: in 1923 the plan was to settle 6000 families though this was subsequently much reduced. In the event only 336 settlers were placed between 1923 and 1925. The land schemes were associated with the highest hopes and their subsequent widespread failures caused intense criticism and ill feeling. The land was unresponsive, yields were low, prices were down – all contributing to the broken spirits of the settlers.

The entire nation suffered in the Great Depression. In the aftermath a Victorian Royal Commission conceded that settlers had been put on 'a wilderness of eucalyptus scrub', but the new British immigrants were among the most vulnerable and they became vociferous about their plight. Who was or what was to blame for their catastrophe? Some said that the poor quality of the immigrants had been a factor in their own unhappiness, but the evidence was not clear, though it is likely that the British migrants of the 1920s were less suited to pioneering than their predecessors in the 19th century. Michael Roe found that many of the migrants were poor, some even destitute. These were the migrants who clustered in the cities and their skill levels were allegedly falling. Despite medical examinations, there were recurring complaints about 'degenerates' and 'imbeciles' among the immigrants. Simultaneously it was claimed that too many public-school educated urbanites were recruited, men entirely unfitted for life in the Australia bush. In reality there is no decisive evidence that the immigrants were any better or worse than previous or later cohorts. They were overtaken by the Depression, which had no respect for class or origins, especially on the land.[52]

The majority of immigrants left no record, though some certainly succeeded and were indeed ecstatic: a young British migrant in South Australia in 1926 declared that in Australia 'Jack is as good as his master' and that it was 'really marvelous how quick the English do get to the top'. One was sending home £32 for his mother. But when conditions in Australia deteriorated in the late 1920s stories of hardship, exploitation, neglect and suicide among British immigrants multiplied. The schemes in Victoria and West Australia were fiascos in which 'abounded epics of human misery and governmental crassness'. Subsequent inquiries in England and Australia exposed stories of desperation, poverty and despair. A House of Commons petition from Australian immigrants spoke of people losing their reason and reported many suicides. A South Australian parliamentary inquiry in 1924 found that wages paid to teenage-boy migrants were in some cases seriously insufficient. Witnesses alleged instances of ill-treatment by employers and some cases of premature death – perhaps suicide.[53] There were accounts of anti-immigrant discrimination to be set beside many stories of kindness.

The troubles surrounding the land schemes were concentrated in the lives of many young migrants brought from Britain by special schemes as part of the push to achieve closer settlement. Voluntary organisations in Britain were heavily involved in Australian immigration: the Salvation Army was the most influential and between 1903 and 1938 it resettled 250 000 migrants in Canada, Australia and New Zealand and South Africa. The open vistas of rural expansion seemed to offer perfect opportunities for young adventurous men of every class – from urban orphans to public-school boys. Many charitable organisations were involved in the channelling of thousands of these 'boys' to the Australian outback. Such parallel schemes were designed to facilitate the introduction of young British males to rural employment and, taken together, they accounted for 10 per cent of all assisted immigration in the 1920s. In New South Wales, for instance, the Dreadnought Trust was revived and brought out 5659 immigrants between 1921 and 1930, and provided training facilities outside Sydney and elsewhere.[54]

Between 1922 and 1927 a total of 14 000 boys and 2000 girls, sponsored by juvenile migration schemes, were settled in Australia. The rhetoric of empire was powerful especially in the propaganda offered to Boy Scouts, who were promoted as the best of emigrants: 'The call of empire comes [to scouts] from the prairie lands, lakes and forests, of Canada – [and] from the vast unoccupied lands of Australia and New Zealand'. It was the noble ideal of the good life across the seas: the longing for the open air life would be fulfilled while also 'helping to build up the Empire' – as opposed to staying in Britain and 'dawdling about in smoky streets, looking for scanty and poorly paid jobs which lead nowhere in the end'. Those recruited by the Scouts Association for Queensland were provided with passage and landing money and the prospect of employment on the land at 15 shilling per week and board. Those chosen met certain specifications: at 18 they would be at least 5 feet 7 inches and 9 stone, 'and <u>must not wear glasses</u>'.[55] Similar schemes, such as the Barwell Boys, operated in South Australia; a Church of England scheme brought 4095 juvenile farm workers to Queensland; and a series of child migration schemes including the Fairbridge enterprise in Western Australia and New South Wales yielded 1500 in the period 1921–30, while a Barnardo scheme conveyed 683 boys and 404 girls in the 1920s. Often these organisations offered minimum training and apprenticeship for rural work.[56] Return migration rates were high though many persisted on the land even in the worst of times.[57] According to Michael Roe, the Boy Schemes were a 'supreme example of bourgeois – bureaucratic paternalism' and indeed the arrangements smacked of indenturing of an earlier era.[58] The legacy of these schemes lingered on throughout the century and belatedly erupted into public controversy in the 1990s.[59]

The tribulations surrounding these Anglo-Australian schemes were exemplified in the most distressing form in Western Australia. The state had expanded disproportionately even in the 1890s, and between 1903 and 1914 attracted nearly 55 000 British immigrants. Its immigration, according to Geoffrey Bolton, was partly a response to the 'nostalgia professed by many prominent urban British for the elemental simplicities of rural life'.[60] Ideas of semi-communal land settlement had been circulating for many years[61] and in March 1921 substantial plans for opening up the southeast were publicised – based on the notion that experienced farmers would lead the way for the immigrants. British newspapers became warmly enthusiastic and by February 1923 the Western Australian government was committed to settling 6000 suitable immigrant families in 'group settlements' with the help of loans provided through the British and Australian governments. It was heralded by excited propaganda and talk of 'a bold yeomanry' which Billy Hughes and overseas visitors helped to circulate. As Bolton says, 'It was curious how long this dream of transporting English village life to the Antipodes lingered among British visitors'. The investment was colossal.[62]

In reality too many migrants were sent out too quickly. Who were the settlers? A contemporary said they were 'mainly "dusted" gold miners, ex-slum dwellers, and Britain's unwanted'. In fact they rarely came from the poorest classes. They included clerks, tradesmen, artisans, often with a war record: 'these were migrants who saw the future constricting before them in the Britain of the 1920s and elected to try their fortunes with the groups'. One of them ruminated:

> We are not all from the slums as some people like to
> make out. Small middle-class people we come from.
> My own people were skilled artisans. My father was

a boiler-maker, my grandfather an engineer and my great grandfather an engine driver.

After a drab reception at Fremantle they pushed out into untested outback areas which were entirely unsuited. They faced a 'hungry ugly country, swampy and ill drained'. Most of them failed and it was heartbreaking, the land not fit for grazing let alone cultivation. And prices were falling as early as 1922: 'In short, the group settlers were the victims of a government which thought that enthusiasm and good intentions were an adequate substitute for planning and research'.

In April 1924 it was estimated that 30 per cent of immigrant group settlers and 42 per cent of Australians had already walked away from their holdings. The bitterness and ill feeling surfaced at various moments. A West Countryman issued a 'Warning to Migrants', saying that 'we were treated like a Damn lot of Dogs'. Migrants were greeted at the wharf with the cry, 'Go away – there is no work here for you', and there was a great deal of anti-immigrant feeling at large.[63]

In 1927 the downswing began but the inflow of immigrants to Australia continued – accompanied by jibes aimed at 'foreign cheap labour' and a call for new restrictions. Domestic servants were still in short supply but in December 1929 all assistance was terminated: many distraught immigrants were now stranded in Australia and the human cost was incalculable. The music had stopped; the tables were bare; most of the immigrants could not get back home. Imperial goodwill had been stretched too far.

Non-Britishers and everyday racism

Opposition to immigration was recurrent and easily fermented and did not exclude British immigrants. James Scullin, in Opposition in August 1922, vehemently demanded the reduction of assisted immigration. Immigration, he insisted, increased unemployment: 'The Government is dumping immigrants here by every ship that is arriving'. He condemned false advertising in Britain to attract immigrants and told the Richmond branch of the Australian Labor Party that 'he had been inundated with letters and personal visits from new arrivals complaining that they had been tricked into migrating by inaccurate information ... the accommodation that immigrants were forced to accept in Yarra was disgraceful'. He also asserted that large-scale immigration of southern Europeans and other foreigners would destroy the standard of living of returned soldiers in the grape-growing areas. The labour market was already overcrowded, he claimed.

The trade unions were always wary of assisted migration on the assumption that it 'depressed wages and threatened to cause unemployment'.[64] But Scullin admitted that there was no dispute that an increase of population was wise – he indeed predicted that in a few generations the population of Australia would be 100 million. But this target first required Australia to get its house in order. In the meantime he believed in tariffs and a reduction in immigration.[65]

In 1924 Prime Minister Bruce declared that his policy was to keep Australia 98 per cent British. The White Australia policy was in no doubt. Nevertheless the actual proportion of British immigrants in the total intakes declined in the 1920s. This was accounted for almost entirely by the increased inflow of Italians, which became a test of Australian regulations and cultural tolerance. The great Italian diaspora had developed swiftly after 1870 and soon overtook other flows out of Europe, but overwhelmingly Italians emigrated to the United States. Small numbers of Italians had reached Australia before the war, about 1745 per annum in the years 1912–14. American restrictions in the 1920s may have caused some diversion to Australia.[66] Australia, in company with most other countries, introduced immigrant quotas (for example on Maltese immigration in 1920); in 1925 a quota was extended to Greeks, Albanians, Yugoslavs, Estonians, Poles, Bulgarians and Czechs.[67] Alien immigrants were accorded few of the advantages possessed by the British; all Australian regulations were weighted against them. In 1924 aliens had to carry a guarantee of £40 from their Australian sponsors; in 1928 more stringent quotas on visa entries were instituted and the landing requirement was raised from £50 to £200. This was at a time when the British immigrants needed only £3. Italians dominated the non-British category – constituting 70 per cent of non-British immigrants in 1925. A Commercial Treaty in 1883 between the United Kingdom and Italy gave Italian subjects freedom of entry, residence and travel and the right to acquire property.[68] Italian immigration rose from 631 in 1920 to a peak of 7884 in 1927 – at which time the southern European numbers were up to 12 per cent of the British total. In 1928 there was an agreement with the Italian government to restrict arrivals to 3000 per annum, which was cut to 1500 in 1929; and in 1930 the dictation test was applied to people arriving on Italian ships.

In most respects (apart from their non-Britishness) the Italians fitted Australian needs ideally – they were mainly rural folk, they had few dependents and located themselves in parts of Australia where labour was most scarce, most notably on the North Queensland cane fields. Italian immigration was nonetheless controversial, especially when labour markets became oversupplied in the later 1920s. There were underlying questions about assimilation and recurrent eruptions of outright racism against southern Europeans. As Pope noted, 'Through many Australian eyes this was an invasion'. Italian immigration seemed to threaten the racial identity of Australia. WA Osborne at Melbourne University said it was a racial menace, a new 'young Frankenstein'.[69] The federal election of 1925 produced an outburst of scaremongering and Italian immigrants were the prime target. The unions were vociferous and regarded Italians as a threat to wages and conditions in Australia. They were 'a menace to Australian standards', said the Melbourne Trades Hall Council in January 1925, claiming also that illiteracy among foreigners increased crime and poverty. There was dark talk of Australia becoming a 'polyglot nation'.[70] Three years later the Labor leader, Ben Chifley, appealed to the racism and insecurity of ordinary Australians when, at a meeting at Lagoon, he denounced the government's policy to give 'preference to Dagoes – not heroes'. Australia had 'allowed so many Dagoes and Aliens into Australia that to-day they are all over the country taking work which rightly belonged to Australians'. Consequently 'thousands of Australians were walking about the Commonwealth out of work – penniless and almost starving'. He referred to newspaper reports of a fight in Melbourne between 'Dagoes and Australians' – it was a 'forerunner of what was likely to happen in the future unless the stream of these undesirable immigrants was stemmed'. Chifley added that 'Australia was supposed to be a white man's country, but Mr Bruce and his Government were fast making it hybrid'. Once more labour protectionism and racial attitudes rode in tandem. It became a greater issue in the 1928 election. The demand was that Australia remain as 'British' as it was in the 1921 census – that is, 98 per cent.[71]

Politicising the non-British immigrant issue induced the Queensland government to institute an inquiry, the Ferry Commission, in 1924–25. It was already evident that the Italians indeed tended to cluster, especially in Queensland among the cane growers in the Herbert River District. Such pockets of aliens generated adverse reactions which led to apprehension. The commission showed that the number of Italians arriving had increased from 150 per annum in 1901 to 6854 in 1924, and 5662 more arrived in 1925. The commission also ventilated feelings against southern Italians who were alleged to lower standards of hygiene and morality. The Ferry Commissioners took evidence of the appalling conditions in some of the Italian locations – especially drawing attention to the 'very dirty class of boarding house'. They recommended controls without which such immigration would damage the racial composition of Australia. In 1930 there was an agreement that in future three-quarters of canecutters should be British in character. It was transparently a discriminatory policy designed to prevent the British component of the population dropping below 98 per cent and it was reinforced by increased landing fees and capital requirements. The policy was self-policing since shippers faced a £100 fine for conveying illegal immigrants – and they were required to return such immigrants to the port of embarkation and pay for their interim maintenance.[72]

Another national leader, Billy Hughes, also appealed to popular feeling and repeatedly voiced intemperate opinion. In 1928 the government had agreed with the Italian government (which was keen to limit emigration anyway) to restrict the immigration to 400 a month. But Hughes went further and alleged that the Australian government was allowing the re-entry of Russian agents and was failing to enforce the White Australia policy by admitting undesirable American negro entertainers.[73] Along similar lines HV Evatt declared that migration should be regarded as 'a scientific redistribution of population' and that certain racial types could not be assimilated in Australia without endangering living standards.[74]

Italian and Maltese immigration aroused various shades of opposition but mostly from the trade unions. On the extreme fringe, the *Australian Worker* described southern Europeans as 'the scum of Europe', as 'cheap, ignorant and low grade', 'miserable semi-slaves', 'backward and degraded' as well as 'simian' in appearance.[75] Southern Europeans were only 'part-white' and even the French were 'part Negroid'. The Maltese were regarded as 'an influx of inferior races' and were not even allowed to join unions. These passions deepened in the Depression.

Most of the immigration restrictions were largely inoperative simply because Australia was too expensive a destination for almost all unassisted migrants. In 1925 Stephen Roberts (later Professor of History at Sydney University) urged a greater public debate on immigration and believed that the idea of White Australia hampered economic growth, fostered higher wages and an uncompetitive labour market. There was indeed considerable academic despair regarding Australia's 'racial paranoia'. It is clear that landing fees, quotas and the dictation test amounted to a formidable armoury of restriction and showed that Australia could have increased its immigration had it not adhered so firmly to White Australia.[76]

Between times, in some of the remote parts of Australia, quiet improvisations were employed to meet local labour shortages, even subverting some parts of the White Australia policy. Thus in the Northern Territory the local population comprised 60 per cent Chinese with small numbers of Greeks/Turks, Patagonians and Maltese. But in the rest of Australia opinion was hardening and, in 1928 Scullin declared that there were too many immigrants and too much had been spent on them. He blamed current unemployment on 'the influx of new arrivals', and Greeks and Italians were worsening the situation because they accepted low wages. The decade thus ended in black despair. The government abandoned the Development and Migration Committee in May 1930 and cancelled the £34 million agreement. Immigration plummeted.[77]

The last hurrah

Yet enthusiasm for immigration was not easily deterred. Even in the late 1920s the spirit of expansion remained. Thus in 1928 a 'Scottish delegation' of 640 passengers from all over Australia sailed aboard the *Hobson's Bay* from Outer Harbour, Adelaide to Scotland to push sales of Australian produce 'and also induce Scots of the right class to settle in Australia'.[78] They were evidently unaware of the calamity about to engulf them all. Some of the delegates had emigrated from Scotland some 50 years before and recalled 'the old days in the wind jammers'. The tour was documented by a journalist who caught the prevailing attitudes well enough – in Colombo it was reported that 'the natives are as thick as bees … and their ways of work are primitive', and it was worth noting that 'the chocolate brigade' was mainly begging. The delegation took the view that:

Alarm against immigrants before The Great Crash – Labor propaganda, 1928. *Theodore Papers, MS 7222, National Library of Australia*

In the Empire scheme of things we are still pioneers.
We are pressing forward with determination, and
the busy present is hurrying to as busier a future.
Inquiries regarding industries and land settlement
have poured in of late years from all points of the
world, and will do so to a greater extent after the
mission has finished its job. An infectious spirit
of optimism prevails, and faith in the future of
the Commonwealth is unbounded. There are no
croakers on the *Hobson's Bay*.

But they were prepared to concede that 'the majority of our delegates recognises and repeatedly say, that we in Australia are lax in our manner of welcoming visitors and immigrants from the Homeland'. There was a pressing need for advertising and greater distribution of propaganda.

In retrospect it is clear that Australian immigration in the 1920s was at the centre of a grand imperial intergovernmental project entailing the long-distance transfer of labour and capital. Its unhappy fate caused deep pessimism at every level, including the very idea of migration and the development of the country. It was a comedy and tragedy of misplaced predictions and the powerlessness of a country to mould its own future.

5 Malaise, recrimination and demographic pessimism: the 1930s

Immigrants of the Depression

The young English immigrant, Robert Keen, felt the full blast of the economic blizzard that descended on rural Australia in the Great Depression. Rebellious son of a wealthy farmer's family from Oxfordshire (as we saw in the previous chapter), he had emigrated under the auspices of the Church of England Schoolboys Emigration Scheme to Western Australia in 1928, where he found a 'wonderful climate and plenty of opportunity'. He had set himself up as a farmer. In September 1930 he wrote to tell his parents that 'the price of wheat is down to 2/6 per bushel now and things begin to look fairly serious for all of us'. But, he said, 'we shall pull through somehow, there are hundreds of thousands worse off than I am'. When prices collapsed he was caught in the classic rural debt trap: 'what kills most farmers is interest on borrowed money and most of them have their places mortgaged to get clearing and fencing and water supplies etc'.

By Christmas 1930 Keen was desolated. He had run through

the money sent from home, and he now wanted to return. He wrote bitterly to his parents (themselves no doubt much devastated by the same course of agricultural prices in England itself):

> you seem to think I am doing alright out in the wild west, when I have done my best but I am afraid it is not much good this year from a financial point of view, the fall in the wheat prices has settled any chance of making anything of it ... I have been unlucky in Aussie but will try again at home. I have all my eggs in one basket so there you are.

He had been overtaken by disaster: 'the game is not worth the candle, one even has to cut down the food expenses to a minimum'.

One month later Keen said he would soon be existing on boiled wheat and rabbits: 'but we shall get through, we are all broke every one of us ... but there are better times ahead, there have been slumps before and there have booms, and they will come again but we must hang on and keep our peckers up'. By this time he was aware that conditions in England were also very poor and chided his family for keeping their two cars: 'if you are so terribly hard up that can hardly be called economy these days'. Keen put off his idea of returning to England and was about to take to the road, to join his brother on the goldfields: 'a man may as well starve to death there as anywhere else. I am fed up to the teeth with this, and I know if I go on again I shall be just as badly off next year, we cant grow wheat at 1/6'. He became utterly broke and gave up his farm and walked off the land. In July he reported: 'I did not hand everything over to those dashed creditors, I have learnt a little since I have been an Aussie'.

Wheat prices fell from 5 shillings to 1s 8d a bushel during the time Keen farmed: he told his brother, 'I have hit the worst year in the history of wheat farming (I am fed up with explaining the position) ... I have lost every penny I have put into it and am now going to have a go at the biggest gamble in the world, namely gold

In 1913 Robert Keen tried his luck in the Western Australia goldfields (Kalgoorlie region) after his disasters in wheat farming. *From RC Keen,* Big Men, Little Men and Men in between, *self-published, Tebworth UK, 1965*

digging'. It had cost Keen's parents £500 to send him to Australia, which he regarded as a lottery. He faced the harshest edge of the Depression, and he eventually returned to England, a failed emigrant.[1]

The British were the most numerous and the most vocal of the immigrants who were laid low by the Depression. But they were better placed than other immigrant groups who were virtually invisible. One was Emmanuel Attard, who had emigrated from Malta in 1916 and was interviewed much later about his hardships during the Depression in Adelaide. He recollected the humiliations of the unemployed and the severity of the wage reductions, and people sleeping in tents along the banks of the River Torrens. He spoke vividly of the sheer worry and pessimism of it all: the great thing was to survive.[2] The years from 1929 were damaged by depression, pessimism and finally war which, together, caused a radical reconsideration of the immigration horizons of Australia.

The post-mortem

The Depression in 1929 immediately terminated most immigration. In the post-mortem on the previous decade, immigration was itself roundly blamed for much of the subsequent collapse; at the same time many of the immigrants, including Robert Keen, were bitterly critical of the failure of the Australian promise.

The land settlement schemes of the 1920s mainly ended in fiasco, even though they had been the most fully coordinated migrant projects since the start of colonisation. Hopes had been highest in Western Australia, where they were most comprehensively dashed: the idea had been to settle 75 000 migrants on 2 million hectares of dairying land in the southwest, often on virgin land which first required clearing. There had been a running trace of socialism in these schemes: the settlers started in groups of 20, clearing off the timber, and then were provided with 25-acre blocks by ballot – the interim development costs were borne by bank loans. Most of the schemes turned into painful fantasy: much of the land was not good enough; the immigrant recruits lacked the requisite knowledge and experience; the planning was poor, and, most of all, the times turned very bad. Many of those who had left were broken and embittered, returning to England or retreating to the cities.[3]

The story was replicated across rural Australia. In aggregate the schemes had aimed to establish 22 000 farms at a cost of £14 million; in the outcome only 478 farmers were settled at a cost of £15 million. Farms were abandoned in every state.[4] The raw statistics of the land schemes masked the human catastrophes contained in that experience. The misery was concentrated in the years after 1928 when collapsing commodity prices sealed the fate of the immigrant farmers.

Recrimination was widespread and the emotions were stoked by publicity in noisy British newspapers. The plight of young British boys in jeopardy now became the focus of indignation, and there were reports of 20 000 immigrants stranded in Australia. Before long a petition from 50 000 British immigrants was presented to the House of Commons, speaking of misery, semi-starvation and despair. These Britons, it was claimed, had been induced to emigrate by the false propaganda of the Australian government:

> Our members have been, in consequence, reduced
> to misery, semi-starvation and despair. Suicides are
> frequent. Some have lost their reason. Young women
> have sold their virtue, and many of our young men
> are herded together in camps of unemployed in
> conditions hardly better than the conditions of
> convicts in British prisons.

The migration agreements had been 'dishonoured by the Australian Government'. They wanted compensation and repatriation.[5] The whole issue threatened to poison relations between the two countries, not helped by the 'Bodyline' series in 1932–33. (The main strike bowler of the English cricket team, Harold Larwood, a proletarian commanded by his patrician skipper Douglas Jardine, later became an emigrant to Sydney.)

Referring to the operations of the Empire Settlement Act in the House of Commons, in November 1930, Major RGC Glyn asked about British families in Victoria who were allegedly 'reduced to receiving supplies of food and clothing from the Salvation Army' and other charities. Glyn was unable to budge the British government, which told him that it could accept no responsibility for these people, who are 'in great distress and have neither food nor clothing'. A Royal Commission met in Victoria from 1930 and finally conceded that many of the migrants had indeed confronted 'a wilderness of eucalyptus scrub', and the Victorian government, after long delays, paid out £5 million in compensation.[6] The state allocated extra land to the remaining settlers, wrote off debts and did rather more for them than for the unprecedented number of Victoria's own urban unemployed of the time.[7]

The 1925 Empire Settlement Act had planned for the expenditure of £34 million with 450 000 immigrants within 10 years, but these targets were never met. On the other side it was true that assisted immigration in the 1920s was greater than it would otherwise have been, and that 4000 miles of railways had been built, together with irrigation works, electricity schemes, as well as soldier and farm settlements. In a masterpiece of understatement, Herbert Gepp looked back on the scheme and declared that the efforts to settle British migrants on the land 'were not proving outstandingly successful'. He blamed the unexpectedly high costs of clearing land and the lack of knowledge of trace elements, fertilisers and the role of subterranean clover. About half of the settlers had eventually abandoned their blocks. The plans in Victoria and New South Wales to settle 8000

British families struck the same difficulties and only 730 families in all were established on the land. As Gepp put it, the plans were swept away by the 'tidal wave of the Great World Depression', though in reality they were sickly long before that event. Gepp claimed that the commission did not achieve the miracles expected but had raised the rate of immigration from 20 700 to 24 200 per annum, and saved the country from a mad spate of wild cat schemes.[8]

Later verdicts were distinctly less benign. The plans of the 1920s had been slave to the 'rural myth' and to increasingly anachronistic ideas about imperial reciprocity between industrial Britain and the primary-producing dominions.[9] The grand imperial plans for accelerated and synchronised immigration and closer settlement were not only unlucky in the collapse of commodity prices, but were founded on a false assumption about the foundations of future economic development. There had been a mammoth miscalculation in which the British government had taken the responsibility to facilitate the flow of capital from the imperial centre to the dominions, which would give preferential treatment to imports of British manufactured goods. This was the idée fixe of the times. The trouble was that the agricultural land available was increasingly marginal: according to WA Sinclair, 'A stage had apparently been reached at which Australia's natural advantage of under-utilised land was beginning to lose its force as a basis for economic growth'. It was the end of the colonial frontier as far as Australian development was concerned.[10]

In summary, the immigration story in the 1920s was disappointing in scale and consequence and the efforts to harmonise imperial preference, imperial investment and migration failed. In future the relationships between the sending and the receiving countries required radical revision; meantime the Depression put paid to any thought of renewed emigration to Australia.

The Depression in Australia

The Depression was exceptionally severe in Australia and most economists say that Australian unemployment was as bad as anywhere in the industrial world. Prosperity had reached a peak in the mid 1920s and then levelled off and decline set in by 1929, somewhat earlier in Australia than elsewhere. National income per head probably fell by 35 per cent between 1928/29 and 1931/32. Unemployment, which had been 105 000 in 1925/56, rose to 205 000 in 1927/28 and then crested in 1931/32 at 560 000, probably close to 29 per cent of the civilian workforce. Unemployment subsided only slowly and remained above 250 000 until 1941. Meanwhile wages fell more than prices and there were drastic cuts in living standards. There was no regular governmental relief system, but food was doled out.

The Depression showed the extreme vulnerability of Australia to fluctuations in international commodity prices and the capital market. Wheat prices plummeted from 7 shillings a bushel in the 1920s to less than 2 shillings in 1930/31: yet producers continued to produce more than ever and thus pushed prices down further. There was a collapse of demand for Australian exports and 'by 1931 foreign capital inflow virtually ceased and the prospects of expanding exports were poor'.[11] There had been an 'orgy of foreign borrowing' in the 1920s and the precipitous decline of capital flows instantly affected the need for labour. The flow of migrants in the 1920s had been closely connected with these heavy capital inflows, artificially stimulated by governmental intervention. Consequently immigration was promptly terminated. As Carl Strikwerda says, 'the collapse of the gold standard and international financial cooperation meant ... that one of the crucial sinews of the 19th century economic expansion had gone' and with it, of course, the benign climate which had facilitated almost unrestricted international migration.[12]

LF Giblin, the influential Tasmanian economist who came

to exert an almost Keynes-like authority, surveyed the scene in Australia in 1930. He declared that its high standard of living was not being earned – he calculated that it was 30 per cent higher than that prevailing in England and Northern Europe. Australians were living beyond their means and the debt position was worsening each day. The Depression was already a terrible blight and Giblin gave small comfort: 'it is only after some measure of Purgatory that we shall pluck again the amaranths of our desire'.[13]

The image of the 1930s in Australia is one of unrelieved gloom, of joblessness, evictions, dislocation, humiliation, boredom, callous bankers, floundering governments, with a third of the population affected by unemployment and distress. Sometimes there were claims regarding widespread malnutrition, increased disease and mortality. But the Depression was not universally negative – in particular, those in employment received the benefit of lower prices for everything. For instance, there was an increasing demand for domestic servants in the middle years of the Depression, which probably expressed the widened gap between the well-off and the true victims of adverse times. Moreover even though a quarter of the work force was unemployed, it is likely that public health continued to improve: infant death rates fell, partly because the birth rate was also falling, people were better nourished and the water supplies were safer. More obviously there was a spectacular fall in the death rate across all age groups during the Depression. Even mental health may have benefited. As FB Smith explained:

> Altogether the mortality and morbidity measures
> suggest that the Depression internalised discipline
> and promoted life-preserving behaviour among
> Australians of both sexes and particularly, perhaps,
> at younger ages. The slump enjoined frugality,
> family support, stoicism, caution, a curtailment of
> the imagination.

Altogether there was an improvement in life expectancy and the quality of life.[14] It is clear, however, that this reality was unknown to prospective emigrants who might otherwise have been attracted to Australia.

Recovery out of the Depression was slow though perceptible by 1936 and exports began to revive in 1937/38. Recovery was mild to 1938 and then seemed to dip again. Economic performance by 1938 did not reach quite the level of 1928. A manpower survey in 1939, in the National Register, found that at least 15 per cent of men between 18 and 64 were out of work. 'The Australian economy had settled into a steady state of poor performance between 1937 and 1940', and government policies did little to affect the outcome.[15]

In the few years of recovery before the Second World War, manufacturing accounted for 42 per cent of the growth in employment and 18 per cent of money income increase.[16] Gold did especially well and wool prices strengthened. Some of this may have anticipated the changing shape of the Australian economy, partly induced by the trade diversion policy adopted in favour of the Empire. This in itself caused diplomatic problems with various countries including the United States; it was especially provocative in the burgeoning relationship with Japan. The diversion of trade away from Japan was 'reckless':

> Its rulers believed that Australia's refusal to negotiate
> sprang from racism, a refusal to modify the White
> Australia policy so that Japanese nationals could
> move freely on business into and out of the country.
> The trade diversion measures were interpreted as a
> racist insult as well as an economic injury.[17]

There was indeed a great deal of anti-Japanese activity, including the prohibition of Japanese investment in Western Australian ore deposits, for fear of being incorporated in Japan's economic empire.

Up to 1930 wages in Australia had been much higher than in the United Kingdom, but the subsequent wage-cuts together with the depreciation of the currency brought British and Australian wage-levels roughly to parity. Despite the great upheavals of the Depression a marked shift in the economy was manifested in the emergence of new industries, a tendency already perceptible before full recovery set in. Thus by 1939 manufactures contributed nearly two-fifths of the annual value of production, almost double the proportion of 1911.[18] This sea change in the economic life of Australia presaged a radical alteration in future labour needs.

Rarely was the voice of the migrant recorded during the 1930s. An exception was the industrialist HV Wilson, who had left Australia for Chicago in 1909 and eventually worked for the Illinois Steel Company in Milwaukee. He celebrated his successful American career by a grand tour of Australia in 1936/37. Reflecting on his feelings for Australia, especially in the west, he remarked, 'the West Australians are great boosters but I am not impressed with the country. I am quite satisfied that I went to the USA instead of WA in 1909'. As an Australian emigrant, a growing category, he declared forthrightly, 'I am very happy to have this the opportunity to revisit Australia, but the USA is my choice'.[19] Wilson captured the decline of Australia as a desirable destination in the mid 1930s.

The cessation of immigration and restrictions

When, in December 1929, all assistance to immigration was terminated, Archbishop Mannix of Melbourne said immigration should have been ended long before. He declared that Australia could not support its own population and that immigration simply created new unemployment.[20] By May 1930 labour was in surplus, even among domestic servants in Melbourne: 'there was a small army of single unemployed girls roaming the city in search of employment', according to the *Herald*. Recruitment overseas had stopped and the existing supply of domestics was sufficient for the next 5 years. In Tasmania there were no immigrant arrivals after 1930. Immigrants were indeed leaving, citing reasons such as unemployment, factory closures, and also their mental health; some of them had been in receipt of government assistance for a long time. Few had any intention of returning to Tasmania.[21]

Immigration had already been falling in the late 1920s: from 51 000 in 1927 down to 30 000 in 1928 and 11 800 in 1929. Another symptom of depression was the exercise of a more rigid control of alien immigration. The landing requirement was raised to £500.[22] The Depression sharpened antagonisms towards migrants which had been simmering in some states even before the onset of high unemployment. Tension in the labour market expressed itself, as always, against newcomers. The hardening of attitudes to aliens was displayed most violently in a widely publicised riot in Kalgoorlie in 1934. The incident began as a brawl in which an Italian barman accidentally killed a customer, and led to an anti-Italian riot involving looting and arson, undoubtedly inflamed by general xenophobic feelings.

Australia at large continued to fear 'the melting pot', and this was reinforced by hard times even though there was little prospect of renewed immigration from any source during the Depression.[23] Externally, the White Australia policy continued to generate offence by its principle rather than its actual operation, and Australia was far from unique: New Zealand, South Africa, Argentina and the United States all enacted entry restrictions based on race, health, age and disability in common with Australia. Japan was particularly sensitive and regarded itself as disrespected by Australia's policy, which may have contributed to the psychological tensions leading to the coming world war.[24]

The dictation test remained the supremely effective barrier against unwanted immigrants. Indeed from 1912 it was sometimes used to exclude Europeans who were deemed 'undesirable'. Any potential immigrant who happened to know the English language could be set 'a dictation test of fifty words in any prescribed language'. In 1914 in Adelaide a young Irish woman – a British subject of European race – was rejected after failing a test in Swedish. It was principally directed against the Chinese, without giving collateral offence to Japan. In the 1930s the test generated great publicity as a consequence of 'the Kisch Case, which had nothing to do with China or immigration'. This celebrated episode concerned a French/Jewish, socialist/communist journalist, Egon Kisch, an expert linguist who had been released from a Nazi prison and taken up Czech citizenship. In October 1934 he was invited to Melbourne to address the All Australia Congress Against War and Fascism. Kisch was in Australia for less than six months but achieved lasting celebrity: he had received his visa in Paris from a British official but in Australia was declared a prohibited immigrant, evidently on political grounds. He was prohibited from landing in Perth but in Port Melbourne he literally jumped ship, broke his leg and was carried back onto the ship and taken further to Sydney, where he was released under a court application: he was 'carried down the gang-plank by four stewards and deposited on the sacred soil. Within two minutes he was given a language test in Gaelic'. He failed, but was given bail. On appeal the High Court reversed the decision on the grounds that Gaelic was not a European language [sic]. Kisch eventually addressed a crowd of 20 000 on the German situation in Sydney Domain, as well as large crowds in West Melbourne. The Duke of Gloucester, John Masefield and Baden Powell were all in Australia at the time but Kisch outshone them all.[25] A subscription eventually paid his legal costs and he left voluntarily in March 1935.[26] He later recalled his escapades in his well-titled reminiscence, *Australian Landfall* (1937).

'The Kisch case' was a direct challenge to the dictation test employed, in this instance, on the grounds of political affiliation rather than race. It registered the all-purpose potential of the test, which was transparently designed to be failed at all times. If a person began to show signs of passing the test it could be changed to any other European language. It produced bizarre examples of the English language in translation, such as:

> The hairy adornment of the lion renders him more
> formidable in appearance. But the plain fact is that
> the tiger's head and jaws are more solid, heavy
> and powerful than the lion's. We can only tell the
> difference when examining the skeleton's [sic] of the
> two animals with a skilled anatomist.[27]

Over the period 1901–58 about 2000 immigrants were stopped by the test, but mainly in the early years of the Federation. After 1930 it ceased to be the main means of exclusion. The outstanding success of the policy was demonstrated by the fact that between 1901 and 1947 the absolute numbers of Japanese, Chinese, Pacific Islanders, Indians and Afghans all declined steeply; their percentage in the Australian population fell from 1.3 per cent in 1901 to 0.2 per cent in 1947. The side effects of the policy were political and international, and the full diplomatic costs were counted only in later decades.[28]

Australia's immigration regulations, as well as checking unwanted political and racial incursions, also gave thorough control over other requirements, such as health and dependency. For instance, South Australia and New South Wales were prepared to accept one-eyed ex-servicemen, but Victoria refused such men. Premier HSW Lawson remarked that 'maimed men, generally speaking, should not be eligible for subsidised passages'. Men wearing glasses were also suspect.[29] Morals entered the unspoken criteria as in the case of an English woman who was given a dictation test in Italian to keep her out for nearly a year 'because a minister of the Crown had heard a rumour that she might "break up an Australian home"'.[30]

In 1936 the Australian Institute of International Affairs commissioned a review of the efficacy of the White Australia policy: R Jay observed that, despite heavy initial criticism (by the Chinese and

Japanese) the dictation test had 'worked extremely well in practice' and was 'highly discretionary'; 'Few immigrants are turned back, because those at whom it is aimed do not attempt to enter, knowing that it would be useless'. Jay noted that in the 1920s an increased stream of immigrants had arisen from Mediterranean countries, 'diverted from the United States' by legislation. There had been a clamour against them because they settled in groups and 'did not assimilate with the existing population'; they also had 'a lower standard of living, and were entering the country in excessive numbers'. This led to an amendment of the Immigration Restriction Act in 1925 which extended the power to restrict aliens of any race for economic and assimilation reasons. Public opinion accepted northern Italians as satisfactory immigrants but not southerners, and the Italian government (which did not in any case favour emigration) agreed to limit passports to 100 per month. The only direct prohibition applied to enemy countries – Germans, Austro-Germans, Bulgarians and Ottoman Turks.[31]

Population and policy

Behind the politics of immigration was the broad stream of Australia's evolving population history. Despite a sense of general disappointment, population growth in Australia in the decades 1900–30 was faster than in most of Europe and North America. Net immigration had significantly enhanced the workforce, contributing more than 34 per cent of the employment growth before 1914, and up to 40 per cent in the years 1921 to 1927.[32] This was, of course, set in a very small national population (still less than 5.5 million in 1921). Moreover the priority which the nation had invested in populating rural Australia had simply failed. The number of new British migrants who were located in rural areas was too small, even if they had stayed on the land, to compensate for the larger drift to the cities.

During the Depression ideas of settling British immigrants on small-scale Australian farms withered away and the old assumptions were severely questioned. Indeed the likelihood of renewed British emigration was itself severely diminished by the fall in the British birth rate. For several years there was a net loss of population from Australia by out-migration and this inevitably deepened the demographic pessimism. The annual increase of population was slow and fell from 2.04 per cent per annum in 1913–23 to 1.88 per cent in 1923–29 and less than 1 per cent in the years 1933–39. In the 1930s the birth rate declined further as a consequence of fewer marriages and fewer children per family.[33] In combination with negative migration this produced the lowest rate of population growth in Australia for at least a century. Consequently almost all indicators of the nation's demographic vigour in the 1930s were dismal.

Given the sickly state of the nation's psyche the debate on population took a new turn. The statistician, CH Wickens had famously likened the immigration into Australia to a boa constrictor: 'we were in the habit of bolting our immigrants and then resting until we had digested them'.[34] In the 1930s some parts of the nation thought the appetite had died altogether. Whereas in the 1920s influential opinion advocated the expansion of British settlement across the continent, in the 1930s the channelling of immigrants to the 'empty spaces' lost its credibility.[35] Now the population debate was concerned with Australia's capacity to absorb immigrants, and the new and alarming emphasis was the allegedly limited population potential of the continent.[36] The economist Giblin, in 1930, thought that the population of Australia could be larger because there existed unused resources, which might support an additional 3 million people at a lower living standard. But he also warned that Australia was living beyond its means and that this simply generated 'the envy of less happy lands'. He pointed out that the League of Nations could not defend Australia in such circumstances and he confessed he had ' no solution to offer you'.[37]

The debate on population in Australia was always divisive.

Throughout the middle decades of the 20th century there were wildly divergent predictions, both in terms of what was likely, and what was desirable. Thus in 1930 AM Carr Saunders said Australasia could absorb 1 million immigrants per annum. RG Menzies thought that the future population of Australia would be about 20 million, while the economist JW Gregory talked of a future population of 100 million. More conservative were Earle Page, foreseeing a population of 30 million, and the economist FC Benham predicting 10–15 million as the most likely outcome.[38] Alarmingly unsuccessful population forecasts were not, of course, exclusive to Australia. Demographers are prepared to conceded that 'The irritating failure of most attempts to forecast population ... is a humbling example of the limits even of restricted working hypotheses'.[39] Jonathan Stone, Professor of Anatomy at Sydney, was sharply critical when, in 1994, he remarked that the 70-year-old debate on the optimum population of Australia had 'yielded no consensus, for either expansion or contraction'.[40] It was little wonder that the question of optimal immigration was wrapped in uncertainty and ill-placed dogmatism.

The most divisive figure in all these debates was T Griffith Taylor, the geographer who argued that Australia could never support 60 million people and that there would be no more than 20 million at the end of the century. His views were not popular and he was regarded as a demographic pessimist and an environmental determinist and, under a cloud, he resigned his chair at the University of Sydney in 1928 and left for Chicago. He believed that the size of the population depended on the size of a country's coal deposits, which would determine close settlement. On this basis he predicated the massive industrialisation of Australia. Some of Taylor's views were distinctly bizarre: he compared Townsville to Calcutta and appeared to advocate miscegenation and some mixing of the inhabitants with non-Europeans, mainly broad-headed alpine types. On the basis of his theories he gave some support to the idea of Asian immigration (partly on climatological grounds and partly because such people as the Chinese were *brachycephalic*, or broad-headed).[41] His views ran counter to the conventional White Australia policy, and Taylor found himself the subject of vituperative attacks in the press.[42] Europeans in the tropics were few in number, but a report in 1937 suggested that 'Through the cultivation of sugarcane it has been able to settle the tropic north of Queensland with permanent white population – and the most striking feature of this settlement is the fact that the increase in the birth rate in Australia's tropical areas at the last census was greater than in the non-tropical areas'.[43]

The racial question remained central to Australia's population policy though stasis seemed to hang over the debate in the 1930s and the government could find little clear guidance from the social scientists of the time. Caution was the watchword. In 1927 J Lynge, a Danish writer, published a book on 'non-Britishers' in Australia which argued that the common idea that Australia was 98 per cent British was false. He claimed that only 89 per cent were British while 9.5 per cent were non-British like himself. He also claimed that the 'non-Britishers' had made a substantial impact (including Resch's beer), and a sympathetic reviewer said that 'variety is the spice of life' and pleaded for the return of the 'lovely German place-names so ruthlessly eradicated during the War'.[44] With immigration at so low an ebb in the 1930s there was little testing of the limits of Australian tolerance, though when migration again resumed so too did the old question of who should be allowed to enter Australia.

Revival

Australia surfaced only slowly from the Great Depression but, by the end of 1935, specific labour shortages were emerging. Prime Minister Joseph Lyons was reluctant to reactivate the program of assisted immigration, but the national mood was shifting. AV Alexander, the British Labour MP, told Lyons: 'It is clearly our duty to settle the peoples of the earth as far as lies in our power, and as rapidly

Noorla Boarding House, Ingham, North Queensland, run by the De Giovanni family, often accommodated Italian canecutters in the inter-war years. *Italian Historical Association (COASIT)*

as possible; that, and that alone, can prevent, within the next years, War'. Lyons said straightforwardly in September 1936 that Australia had experienced 'a very unsatisfactory' net loss of British population since the Depression, and meanwhile the 'white alien population' had increased, including southern Europeans. He proposed a partial resumption of assisted immigration, directed particularly at 'female household workers and/or youths for farm work'.[45] The Lyons government took the view that the resumption of assisted immigration must entail the sharing of the cost between Australia and England and that the arrangement would be linked to markets: 'the Australian ministers have told the English Government that a renewal of immigration is dependent upon an extension of the English market for Australia's products'.[46] Australia indeed compelled the British government to discuss the sensitive matter of preferential access for Australian produce into British markets.

Over the following 18 months the signs of revival were confirmed and negotiations with Britain led to the resuscitation of the Empire Emigration Development Conference in October 1937. The swing in policy was heralded in a speech by Lyons, in September 1937, entitled 'More People Imperative'. In January 1938 South Australia was prepared to accept more domestic servants; and New South Wales wanted to resume assisted immigration, specifically for juveniles, farm lads, domestics and special nominations through families. In March 1938 the prime minister put out a circular to the states, 'To Restore British Migration'.[47] In that year the British and Australian governments signed an Assisted Passage Act for prospective emigrants: the conditions were now more stringent – thus passages for a family were offered at two-thirds cost, but the family was required to demonstrate capital assets to the value of £3000 capital, or a pension of £100. A single person had to prove assets of £50. These were relatively tight conditions and the results were modest: in 1938/39 only 3538 migrants took advantage of the opportunity.[48] In effect the British source of migrants had shrunk. The fact that Australia signed small parallel agreements with the Dutch and Swiss governments in 1939 set a precedent for the postwar years.

Australia seemed to grow away from Britain in the interwar years; certainly the ratio of home population to immigrants from the home country declined. The distinguished music and cricket correspondent, Neville Cardus, accompanying the Test tour of Australia 1936/37, contemplated the country thus: 'Australia is abroad, an unusual civilization, only English by accident of blood relationship'. It was 'a happy land. The first thing that strikes the English visitor … is the carefree, almost reckless, high spirits of everybody'. But he complained of the lack of intellectual and cultural life, and spoke of 'the heartiness of a nation not grown up'. Yet he confessed that 'I could live at Vaucluse or Watson's Bay and be happy, given a gramophone and Test matches only once every few years'.[49]

Despite such enthusiasm, the revival of British emigration was very small in scale. Nor were the signs in Britain encouraging for a renewal of mass emigration. For instance, a Salvation Army survey of 30 000 families in the United Kingdom revealed very little interest in emigration. The resumption of assisted immigration began in the context of a realisation that Britain had 'ceased to be a major emigrant country'. By 1938 the Oversea Settlement Board warned the Dominions that Britain no longer possessed 'a surplus population waiting to be enticed to move and that demographic decline is the more likely tendency'.[50]

The stuttering resumption of immigration from Britain in the late 1930s brought a few thousand before the Second World War. One was Albert Pace, a young man with his wife and child, from Wolverhampton in the English Midlands, who arrived in 1936/37. Pace had been out of work before the emigration and, writing home, he reminded his mother that 'The life while I was waiting for it to pick up was getting on my <u>nerves</u>'. His mother had been unhappy about the emigration and told Albert that he should have waited until things got better in England. Instead he settled into his new life in Bassendean in Western Australia whence he reported, 'I have a nice house and well furnished and [it] will be paid for in a few years'. Albert Pace felt the shrinking horizons of the Depression in England, and the shadow of war approaching. Western Australia, he decided, was a better place. But he was concerned about the ill health of his mother back in Wolverhampton. He sent a 10 shilling note home and wanted to send more but he also had incurred medical expenses: 'I have not given up hope of seeing you', he said.[51] The Paces were unpretentious folk with modest expectations and they had found life hard in both countries. As emigrants they were typically ambivalent about the loss of home and Albert Pace remarked tellingly that, 'Its just your faces I would like to see, but I don't think

I would like all the Old War scare around me'. Albert Pace was an unsuspecting harbinger of the coming war.

During this modest revival of immigration a significant transition in Australia was becoming evident. Various new Empire plans for migration raised their heads. But there was a swift rejection of any return to the thinking of the 1920s: 'It was pointed out by the Secretary, Department of the Interior, that schemes involving the settlement of migrants from the United Kingdom on land in Australia had not been a success'.[52] It was crystal clear that there would be no revival of land settlement schemes. The traditional belief that Australia's future was unshakably founded on the rural sector was no longer an article of faith. The diversification of the economy now became the central issue. The economy had shifted away from intensive agricultural production and it was acknowledged that the Soldier Settlements and Empire Settlement Schemes could not be repeated. The future rested on industrialisation though the ramifications of this structural shift remained unexamined until the war itself jolted the nation into an unreserved commitment to a new future. But the signs were already manifest in the prewar revival. As Michael Roe says, 'in the inter war years British and Australian commentators came to believe that only an industrialised Australia could sustain a much increased population, and events have proved them right'.[53] To their credit a few Australian planners had argued for industrialisation as early as the 1920s, and a British Trade Commissioner had captured its essence in 1923 when he remarked:

> The main argument for pushing on with the
> development of Australian manufacturing is that
> such industries permit a far more rapid increase
> of population than land settlement. In addition to
> this, the average person of British stock appears to
> prefer to live in cities and to devote his energies to
> manufacturing and commerce rather than settle on
> the land.[54]

In the late 1930s particular labour shortages were exposed in certain parts of the Australian economy which caused a chorus of demand for special concessions to import migrants. Some sections of the community declared that it was essential to look beyond the British Isles to fulfil their needs – which, inevitably, roused 'the bogey of the White Australia policy'. Various employers wanted to import Asian labour for domestic service. Such a recourse remained blocked, though there were already a few minor exceptions to the remarkably comprehensive character of White Australia. Thus Japanese pearl-shell divers were regarded as indispensable in the remote north coasts: 'The pearl-divers of Broome provided an exception but were not allowed to serve as a precedent'.[55]

There was a serious and recurrent shortage of domestic servants, especially in the remote pastoral and tropical zones. The problem was that wages were now as good in the United Kingdom as in Australia. Some outback graziers claimed that the lack of domestic help was causing the closure of homesteads because of the excessive strain on farmers' wives. There was a perennial shortage of domestic servants in Darwin, where it was said that 'life ... for many of the white families would be almost impossible without some cheap domestic labour, and the aboriginal is the only suitable labour of the kind procurable'. This was the basis of a policy to collect 'half-castes from native camps at a early age and transfer them to government institutions at Darwin and Alice Springs'.[56] It was claimed also that the scarcity of domestic servants deterred white families in the north, and this led to special pleading for permission to import coloured servants. There had been persistent but unrequited requests for a relaxation of the policy through the 1920s. The Graziers' Association of New South Wales said they would have to look beyond Britain and proposed a search for supplies of domestics from Germany, Austria, Finland, Estonia, Poland, Czechoslovakia and Scandinavia. Philip (later Sir Philip) Goldfinch, general manager of Colonial Sugar Refining Company, said that the British owed much to the Continental peoples who had come to live among them, but had been careful to avoid an 'overdose'. Goldfinch noted the recent loss of 'persons of British blood' from the Australian population and the beginnings of a balancing influx of 'foreigners'.

The government was reluctant to extend assistance to European immigrants, even for domestic servants, and there was specific opposition to Jewish recruitment even in this field. More encouragement was given to other categories, which included the possible recruitment of foreign domestics who had already worked in the United Kingdom, especially if they were 'Teutonic girls. Good house women, Marriageable. Broadbeamed (mostly). Good breeders (probably)', none of whom would arouse any political objection. Correspondents in Tasmania recommended recruitment among the Dutch, Swedes, Danes and Finns.[57] The prewar exchange of government memoranda on the question of domestic servants revealed a more encouraging attitude to certain types of European immigration in the face of particular labour shortages (especially for rural households in this case). It suggested a very small relaxation towards 'white aliens', though the essential racial criteria remained unbreached.

The White Australia policy therefore had denied several sectors of the Australian society, notably the sugar industry and domestic service, the labour they craved. From these sectors came choruses of vociferous pleading for exceptional dispensation, but no half measures were entertained and this demonstrated the absolute character of the policy. As BW Higman observed, the prewar policy was designed 'to increase the nation's population absolutely while at the same time ensuring its ethnic homogeneity'. These twin objectives were in contradiction, 'and the balance was overwhelmingly weighted in favor of the primacy of racial purity'.[58]

The population question was affected also by the changing demographic relationship between Australia and her traditional purveyor of people, Britain. In 1937 Prime Minister Lyons linked future population growth with industrial policy. But most of all, he said, 'the problem of the declining birth rate overshadows all others.

It must be squarely faced'.[59] Population increase was necessary for industry and defence. Throughout the Western world in the 1930s there was growing awareness of the declining birth rate in most countries.

In 1938 Archbishop Mannix again spoke of the 'curse of race suicide':

> Unlike other countries Australia has vast empty spaces. Race suicide was bringing older nations to their graves through artificial sterility, yet little or nothing is being done by the authorities. The Post Office here is at the disposal of people to send around anonymous circulars, and in the windows of chemists' shops things are displayed that decent people should be ashamed to look on, much less use.[60]

The archbishop evidently had little influence over the course of fertility; statisticians calculated that Australia's reproduction rate was falling towards zero. One authority predicted that Australia would experience negative population growth unless it began to recruit more than 40000 immigrants per annum. But falling birthrates and family sizes were now recognised as a general Western European phenomenon. Not even Italy and Germany had been able to reverse the trend. British emigration could not be relied on: its own birth rate was below replacement level and its population was predicted to decline by 1950. In the interwar years internal migration in the United Kingdom increased while the propensity to emigrate weakened.[61]

These emerging trends (as well as the state of labour markets) affected official British policy towards emigration. The British government was now more hesitant to encourage emigration. The British sociologist, Carr-Saunders, had already declared that British emigration could no longer be relied upon; he pointed out that 'the reproduction rate in this country is now well below replacement rate, [and] it is evident that it will soon become impossible to carry on the traditional role of a country of emigration by parting with a fraction of the natural increase'. He noted that United Kingdom emigrants had not filled their quota entitlement for entry into the United States. If countries such as Australia were to depend on immigration to build up their populations, 'they must look to countries other than Great Britain'.[62]

When, in 1937, the Empire Settlement Act was ratified for 15 years, Britain decided against a vigorous new program. The 1920s schemes had been discredited; now the talk was of modest voluntary emigration. In 1938 the Overseas Settlement Board suggested that the dominions should look for 'a carefully regulated flow of foreign immigrants of assimilated types', of northern European extraction. In the context of the traditional British White Australia policy these suggestions of a shift towards European sources were regarded as radical and aroused immediate anxiety within Australia. In 1936 the Australian government remained tentative about the encouragement of non-British immigration, even of so-called 'Nordic' immigrants. Trade unions still feared the competition of migrants and the 'transfer of unemployed' from one side of the world to the other.[63] The resumption of southern European immigration in the late 1930s reactivated 'Australia's Anglo-Celtic xenophobia'.[64] It is clear that, despite the mounting demographic anxieties, there was formidable resistance to any widening of the migrant catchments. Michele Langfield asks the crucial question: 'Why were the restrictions on European immigrants maintained in the late 1930s in the face of widespread alarm over the declining birth rate and the reduced availability of British immigrants?'.[65] Nevertheless there was a small liberalisation of policy towards non-British white immigration, which was registered in 1936 when Australia's landing fee was reduced to £50. Orthodox opinion continued to express concern about the creation of 'alien blocs', and the preference for northern over southern Italians. Racial categorisation of immigrants remained entirely commonplace.

Refugees from Nazi Europe: Jewish migrants arriving in Australia in 1939.
National Library of Australia

Liberalisation was put to a new test before the outbreak of war with a swelling contingent of refugees. Indeed the refugee question in Australian immigration policy had not arisen until the late 1930s. Australia was a reluctant signatory to the Evian conference (1938), which organised asylum for the Jews fleeing Nazi Germany. Eventually Australia agreed to take small numbers,[66] the Australian delegate, TW White, claiming that it would 'no doubt be appreciated that as we have no racial problem we are not desirous of importing one'.[67] In 1935 the Australian intake was less than 100; in 1936 more than 150, and in 1937 it was 500. Thereafter a great pressure of refugees mounted: there were 300 applications per week at Australia House, equal to 50 000 per annum. In the outcome only 1556 were admitted in 1938, and 5058 in 1939. Their entry and control raised the racial issue and aroused strong passions: the most newsworthy was the claim that the Jews were a 'non-assimilable' people.[68] It was claimed in 1939 that Polish, Russian, Lithuanian and Rumanian Jews in the clothing trade were promoting the worst sorts of sweated labour.[69] It was a prelude to the great refugee question after the war which now loomed. Australia at all times remained guarded about the rights of people to enter the country and the meaning of asylum.

6 Race, refugees, war and the future: 1939–45

War fears

When the British novelist HG Wells visited Australia in 1939 he witnessed dramatic and terrible bushfires around the new 'bush capital', Canberra, and wrote a moving description of the firefighters. He also registered his dismay at the lack of preparations for the defence of Australia (he was a vocal critic of British defence arrangements at that time): 'The plain truth of the case is that Australia is absolutely defenceless against competent raider attacks, because of its sprawling extension. It exaggerates the general position of the British empire in this respect'. He pointed out that the 'desiccated, thinly populated hinterlands' of Australian cities promised no chance of 'retreat or reinforcement against air or sea raids'. He declared that Australia must have powerful air forces 'capable of bold offensive and stationed along the northern sphere of influence', coupled with close coordination not only with the rest of the Empire but with the Americans and the Dutch. Wells believed that the Empire must be able to strike at the enemy before it arrived.[1] In the following 6 years the vulnerability of Australia was fully exposed and its ingrained fear of oriental invasion and domination – the 'Yellow Peril' – became, at last, a reality. War entrenched 'White Australia' and made it more urgent. The war with Japan was regarded as its ultimate justification.

The war began in Europe in September 1939 but was preceded by anti-Semitic convulsions in Germany which reverberated as far as Australia. The human faces of these traumas were the Jewish refugees arriving from 1938 onwards, the fraught and dramatic precursors of postwar refugee intakes. They were a new test of Australian immigration policies. Some of these Jewish refugees gathered vivid impressions of their first sight of Australia in late 1938, Sydney in 114 degrees Fahrenheit (nearly 46° C) with the smell of smoke from bushfires 'all around the harbour'.[2]

Australian authorities were afraid of fifth columnists and interned many aliens, including Jews, throughout the war. Paul Herzfeld, aged 21, arrived in Australia in 1939 having left Austria, where he regarded himself as an anti-Nazi monarchist. He tried to join the RAAF to fight against Germany but, instead, found himself categorised as an enemy alien and was held in remote internment camps at Tatura and Loveday. Herzfeld was among other long-time German residents interned in Australia: they included 'non-Aryan Christians' (who were Jews according to Nazi racial laws), socialists, Jehovah's Witnesses and other fleeing people. To their mounting horror they were mixed in with genuine Nazis who, Herzfeld reported, celebrated Hitler's birthday and greeted each other with 'Heil Hitler'.

In June 1940 Joe Cantamessa, from near Ingham in northern Queensland, was taken away by local police and interned. He was a leading citizen of the Herbert River district, a fifth-term councillor, chairman of Ingham Cane Growers' Council, president of Ingham Bowling Club and the tennis club and recognised as a great moderator of local life. Cantamessa had been born in Piedmont, Italy and had arrived in Australia aged 15 in 1907; he became a sugar grower and a naturalised British subject; he was highly assimilated. But he was locked up for 3 years in New South Wales and South Australia. Eventually 4727 Italians, 1115 Germans, 587 Japanese and some 550 others were interned even though Arthur Calwell intervened in 1943, protesting that there had been 'too much racial and other prejudice' against 'many naturalised British Subjects living in Queensland'.[3]

Wolf Klaphake was another prewar immigrant from Germany who passed along the unhappy path to Tatura as an enemy alien. Six feet 8 inches tall, this scientist and inventor was interned for the duration of the war, despite his anti-Nazi credentials. His wife was a sex psychologist and they had been targeted by the Nazis; Klaphake decided to emigrate to South Australia in 1935. He developed a dew condenser, which possessed considerable potential in Australia. But in June 1940 the German Consulate in Sydney was raided by police and they found Klaphake's name among Nazi Party membership records and were convinced he was a Nazi agent. He claimed that he had been a party member only as a convenience to sell his work in Germany: this was disregarded and he was interned for 4 years at Orange and Tatura; during this time he wrote many letters to authorities protesting his innocence and made strenuous attempts to assist the war effort. He was never told why he was interned or placed among Nazi sympathisers. In August 1944 he was released and became a consultant chemist, maintaining his rage against the Australian government that had detained him without explanation.[4]

The war

On John Curtin's death, in 1945, Acting Prime Minister Frank Forde, remarked, 'History will some day record how close Australia was to being overrun'. Australia had always feared invasion, either by irresistible unwanted immigration or by force of arms. The second of these nightmares became reality in early 1942. In December 1941 Curtin had already appealed to the United States over the United Kingdom. The sinking of the *Prince of Wales* and the *Repulse* and then, in mid-February 1942, the fall of the supposedly impregnable Singapore, was followed by the invasion of New Guinea. Four days after the capitulation of Singapore, Japanese bombs began to fall on Australian soil for the first time: Darwin was attacked by 188 carrier-borne Japanese airplanes specifically to prevent any Australian interference with their planned Timor landings on the following day. Darwin was assaulted in two raids in which at least 243 people were killed and many others injured; 6 ships were destroyed and 3 more badly damaged. Darwin experienced another 62 raids by November 1943 though the first strike was the worst. Confusion and panic had followed. The awful fear of an 'invasion of Australia by a yellow peril from the north' was now upon the country.[5]

Military historians point out that the Japanese did not have a policy or a plan for the invasion of Australia. Rather they sought to contain Australia and isolate it from the western coast of America. They 'sought to prevent the build-up of significant offensive capabilities in Australia' that might 'strike at [Japan's] southern defensive perimeter'. The attacks on Darwin and Sydney were not preliminary to an invasion though it suited Australian politicians to maintain this view for wartime purposes.[6]

Australia had joined the war in 1939 and fought on behalf of Britain in Europe and Africa. British and Australian troops in the war were interchangeable.[7] It became undeniable by early 1942 that Australia could no longer depend on Britain for its defence. Some Australian historians argue that the British government was already prepared to abandon Australia and that it would have to be recaptured after the war. Ill will was certainly generated in the moment of crisis. Thus, when Curtin adopted his realignment towards the United States, deep British prejudices against Australia were exposed. The British High Commissioner Ronald (later Sir Ronald) Cross described Australians as 'inferior people', and

Churchill himself declared that Australians were cowards born of bad stock.

These words were doubtless spoken in extremis but the policy shift had, in fact, been long anticipated. Curtin said in November 1936 that 'The dependence of Australia upon the competence, let alone the readiness, of British statesmen to send forces to our aid is too dangerous a hazard upon which to found Australia's defence policy'.[8] He already believed that the basis of Australia's defence must be its own industrial strength, associated with increased migration and a stronger population. But the rhetoric of Empire remained in his mind and at the time of the attack on Pearl Harbor Curtin said: 'We Australians have imperishable traditions. We shall maintain them ... We shall hold this country and keep it as a citadel for the British-speaking race and as a place where civilization will persist'. More famously he also declared that 'Australia looks to America, free of any pangs as to our traditional links or kinship with the United Kingdom'. He was then stating the obvious even though Churchill found this turn highly objectionable. According to Geoffrey Serle, 'As invasion appeared imminent, both government and people began to develop the jitters'.[9] Yet by mid-1942 the acute danger was over; within two years the reconquest of New Guinea was completed and by September 1944 200000 Japanese troops had been cut off from their home base.

Meanwhile, of course, Australia had long marshalled all its resources to meet the exigencies of war. The economy was placed on a total war footing with such a rapid mobilisation of labour that the unemployment problem that had racked the 1930s was almost instantly nullified. Arms and munitions production absorbed a great deal of the slack labour. In the process the production of guns, ships and planes, and the rise of the chemical and metallurgical industries, became part of a great structural shift in the economy which helped greatly to accelerate the still incipient industrialisation of Australia The demands of the war helped to reshape the economy, with permanent implications for future planning and national labour requirements. Rural production was similarly enhanced despite serious droughts in 1944–45. The context of war was exceptional: Australia soon found itself pushing against the limits of its labour supply at a time when net immigration was impossible. War indeed created peculiar problems in terms of immigration, but some were inherited from before the war.

Causalities of war

The arrival in Australia of Jewish refugees before 1939 had (as we saw in the previous chapter) aroused a renewal of public apprehension about the acceptability of alien immigration. Apart from the recurrent tensions associated with earlier Italian immigration, the operation of the White Australia policy was effective in masking most racial issues in Australia throughout the first half of the 20th century. Indeed very few alien and un-white immigrants had been allowed into the country. Racial antagonism, and even ordinary xenophobia, were little in evidence, essentially because the policy excluded most non-British immigrants. This was, of course, one of the most important justifications of the policy.

But there had always been small pockets of non-Europeans in Australia (apart of course from the Aborigines) and their presence reminded the country of its racial assumptions even before the war. The pearl-shell industry (the collection of valuable shells used for commercial button making and mother-of-pearl) had been established at Broome in 1889, when it was mainly in the hands of a London Hatton Garden jeweller. The industry depended greatly on non-white labour, and employed thousands of indentured workers including many highly skilled and intrepid Japanese divers (as well as Aboriginal and Torres Strait Islander and Timorese labour).[10] A very high proportion of the Broome population was non-British and a fierce racism affected the industry and the town. In the off-season about 1000 Japanese entered the town for weeks at a time accompanied by their women and prostitutes.

The Sunlight Cinema in Broome was famously segregated, but some of the expatriate British broke the racial rules and 'alienated their peers by forming alliances with Asian and Aboriginal people'. Pearl-shelling slumped in the mid 1930s because the sea beds were exhausted, which reduced the immediacy of the question. In general, however, a blind eye was turned to this gap in the White Australia policy – the Japanese incursion was small and remote and declining. But as soon as the Second World War broke out virtually the entire Japanese population in Australia was interned. They numbered 1068, many of them from the pearling luggers, and they were sent to camps in Hay, Loveday and Tatura. At the end of the war most of them were deported.[11]

The arrival of Jewish refugees in Australia in the late 1930s posed a much larger challenge, though their reception was often little different from that of other non-British immigrants, typically a combination of hostility and condescension. Many of the Jews were from the Viennese middle class, 'professionals, manufacturers, and highly skilled tradesmen' – escaping Hitler rather than the Depression as such. It was expensive to get to Australia. The emigrants were not allowed to take money from their homeland and were compelled to bribe officials, and also needed £200 capital to enter Australia. Often they carried portable valuables such as jewellery and furs and appeared highly cultured and sophisticated people, many with contacts in Australia. But they also faced 'culture- shock' and some of the newcomers soon came to regard Australia as a barren waste and a cultural void. Though relatively liberal and generous in its acceptance compared with other countries, Australia had little understanding of their background. The Jews found themselves in the familiar situation of new migrants, striving to recover from the exhausting cost of their migration.

Existing Jewish communities in Australia mounted a campaign to persuade the government to reduce the landing requirements to £50, and permits were issued for considerable numbers until Australia became alarmed at the growing scale of the Jewish migration. The

pressure of refugees mounted and by 1938 the large number of applications was threatening to overwhelm Australia House in London. A
quota of 5100 was adopted by Cabinet in June 1938, the new limit
being justified by the classic social argument, namely that the Jews
were a separate and non-assimilable people and likely to inflame anti-
Semitism in the wider community.[12] There was also concern about
the propensity of Jews in Sydney to congregate too closely in places
such as Bondi, Kings Cross, Kirribilli and Neutral Bay.

Resistance to the Jewish inflows in general was not specifically
anti-Semitic in tone or urgency. As one historian puts it, 'Far from
being made in a vacuum, Jewish refugee policy [was] the product
of what were, by 1933, already long-established practices' which
were commonly applied to all aliens entering Australia.[13] Some of
the new Jewish immigrants were poor Eastern Europeans, not unlike
the Jews of East Side New York, and many congregated in certain
parts of Melbourne. Even the old-established Anglo-Jewry in Australia was ambivalent about the inflow of these alien co-religionists.
But there were several groups in Australia in the late 1930s prepared
to support the intake of refugees, including Theosophists, the Communist Party, Quakers and various Leagues of Peace seeking to give
aid to the victims of European fascism.

Outright opposition to the Jews was vocal and included the
Business Brokers Association of New South Wales and even the
manufacturers of artificial flowers, who feared competition from the
refugees. Some critics of the refugee intake advocated the restriction of asylum to British Jews only; others suggested that the fleeing Jews should be redirected to Papua and New Guinea, Malaya
or Borneo; the Congregational Union of Victoria said that refugees should be required to learn English and be strictly controlled
on arrival. Anti-Jewish feeling in mid-1939 was fanned by Sir Frank
Clarke, who claimed that the new intake of Jews was undercutting
wages especially in the clothing trades in Carlton. Reference was
made to the poor physique of the Eastern European Jews working in
slave-like conditions – in contrast with earlier Austrian and German

Jews who had settled in the better suburbs. It was claimed that it would take two generations to assimilate the new wave of Jews.[14] Meanwhile the credentials of skilled immigrants, including those of doctors, were questioned.

Group settlement by aliens in Australia had been attempted before the First World War. Leopoldo Zunini, the Italian Consul in Perth between 1905 and 1908, instigated a relatively well-planned scheme to bring to Western Australia a substantial number of Italian farmers. At the time it chimed well with reigning assumptions for closer settlement and the introduction of yeoman-type stock into new districts for the purpose of pioneering at a time when British migrants were difficult to recruit. The Italian government had also been interested in the better organisation of emigration. Zunini's ideas met a good reception in the Northam district and enthusiasm seemed to swell. But the scheme petered out partly because of rumours that the proposed colonists were socialists. The scheme also aroused a certain amount of xenophobia abetted by the notion that Australia was reserved for 'purely Anglo-Saxon' peoples. Group settlement ideas continued to simmer, including the ambitious notions of introducing 100 000 Maltese in the Kimberley in 1922, but the plan never reached fulfilment. Italian and Maltese immigration, in reality, mainly occurred by way of low-key chain migration – individual migrants like Giuseppe Torrisi, a young Sicilian farmer and viticulturalist who had first tried Argentina and returned to Naples in 1908 and then decided on Australia. He worked in Fremantle and accumulated capital; in 1913 he bought land, developed his crops experimentally and became the first link in a classic connection between the village of Trecastagni and the Donnybrook district.[15]

On an entirely different scale was the ambitious 'free land' proposal made by overseas Jewish interests at the end of the 1930s to create a large and completely new community in the Kimberley, virtually a Jewish colony in the northwest of Western Australia. This idea was advanced in 1939 amid the international crisis of Jewish asylum. Parallel proposals included Jewish resettlement in the Dominican Republic, and various African countries including Madagascar, 'in a bid to find a home for refugees that no country wanted'. Among these exotic suggestions was the proposal for a Jewish Settlement in the East Kimberley region inaugurated by a body wishing to promote the 'Freeland League for Jewish Territorial Colonisation overseas'. This generated extensive discussion about the feasibility of the plan and its implications for defence, population distribution and the idea of alien colonies within Australia and, more broadly, the limits of closer settlement in the north.[16]

The leader of the Freeland League, Dr Isaac Steinberg, visited Australia in May 1939 to investigate possibilities in the Ord River Scheme zone. He made it clear that the project did not entail any notion of political autonomy. His visit aroused great interest and even Arthur Calwell, who eventually opposed the scheme, spoke well of Steinberg. In essence the idea was to take possession of 7 million square miles inland from Wyndham: indeed landowners in the region were prepared to sell them land for £180000. The expectation entailed 500–600 young Jewish colonists sent forth to pioneer the infrastructure (for a mixed economy) with an eventual settlement of 50000 refugees, funded by Jewish interests overseas. Steinberg persuasively argued that the scheme would address both the population and defence priorities of the region and of the nation: he pointed out that Australia had suffered a net loss of 4000 British settlers in the years 1935 to 1937; he also highlighted the dangers posed by Japan, and the strategic value of a new immigrant population in the north of the continent. Some Australians in 1936 indeed feared that their own expansive and lightly populated continent, rather than India, would be seen by Japan as the more desirable place to conquer.[17]

The humanitarian response to the Freeland scheme in Australia was considerable and attracted several influential supporters including Walter Murdoch. But serious public doubts were aroused: for instance, there was continuing opposition to Jewish refugees at a time when unemployment was running at 8.7 per cent; it was also contended that the Jewish immigrants would soon forsake the Kimberley, migrating to the cities to compete for jobs. Negative claims about the assimilability of the Jews were repeated vociferously. Labor was divided, and heated discussion ensued within the movement. Established Australian Jews were also lukewarm about the Freeland idea: there was a general lack of support and, from most of them, a stony silence. They too feared a generalised spread of anti-Semitism. Enthusiasts for northern development were favourable but there was, in other quarters, a growing scepticism about 'the myth of the open spaces' which scorned the idea of northern development regardless of the origin of settlers. The Commonwealth government insisted on an assimilationist philosophy and was opposed to the idea of group blocs of immigration. It did not want a cell of alien immigrants in Australia.

In the outcome the decisive factor in the rejection of the Freeland scheme was the Commonwealth attitude to assimilation. In 1938 the government had already moved against any further concentration of Italians on the Queensland cane fields. In July 1944 Curtin told Steinberg that the government could not depart from its 'long-established policy in regard to alien settlement in Australia'. The Freeland idea was therefore stillborn.

When the war came all movement of people was subject to close containment: new immigration, of course, ceased. Labour was conscripted into war service and there was a great commitment to equality of sacrifice in the community. The only inflow of new labour comprised prisoners of war who were brought to Australia for internment. The process began badly with the *Dunera* episode. This was a ship from Britain which arrived in Sydney in September 1940 carrying 2542 refugee internees from Britain, a mixture of German and Austrian refugees, prisoners of war and Nazis who had been indiscriminately interned in Britain and then arbitrarily transported to Australia and other places. The *Dunera* sailed to Australia in 1940 with appalling shipboard conditions, the passengers treated as trash. On arrival the *Dunera* internees were sent to concentration camps in Hay and Tatura as a precautionary measure. It was part of the internment of aliens in World War Two which eventually numbered 9000, including 2000 German nationals, though at the end of the war only 600 remained under guard. This was coerced immigration and included many very talented young men who were subjected to outrageous injustice since they had no political connections with the Nazis. Some famously became distinguished Australians after the war, including for example Henry Mayer, Fred Gruen and Henry Wolfsohn. About half stayed on in Australia, the others returning to Britain at the end of the war.[18]

The treatment of internees in the war demonstrated cruelly how ordinary people were caught up in the global conflicts, often when they were specifically trying to escape fascism. Dr Evatt, the attorney-general, made special efforts to ameliorate the conditions of internment. During the wartime crises Australia also reluctantly accepted token numbers of refugees from nearby countries fleeing the Japanese invasions. Strictly limited acceptance was allowed to small numbers of Chinese and Eurasian women and children, and some men above military age. These restrictions on asylum caused great offence among Singaporeans.

Another testing incursion of aliens was the substantial number of allied troops who were based in or passed through in the course of the war. Most notable were the United States servicemen who made a noisy impact in several Australian cities, igniting a number of heavily publicised fracas from time to time. But the most politically sensitive question was the inclusion of coloured servicemen among the United States troops. There were delicate negotiations before their actual arrival, exposing the awkward position of the Australian government in terms of its racial values. The tenacity and the severity of the White Australia policy was exposed most precisely in the emergency of war in 1942 when the United States sent its own troops to Australia. The United States government asked directly: 'what would be your reaction to a proposal that a proportion of these troops should be colored (Negro)?' noting that they would be mainly involved in anti-aircraft units to be stationed in Australia. The Australian response was unambiguous, RG Casey, Minister to the United States, making it clear, in a cable, that 'we are not prepared to agree proposal that proportion of United States troops to be despatched to Australia should be coloured". Evatt reinforced this policy, saying that he would rely on the United States government's understanding of 'Australia's susceptibilities'.[19]

These episodes throw light on the limits of Australian thinking on the question of immigration on the eve of the war, and on the extra challenges to White Australia which were generated by the inevitable interchanges of personnel and refugees brought on by wartime conditions.

Planning for the postwar world

Planning for the reconstruction of Australia after the war was an overriding priority in government throughout the later stages of the great conflict. In the wider community there was also a new mood of questioning the fundamental assumptions upon which the economy and the peopling of Australia had been based over the previous 160 years. These foundations were the subject of an unusual and eventually seminal book by William Douglass Forsyth (1909–93) published in 1942 under the title *The Myth of Open Spaces*.[20] It registered a shift in thinking about Australian population and the ultimate demographic capacity of the continent. Forsyth argued that Australia was not a great fertile land selfishly excluding the teeming millions of Asians by the operation of the White Australia policy. In reality most of Australia was uninhabitable and, in any case, most of the people lived in cities; for the rest, Australia was empty simply because it could not support any population. Australia, in effect, was an optical and demographic illusion.

Forsyth cited the Freeland proposal to settle a Jewish colony in the Kimberley region, pointing out that 'any land settlement scheme which aims at placing thousands of farms in the far North is doomed to certain failure'. He was emphatic: crying 'back to the land' was absurd. In Australia there were fewer men on the land in 1935 than in 1913. The modern trend was unmistakable and the drift to the cities was inexorable.[21] In modern times industrial places attracted migrants rather than the countryside or overseas destinations. Forsyth also believed that the long era of international migration was coming to an end and that 'nations can no longer hope to solve or even much alleviate their difficulties by shifting people about the globe'. Overseas migration was a phenomenon of the 19th century and it had now run its course.[22]

Forsyth identified a new direction in modern migration. He pointed out that, in the modern age, migrant people were overwhelmingly drawn into the great industrial and commercial cites of Europe: 'This centripetal tendency has made migration within continents (continental) much more important than between continents (inter-continental)'. Within Britain internal migration from the northern and western districts to the southeastern cities 'has been very important during the post First World War years. Between 1921 and 1931 twice as many Englishmen migrated into the areas about Greater London as into Australia and New Zealand'. All this had undeniable implications for Australia and its future.

'We have reached the end of an era of unprecedented European emigration', said Forsyth, and he warned of the 'drying reservoir of migrants', a consequence of declining birth rates and the greater attraction of the cities. Australia was most likely to experience a stagnation of numbers in the immediate future and by 1970–80, he predicted, population would fall; immigration could not be relied upon, especially while birth rates were falling. Large-scale migration from Britain would become a thing of the past, and northwest Europe would not perform as a substitute source: secondary and tertiary industrial development in Australia would support moderate immigration, but the new immigrants would have to be drawn from southern and eastern Europe. Forsyth warned that Australia would inevitably be required to overcome its prejudice about alien non-British immigrants. By contrast, he was much more sceptical about the possibilities of Asian immigration which, he predicted, would create very heavy social costs and would not solve Asia's problems: 'Asiatic sources are vast, but emigration would only be a palliative for the Asiatic population problem, while its social costs in lands settled by white people would be very great'. Nevertheless he suggested tentatively that 'carefully-planned settlements may be possible':

> In prosperous world conditions secondary and
> tertiary industrial development in Australia would be
> likely to provide a basis for a moderate immigration,
> but in such conditions the migrants could be found
> only in southern and eastern Europe over a long
> period, Asiatic sources aside.[23]

Forsyth therefore had identified several great shifts in the world which posed fundamental problems for Australia's middle-term future, namely the falling birth rate, the rising vitality of industrial growth and the decline of migration from traditional sources. Much of this was worrying and, indeed, prescient. One of Forsyth's reviewers, however, pointed out 'the possibility that the war devastation and political oppression in Europe will increase [rather than diminish] the desire to migrate overseas'. But the most crucial proposition in Forsyth's analysis was its signal of the end of the post First World War optimism which had fuelled the policy of 'closer settlement'. The 'empty spaces' idea had now been exploded. His notion that Australia had a much more restricted capacity to take immigrants was a product of the interwar population debate. As things turned out, he predicted (but seriously underestimated) the impact of industrialisation on Australia's capacity to attract and employ migrants and, equally, its capacity to diversify the origins of its immigrants. But Forsyth also stated, with unprecedented clarity, the fact that refugee migration could be regarded as a future source reservoir of selected new citizens. His accurate prediction was marred only by his overriding belief that 'the principal population problem of Australia is not migration but fertility'.

Shortages emerge

Planning Australia's postwar world was heavily overshadowed by the ominous lingering clouds of the 1930s and also by the experience of the war itself, especially its decisive impact on the national labour supply. The immediate stress of war was demonstrated with the scale of the national call-up which, by March 1942, siphoned off 554 700 men and women into the armed forces from a population of 7 million.[24] This inevitably stretched the nation to its limits. It was manifested in many parts of the economy but perhaps most critically in the housing sector – thus by 1941 new housing construction had virtually ceased. During the war years housing shortages created difficulties even for armed personnel on the move. Shortages accumulated in all sectors in the last four years of the war.[25] Predicting the postwar context was extremely hazardous and the planners swung between two opposite possibilities. First, there was an understandable fear of a sudden recrudescence of interwar levels of unemployment at the end of hostilities; the second was the opposite danger of the onset of paralysing manpower shortages which could prevent the reshaping of the economy. The planners had no model to follow, except that of the aftermath of the First World War, which suggested a mainly negative and depressed prospect for the nation.

Labour planning and population growth were quickly instated as central policy targets – that is, how best to boost the national population and provide labour for the complementary acceleration of Australia's economic development? The official war historians claimed that 'the genesis of the actual programme [of long-term population policy] was to be found in the importation of about 12 000 Italian prisoners of war (mainly from India) in 1943 and 1944 to work in rural industries'. This was 'the Italian prisoner of war immigration programme': and, remarkably, the Italians soon proved their worth.[26] They performed an excellent demonstration effect for the future use of southern Europeans in the Australian economy. By 1944 the Italians were employed throughout the country and the original limitations on the conditions of their employment were soon relaxed. By the end of 1943 it was estimated that up to 20 000 of such prisoners of war could easily be absorbed; it was a message in alien labour recruitment which could not easily be ignored.

The long-run consideration of Australia's future was less urgent than immediate concerns about the possible reversion to depression after the war. In fact the essential context had changed early in the war: the Australian economy, by necessity, switched decisively in the direction of manufacturing, with prompt expansion in industries such as oil production, munitions, steel and many sorts of engineering, all indispensable in terms of import-replacement and defence supplies. This shift became entirely consistent with the longer term planning of industrial development.[27] Industrialisation emerged as the vital turning point in the economy, and wartime needs accelerated and directed its evolution until it became crystal clear that the new industries would become the basis of future growth in Australia. One implication was that skilled immigration would be an immediate priority in any likely postwar setting.

As early as 1941 the future of population and immigration policy was well established in the planning agendas. Defence was already connected with the fear of a falling population, itself a legacy of the 1930s.[28] The Commonwealth government now saw that immigration transcended state interests and was an imperative lever of control in national planning and its orchestration. A paper by the Department of the Interior, the responsible Commonwealth ministry, accorded immigration high priority in reconstruction planning, asserting that 'We must build up our population to the extent that we shall be able to defend ourselves, and also have a more balanced economy – especially from the point of view of our primary export industries'.[29]

LF Giblin was influential in early identifying the practical questions of planning the postwar world: Giblin famously made the off-the-cuff calculation that a net population growth of 1 per cent per annum (from natural increase and immigration) was feasible. This was perhaps the start of 'immigration planning', based on Giblin's slender foundations.[30] Giblin worked closely with the Commonwealth statistician, CH Wickens, in the key planning offices of the Finance and Economic Committees. Though Giblin expected problems in postwar reconstruction he was nevertheless optimistic about the recovery of demand for Australian exports and, by late 1943, he was also anticipating a rise in employment after the war.[31]

In 1943 Giblin lectured on likely postwar needs and not surprisingly gave special emphasis to the problem of anticipated unemployment – the anxiety of the interwar years which still hung over the country. As he said, 'In the 1930s when the depression struck Australia, there was one man in three unemployed. I think the sort of thing Australian people want more than anything else after the war is the prevention of unemployment'. There would be a demand to achieve a very high level of employment, and here he was talking about 3 to 4 per cent on current definitions. He expected 650 000 people, fit for work, to be released at the end of the war from their wartime duties, plus 200 000 others. Eventually it would pack down to 600 000. He expected public works to mop up many of them, 'to bridge the gap to an ordinary civilian peace-time economy'. He was optimistic about the idea of managing the economy to this end. He expected scarcities at the end of the war. But in 1943 he made no mention of immigration or labour shortage.

Optimism was difficult to sustain especially when labour shortages emerged as a critical issue in 1944–45. As the official historians put it:

> Unless industrial reconversion and the restoration
> of housing construction were well advanced by the
> end of the war, it was anticipated that demand for
> consumer goods and housing would exceed supply
> to such an extent that a period of rapid inflation
> would be followed by a sharp depression.

Hence there was already a recognition that some diversion of manpower would be unavoidable even before the end of the war. Manpower became the central issue. HC (Nugget) Coombs was appointed as Director-General of Post-War Reconstruction in January 1943. The fear of heavy unemployment remained central and the question of immigration was not resolvable until greater clarity was achieved. Yet, despite this uncertainty, a powerful countervailing instinct was at work – it told the nation that it must 'populate and develop or face a full-scale "yellow" invasion from the north'.[32]

Out of these cross-cutting ideas about the needs of postwar reconstruction eventually emerged new formulations for demobilisation and for large-scale immigration. Such plans began to take shape in 1943–44 when gloom still shadowed postwar prospects – it was 'testimony to the strength of the Australian faith in development through population growth'. There was a historical dimension: Australia's population growth rate had been one of the highest in the world before 1914 with a natural increase of 17 per thousand per annum, but this fell to 7 by 1934. It had risen to 11.5 by 1943 though forecasts suggested that it would then stabilise at no more than replacement levels. In 1942 a number of politicians were saying that the population needed to rise to 20 million within 20 years and it was calculated that this would require very much larger immigration programs. Giblin pointed out that the plan would require 11 million immigrants and a substantial reduction in postwar consumption to create the infrastructure. But he was prepared to say that a 2 per cent per annum growth rate was heroic yet also feasible, half to be achieved by a surplus of births over deaths, and half by net immigration. The 2 per cent number soon became an accepted official growth objective, elevated as an article of faith, an authentic symbol and target for the postwar generation.

Immigration therefore became a central pillar of postwar Australian planning almost from the start. The first move in its practical initiation was made by the British government in April 1943 when it asked Australia if it would be prepared to accept Empire Settlement after the war. The proposal would, in the first instance, offer free passages to ex-servicemen paid by the United Kingdom government. Australia was immediately enthusiastic and there was clear unanimity about the idea of a rapid increase of immigration at the end of the war. In May 1944 policy details were worked out in full Cabinet for use by Curtin at the Commonwealth Prime Ministers' Conference in London. This was the origin of the March 1946 agreement between Australia and Britain. Australia would accept Britain's offer of free passages of medically fit ex-servicemen and dependents; beyond this an assisted passage scheme would be created to provide passages for the very cheap sum of £10, with the generous subsidy paid equally by Australia and the United Kingdom. The machinery of information was to be created in Britain; voluntary associations were to be drawn in and a reciprocity on social security payments was negotiated. It was accepted that the Maltese would be treated equally if they had good English; by contrast the Freeland League for Jewish Territorial Colonization in the Kimberleys (as we have seen) was rejected.[33] In November 1944 the idea of British and European child migrants was also brought forward, involving plans to recruit children who had been orphaned in the war and who would soon provide future stock for Australia. In collaboration with United Nations Relief and Rehabilitation Administration as many as 17 000 children were recruited and were regarded as a way of guaranteeing future fertility in Australia.

Negotiations were much more cautious on the question of white alien immigration. A report in January 1944 reiterated the primacy of United Kingdom migrants to fit Australia's needs. It concluded however that:

> So great is Australia's need for population that it
> cannot afford to be too exclusive as to categories
> to be regarded as eligible for admission ... the
> Commonwealth should be prepared to accept
> any white aliens who are considered likely to
> assimilate and contribute satisfactorily to economic
> development, and against whom there are not
> objections on the grounds of health, character, or
> (while the ban is in force) enemy alien nationality.[34]

This was conservative in outlook but it was also clear that southern Europe was now being regarded as a likely source of migrants. The ground had shifted substantially.

Thus the blueprint for immigration policy in the postwar world, bipartisan in character, was already drawn up by the end of 1944, even if the alien element was still under wraps. Everyone agreed that the nation's population should be doubled by the end of the century. This priority was recognised in July 1945 with the creation of the new Ministry of Immigration under Arthur Calwell. The annual population growth target was set at 140 000, which was equal to the magnetic 2 per cent per annum. Since it was unrealistic to expect 70 000 British immigrants each year, Calwell was carefully vague about the non-British element which was implied in the statistical projections. Soon the lingering fear of depression

Child migrants from the Blitz arriving in 1940. Arthur Calwell later remarked, 'Australia needs children like these as new citizens'. *From AA Calwell,* How Many Australians Tomorrow?, *1945*

dispersed and the shortage of labour became manifest: 'The marriage of full employment and rapid population growth had been
consummated'.[35] Curtin was himself enthusiastic for Keynesian
approaches to the question of full-employment which were finally
articulated in a White Paper published in 1945, based on the
British model.[36]

Australia and Britain

The strategic and emotional shifts imposed in the war did not
erase Australia's traditional assumptions and allegiances. Thus,
despite Curtin's appeal to the United States at the time of Pearl
Harbor, he retained a deep commitment to the British connection.
In the second half of 1943 he formulated his views on the future of
the Commonwealth. This was partly about war decisions and the
role of the Commonwealth:

> I do not believe that Britain can manage the Empire
> on the basis purely of a government sitting in
> London. I believe some Imperial authority must
> be evolved so that the British Commonwealth of
> Nations will have, if not an executive body, at least a
> standing consultative body.[37]

He began to visualise a representative council which would be
consulted. Indeed he had serious-minded plans for the Commonwealth in reconstruction and international peace after the war.
He spoke of the idea of a fourth Empire of equal and independent
nations devoted, in Burke's words, to freedom and liberty for the
'chosen race and sons of England'. In 1944 Curtin was in London
and uttered remarkably imperial sentiments including the proposition that 'Once the King of England was at war the King of Australia was at war ... We carry on out there a British community in

the South Seas and we regard ourselves as trustees for the British way of life'. He remained warm on the unity of the Empire yet regarded himself as 'a natural Australian, impervious to imperial ideology'. Nor did he make political capital of his Irish heritage (about which he was anyway somewhat sceptical).

Similarly, population planning in Australia was preparing to renew the old rhetoric of Empire and the British heritage. The Australian Labor Party planned a new era of economic security and social justice and both Government and Opposition now assumed a doubling and even trebling of the population in 20 years; 20 million Australians by the end of the century became the common target. The traditional preference for British migrants was reasserted and given immediate priority in the recruitment of orphans and ex-servicemen. The broader assisted passage scheme was agreed in principle in London in May 1944 and announced in June 1945. At the same time there was already a growing aware-ness that unique opportunities to take European refugees were looming; some even realised that it was now a moment to seize.

In May 1945 Chifley assumed power, with Calwell as his Min-ister of Immigration. Calwell was an enthusiast for a 'polyglot Aus-tralia' on the American model. The great postwar immigration program was begun by Calwell two weeks after the Japanese sur-render. He assumed that the Japanese threat would recur quickly enough – that Australia had only a short breathing space. There-fore he promptly adopted the 2 per cent per annum population growth target, half by natural increase, half by net immigration. In 1945 Calwell published a booklet called *How Many Austral-ians Tomorrow?* Some of his propositions were emphatic: he again affirmed that Australia would need 20 million people to be secure; but sheer numbers were not the only consideration. Echoing the anxieties of an earlier time, Calwell continued to decry urbanisa-tion which, he felt, smacked too much of the worship of money and developed unsatisfactory patterns of social life. Moreover, he noted:

Britain can ill afford to lose emigrants and will make every attempt to keep her people at home … Southern Europe may provide us with some immigrants, but are Australians willing to accept more of these people if settlers are not available from British sources?'

This was the crucial question.

Calwell at this stage possessed little definite idea about what was to be done, but the implications of his line of thought were taking shape.[38] The reality by 1946 was as plain as a pikestaff – in that year there was a net outflow from Australia of 15 148 people.

7 Arthur Calwell and the new Australia: 1945–51

The immigrants

By 1947 Australia was recruiting immigrants from dramatically new sources. The forerunners were mainly survivors and escapees out of dislocated Europe. For Australia, if not for the rest of the world, it was a social revolution. The roots of the change grew out of war conditions which had shaped the lives of these postwar migrants.

One was Petronella Wensing, born in Breda in Holland in 1924. Her career captured some of the central themes of mid 20th century European migration. Many years later, from the quiet repose of Canberra, she recollected the saga that overwhelmed her family in the decade before her emigration. She was a Catholic, the fourteenth of 17 children, six of whom died soon after birth, and she herself suffered rickets. Her father was employed on the railways and the family experienced severe privation in the Depression. At the time of the German invasion of Holland he escaped to Marseilles but then returned to face the conquerors. Petronella witnessed some of the horrors of the war in Holland. After the war, in 1948, she married and had two sons by 1952. Her husband was 12 years older, from Rotterdam, a house-painter and, though not in severe circumstances, they suffered bouts of unemployment and were receptive to ideas of emigration – especially since their government was positively enthusiastic about thinning the Dutch population. The Wensings had the choice of several subsidised destinations. Canada was eliminated as too cold; New Zealand did not want families; South Africa was unattractive; Australia offered the best terms. Dutch regulations, imposed during the postwar currency crises, prevented them from taking money out of the country and they were allowed only 1 cubic foot of luggage per adult. The Wensings were virtually penniless, though they were given £50 to set up in Australia. On arrival they passed though the migrant camps and on to Canberra for employment – Petronella Wensing eventually became prominent in the immigrant community.[1] She was the very model of the new Australian immigrant – highly assimilable, very close to the British, white, positive, successful and reproductive.

Australian immigration in these years, 1947–53, intersected with epic currents of change on the other side of the globe. There were thousands of remarkable stories, some captured in later memoirs. Especially evocative is Raimond Gaita's recollection of his parents in *Romulus, My Father,* which began with his father, born in the Romanian-speaking part of Yugoslavia. After serving as an apprentice blacksmith Romulus Gaita moved to Germany for employment. In 1944 he was conscripted into the army of foreign workers in a labour camp in Dortmund. There he met a 16-year-old girl, socially superior to him and with whom any alliance was forbidden by Nazi racial laws. Raimond was probably conceived in a cemetery and the fugitive family fled and became refugees at the end of the war. Gaita's wife suffered from asthma and sought the warmer air of Australia. Thus, with a 4-year-old son, they arrived at the migrant camp at Bonegilla in early 1950. Romulus was sent to work at Cairn Curran dam near Maldon in central Victoria. There he teamed up with two other Romanians, refugees from 'communism's oppressive apparatus', together with a Lithuanian going out of his mind. They lived precariously on the edge of sanity, by turns promiscuous and suicidal. Romulus's son, Raimond, survived all the horrors of migration and subsequent tragic family traumas after they left the camps, and eventually became a distinguished Australian philosopher.[2]

Immigrants carried psychic baggage, some heavier than others. For many Europeans, especially the 'displaced persons', emigration was an escape and many of their stories were later excavated, sometimes by their own families. Half of the Polish refugees to Australia had already passed through work and concentration camps in Germany, usually as coerced semi-servile labour under the Nazis. The experience of forced labour remained vivid in the memories of Polish community members when interviewed in 1994. Thus the 19-year-old, Maciek, had been caught by the Gestapo in Lwów in January 1942 and locked up before being taken to Germany and eventually forced into a factory near Dresden until the end of the war. He was a valued employee, an electrician, and lived reasonably well because of the shortage of tradesmen in Germany. He survived in good shape but, at the end of the war, he could not return to Poland under Soviet control and instead came to Australia.

Also Polish was Jan, living in Poznan in 1939 when the Gestapo seized his father to be taken first to Dachau and later to a worse place, Oranienburg. His mother was also taken by the Gestapo but Jan, at 14 years of age, escaped and ended up working for an anti-Hitler aristocrat. He was severely beaten by the Gestapo for failing to volunteer as an ethnic German but was protected by his employer. At the end of the war he had another narrow squeak when British troops mistook his employer for a German SS, but eventually he found his way to Australia. Another Pole recounted how he had survived Auschwitz, Flossenburg and Dachau and then returned to Poland to find the Russians in control, and therefore escaped back to Germany where he worked in quarries for 2 years.

Recaptured and sent to a concentration camp he was saved from the gas chambers by the arrival of the Americans. He then also found his way to Australia.[3]

Among the European migrants there were markedly different experiences, but many suffered great deprivations before their emigration to Australia. By contrast many of the British emigrants, arriving in parallel with the European refugee recruits, came from less dramatic backgrounds. Even though their numbers in Australia were much greater, collectively they were less visible, less heroic, perhaps more ordinary. Yet many of them had lived though Depression and war, and every variety of shortage and dislocation. Robert Keen from Oxfordshire, as we saw in chapter 5, had suffered the fate of many unlucky British immigrants in the rural devastation in Western Australia in the 1930s. Keen managed to get back to England but in 1947 returned to Australia as a successful agricultural vehicle manufacturer and was determined to make a new fortune in the goldfields. Keen voiced some of the racial anxieties exacerbated by the war and its immediate aftermath. He spoke of the imminent dangers of the 'Yellow Peril'. Australia, he opined, was 'a vacuum' waiting to be filled and the entire British world had become precarious, and meanwhile 'we harass white South Africans and insult the Dutch out of New Guinea'. He declared that 'God only can save Australia from the little brown or yellow men wedged into the top of a V pointing at Australia ... Australia could use five hundred million white men to make it the America of tomorrow'. He remained pessimistic.[4]

Postwar dislocation and the first refugees

In 1945 the National Health and Medical Research Council, echoing the anxieties of the 1930s, warned that Australian fertility had fallen below replacement level and that the Australian population of 7.3 million could not be expected to grow beyond 9 million. Recon-

Women and children learn English at Woodside Migrant Centre in the Adelaide Hills, 1952. *From Bureau of Immigration Research,* Immigration in Focus 1946–1990: A Photographic Archive, *1990*

struction would be crippled and the population would become aged. It was agreed that a return to large-scale planned immigration was indispensable.[5] But in 1945 the entire question of migration and its renewal was still shrouded in doubt. In Britain especially, prospects were negative, its own population expected to fall. It was remarked at the time that 'The cancer of the population is the failure of women to bear children'. Nor did it seem that any demand for emigration would develop. Despite the early stirrings in Australia, the

Economist reported a 'lack of enthusiasm' among the dominions for any large-scale immigration programs. This was just as well because the United Kingdom could 'ill spare any of its young and skilled ... But it is disheartening that the Dominion Governments still appear to fear that imported manpower will take jobs away from their own countrymen'.[6] There was a distinct feeling in Australia of 'the rapidly drying up pool of surplus Western European population' and even if Australia could locate prospective migrants she would face serious competition.[7] JP Belshaw, the economist, wondered whether emigration from Europe would ever revive, or indeed be permitted by European governments.[8]

The immediate postwar world was a shambles at home and abroad. It was a world of shortages, dislocation, uncertainty and then the rapidly rising fear of the atomic bomb. It was a poor context for planning a new population policy. When Frank Clune visited Britain for the first time in 1947 it was to his remote grandmotherland: 'I was visiting Britain at the end of a disastrous, victorious war, when the people were "punch drunk", still reeling from the force of blows they have given and received'.[9] Yet the social and economic degradation of Britain at the end of the long war might create favourable opportunities in which to recruit migrants for Australia. The immediate situation seemed too chaotic for any kind of concerted new program. The shock of British conditions affected all the postwar visitors. When Noel Lamidey became Chief Migration Officer in London, after 25 years absence from England, he exclaimed that everyone on the Underground seemed tired and broken:

> Moreover they had lost the art of laughter ... They
> were sick in both body and mind ... One could
> not escape noting the hollow-eyed tragedy of the
> women folk whose husbands, sons and lovers were
> never to return, the look of bewildered resignation
> on the faces of many of the returned men, and the
> pallid complexion of many of the children.[10]

Out of this immediate disillusion there eventually emerged signs of recovery and new plans. The propensity to emigrate itself began to revive, possibly from a pent-up demand now given urgency by the severe austerity that descended on Britain at the end of the war. In 1946 Australia House and South Africa House gathered inquiries at the rate of 1000 per week and New Zealand at 300 per week; Canada was also inundated with inquiries. At the start of 1947 the number waiting to go to the four dominions reached an estimated 500 000 and many others were too discouraged by the delays. Emigration was in the air – and 'the newspapers were giving it high coverage'.[11] In 1946 an agreement was signed to promote free assisted passages for British ex-servicemen and their dependents and also to assist selected civilian immigrants. Australia House soon inaugurated a new propaganda drive for British migrants. A Gallup poll in the United Kingdom in March 1948 suggested that the demand for emigration was actually rising rapidly.[12] The subsidies for immigrants were soon extended first to Polish ex-servicemen in Britain who were unwilling to return to their occupied homeland, and later also to ex-servicemen of the United States, Netherlands, Norway, France, Belgium and Denmark. This was the prelude to a much greater widening of Australia's recruitment net.

Thus the question of a radically diversified catchment of immigrants was broached very soon after the war and there was a new expansiveness even in the minds of conservatives. The Opposition leader, Robert Menzies, in August 1945 was already reading the times in surprisingly new ways. He urged the government:

> Take risks with some of our standards of perfection,
> with some of our problems, in order to get people
> to come here … if we are prepared to avoid the
> undoubted risk that will exist should our population
> remain low; in other words, should we postpone
> our attack upon the migration problem until all our
> domestic and economic problems have been solved,

First priority: Calwell welcoming British migrants after World War II.
National Library of Australia, vn3311968

we shall probably postpone it so long that we may
abandon any chance of getting real migrants from
the other side of the world.[13]

Menzies was evidently well in tune with the thinking of the Labor
government which soon presided over the great transformation of
Australian immigration. But Menzies was unhappy with the attitude
of England under its own Labour government in these years. When
he visited England in 1948 he was particularly critical of Attlee's government for what he alleged to be its 'chilly' attitude to emigration.
He was certainly critical of the march of socialism in Britain and of
Attlee's policies towards the Commonwealth. Menzies was opposed
to the removal of the word 'British' from before 'The Commonwealth'
and even more opposed the 'extraordinary idea that there can be a
new formula which will include republics as well as monarchies'.[14]

The forces of Australian conservatism were, notwithstanding
Menzies' open-mindedness, still suspicious of any non-British immigration. This was captured in the words of former Prime Minister Bruce. Interviewed after his retirement he recalled how he had
stood firm on the question and had denounced the way in which
Labor (and presumably Menzies too) had changed their tune about
non-British immigration after the Second World War, and had welcomed foreigners. White Australia, he asserted, was indispensable:
'Watch it! Watch it! Watch it! Think what's going on in America
now, and what's developing in Britain. Anyone who suggests that we
were unwise to have adopted this policy [White Australia] is talking
the most frightful nonsense'.[15]

In the immediate postwar years the very first test of this resolve
was the contentious question of Jewish immigration. Yiddish-speak-
ing Jews had arrived in the 1920s and then 8000 German, Austrian
and Czech Jews were permitted to settle between 1933 and 1940,
escaping the Nazis. As we have seen, they met a mixed response. At
the end of the war the humanitarian crisis was even more urgent and
2000 permits were granted in March 1946 for people, mainly Jewish,

who had been in places such as Buchenwald and Belsen, or were homeless and destitute. The outspoken Henry Gullett was outraged by the entry of Jewish refugees in 1947, warning that Australia was taking far too many. He remarked, 'They [the Jews] secured a stranglehold on Germany after the last war during the inflation period, and in a very large part brought upon themselves the persecution which they subsequently suffered'.[16] By sharp contrast, the young Eugene Kamenka met the immigrant ship *Johan De Witt* at the docks in Melbourne and reported movingly on the emotions released by the arrival of the victims of the concentration camps; he predicted the rich cultural potential of such people for Australia. But the spasm of public vituperation caused the government to declare that it had done as much as it could for such people. Calwell now promised that no more than 25 per cent of Australia's immigrants would be refugees. The issue was highly sensitive and though the government stated that religion would not be a basis for the selection of migrants, it was not convincing.

The reception of the Jewish refugees was a sharp warning that the minister would need to tread carefully at the very time when Australia was about to overturn its policy on its most controversial and potentially explosive issue, namely non-British alien immigration. Between 1938 and 1954 Australia received more than 25 000 European Jews who had survived the Holocaust, and many others from Egypt, Russia, Israel, South Africa and Britain. It was claimed that Australia absorbed the highest rate of Holocaust survivors per thousand of its population.[17] This was a small part of the much greater diversification of Australian immigration which was achieved in a series of policy changes soon after the end of the war.

Calwell's revolution

The momentous shift in Australia's immigration was substantially attributable to the forthright leadership of the first Minister of Immigration in the Chifley government, Arthur Calwell, remembered as the architect of the 'massive European immigration'. His own life mirrored the changing currents in Australian attitudes. The slow evolution of his thinking captured the apprehension and ambivalence of the nation at large. On his father's side he possessed Welsh origins, but his mother's Irish background clearly dominated his upbringing while his Catholic education seemed to invest him with a certain degree of Anglophobia. One of Calwell's grandfathers was an American sailor who deserted ship in Melbourne in 1847 and was, therefore, an unofficial immigrant.[18] Calwell himself joined the Victorian public service at 16 and was politically active by 19; he was rejected for war service and was involved in the Young Ireland Movement after the 1916 Rising; he married into another Irish family. His attitude to immigration was nationalistic and he declared: 'I hope we don't find Australia after the war being used as a dumping ground for "pommies" and cockney outcasts ... We want men who are our equals not our inferiors'. He had never wanted Australia to be a 'little England' in the southern hemisphere.

By 1930 Calwell was president of the Victorian branch of the Australian Labor Party and categorically opposed immigration in the Depression. In 1938 he opposed the renewal of immigration on the grounds that it created unemployment. In this respect he simply gave voice to the prevailing trade union opinion on the subject. He declared that 'as things are today we are not prepared or capable of absorbing any of Britain's surplus population'. The war caused Calwell to rethink radically his position on the question. By 1942 he was already presaging a renewal of immigration, telling parliament that white immigration was always desirable in the right conditions. Calwell was moving ahead of his party. He believed that a new social order could be established after the war, a new workers' paradise. By 1943 he recognised that a new national population policy was imperative. In February he said that 'an increasing population might well be classed as the first objective of national policy'. Prosperity and defence could only be built on a much greater population. Calwell now 'believed that an influx of migrants would stimulate economic growth and would banish the dreaded spectre of depression'. He had reversed his ideas which then grew in scale. In September 1942 he asserted: 'Australia will not continue to be a white man's country even if we win this war, unless it has a population of approximately 40,000,000'.[19]

Thus Calwell's views were essentially traditional but new policies were dawning in his mind. He feared a future militarised Asia moving southwards, leaving Australia with no European or American aid to call upon. White Australia was the uncontested and entirely popular basis of national policy and, according to Calwell, irreversible:

> If we are to remain a white race, we can do nothing
> else but maintain the White Australia policy. If we
> cannot get a population of 20 million or 30 million
> people in this country within a generation or so
> by means of immigration and an increase of the
> birthrate the day of the white man in Australia will
> be finished.

But this diagnosis moved Calwell to another radical viewpoint: he began to espouse the notion that the sources of White Australia needed to be widened even if only marginally. He remarked that

> It would be far better for us to have in Australia
> 20 million or 30 million people of 100% white
> extraction than to continue the narrow policy of
> having a population of 7 million people who are 98%
> British.[20]

Calwell regarded Australia as 'a citadel of European civilization in this part of the world' and judged that Australia needed to introduce 15–20 million people within a generation. He was already critical of the Curtin government for not moving quickly enough in this direction. He was acutely conscious of the scale of the political challenge when he remarked that 'Southern Europe may provide us with some immigrants, but are Australians willing to accept more of these people if settlers are not available from British sources?' Despite his new-found radicalism on immigration, Calwell's clarion calls still echoed within the old framework. Thus the White Australia policy was not negotiable and immigration should remain primarily rural and directed away from current centres of urban population. He continued to believe in 1942 for instance that 'The continued prosperity of the countryside is the only foundation upon which the greatness of Australia can rest'.[21] He took the view that cities in Australia grew only at the expense of the rural areas; cities were not a reproductive population; cities lived off the rural population and would negate rural population growth.

Between 1942 and 1945, when he became Minister of Immigration, Calwell began slowly to realise that Australia's future was in industrialisation. Industrialisation and suburbanisation eventually became the twin pillars of postwar reconstruction. Already in 1947, 54 per cent of the Australian population lived in the capital cities.[22] Moving ahead of most Australians, Calwell also began to realise that its immigrants must become more heterogeneous. Perhaps influenced by the ideas of WD Forsyth, he foresaw a more diversified immigration program for Australia, which would require more Europeans and more Catholics. The Haylen Report (1946) declared that 'the hammers and chisels of Australian progress can be heard in the remotest villages of Europe'.[23]

Calwell was essentially a nationalist and he was not wedded to the endless dominance of English Australia. His own American and Irish roots may have played a part in his attitudes: he was evidently inspired by the great example of the United States in the nineteenth century, the melting pot. But he never accepted that the ingredients could be anything other than white. He also continued to believe that northern Australia was a priority for development by immigrants, specifically as a bastion against Indonesian and Japanese expansionism.

The possibilities of Britain supplying Australia's needs were dubious. The British birth rate was simply too low to furnish migrants in the numbers required.[24] In November 1946 Mannix said that 'If Australia does not act within the next year or two to bring immigrants from Europe, she will lose forever a great opportunity. They will go to America or South Africa'. Mannix advocated rural settlement as the best plan.[25]

The new policy emerges

In the last year of the war, planning for immigration began to emerge, somewhat ahead of Calwell's involvement. On 15 November 1944 Acting Prime Minister Forde appointed a new committee to develop a revised immigration program, pointing to a return to conventional British sources but making special reference to British ex-servicemen and child migration. In 1946 a symposium in Goulburn discussed the vulnerability of an under-populated Australia, and GL Wood spoke about the eugenic priorities of the country.[26] The population imperative was activated in several quarters.

The Australian Labor Party remained anxious about the return of high levels of unemployment but Calwell, a close associate of Chifley, carefully broached the possible reorientation of policy towards continental Europe. When Chifley gained power (in July 1945) Calwell swiftly assumed leadership on immigration issues. His 1945 pamphlet, *How Many Australians Tomorrow?* declared that 'it is from the great reservoir of central and eastern Europe that Australia must in the long run draw a considerable proportion of her migrants'.[27] For the moment, however, the new immigration policy, launched in parliament by Calwell on 2 August 1945, was essentially a commitment to a rapid renewal of traditional immigration rather than its immediate diversification. It was well received and regarded as uncontroversial. The nation was united on the question but there were clouds on the immediate horizon and Calwell needed patience.

Curtin had convinced Cabinet that a new wave of immigration was vital for defence and development purposes. Calwell himself advanced the concept of 'maximum effective absorptive capacity', which (with the prompting of HC Coombs) he calculated at 2 per cent per annum. He was advocating a future Australian population in the ambitious range of 20–30 million while also assuming the grand priority of full employment, which would be essential for successful absorption. White Australia remained the cornerstone of the policy; natural increase would provide half of the required demographic target; the immigration of young immigrants with small families would yield the remainder of the desired equation. It was expected that the United Kingdom would provide 90 per cent of the intake, at least in the first phase. As Calwell said:

> We all know what is in store for Australia unless it is
> peopled, unless it is filled with good healthy persons
> of the type from which we sprung, whom we hope
> to bring from Great Britain in the proportion
> of anything up to ten to one of people from the
> continent.[28]

The first new agreement with the United Kingdom was signed in March 1946 and it provided free passages for ex-servicemen and their families. Calwell's associate Noel Lamidey observed that 'we had learnt our lesson and realized that without a vast immigration we would as a nation remain in the world's backwater; if indeed we did not sink altogether'.[29] Calwell was conscious of the demographic problem in Britain and even talked about the possibility of bringing to Australia 50 000 British orphans from the Blitz.[30] Soon active recruitment of selected British civilian migrants was sanctioned, though Calwell jumped the gun and authorised the dispatch of 1000 building tradesmen by the *Largs Bay* in December 1946.

Already it was clear that the immigration policy was geared not to rural development but to industrialisation. The conservatism and outright opposition of sections of the trade union movement was a serious obstacle and Calwell exercised great persuasion; according to RJL (Bob) Hawke, Albert Monk, the London-born trade unionist leader, was decisive in his 'strong and courageous support'.[31] The outcome was a major political victory which rested on practical negotiations governing award wages and the encouragement of new migrants to join the unions. It was a clever and workable compromise essential to the grand scheme. In 1947 23 000 British migrants were recruited together with 9000 non-British. Phillip Knightley interviewed migrants a few years later and remembered especially the 19-strong Davis family from Leigh-on-Sea in Essex; also memorable was 24-year-old Margaret Jarrett, from London, who had written to the mayor of Sydney saying she 'wanted to marry an Australian' and who 'received 800 responses of proposal'.[32]

The demand for immigrants was now incontrovertible; but the supply side was seriously problematic. There were severe shipping shortages for the delivery of migrants of any sort at the end of the war. Moreover Britain itself soon identified its own labour shortages (and began recruiting its own immigrants from Europe at this time). Not surprisingly, in this context, Britain was reluctant to finance emigration. Calwell came to the view that he would be able to recruit no more that 30 000 British emigrants per annum, which would not satisfy the urgent demands of his new policy. It became transparently clear that the new immigration policy would not be fulfilled if confined to Britain and Calwell knew that the proportion of foreigners would inevitably have to increase. Britain simply could not supply the target of 70 000 per annum. Over the following decade it proved almost impossible to find even a third of all immigrants among the British. The sea change had become inescapable.[33]

In 1947 Calwell made a 12-week tour of 23 countries and returned convinced that European refugees were the best immediate pool of mass migration. It was a time for quick decisions and Calwell was equal to the moment: the refugees were judged to be of good quality at low cost, and were subsidised by the International Refugee Organization (IRO). He finalised an agreement with the IRO for 4000 recruits in 1947 and 12 000 in 1948, on condition that it find the shipping. He pointed out that 'If we did not take the excellent displaced persons we are now bringing from Europe the ships that are carrying them would take them elsewhere'.[34] He persuaded the IRO that Australia could take the migrants instead of South America by paying the extra £10 required for the passage. In America Calwell said he wanted a million Americans to come to Australia, whites only of course. In 1947 he had already coined the 'New Australian' tag for the migrants from Europe and by 1949 it was in general use. Having secured shipping, Calwell doused the fires of anti-Semitism and avoided a likely electoral backlash on the issue of Jewish immigration. As he confessed, 'We had to insist that half the accommodation in these wretched vessels must be sold to non-Jewish people. It would have created a great wave of anti-Semitism and would have been electorally disastrous for the Labor Party had we not made this decision'. Calwell pressed for the acceptance of allied and Empire ex-servicemen 'of pure European descent', not otherwise acceptable under Australian–British agreements. There was an ancillary flow of people of Dutch descent leaving troubled and decolonising Indonesia in the years 1947–56. Overwhelmingly, however, Australia recruited its immigrants 'from the far side of the globe, from Europe alone, to form a bulwark against Australia's neighbours'.[35]

Calwell carried through the transition towards the European-isation of Australia's immigration with outstanding success, and the policy achieved whole-hearted bipartisan support and continued beyond the demise of the Labor government in 1949. Calwell's achievement depended on his own determination and also on his credentials with the trade unions. He guided the new policy around dangerous shoals within conventional Australia – for instance, he was extremely careful in his treatment of industrial sensitivities so that the unions did not feel their power undercut by the new immigration;[36] he maintained robust and effective relations with the public service, especially in his creative partnership with Sir Tasman Heyes; most of all he assured the nation that the White Australia policy would be unaffected, indeed buttressed, by his administration. In practice this meant a severe enforcement of discrimination and Calwell used his ministerial power with great rigour in a series of contentious individual cases, strictly upholding the White Australia policy. Calwell was adamantly opposed to Asian immigration yet he conducted warm and comradely personal relations with Asian people on an individual basis, and he was a vocal supporter of Aboriginal rights. He never denied the racially discriminatory character of the immigration policy: he wanted racial homogeneity and was forthright in his advocacy. He had a blunt and colourful turn of phrase. At one point he declared that 'No red-blooded Australian wants to see a chocolate-coloured Australia in the 1980s', and he once called Japanese women, wives of Australian servicemen, 'pollutants'.[37]

The new policy of Europeanisation began to take effect in the crisis year of 1947 when it became clear that Britain would not be able to fill Australian migration expectations, leaving a great shortfall. The omens were poor: in 1945/46 Australia suffered a net loss of 10000 migrants and another loss of 6500 in the following year. At last, in 1948, Australia's migrant balance sheet showed a small net gain of 29365 (which was much less than levels achieved one hundred years earlier). The first non-Jewish European immigrants were 1457 former Polish soldiers in the United Kingdom who were directly recruited to a Tasmanian hydro-electric scheme in late 1947. The formal refugee scheme began with the arrival of the *General Heintzelman* in Fremantle in November 1947, carrying mainly single Baltic men with an average age of 24: they conformed perfectly to the Nordic image and went directly

Baltic migrants working at a limestone quarry in southeastern Tasmania,
employed by the Australian Carbide Company. *From Ramunas Tarvydas,
From Amber Coast to Apple Isle, 1997*

to ex-army camps and then to employment under the terms of the agreement with the IRO.

By 1949 Calwell was bursting with optimism about immigration. He had secured 10 ships of 170000 tons which were now devoted exclusively to immigration; reception camps were also being developed. In effect, Australia became part of a much larger exchange of population. In 1945 there were 12 million displaced persons in Europe; from mid-1947 to the end of 1951, 1 million of these were settled overseas; in 6 years Australia received 170000 IRO refugees, and another 11000 came under the assistance of the local Jewish agencies.[38] Australia had to strain its international credentials to secure these people, most of whom regarded Australia as their fourth preference after the United States, Canada and Argentina. Those who came included 60000 Poles, 24000 Yugoslavs, 19000 Latvians, 17000 Ukrainians, 12000 Hungarians, 10000 Lithuanians; 10000 Czechs and 9000 Estonians. They were not a random selection: Calwell was determined to recruit only the best and the healthiest of the refugees – they were in the proportion of 10 males to 7 females; they were almost all under 40 years of age; 6 per cent were graduates (twice the prevailing Australian level at the time). On most criteria they were ideal immigrants, as they were immediately inductable into the labour force and were also highly reproductive. Their entry into Australia was very closely directed: they were provided with rough accommodation, often in remote locations, with some language facilities. Yet, in reality, they were indentured workers, subject to control for 2 years. They fitted Australia's immediate need for unskilled labour and were not in direct competition with Australian workers (though they received the same terms as Australian workers). Many found that their skills and qualifications were unrecognised and they experienced considerable hardship in conditions not much better than those they had experienced in European refugee camps.

The numbers at the time seemed heroic, but they were not enough and the supply of displaced persons was soon exhausted.

All the immigrant-seeking countries began to look to Europe at large for new recruits. In practice there emerged a tacit (and sometimes explicit) hierarchy of choice among potential emigrants. For Australia the most preferred were those of northern European appearance who would create 'a reasonable balance of nationalities'. Thus the virtues and physical appearance of the Baltic and Dutch migrants were greatly amplified to reassure the Australian public in the first stages of the diversification of the migration program.

The recruitment of refugees in the immediate postwar years wound down but became a precedent for later episodes – thus in 1956–58, some 14000 Hungarian refugees were received and 6000 Czechs in 1968–70.[39] In this way refugees became part of Australia's immigration system as it interlocked with various international conventions and agreements. These recruitments were inevitably sporadic, responding to particular episodes. More immediate was the implementation of new agreements with a widening range of governments, first in Western Europe, to recruit immigrants on a regular basis agreeable to both countries. This was a further radical shift of Australian policy and reflected the success of the refugee experiment, the shortfall of British emigrants, and the continuing appetite for more labour in the rapidly expanding Australian economy. The new arrangements began with Malta in 1948 (which was in a special relationship with Britain and the Empire) and then expanded, first to the Netherlands in 1951, then to Italy in 1952, Germany in 1952 and later Greece, Spain, Sweden and beyond. The telling aspect of these developments was, first, the fact that former enemy countries (not including Japan) were quickly brought into the net, and second that, in contrast to the British, most of the foreign immigrants received little if any assistance.

The scale and velocity of the new program was impressive. In 1950 net migration reached 153 685, which was the third highest intake of the 20th century.

Recruitment

Having established the new policy, the prime task was to implement its aims and to reach the ambitious and urgent targets set by Calwell. The memories of the people engaged in the recruitment system immediately after the war provided a graphic account of the campaign for new migrants.[40] Eventually several thousand officers were employed by the Department of Immigration, many of whose initial plans were announced before facilities were available. At the start there was a deluge of 750000 British enquires even before the application forms were ready: some of the immediate interest in emigration to Australia was lost. Great queues collected outside Australia House in London, reaching along the Strand; in the first phase single ex-servicemen with building experience were given priority, and a group travelled on the *Largs Bay* in December 1945, some of them soon helping to build Canberra.

The austere conditions in postwar Britain were exacerbated by severe weather while the long food crisis worsened. The Australian recruiting officers remembered the haste with which selections of migrants were made and the narrowness of life in postwar Britain, with its pinched hotels without showers, and coal stored in domestic baths. In England there were still only 6 selection officers in 1947, plus some local assistants in the office of the High Commissioner. They had to address specific labour demands for skilled tradesmen: thus the Victorian Railways wanted particular workers whom they supplied with imported prefabricated houses. The State Electricity Commission of Victoria built Yallourn with migrant labour. The shipping shortage initially meant that only single men were selected and the British were given preferential treatment at all times: consequently no British migrant travelled on unconverted ships.

By August 1947 Australian emigration officers were making helter-skelter preparations in Germany in conjunction with the Australian Military Mission, and were immediately given the task of filling a ship with refugees within 6 weeks. German people were still in a state of shock after the war: the officers found themselves choosing candidates amid myriad tragedies, and aware that they were not allowed to take people originating from countries now under Russian control. The recruiting teams moved about Europe selecting people for Australia, many of them desperate to leave and prepared to accept any conditions imposed by the Australian scheme. The recruitment officers came face to face with the personal tragedies of so many of the displaced persons. George Kiddle recollected that refugees able to speak English had the best chance of selection. He was involved with the earliest and very hurried efforts to get a train load of migrants to a ship leaving Diepholz for Bremerhaven: they had no alternative but to use cattle wagons, the only rolling stock available. He remembered, 'That was quite an emotional moment for us, I think, to see people really being herded around like cattle'. There were similar problems with the unavoidable use of old and decrepit shipping during the first years of recruitment.

Jaroslav Havir was a Czech refugee who had escaped into Germany and then into the IRO camps. Seeking emigration, he confronted the intensely frustrating problems of providing satisfactory documentation; his own case was complicated because he was coupled with a British woman who became a voluntary Displaced Person (DP) for the purpose of emigration to Australia. The Australian immigration officers were shocked by the food shortages, the lack of soap and the smell of the refugee camps, which left an indelible impression. 'Conditions of the first ships, usually very old unconverted American troop ships, were virtually Dickensian', racked with sickness and bearing large numbers of children, they were reminiscent of 19th century shipping conditions. In late 1948 Abraham Cykiert, a survivor from the Buchenwald concentration camp who had been helped by the Jewish community, was appalled by conditions, including dysentery, on his ship and welcomed the outrage expressed by journalists who met the ship at Fremantle. On arrival in Australia many of the immigrants were stunned by the signs of wealth and the astonishing availability of nourishing and attractive food.

Meanwhile the recruiting officers perambulated Europe in search of more people to supply the needs of such projects as the Snowy Mountains hydro-electricity scheme and the Bell Bay aluminium enterprise in Tasmania. One officer could not forget the devastation in Cologne, the bombed-out buildings and its ruined cathedral. Selection at the start was rough and ready at the hands of interviewers who had received virtually no training. As it happened existing German records were remarkably detailed and this helped with the sifting. But there was a great imbalance of single males in the general migration, though many proxy marriages were contracted to qualify for the migration and there followed strings of broken romances. 'Assimilability' was the unspoken rule for selection. No disabled or disfigured were selected because 'it would not be fair to Australia'. The recruiters were acutely aware of the fear of Russia that clouded the atmosphere of the emigrants' exodus, many of them paralysed by fear of another war. The Australian officers worked in teams of 2–4 and commonly interviewed 20 prospective recruits per day. The interrogation took them through a standard list of points on a card which led to the fateful decisions: 'accept' or 'not accept'. The officers were vigilant for Communist or criminal elements and they were warned of Nazis channelling themselves through the Trieste camp to emigrate to Australia.

There were thousands of dramatic stories of escape and trauma among the people who eventually reached Australia out of postwar Europe. After the Yalta Conference many of those from the east, including the Ukraine, had been terrified of being returned to the USSR and sent to Siberia. False papers were common and many people passed as 'Poles', being in fact Ukrainians. They often suffered badly in Australia, feeling despised, and descended into mental illness. One such story was that of the parents of Eva Maria Chapman, who wrote a book about it all, the sort of account that challenged some of the celebratory versions of the reception of refugees in postwar Australia.[41]

Holland, which had suffered severely in the war, was one of the first countries to sign a bilateral migration agreement with Australia and three selection centres were soon established. One of the early migrants, Catherine Vanderhorst, recollected the terrible housing shortage in Holland which had prevented people from marrying: she was very pleased with her reception in Australia. But professional people in Holland were deterred by the refusal of Australia to recognise foreign qualifications, and this twisted the pattern of recruitment. Australian officers were intensely alert for Dutch 'collaborators' and also for communists, any affiliation with communism being an automatic bar to acceptance. One officer claimed that rejected Nazis went to South Africa: 'The South Africans apparently didn't find this an objection'.[42] Later, in Italy, the Australian recruiters made their selections in close association with local doctors.

German immigration was accepted with surprising alacrity soon after the war, the former enemy suddenly turned into bona fide migrant. Two circumstances favoured the transition: first, the devastation of the German economy created a great pool of surplus labour, and second, the voracious appetite for labour occasioned by Australia's manpower shortages. Some of the earliest migrants (240 in 1947–52) were scientists, some expert in the extraction of oil from coal; and there were about 5000 German wives of DPs in that phase also. In 1947 an Australian opinion poll showed that 53 per cent said they were friendly to German people, and 34 per cent unfriendly. But opinion was shifting so that in 1953, 65 per cent favoured German immigration, and only 24 per cent were opposed. In 1952 an agreement with West Germany arranged to subsidise 3000 immigrants and allowed for 1000 others to enter on 2-year work contracts. There were several other categories of Germans, some of whom had been interned in the war, and former prisoners of war, who were able to enter Australia. Opposition to the people from recent enemy countries was short-lived and mainly derived from the Jewish lobby.[43] There appears to have been little friction generated against German immigration despite the scale of the influx.

Australian attitudes to different categories of immigrants were registered in opinion surveys. For instance, a survey in Melbourne in 1948 demonstrated preferences first for English migrants, followed by the Irish and Germans, all well ahead of southern Europeans, Jews and Negroes. Another poll showed that the Germans came third after the Dutch and the Scandinavians in the hierarchy of preference. Italians also entered the league table but the other former enemy, the Japanese, remained totally unconsidered.

Test cases

Calwell in 1947 had embarked on a risky policy which stretched ahead of public opinion regarding the radical dilution of the British character of Australia.[44] The Australian public needed reassurance. The sudden widening of immigration intakes was associated with extra demonstrations of vigilance for the continuing integrity of the White Australia policy. Calwell represented himself as the guardian of the old policy and, indeed, insisted that the 'New Australia' would be more effectively able to resist the incursion of Asians. The Europeanisation of immigration was a 'bold experiment' which rested on bipartisan foundations. In later years, when the success of the experiment was manifest, politicians of the time congratulated themselves on the courage and humanity of the great program of postwar immigration. Discordant voices, however, questioned its credentials as a generous response to fascist terror and the refugee crisis: Australia's policies, in this view, were seen more as 'calculatingly and selfishly opportunistic', supplying its appetite for cheap labour and for augmenting its white population. Australia had extended its migrant net because Britain was unable to supply enough people. Australia, despite the changes, remained deeply xenophobic.[45]

Certainly Calwell continued to blazon the policy with which Australia remained most associated across the world: he trumpeted the view that 'the flag of White Australia will not be lowered'.[46] Calwell's attitude to race was complicated and his own family always denied that the White Australia policy was based on the assumption of racial superiority. He had many Chinese friends and spoke some Mandarin and, in 1947, had recommended naturalisation of Chinese residents, which was rejected by Cabinet. But Calwell also insisted that Australia could not solve Asia's poverty problems: the best way was to educate their students. He feared the incursion of a cheap-labour system which would destroy Australia's progressive social experiments: 'the blackbirders have gone but their spirit lives on', he said.[47] He conceded that the term 'White Australia' was offensive to Asians, but was essentially misunderstood. Calwell believed that Australians were united to retain the policy.

The idea of 'assimilation', similarly, was a fundamental and uncontested assumption of the policy and a requirement upon all immigrants. As the demographer WD Borrie remarked, 'Here in Australia we have never really had to face this problem of assimilation until the post-war years'.[48] The danger of importing unassimilable elements from non-British countries continued to prey on the minds of the planners and any sign of inter-communal tension was rapidly identified and condemned. Australia set its face against the introduction of alien antagonisms and inter-ethnic conflicts; such tensions were utterly anathema. In the event there was surprisingly little imported conflict and every slight symptom was given short shrift. From the Liberal side of politics the message was unambiguous. In 1950 Menzies spoke openly against sectarianism: 'Prejudice against a migrant because of race or origin is not a sign of pride but a sign of stupidity'. He insisted that the British themselves were a very mixed group: 'we are, of all people, the most mixed. We are the product of wave after wave of movement of peoples from the Caucasus westward'. He pointed out that Australia's greatest soldier was a Jew (Monash) and that the Germans had been the best of settlers. 'We must receive them as Australians ... when they have lived here for a few years, they will all be Australians, they will all be British, and they will all be, as we are, the King's men, and the King's women'.[49] This was the prevailing and all-embracing philosophy of Australian immigration.

Nevertheless, White Australia remained deeply entrenched and policed with extra vigour. Calwell reaffirmed the policy wherever it was tested. Thus the treatment of Asian entrants was rigorous – from war brides to seamen. Individual cases sprang up recurrently – such as that of Arthur Gar-Lock Chang who had waited 40 years to gain naturalisation but was defeated by the impregnable dictation test which continued to protect the White Australia policy.[50] During the war about 15 000 people had been evacuated to Australia from neighbouring countries and of these 5473 were non-Europeans. At the end of the war Australia paid for the repatriation of 3768 Indonesians. In 1949 Calwell refused to allow the Philippines-born United States serviceman Sergeant Gamboa to take up residence with his Australian-born wife. In 1949 he also stood firm on the O'Keefe case: this involved a refugee woman whose first husband was a Dutchmen killed in an airplane crash serving the wartime allies; she had subsequently married an Australian citizen, John William O'Keefe. Mrs O'Keefe and her family were deported despite a great furore in the newspapers.[51] Calwell responded to Menzies' taunts, 'We can have a white Australia, we can have a black Australia, but a mongrel Australia is impossible and I shall not take the first step to establish precedents which will allow the flood gates to be opened'.[52] Calwell regarded it as a test of White Australia: 'We do not want in Australia a reproduction of conditions in Singapore, Surabaya, Fiji and the Harlem section of New York'. The O'Keefe case became a rod for his unbending back and meanwhile the newspapers, the rabble-rousing *Truth* in particular, continued to attack the authorities for being too slack.

In reality there were few episodes and the dictation test had little use: only eight cases were tested in the years 1942–56 (5 were Europeans, 3 Indians, and one Chinese). Among them were Mohammed Razak and Mohammed Sadiq, both Muslim Indians from Fiji who jumped ship in Sydney to become immigrants. They were interviewed by the Immigration Department and given the 50-word dictation test in Italian and failed. They were sentenced to 3 months imprisonment and deported. The policy remained unbreached.[53]

Trickier were the cases which inevitably arose within the normal selection procedures in Britain. Generally there were very few non-white applications to Australia House. But an immigration officer remembered a particular case in 1948: a family in Nottingham with 13 children applied to Australia House and was greeted as a splendid case for publicity. The newspapers and cameramen were alerted and the family assembled (except for the most recent baby – asleep in a cot upstairs). The press pleaded with the parents to bring the baby to complete the photo call. As the recruiting officer put it, 'And then, lo and behold, the thirteenth child, as black as the ace of Spades. The rest of the 'family was completely European white. The mother was the grand daughter of a Jamaican seaman and her thirteenth child was thrown back to that colour'. The press cooperated and agreed not use the story. One month later the family was told that they had been rejected. As the Immigration Officer noted, 'coloured people simply accepted the fact that they couldn't migrate to Australia'.[54] Not even the British could be relied upon to be consistently white and the selection methods occasionally lapsed into farce. But the implementation of the policy was never less than serious in terms of the expectations of the Australian public.

A different sort of discrimination applied to any immigrant tainted by association with the Nazis, most notably the *Schutzstaffel* (SS), all of whom had been tattooed on the left arm. This led to very intrusive scrutiny of all German emigrants – trying 'to flush out the SS'.[55] In 1947 Frederick Galleghan was appointed head of the Australian Military Mission in Berlin, responsible for liaising with the IRO regarding refugee recruitment for Australia. He believed that Australia should be a 'haven for people who by the fortunes of war had become stateless'; he was horrified by conditions he witnessed in the DP camps. But Galleghan was sceptical of 'de-

nazification' and was in principle adamantly opposed to their recruitment to Australia. In practice he began to see the value of former
Waffen SS recruits. As Galleghan's biographer put it:

> they were all magnificent specimens of German
> manhood and fitted perfectly into Hitler's Aryan
> ideal. Galleghan examined many of these ex-soldiers
> and came to the conclusion that many would make
> an excellent contribution to Australia as immigrants
> to work on the Snowy Mountain Scheme and the
> South Australian Railways project.[56]

Inevitably various unwanted migrants squeezed through the system, and the story-seeking journalist Phillip Knightley reported
evidence of Nazi sympathisers in the Australian reception camp at
Bonegilla in the early phase. The hunt for Nazis was a long-running
campaign in postwar Australia as it was in many other parts of the
world. Australia was slow to investigate suspected war criminals:
several decades passed before any real action was taken. Eventually 200 residents in Australia were investigated, but very few were
charged with war crimes.[57] The 1988 War Crimes Amendment Act
sanctioned the use of Australian courts to try suspected war criminals resident in Australia, all men in their seventies who had emigrated from Eastern Europe.[58] These trials did not convict but they
exposed the unutterable horrors of the wartime massacres which
people remembered all too vividly. The immigrant experience did
not expunge the past.

The camps

The reception of unprecedented numbers of immigrants from
highly varied origins was one of the greatest challenges not only to
the immigrants but also to Australian society at large. One of the

largest tasks was sheer accommodation – Australia's housing stock was badly rundown in wartime and the creation of new infrastructure, industry and, indeed, new housing was the first task of the immigrant workforce. Naturally, in the first instance, their arrival worsened the housing crisis before they could help solve the problem. There were bound to be tensions and temporary hardships for all classes of immigrant. The travelling British journalist Roy Lewis noted the housing problem created by emigrants wherever they went after the war: 'It is a pity that nobody has yet been able to devise a plan whereby each migrating family could be shipped together with a pre-fabricated house. Meanwhile single men and women get priority'.[59]

Many of the emigrants were absorbed through the receiving community with little trace and joined the community relatively quietly, often helped by relatives and church organisations. But tens of thousands of immigrants passed though makeshift facilities which tested the tolerance of all parties. The best known was the reception camp at Bonegilla, a remote location on the border of Victoria and New South Wales, and 8 miles from Albury, 6 hours by train from Melbourne. Bonegilla was part of the deliberate dispersal policy designed to minimise close confrontation between the immigrants and the established population. Part of the purpose of the camps was to prepare the migrants for employment on great schemes in remote areas, but they were also designed to avoid large concentrations of aliens close to the existing centres of urban population. Moreover the conscripted labour of immigrants would compete less directly with unionised labour if they were sent to remote locations. The refugee immigrants (such as Romulus Gaita) were often required to work for most of 2 years away from their families on projects such as the Snowy Mountains Scheme.

But facilities at Bonegilla (and the other immigrant camps) were spartan at best, and led to considerable alienation among the people who passed through their doors. For the displaced

The first Displaced Persons from Europe leaving Port Melbourne by train for Bonegilla, December 1947. *Postcard, Immigration Museum, Melbourne*

people of Europe there was a psychological reaction because Bonegilla was an ex-army training camp which had been converted into a prisoner-of-war camp and then reopened in 1947 as a 'reception and training centre' for newly arrived immigrants. At its peak in 1950 there were 7700 migrants housed in unlined corrugated-iron huts and 1600 in tents, and managed by ex-military personnel. Over the following two and a half decades more than 320 000 migrants passed through Bonegilla, some for a few days, others for extended stays. They were refugees and voluntary immigrants who had 'exchanged two years of their labour for an assisted or free passage', destined 'to be placed in jobs which Anglo-Australians did not want to do'. Bonegilla was a sorting house for further employment and the start of the immigrants' assimilation.[60]

The reactions of most of the European migrants to their reception was not known until much later when many of them wrote their memoirs. The official requirement was that the refugees would not threaten prevailing wage conditions in Australia; this was a two-edged matter since it ensured basic wage levels for the migrants; but it also channelled them into some of the least desirable and dirtiest jobs under harsh contract conditions and in the worst living conditions. Later verdicts claimed that the refugee and civilian intakes were unbalanced in terms of ethnicity, age and gender and that these combinations generated high levels of 'loneliness, alcoholism and mental breakdown among an already vulnerable people'.[61]

At the time the work of the sociologist Jean Martin provided the first systematic investigation of the intersection of Australian society with the exotic newcomers. She discovered the undertow of anti-European prejudice in Australia, though the government introduced concerted schemes to counteract the problem, with some success. Indeed the great immigrant experiment, fraught with dangers to the social balance and general amity of Australian society, was achieved with extraordinary peaceabililty and little inter-communal aggravation. But the great achievement was punctuated by small and large episodes of tension and social breakdown. The levels of psychological trauma in the camps was widely acknowledged; and sometimes (as we shall see in the next chapter) relations reached the very point of violence. Bonegilla was itself described as a degrading place; on the other hand the same migrant's daughter spoke fondly of her time at Bonegilla.[62]

The thinking

For Australia, a profoundly monocultural country, the new waves of European immigrants were the onset of a social revolution the quietness and peaceability of which surprised even its instigators. It was, of course, a planned change prompted by postwar fears in a new age of planning. The immigration policy was a great national project supported by all political parties. It entailed a swift shift from an all-British population to a European population designed to strengthen the foundations of White Australia.

Despite the sudden increase of European immigration, the British component was sustained at 41 per cent in the years 1947 to 1951, though it fell to 33 per cent in the following decade; British-born residents increased by 193 000. British immigrants were now almost entirely urban in origin and their passages were greatly facilitated by very generous and preferential assistance which helped to counteract the declining propensity to emigrate (shown by the radical decline of emigration to the United States over these decades).[63]

Calwell believed a population of 15 million would greatly increase industrial output; with capital deepening Australia could double its population and treble its productivity. The Snowy Mountains Hydro-electric Scheme symbolised the determination of the Chifley government to accelerate national development. This project diverted the headwaters of the river system and also involved a vast extension of irrigation over a wide area; it took 25 years to complete; almost two-thirds of the 100 000 people engaged in the construction scheme were drawn from the newly arrived migrants, many of them well qualified and most of them working under conditions similar to an indentured system.

The Snowy Mountains project also symbolised the strictly national purposes of the immigration schemes. It was never presented as a humanitarian refugee program: Australia was pursuing its own national agenda, its own priorities, which happened to interlock satisfactorily with the availability of acceptable postwar refugees. There was virtually no claim that its purpose had been to succour the casualties of world war. The immigration program was hard-boiled: as Calwell said, these were economic migrants as far as Australia was concerned, their status as refugees was essentially secondary. Australia may have been sentimental about the British connection but its severe demand for labour also transcended these considerations.

The refugee issue was treated warily by the government and its advisors. In 1948 Tasman Heyes was clear about its dangers when he declared that:

> If it is intended to mean that any person or body of persons who may suffer persecution in a particular country shall have the right to enter another country irrespective of their suitability as settlers in the second country this would not be acceptable to Australia as it would be tantamount to the abandonment of the right which every sovereign state possesses to determine the composition of its own population, and who shall be admitted to its territories.[64]

The postwar immigration policy was clearly not designed to convert Australia into a multicultural society; the first European immigrants were treated as second-class entrants with few rights; they were part of a strictly mundane priority, not the basis of a new vision of Australian society. They were simply required to assimilate. As late as 1951 and beyond, newspaper editors in Australia continued to regard the dilution of the British monopoly as a 'temporary aberration'.[65] The wider context was Australia's own relationship with Britain in which there was a renewed effort in these years to keep the Empire stocked with 'the British race'.[66]

Australia was surprisingly successful in reviving British emigration when demographic and economic conditions seemed against it. British attitudes to Australia were finely captured in 1948 by the visiting writer, David Esdaile Walker. He recorded British fears and hardships: 'At home in England there were millions looking to the possibility of starting life afresh in a new country, as soon as ships could be found to carry them. In an atomic age, common sense demanded the dispersal of British industry, if this were feasible'. Walker interviewed Calwell, who told him he wanted to treble the Australian population to 20 million within three generations and this depended on getting 'the shipping and the houses. This is absolutely necessary if Australia is to enjoy a sense of security'. Calwell reflected:

> The sad truth is that Australia as we know it is
> only 150 years old but we are slowly bleeding to
> death ... Unless the situation can be remedied by
> the immigration of women, Australia's population
> will never reach eight million ... If the net rate of
> reproduction does not improve, we will be finished
> as a nation at the end of fifty years.[67]

Walker reported: 'The average Australian family of four had dropped to two since the turn of the century'; by 1948, 20 per cent of Australian marriages were childless. According to the Commonwealth statistician, there had been an 'alarming turn for the worse' in demographic matters: Australia already had an ageing population, with twice as many over 65 than in 1900.[68]

Calwell told Walker that Australia could easily support 30 million, but 'To the north and the west live 1,200 million Asiatics, a potential threat not far distant in this jet-propelled age. The Japanese have been near enough and that is a lesson and a warning'. He said, 'I would like 70,000 migrants [per annum] if only we could get the ships. Even so that would be a drop in the ocean compared with the annual increase of such nations as the Chinese and the Japs'. Tens of millions of undernourished Asiatics 'whose eyes quite naturally begin hungrily to turn towards the undeveloped spaces of the south … History might at any moment prove that the echoes of that cry for *Lebensraum* had not altogether died away'. Walker quoted a recent government report which declared that 'to maintain the northern portion of this continent as a heritage for the white race, Australia is committed to an heroic task, the like of which has no parallel in the history of mankind'.[69]

Walker toured the streets of Sydney and found no slums or beggars. Australia had been extraordinarily generous in its response to the recent campaign for 'Food for Britain' – appeals had gone out from the streets, the pulpits and the press, and produced 'a fantastic national act of goodwill from 7 million to 50 million other people over the seas'. Calwell had told him that 'We would like the British and the Nordic races as first priority. Government policy forbids the immigration of male enemy aliens, though the Germans have proved good colonists in the past'. In North Queensland Walker found many Italians and the local police said that 'the Italians gave no trouble at all, with the exception of the Sicilians'. They looked just like Australians and, though the 'Wops' and 'dagoes' had generated resentment at first, they were now fully accepted: 'The newcomers are practically "dinkum Ausssies" before they knew it'. Calwell himself said that it was the Scots and the Irish who had built Australia; 'The English never did much of the labourer's work', and now the dams were being built by Welsh, Cornish, Italians, Maltese and Yugoslavs.[70]

Walker advocated much higher emigration from Britain, partly for strategic reasons. The atomic bomb had made the dispersion of British interests and its people a new imperative. There were hundreds of thousands of people in Britain anxious to emigrate, 'but there are no ships. British firms are investing in Australia which is making a difference'. Britain would be the first target in an atomic war and Australia beckoned: 'Here we've enormous spaces offering a genuine invitation towards dispersal, inside the Commonwealth of Nations. To ignore such an offer seemed imperial folly'. He quoted

Mr Hambleton of the engineering firm Rubery Owen – an English industrialist about to set up in Adelaide:

> There is absolutely not a shadow of doubt that the industrial potentialities of Australia are immense.
> The problem is surely not so much a matter of saving the English peoples as of preserving the British <u>race</u>.
> We <u>must</u> become Empire-minded. This isn't mere sentiment or emotionalism. It is blunt common sense from any point of view and particularly in view of defence.[71]

In the Calwellian years the British remained the largest supply of migrants but the transition to a much more diversified Australia had been inaugurated with astonishing speed and resolve.[72]

8 The great diversification: the 1950s and 1960s

Migrant experiences

Galvanised by fear and hope, Australia during the late 1940s had embarked on a concerted program of demographic renewal and economic development. In the following 24 years (1947–71) 2.5 million people from all over Europe were persuaded, assisted and conveyed to Australia. It was an extraordinary inrush of immigrants propelled in a mood of national unity. It happened in a highly favourable context: these years were set in the longest and most dynamic surge in economic growth ever experienced in Australian history. This convergence of positive circumstances, against expectations, filled most of the population void which had haunted the country during the previous five decades. The immigrants themselves were more diverse than ever before. It was the heroic age in the project to populate Australia and to secure its future.

The British remained the most favoured and numerous of the immigrants. They seemed at times to arrive with barely a care in the world. Several decades later a Canberra humourist and migrant recollected how he had departed Cromer in Norfolk in England: 'I came to Australia when I was eighteen because I was bored, because it was free and because I had been told that Ken Rosewall was Australia's Prime Minister. I was misinformed but I stayed'.[1]

Elizabeth Jolley, later a distinguished Australian novelist, was born in the English Midlands. Like many other migrants her family had already experienced migration within Britain – to cold hostile Edinburgh and also to affable but exclusive Glasgow. They then, in the 1950s, decided on Australia. Jolley recalled the anxieties of the sea voyage and captured the emotions of the time, particularly the flocking of migrants at the wharves. Most memorable was the passage of the emigrant ship through the Great Bitter Lake and its arrival at Fremantle – and the crowds. She remembered medical officers examining fingernails for ridging, the tell-tale sign of tuberculosis, and the equal vigilance for evidence of venereal disease. She also observed a customs officer injuring himself in his overzealous search for obscene literature in crates of books brought in by immigrants.[2]

The British migrants have been much neglected in the annals of Australian immigration, partly because it was assumed that 'British settlers were a homogenous group and somehow indistinguishable from native or so-called Anglo-Celtic Australians'. Between 1947 and 1974, 86 per cent of British migrants received assisted passages; they were mostly skilled or semi-skilled men and women, derived from suburbs surrounding Britain's industrial cities. Australia's new manufacturing industries were hungry for their services; in 1966 two-thirds of the population of the new town of Elizabeth in South Australia were British, with a disproportion from Lancashire and London and with many trade unionists among them. As Mark Peel points out, the great benefit of leaving England for Australia was that 'you could start to forget the careful balances and deferences of the British class system, happy to be out of England, happy to be in a place where you had a decent house, an indoor toilet and a proper bathroom, a bit of

Legendary English cricketer leads his own team to Australia: Harold Larwood and family became immigrants in 1950. *From Bureau of Immigration Research,* Immigration in Focus 1946–1990: A Photographic Archive, *1990*

space and a bit of privacy'. Moreover 'British migrants were ... never subject to the assimilationist demands Australia made on Southern and Eastern European migrants'. In the 1960s they were generally satisfied as migrants though their optimism faded some-what in the subsequent decades.[3]

The best known Australian immigrant story was the literary spoof entitled *They're a Weird Mob* (1957), a novel written under the pseudonym of Nino Culotta, supposedly an Italian builder's labourer cum journalist, and his account of coming to Australia from Italy. The author in reality was John O'Grady, born in Sydney in 1907, and his book was immensely popular, reprinted 21 times by 1959. Written in pseudo-broken English, Culotta plays the part of a fully assimilating Italian migrant who adopts all the local bigotries. O'Grady used the device to gently mock both the Australians and the immigrants, but it carried clear propaganda intent, concluding that

> There is no better way of life in the world than that
> of the Australian. The grumbling, growling, profane,
> laughing, beer-drinking, abusive, loyal-to-his-mates
> Australian is one of the few free men left on this
> earth. Learn his way. Learn his language.

As a later critic observed, it was a 'faintly amusing and energetic opus, probably racist ... [and] a repository of outdated attitudes'.[4]

The direct and authentic testimony of the European migrant emerged only slowly but by 1960 new voices were heard in the immigrants' own languages. The prewar experience had been told by Pinchas Goldhar, a Polish Jew, in his *Tales from Australia*, first published in Yiddish in 1939, carrying the scars of Nazi brutality as well as the fear of anti-Semitism. Other Jews, and then Italians and Greeks, began to relive and give shape to their migrations, still largely unnoticed in the mainstream of Australian literature. Second and later generations of migrant families were much more vocal, and eventually gave expression to their often confused transition into the receiving society of postwar Australia.[5]

The best example was Raimond Gaita's searing account of his family's experience, which made no bones about the reality that was immigrant life for people such as his parents and their friends (already mentioned in the previous chapter). But Gaita made it clear that immigration was complicated by earlier factors in such lives. Typically they had transported with them their hatreds of communism and the scars of war itself.[6] For these migrants, coming to Australia was the tailpiece to a much more dramatic story played out in Europe before emigration.

Another literary version of the European experience was evoked by Andrew Riemer, about the trials of his Hungarian parents and family in getting to Australia in 1947: 'We were among the first of those waves of postwar European migrants who were to influence the nature of Australian society in various and at times unexpected ways'. Riemer captured the cultural adjustment forced on immigrants, most notably the widespread language problem of the elderly, often magnified by the confusions and barbs of ordinary social interactions they faced day by day in suburbia. Australians treated such folk with sharp disregard and little understanding of the severe experiences which had already marked many European immigrants before they arrived. Many of these people had been on the move for many years, often out of profoundly disturbed and impoverished places. They arrived in a booming and affluent industrialising society and fended for themselves in the hubbub. Riemer, several decades later, observed that the end of the century was 'a time when the seeds sown by the postwar Government's policies of mass migration were bearing fruit in a manner that the people who had shaped those policies may not have anticipated'.[7] Other compatriots told of growing up as Hungarian-Australians in the 1950s and 1960s, of the pressures to assimilate socially and culturally as well as the need to adapt in economic terms. They remembered the prejudice against 'reffos' mixed in with common kindness from Australians, the balance of sensitivities on both sides

Memories of immigration were often unreliable and subject to challenge: for instance, the notion that the British migrants had travelled in luxury, unlike the stoical Europeans. Sometimes the British migrant was singled out for mockery as unheroic, pampered and typically complaining. Such insults were angrily rejected by British migrants of the late 1940s who recollected the journey in, for instance, the *Ranchi*, which was built in 1925 for 500 passengers and had been refitted for troops and refugees and then converted to carry 940 emigrants, all 'crammed in'. The cabins housed 8, 10 or 12 and the sexes were segregated over five weeks. Babies and small children were accommodated in un-airconditioned areas. One of the migrants fulminated, 'Yes, I was a 10 quid migrant, one with more respect for social history than journalists'.[8]

Perhaps most poignant of all was the humorous/bitter prose poetry of the Polish immigrant Ania Walwitz, born in Poland in 1951, arriving in Australia in 1963 with her family to live in Melbourne. Much of her work was both experimental and painfully satirical. In a single short poem she snared all the negative clichés calculated to make Australians cringe, expressed in the words and cadences of an adolescent rebelling against the Australian world:

AUSTRALIA

You big ugly. You too empty. You desert with
nothing, nothing, nothing. You scorched suntanned.
Old too quickly. Acres of suburbs watching the telly.
You bore me. Freckle silly children. You nothing
much. With your big sea. Beach, beach, beach. I've
seen enough already ... And much more.

Walwitz was expressing 'The yearning for a lost place, time and identity' and her poem was described as 'a lovely job of reverse bigotry'.[9]

The policy

As always, the scale of immigration depended on the differential between living standards in the countries of origin and those prevailing in Australia. The gap was wide in the postwar years and favoured the spontaneous flow of migrants. But the pump was vigorously primed by the government. This indeed was the postwar 'age of management'. As Nicholas Brown puts it, there was 'a population to be managed ... [and] ... society could be shaped from above by the ministrations of agencies, primarily the state'.[10] Under Calwell the quasi-socialist state devised an apparatus for the mass recruitment and reception of immigrants which outdid any previous operations. Planning was accepted by all parties as uncontroversial even though the plans depended more on inspiration than calculation. Planning was an inexact science and few of the predictions were strongly based. Nevertheless the central target of 2 per cent per annum population growth was achieved with a generous margin of error. No one really understood the economic and social consequences of the immigration program: it was a leap of faith which succeeded in the most favourable of prevailing contexts. Behind it all was the stark fact of severe labour shortages in the postwar period: at one point the Commonwealth Employment Office in Victoria had more than 50 000 unfilled jobs on its hands.[11]

Immigration policy was married to industrialisation and national security. There was also a grand strategy which would strengthen the Australia economy while simultaneously fostering population control in nearby Asia. Taken together the strategy would reduce the vulnerability of Australia both internally and externally. It was explicit in the words of the influential demographer, WD Borrie, who, in the 1950s argued that Australia's economic development 'was contingent on racial exclusion in immigration to foster a homogenous industrial society'. Controlled fertility in Asia, assisted by countries such as Australia, would help build more prosperous and less aggressive economies in the region.[12]

Immigration was thus incorporated into economic policy of accelerated expansion, industrialisation and urbanisation, which left their permanent mark on the 1950s and 1960s, beginning under Labor reconstruction in 1945 and subsequently merging into the 'Long Boom' under Menzies and succeeding prime ministers, through to 1974.[13] By 1949 labour shortages built up to over-full employment, bidding up wages and making immigration irresistibly attractive. Short-term fluctuations at the time of the Korean War did not shake the drive towards industrial expansion. There were occasional bouts of intellectual recidivism – as in 1951 when the economists Colin Clark and Wilfred Prest advocated a massive reduction in the manufacturing workforce in favour of consolidating rural interests to maximise Australia's role as a primary producer to the rest of the world.[14] In reality markets and planning produced expansion in all sectors of the economy though almost all migrants were channelled into the cities where employment grew much faster than in the rural economy.

The most remarkable aspect of the massive and radically heterogeneous immigrant inflows was how little they impinged on the ordinary flux of policy making. This was a measure of the astonishing success of the policy and the solidity of its bipartisan support. Immigration was not controversial and rarely figured significantly in the memoirs of the leading politicians of the age. Immigration wrought a social revolution in Australia in the 1950s but it was mainly left in the hands of the bureaucracy: it raised barely a ripple in the political world of Canberra. The main concern was the assimilation of immigrants and the maintenance of social equilibrium which was, in reality, not much disturbed. When Menzies visited London in July 1950 he dwelt on Australia's main concerns which were, first, high inflation and, second, the 'absorption of what had become a regularly high immigration intake and economic development generally'. The industrial economy was being held back by shortages of capital goods and raw materials which exacerbated inflation; immigration itself was subsumed under economic development.[15] Mrs Menzies was also sanguine: interviewed by a London newspaper she urged 'professional women – nurses, almoners, doctors, architects, journalists', to think of emigrating to Australia, to 'give us a trial'. She remarked, 'I should be very surprised to hear that any English woman got on badly with her Australian neighbours. We are generally considered a friendly and hospitable people'.

Immigration was subject to central budgetary management and

it was vital to synchronise immigrant intakes with the reigning wage structure and its inflationary tendencies.[16] In 1955 Menzies visited the Netherlands and paid tribute to the Dutch migrants who had already contributed to Australia's population growth. It had been a time of substantial prosperity, good seasons, high earnings and employment levels, and rapidly increasing production in many industries. The essential argument was that more migrants would take the heat out of the Australian labour market and reduce the pressures towards inflation. As Treasurer Arthur Fadden said, Australia's problems were those of prosperity not depression.[17] The Treasury in 1958 declared that expansion at a steady rate was best served by continuing current rates of immigration – it gave industry 'the assurance of steadily expanding markets – an assurance which industry and business recognise and upon which they have come to base their forward plans'. Immigration was therefore a tool of economic management, a stimulus to consumption and investment, adjustable to changing conditions in the economy. Indeed the idea of cutting immigration was dismissed on the grounds that it would depress business at large. This was the philosophy of economic management in the 1950s and into the following decade.[18]

In March 1957 Menzies paid a belated tribute to the postwar work of Calwell and declared that 'whatever price one had to pay for migration, it was worth paying so that this country might have, as it has now, 10,000,000 people, not the 7,000,000 gloomily forecast in my own time – in 1938'.[19] Looking back over the postwar achievement in the same year, Athol Townley, orchestrator of the 'Bring out a Briton' campaign,[20] calculated that it cost £5000 to rear and train an immigrant, i.e. in the countries of their origin. On this basis Australia was acquiring, each year, imported human beings worth £500 000 000. He drew a comparison with the United States in the previous century, when immigrants had been utterly vital for the development of that country: 'That is what Australia is doing today'. Astonishingly, Townley's simple exercise in immigrant economics was as close to precision as any planner had achieved.

The palpable success of the immigration policy meant that little further calculation was required in these decades. The government reiterated its commitment to 1 per cent net immigration per annum and reaffirmed its commitment to British immigration, noting that Australia had secured more British immigrants than any two other countries since the war. But the net had certainly widened:

> Proud though we are of our British heritage,
> determined though we are to maintain undiminished
> the ideals and traditions of that heritage, Australia
> could not, in fact, develop at the desired rate, and
> in the desired direction, if we were to confine our
> intake solely to migrants of British stock.

In the outcome Australia had drawn 'fine people of more than twenty nationalities', 83 per cent of them from northern Europe, though it seemed necessary to add, 'that does not mean that the southern Europeans who we do receive are any less welcome when they come here'.[21] In 1957 Harold Holt still thought of the Commonwealth as a world power of 'the British people'.[22] Indeed the housing problem, rather than any qualms about assimilation or absorption, remained the main impediment in welcoming further immigrants.[23]

The immigration program therefore continued to expand and widen into the 1960s, reaching across Europe towards the eastern Mediterranean. As Sir Alexander Downer declared in his reminiscences, the Liberal governments throughout the 1950s and 1960s 'believed in the wisdom of as large a migrant intake as the national economy could absorb, and Holt's friendly relations with trade union leaders secured their cooperation'.[24] Australia basked in a bipartisan concord throughout the long boom, and recruitment strengthened and grew. To be sure, by 1969 there was growing concern about the capacity of Australia to integrate migrants, but the numbers still grew in the late phases of economic growth.

The entire immigration program was carried forth on the great tide of economic growth through both decades. By the end of the 1950s living standards expanded into unprecedented affluence, manifested in a flood of material goods and a remarkable widening of home ownership.[25] Soon Australians possessed more cars, telephones and radios per head, more television sets, more homes and more homeowners, rising wages and the highest standard of living in the world, next to Canada and the United States. Within Australia there was a great expansion of secondary and primary industries; externally there was a greater sense of security and international respect.[26]

The one millionth immigrant since 1945 arrived in 1955.[27] The immigration program was questioned only when the targets were unfilled or when the economy itself stuttered. Immigration was a tool of planning and could be adjusted to meet economic conditions.[28] In April 1961, for instance, after what Menzies termed 10 years of 'unexampled prosperity', the economy weakened, unemployment rose to 2 percent and a credit squeeze was instituted. Two years later the boom had resumed and there were renewed labour shortages everywhere and a severe shortage of classrooms and teachers.[29] Indeed the Menzies years were remarkable for virtual full employment, great growth and the spread of consumer durables which revolutionised domestic life for the expanded population, including, of course, the immigrants. By the end of the 1960s the face of Australia had changed – nearly 10 per cent of the population had been born in continental Europe; the population approached 12 million; urbanisation now encompassed most of the population; most Australians worked a 40-hour week with continuously rising living standards; one in three owned a car and most houses contained a television set.[30]

The Vernon Committee in 1965 made comprehensive recommendations about economic management, including optimal levels of immigration. Its findings were severely questioned by Menzies, who opposed its managerial and socialistic leanings.[31] Despite such philosophical differences, the immigration program reaped almost universal support; this was a mark of the success of the postwar program, a measure of the bipartisan and self-propelled character of the policy.

The spreading net

Throughout the 1950s and 1960s Calwell's heroic target of 1 per cent per annum immigrant recruitment was easily exceeded. But Calwell had also promised that the British would be 90 per cent of all immigrants and this was not fulfilled. By December 1948 Calwell was already talking of a 50 per cent British content and accorded priority to the 'Nordic races as well as the British'.[32] In the 1950s the British accounted for no more than one-third of the intake, though this remained the largest single element, thus helping to sustain the traditional relationship between Australia and Britain. In some ways the British response was disappointing since it was absolutely and relatively less than before the First World War. On the other hand Australia raised more British emigrants than any other country at a time when many commentators were predicting the end of mass emigration from Britain. Australia applied artificial respiration to the flagging body of the British emigrant.[33]

Gallup public opinion polls measured British attitudes to emigration throughout the postwar years.[34] They show high but varying levels of enthusiasm. The question asked was 'If you were free to do so, would you like to go and settle in another country?' In February 1948, 42 per cent said' yes', 53 per cent 'no' and 5 per cent 'don't know'. Among the positive 42 per cent Australia was the most popular destination. Over the following 20 years polls suggested that attitudes to emigration fluctuated widely; moreover answering hypothetical questions in a social survey was a long way from actual emigration. Conditions in Britain were also relevant, especially in the austere years after the war; but even when British living conditions improved over the following 20 years Australia was able to maintain surprising enthusiasm. The differential between Australian and British living standards prevailed until the 1970s and this was the crucial prerequisite, powerfully reinforced by the generous assistance schemes. There were other positive considerations: the fear of a renewal of war and the perceived imminence of nuclear conflict were heavy in the minds of some of the emigrants; others were clearly attracted by the possibility of an early return home under the conditions of the assistance scheme (which required the migrants to stay for only 2 years); and many emigrated to avoid National Service, and what they regarded as creeping socialism and the influx into Britain of too many coloured migrants.

The vicissitudes of recruitment could not mask the truth that emigration from Britain, though considerable, could not meet Australia's booming demands. The 90 per cent target was not realistic and by the 1950s it was clear that 50 per cent British would be acceptable. But even the reduced target was dubious and special efforts were mounted with the 'Bring out a Briton' scheme in 1957, in which a community in Australia sponsored a particular British family and assisted them to settle. Meanwhile the British government was increasingly ambivalent, and then decidedly sceptical, about the joint subsidisation of its migrants to Australia. In 1950 Britain was paying half the cost of the fare at a time when its own labour supply was beginning to show signs of strain and immigrants were being sought to reinforce certain parts of Britain's own economy. Increasingly the absurdity of the Anglo-Australian arrangement was invoked and it was incrementally curtailed at the British end. Assistance by Britain was limited to £25 pounds per adult and then reduced to a maximum budget of £150000 in 1954. Inflation quickly eroded the value of the assistance and Australia soon shouldered the entire burden. Nevertheless the British remained the greatest proportion of immigration until 1972, after which they fell sharply, though the British remained easily the largest single category of Australia's immigrants.[35]

While the British contribution was relatively reducing, the European component rose under the influence of a succession of immigration ministers. The Displaced Persons immigration was merely a prelude to the much larger intakes from Europe after 1950. Calwell's successor, Harold Holt, confirmed the bipartisan character of the policy and in December 1949 immediately recognised the imperative of new sources of immigrants. Already several large Australian employers in 1950 were seeking special permission to recruit tradesmen from Europe for a 2-year period. Apart from the reigning racial discrimination rules, there were few impediments to unassisted immigration. Conditions were favourable because various European governments were encouraging emigration. Soon agreements were forged to facilitate recruitment and provide passages. It was significant that Australia was soon recruiting in Germany. In 1951 and 1952 the Special Projects Procedure operated and brought in 77 000 male workers, mainly from Germany but also from the Netherlands, France, Austria and Italy. The firms included the Snowy Mountains Authority, the Tasmanian Hydro Electricity Commission, the South Australian Railways and residential contractors in Canberra, notably AV Jennings.

Australia entered into a series of bilateral agreements with European governments which paved the way for large recruitments. Already Malta, by virtue of its close Commonwealth associations, had made an agreement, and 43,000 Maltese were assisted to Australia between 1948 and 1975. In February 1951 the Dutch and Australian governments agreed to share costs and this proved a great spur to chain migration, accumulating from 52 000 in 1954 to 100 000 by 1960. More than half of the Dutch were assisted and more than a quarter assisted by earlier Dutch migrants. An agreement was signed with Italy in 1951 and recruitment was strongly biased towards young Italian couples; over the 1950s an annual average of 4000 arrived but they were outnumbered by the unassisted, who reached 15 000 per annum. Indeed most Italian immigration was self-funded, and by 1971 their numbers accumulated to 300 000 and Italians became the largest non-British group in Australia.

The pronounced representation of the British and northern Europeans in the first phase was part of the psychology to avoid frightening the Australian horses. But the strain of fulfilling Calwell's target of 1 per cent pa caused Australia to stretch its recruitment nets wider and wider. An agreement with West Germany was negotiated by 1952 and mainly comprised assisted migration, and the total number reached 95 000 by the 1970s. An agreement with Greece followed in 1952, supplying 160 000 immigrants by 1971, females in the majority and mostly unassisted. Austria also entered an agreement in 1952 which brought 24 000 by 1961. Spain was added in 1958. Similar agreements were signed with Denmark, Ireland and Belgium and the migrant net spread to the south and the east to incorporate Turkey and Yugoslavia by the late 1960s and extended to Lebanon in the 1970s.[36] But the provision of assistance was differential and Australia retained control over its intakes: there were repeated difficulties in negotiations with foreign governments about the terms of Australia's immigration recruitments and assistance.[37]

In 1966 James Jupp had already detected the likely decline of European interest in Australia as a continuing destination for its migrants. He noted 'the growing difficulty of attracting migrants from northern Europe'.[38] As European living standards rose, he predicted, Australia would have increasing difficulty attracting migrants and it would need to provide greater facilities for their settlement. He also noted that the Australian government spent much more on attracting 'Nordic' migrants, with diminishing success; others were much cheaper: 'To attract and assist a Swede or a Dane may cost anything up to $360, while a Greek or Lebanese may cost almost nothing'. There was a startling difference between the two sorts of migrants.

Australia continued spasmodically to receive refugees, mainly channelled through Trieste, prompted by intermittent crises in Europe. The uprising in Hungary in 1956 produced about 14 000 migrants by the end of the following year; similarly the Soviet invasion of Czechoslovakia in 1968 yielded a further 6000.[39] These were relatively small intakes in the context of the general shift of recruitment away from northern Europe and towards regions which, in living memory, had been regarded as unthinkable to middle Australian society. It was part of the unresisted social revolution of these decades.[40]

Managing the revolution

This great shift was managed, with little fanfare, by a new breed of administrator in the public service. At the start, and at the top, was Tasman (later Sir Tasman) Heyes from Adelaide, who became secretary of the new Department of Immigration in May 1946. With staff inherited from Department of the Interior, he supervised the new level of control over the selection and movement of immigrants. There was a dramatic increase in administrative personnel in continental Europe and the department expanded from 74 in 1946 to 1218 in 1961; overseas its officials increased in number from 14 in 1947 to 390 in 1961. During these years net immigration grew from 11 200 in 1947 to 89 090 in 1960. The actual arrivals increased even more impressively: in the 1950s permanent and long-term arrivals averaged 122 100 per annum. Heyes helped to sell the program to the nation: he was a traditionalist, committed to the concept of assimilation and preferring people of 'Aryan stock'. He was a conservative who did not mince words and pressed for the retention of the White Australia policy and strict rules for non-Europeans. That he was awarded the Nansen medal by the United Nations for his contribution to the resettlement of refugees nicely symbolised the curious liberal and illiberal faces of Australia's migration policies.[41]

Heyes was succeeded as secretary to the Department of Immigration in 1961 by PR (later Sir Peter) Heydon, a former diplomat. Heydon, and the minister Hubert Opperman, later claimed credit for the further liberalisation of the immigration policy in the long transition from racial discrimination. But before that was attained the department had overseen a great expansion of the program and expanded recruitment into Spain, Portugal, Yugoslavia, the Middle East and South America. Turkey became a special focus. At the end of the 1960s there was a great surge of immigration which brought half a million settlers between July 1967 and June 1970.[42] In 1969 Heydon established a committee to facilitate the recognition of foreign professional qualifications, an issue which had always rankled with immigrants to Australia.

In 1965 Heydon provided a formal perspective on the great postwar immigration program. More than 1.7 million settlers had arrived since the war. In 1947 only 9.8 per cent of the population had been born overseas; by 1961 it was 16.9 per cent: this was the 'first stage of a new and more purposeful era' for immigration. He stressed the entirely bipartisan aspect of the context: 'This support encourages vitally the cooperative character of immigration administration in Australia'. The Department of Immigration had been responsible for the attraction, selection and transportation of migrants as well as their reception in Australia and liaison with other bodies in Australia. He noted also that the 'old refugee' problem in Europe had been solved and that the camps were now almost empty: and the flows of migrants out of Eastern Europe were greatly impeded by restrictions imposed by communist regimes, which did not auger well for the future. By contrast, Western Europe in 1965 had become 'prosperous and stable', and the task of attracting migrants was more onerous than ever. He saw the rise of refugee problems in the Middle East and Africa but he was clear that their 'resettlement in Australia is rarely an appropriate solution'.[43]

Heydon's perspective was selective. Unassisted migration remained a large proportion of migration and mainly beyond the influence of the Department of Immigration. Immigrant groups were treated unequally. The preference accorded to the Protestant northwest of Europe was especially clear in the early phases. Thus 100 000 Dutch and German residents and 14 000 Austrians received assisted passages in the 1950s, but only 39 000 Italians and 25 000 Greeks. As Dyster and Meredith point out, 'the British and Americans were prized migrants, but not if they were black'. Former enemy status was not important in the case of Germans, but the Japanese were not considered as potential migrants.[44] White Australia was very rarely breached in these years.

Much earthier perspectives on the realities of recruitment came from the recollections of the recruiting officers themselves. They remembered that the transport of migrants improved when Greek and Italian shipping lines entered the business, setting new standards by 1955 which were exemplified by the *Fairsea* with its airconditioning, though the British emigrants regularly complained about 'foreign' food. Many of the ships accommodated more than 1000 passengers and conditions improved with each year. Migrant transportation indeed required a great flotilla of 169 ships which carried 2 million immigrants to Australia until 1977, when air travel overtook shipping in every sense.[45]

The Australian immigration officers operated in many different contexts. Elva Lynn worked in Britain and remembered the 1200 migrants on the first passage of the *Castel Felice* from Southampton: 'Tired, poor little people they were, mostly working class people'.[46] There were melancholy scenes, people parting, some refusing at the last moment, some in total despair. At times the demand for passages was overwhelming: the Edinburgh office was opened in 1959 and there were 1000 enquiries within three days. The officers admitted that their selections were arbitrary, always looking for 'the cream of the crop'. The campaign in the United Kingdom was conducted with renewed intensity in the 1960s and with remarkable success, spurred on by the 'Bring out a Briton' campaign.[47] But the price of immediate success in recruitment was a high return rate. From 1959 to 1971, 100 000 former settlers from the United Kingdom returned home, which was particularly attributed to the unhappiness of the women migrants who were often left in isolation in Australian suburbia.[48] By 1970 the great migration was petering out.

Recruitment in Europe passed through several phases after the first refugee intakes. Holland provided some of the first migrants but by the late 1950s the situation had changed as home living standards began to rise. Australian recruiters revitalised their propaganda efforts but Dutch employers were increasingly loath to lose their skilled workers; the Dutch Emigration Office began vetting applications in the 1960s[49] and Australia was compelled to accept less skilled migrants. Homesickness was rife and caused many to return: in 1958 the *Flaminia* carried 600 Dutch families returning to Holland, though many of them subsequently re-migrated to Australia.

The immigration officers faced problems of implementing the official, but usually unspoken, racial policy and this sometimes descended into farce. Recruiting in Spain, Australian officials looked for people with 75 per cent European parentage: the recruiters had to imagine whether prospective Spanish migrants might be regarded as non-European in the streets of Australian cities. As one of the immigration officers remarked, 'Until well into the 1960s Australia was strenuous in its efforts to ensure Asians and "coloured" did not, as a general rule, gain admittance as migrants'. In Holland there were many prospective migrants of mixed Asian background, such as the Dutch war pilot who applied with his Indonesian wife; among relatively dark-skinned southern Europeans it was recollected that one doctor 'would get them to strip so that he could see if they were dark all over'; similarly the sons of a British India Army officer and his Indian wife were turned down by the recruiters; in England in 1964 an applicant wanting to join his twin brother, already in Australia, was rejected because he was swarthy and looked non-European.

Australia was moving progressively into new 'migration fields' as it extended its reach eastwards and southwards across Europe. Increasingly it was recruiting in old rural societies, composed of small landowners and artisans, which had been releasing migrants to America in large numbers since the late 19th century. Australia was reactivating and diverting old migrant flows, especially in

Greece and Yugoslavia, where postwar difficulties lasted longer than in the west. In the Mediterranean regions the question of racial characteristics was often problematic. When Peter Edwards was posted to Athens he found that the examination of applicants was stringent; many of them were peasants from third-world backgrounds, people from profoundly rural contexts who rarely shaved and felt uncomfortable in formal clothes. An officer observed that the recruiters were playing God with these people's lives, fulfilling some dreams and destroying others.[50] One of the senior officers admitted that mistakes were often made with the non-British population because 'there is but little opportunity to gauge and weigh the niceties of individual human rights'.[51] But even these flows began to dry up by the 1970s and were replaced by recruitment even further east. It was a moving canvas and a great challenge to the recruiters.[52]

In 1956 the Hungarian crisis produced a new flow of refugees, some 14 000 of whom were channelled to Australia. Many of them fled Budapest in great haste and passed though the Traiskirchen camp in Vienna. They faced a sudden decision about their future and, as an Australian recruiter remembered: 'Some would go one way and some would go the other, and that's the way their new life would start with a decision made in a split second when the bus was about to move off'. As one of the Hungarians (Maria Zsembery) remarked, 'We had to choose between Venezuela, New Zealand, Australia and I think, Sweden. But Sweden was very selective. So we started to think about Australia … We knew about kangaroos'. The Australian immigration officers were under great pressure during the crisis, scrambling to get the refugees to ships in Marseilles. There were also selection doubts. One of the officers was dubious about the swarthy-looking Hungarians. He remembered one he rejected:

> he really was a very dark gipsy with crinkly black
> hair and although I was sympathetic towards him,

> I visualised him walking down Martin Place and
> as such he would have been a 'stare object'. The
> officers were under guidelines which required the
> migrants to be 60 per cent European, 40 per cent
> non European, and I was rejecting him for Australia's
> sake. But I was also rejecting him for his own sake
> because of what he could have suffered when he got
> here and being stared at all the time.

He acknowledged that the policy was 'tricky' and required fine judgment.[53]

Similar dilemmas were commonplace in other recruitment centres. In Austria the authorities permitted no advertising for migrants and the Australian recruiters used table tennis and free beer as a lure. On the other hand the medical vetting was rigorous and many potential emigrants to Australia were disqualified because their X-rays showed old tuberculosis scarring. One medical officer in the refugee camps remembered that 'If the patient wasn't the full quid … we were asked to think very carefully'. In Austria 'Mental retardation was an important aspect but, if a person had a good trade and was generally healthy, and we thought he or she wasn't going to break down mentally or physically within two or three years of arriving in Australia, we would usually accept them'.[54]

As recruitment moved east the problems of selection increased. When an office was opened in Beirut a huge demand was aroused and there were 80 000 applicants within a few months. An agreement was finalised with Turkey in 1967 and great pressure fell upon the department once more. For the applicants the process of interrogation was often humiliating. Yalcin Ener was appalled at the treatment: the people were herded about in military style and he thought that the 'the first migrants must have been the most courageous people'. There was also obvious discrimination since half the Lebanese and Egyptians recruited were Christians; the applicants were subjected to political questioning and preference was clearly given to non-Muslim and non-Communist emigrants.[55]

Although communist governments in Eastern Europe were often suspicious, conditions for recruitment became more favourable in the late 1960s, especially in Yugoslavia, Romania, Bulgaria and Poland, by which time there was little concern about any likely communist infiltration. Recruitment was especially successful in poor regions such as Macedonia though many of the applicants were in poor health, especially with skin conditions and tuberculosis. In a single month in Beograd in 1970 three doctors examined 1219 people: 1046 were accepted, 162 deferred, 59 rejected.[56]

The immigration officers were often under great strain and their reputation was mixed, which was acknowledged by Heydon who warmly defended them:

> [they had organised] annually a greater movement
> of people than any other institution known in the
> free world ... we are giving many individual human
> beings the opportunities of speaking what Franklin
> D. Roosevelt once called 'a single language, the
> universal human language of human aspiration'.

Heydon remarked that it was to 'our material benefit as well as theirs. It is not necessary to claim that we do this from humanitarian or altruistic motives. Frankly, I believe most of what Australia has done had been on grounds of self-interest, which may not be noble but is quite usual, honest and enlightened'.

The great fear in Australia, and among the recruiters, was that the new immigrant groups would not become assimilated and would carry their internecine disputes into the host country. As Heydon remarked, the optimists were rewarded: 'These hopes have been to a very large extent realised, though unfortunately several groups continue to foster national sentiment and political objectives, in an aggressive and objectionable way. The Government expects all migrants to intend to become good Australians'.[57] The policy was also designed to avoid any excessive concentration on any particular source of immigrants (apart from the British). Thus Heydon was concerned that yearly migrant intakes be increased steadily 'without undue dependence on one or two source countries or an undue growth in Australia of a few large national minorities, [and] new countries would have to be tapped along with the old'.

The officers of the department implemented the policy with difficulty, recognised its frequent arbitrariness and illogicality, but realised that the government could not venture far ahead of public opinion. The immigration officers believed in the immigration policy and its purpose to expand Australia's population; many of them were disappointed when the system ran down in the 1970s.

Meanwhile there was the stark achievement: between 1947 and 1972 the population increased from 7.5 to 13 million. Of this, 2.5 million was accounted by net immigration and a further 1 million by their children. Half of the immigration had been non-British; 25 per cent of the non-British were from central and Eastern Europe; 25 per cent from Western Europe, and half from southern Europe. These were the boundaries of the New Australia.

Reception

The first step towards becoming 'good Australians' took place at the docks as the migrants were channelled towards employment, often by way of the hostels. The Bonegilla Reception and Training Centre near Albury became the largest of many camps dotted about Australia, usually ex-army camps. They were, in essence, temporary holding and sorting facilities and 170 000 immigrants had passed through Bonegilla alone by 1952. Conditions were often primitive and congested: newly arrived migrants were located in huts with 26 people, segregated by sex and with little heating. Some were accommodated temporarily in tents and were governed by curfews,

Temporary realities: Gepps Cross Hostel for migrants, Adelaide, 1963.
Migration Museum, Adelaide

with poor bedding and food provision leading to widespread frustration. Eventually by 1971 when it closed, Bonegilla had received and dispersed 300 000 migrants, many of them permanently marked by the experience.

The Department of Immigration faced great problems by the sheer scale of the inflows: it sent out officers every fortnight to inspect conditions in the hostels. The camps were the crucibles of immigration and a severe test of the new policy in difficult times.

The European migrants received the worst of the conditions though many British migrants (generally more favourably dealt with) also passed through the camps. Exposing any British migrant to camp life was heavily criticised, and Calwell in 1953 acknowledged that it had been damaging:

> Whatever the standard of accommodation each one
> left behind in the United Kingdom, it was at least
> a home, a bomb-shattered one, maybe. The result
> could only be psychologically bad for such people
> to find on arrival that, not for a few weeks or a few
> months, but for a year or more, they would find it
> so difficult to establish their families in separate
> comfortable habitations.[58]

Indeed those migrants who passed through the hostels experienced higher rates of return migration than others.[59] In 1958 when visiting British Prime Minister Harold Macmillan asked to see a hostel it caused a flurry of embarrassment.

Bonegilla was always controversial and left mixed memories. Sometimes it was romanticised as a 'Babel of Europe', as a 'multicultural icon' and 'a potential metaphor around the victims of Diaspora'.[60] Some former inmates held warm recollections of the experience but others described it as ' a bit like a concentration camp'.[61] Tensions in these congested and strained facilities were bound to develop. Italian migrants were particularly incensed at their treatment: they and other migrants felt rising frustration about their qualifications going unrecognised, which restricted their search for employment. The Italians in 1952 regarded themselves as economic migrants who had made sacrifices and taken on debts to come to Australia on the promise of employment. They resented the 'patronising and uncompromising attitudes of the Australian authorities' and being viewed as inferior to British migrants at the time.[62] Various tensions came to the surface, precipitated by the spartan conditions in the hostels.

Serious trouble brewed when large numbers of Italian migrants arrived at Bonegilla in 1952. Their immigration was the product of an agreement with Italy by which each of the two governments was committed to pay a quarter of the passage money; the emigrants were able to borrow the rest from charities. There were tensions from the start regarding Australia's preference for migrants from north of Milan and suspicions of residual racial prejudices against people of Mediterranean background (especially Sicilians and Calabrese). The Australian selections were certainly vetted for taints of fascism as well as communism among the migrants.[63]

In mid-1952 a demonstration was mounted at Bonegilla by 2000 migrants, mainly Italians. It was described as a 'riot', primarily induced by the onset of recession but also by cold damp winter conditions in the camp, and great delays in employment opportunities. It was a form of collective protest which aroused enough alarm to cause the government to mobilise the military and remove the main agitators. Italian newspapers then stoked the fires by headlining the event: 'Tanks out in Australia against 2000 Italians'. A right-wing politician in Italy reported to the Chamber of Deputies that the emigrants faced a terrible fate: 'without work and without money, [they were] flung into camps which are alleged to be no more comfortable than concentration camps'. The Australian authorities were denounced for their scandalous treatment of the migrants. In the outcome the riot was limited to some minor violence, and troops reached no nearer than 5 miles from Bonegilla. By December 1952 only 16 Italians remained in Bonegilla. It was nevertheless a chilling spasm in the evolution and management of the migrant program and soured relations with Italy. The next immigration agreement with Italy provided fewer places for Italians, and relations were not repaired until a new agreement was struck in 1954. The Bonegilla 'riot' was a warning for the entire integrity of the European migrant program and the capacity of Australia to cope with the great experiment. As Richard Bosworth suggests, the riot was ' the stuff of a new nightmare – the failure of its attempt to make Australians out of Europeans', and showed the unpreparedness of the Australian authorities for 'a sudden influx of Italians whom they had long been taught were the racial inferiors of their Aryan selves'.[64]

A second riot at Bonegilla in 1961 was blamed on communistic agitators, and the leaders were quickly detained. These events, and the general unsavoury reputation of the camps, threw a question mark over the somewhat triumphalist idea that the new immigration policy was 'one of the great successes in the modern history of migrations'.[65] Undoubtedly the events caused a further shudder of apprehension in Australia and led to concerted efforts to smooth the transition of immigrants into the receiving society. The inauguration of Citizens Conventions, as early as 1950, was an effort to enhance integration and naturalisation, which remained the main focus of policy until the 1960s. The absorption, employment, resettlement and housing of these huge intakes of migrants was a massive challenge to all parts of Australian society. But brief outbreaks of inter-communal tension were never more than sporadic disturbances in the ongoing reshaping of modern Australia.

Work and religion in the immigrant society

Australian immigration did not claim to be a humanitarian project: its overwhelming and overt purpose was to expand the labour force and consolidate European Australia. In the 12 years to 1959 immigrants represented 72 per cent of the increase in the workforce. In most cases the immigrants began at the bottom and worked their way up the social and employment ladder. This after all had been the fate of migrants since the beginning of time. There were anxieties all round: the unions feared a dilution of the workforce and a downward pressure on wage rates; the migrants feared discrimination and exploitation and being regarded as expendable. In the outcome the continuing shortages of labour ironed out many of the problems before they became extreme. Labour was in a good bargaining position and the unions made efforts to accommodate the new workers into their culture (and indeed compelled many migrants to join their unions). Employers were usually so hungry for labour that they interpreted contracts liberally. At the car plant at Geelong migrants made up 47 per cent of Ford's workforce by 1955 and 87 per cent by 1974. It is clear that the immigrants were doing the least attractive work: displaced Europeans and southern Europeans were concentrated in the production areas of the plant – on the assembly line or as body mounters, spray and brush hands, wet rubbers: that is, arduous, dirty, heavy and continuous work shunned by most Australians. 'We work like horses in bad conditions', said one of the migrants. There was a great turnover of labour, but plenty of overtime and few large strikes. There was little obvious prejudice against the migrants, the trade unions were not oppressive (though they called for cessation of migration in times of recession) and the retrenchment policy was evidently not based on ethnicity or gender or marital status.[66]

Australia was conscious that its continuing success in recruiting migrants depended on its reputation as a desirable destination. As HA Bland, Secretary, Department of Labour and National Service, candidly declared in June 1954:

> Australia is [now] forced to attract migrants from
> Europe and the continued flow of migrants depends
> upon the way in which migrants are received
> into the community and reports they send home.
> If migrants were compelled, willy-nilly, to take
> unattractive jobs and thereafter prevented from
> leaving their employment, the prospects of selecting
> suitable migrants in Europe could become more
> difficult than they are at present.[67]

The intensity of the change experienced by Australia after 1947 is

Jobs for migrants: Ford Motor Works, Geelong, 1955.
From Australian Government, Understanding Immigration, *1987*

easily understated. Few societies have accommodated so large an influx of migrants in proportion to its own population; few have suddenly changed the composition of its people so rapidly. Given the extreme homogeneity of Australian society, its capacity to accommodate the change was a matter of high anxiety.

Religion was another potentially divisive force. In the new flood, religion was prominent, if only because the non-British immigrants were not only different from the religious makeup of old Australia; they were also radically different from each other. They included exotic faiths not before seen in Australia, and special tensions were exposed between Australian Christianities and their imported equivalents. After 1947 the Australian churches confronted thousands of newcomers from ostensibly the same faiths but brought up in Dutch, Swedish, Hungarian, Italian, Ukrainian and other traditions. Local churches had developed their own special rituals and styles, some set in amber over the previous century. In 1947, 80 per cent of the population was contained in four groups: Church of England, Roman Catholic, Methodist and Presbyterian. At the start the churches regarded the 'New Australians' like 'the deserving poor' of the early 19th century, as needing ministry from above in a philanthropic mode, and sometimes expected them to demonstrate humble gratitude. Most of all, the churches echoed the community at large: they assumed assimilation.[68]

In reality only 27.5 per cent the immigrants were Protestants while the Roman Catholics accounted for 47.5 per cent and the Orthodox Churches for another 13.6 per cent. This was a geological shift in the foundations of Australian religion and created great challenges, including the very sudden expansion of numbers after a period of quiescence. The Catholic Church found that most of its many new immigrant members were non-English speakers; this exacerbated the existing shortfall in the supply of priests and strained further the educational resources of the church. In 1947 the Catholic Church arranged an annual Immigration Day to raise money for more clergy to serve the migrants.[69] The Catholic Church soon found substantial tension between Rome and Australia, with regional differences prominent, and involving such religious orders as the Capuchins, the Scalabrinians and the Maltese Franciscans, whose members ministered to immigrants. Similarly, existing Australian Presbyterians were now confronted by Calvin-inspired groups from the Dutch, Hungarian and German Presbyteries. The Reformed Churches of Australia was established in 1951 in response to perceived local inadequacies, and the movement became especially strong in Tasmania. Australia was rich soil for schismatic dispute and many immigrant groups set up their own churches, often at odds with each other, notably among the Baltic Lutherans whose divisions were reinforced by political considerations. The growth of the Orthodox Church, and its many versions, similarly reflected the surge of immigration from Eastern Europe by the 1960s, and its theological disputes thrived in the immigrant communities.[70]

Australian Anglicans, perhaps living in a rose-tinted fantasy world, felt some disappointment in the level of faith among the new English immigrants. But there was also the feeling that too many Catholics from southern Europe were entering the country. Traditionalists asserted that the great expansion in Catholic numbers would undermine democracy in Australia and that southern Europeans should really go to South America. Such attitudes, especially among Methodists, increased enthusiasm for the 'Bring out a Briton' campaign. On the other hand many church people provided practical non-sectarian assistance to new migrants and there was a great growth in the number of churches built in these years, notably among the Catholic and the Greek Orthodox communities. The Mass of the Catholic Church by the late 1970s was being said in 20 languages, and the Uniting Church gathered an extraordinary mix of ethnic groups.

The alarming heterogeneity of new religious elements eventually fed into the late 20th century feast of Australian multiculturalism. The potential for social division and internecine conflict was almost entirely averted and the outcome was remarkably benign despite recurrent apprehensions at all levels of society. It was the dog that failed to bark.

Assimilation and White Australia

Immigration policy throughout the 1950s and 1960s maintained its momentum and its determination to expand Australia's population. It did not however compromise its insistence on control over its composition and it retained the principle of racial discrimination despite the Europeanisation of the sources of its new immigration. The policy also remained resolutely bipartisan and within Australia was only mildly controversial.

A summer school in Canberra in April 1953 allocated a brief session to the White Australia policy which encapsulated the assump-

A new wave of refugees: Hungarians disembarking from the *Castel Felice* at Port Melbourne, 1957. *From Bureau of Immigration Research*, Immigration in Focus 1946–1990: A Photographic Archive, *1990*

tions of the times. A delegate from Sydney said that up to 2000 Asians a year should be allowed into Australia to improve relations with Asian countries. He was deeply impressed by 'the resentment expressed by Asians at Australia's unreasonable immigration laws. Discrimination on grounds of colour is an un-Christian approach'. Mrs Kirby of Bellata said the main complaint of cultured Asians was the very name 'White Australia': 'When they were advised that the policy was an attempt to protect Australian living standards they were willing to accept that but felt that the name should be changed'. Senator JA McCallum pointed out that a pan-Asian conference in Pakistan in 1947 had been unanimous that every nation had a sovereign right to determine whom it wants as citizens and noted that Ceylon excluded Indians, and that China was the most exclusive of all: 'The Asians dislike the term 'White Australia', but they do accept the principle'.[71]

The White Australia policy indisputably caused diplomatic irritation, especially in meetings with Commonwealth counterparts among the newly independent nations. This created embarrassment but was usually cavalierly dismissed by Australia's representatives. Australia was not shy about its intentions even in its official language, which declared that 'In pursuance of the established policy, the general practice is not to permit Asiatics or other coloured persons to enter Australia for the purpose of settling permanently'.[72] But the policy was increasingly regarded as Australia's Achilles' heel in the outside world, always vulnerable to criticism and, increasingly, to outright condemnation. It was a sensitive matter even when HV Evatt took a lead in the formation of the United Nations in the mid 1940s. Menzies' attitude towards South Africa's apartheid was conditioned by his defence of White Australia – he insisted that apartheid was an internal matter for the government of South Africa and angrily deplored the attack mounted by the new Afro-Asian nations of the Commonwealth. But his deputy, Jack McEwen, realised that South Africa was being given notice to quit the Commonwealth and that 'In view of our plainly discriminatory immigration policy we have a good chance of being the next in line'. Yet Menzies continued to resist the assault on South Africa and, at the Prime Ministers' Conference in 1960, he passionately urged non-interference. He said, 'I felt that I was defending my own country, its sovereign rights and its future. To do this is no academic exercise; it seemed to me to involve the self-government of Australia'.[73]

Menzies eventually gave way on the apartheid issue even though he realised that Australia might well be next in line. He said privately in 1961 that 'if someone at a future meeting [of the Prime Ministers' Conference] wished to discuss Australia's immigration policy he would simply walk out for good'. Commonwealth leaders, such as Grantley Adams of the West Indies, enjoyed taunting Australia and pointedly raised questions about the movement of population between Commonwealth countries. The racial question was always on the Commonwealth agenda, especially when the White Supremacist regime in Southern Rhodesia declared independence in 1964. Menzies, till the end, tried to maintain the taboo against discussion of the internal policies of Commonwealth countries, partly because Australia was patently vulnerable on immigration restriction and Aboriginal welfare.[74]

Menzies' attitudes were appreciated in South Africa,[75] and he continued to resist major changes to the policy throughout his long reign.[76] The adamant resistance to overseas interference and criticism was continued by one of Menzies' successors, John Gorton. During the East African crisis in 1969 (which created a large flow of Ugandan Asians to Britain) Gorton reasserted the Menzies line, that 'each Government had the right to determine who should be admitted to work and live in its own country'. Gorton believed that Australia's policies were racially based and 'should remain so, in order to preserve cultural homogeneity and to avoid racial conflict. Non-Europeans were welcome but, to become citizens, they must demonstrate a capacity to assimilate'. Gorton said that Australia was perfectly entitled to make its own laws on these matters and would 'brook no interference from outsiders'.[77]

In the face of such unwavering commitment to the standard White Australia policy it was surprising that so much incremental change was effected over these decades. In fact the policy was repeatedly challenged with test cases and subjected to shifts, little by little. Each new case excited a flurry of controversy and pushed public opinion towards greater liberality. PR Heydon, in the

Immigration Department, faced a series of special, awkward and occasionally sensational individual cases. One of the most controversial episodes was the deportation in 1965 of a young Fijian girl of Indian descent, Nancy Prasad. This case aroused widespread dismay about the operation of the policy, which was associated with increased political consciousness of racial issues in the context of greater Aboriginal activism and the 'Freedom Ride' led by Charles Perkins in western New South Wales. The longstanding immigration policy was increasingly questioned and required careful management. Meanwhile the 1958 Revised Migration Act abolished the dictation test and simplified entry permits.

When Heydon joined the Immigration Department he was surprised at its slight political esteem in the government: the Minister of Immigration possessed a relatively lowly standing and did not normally attend Cabinet meetings. Heydon had served as High Commissioner in India and was keenly aware of the embarrassment that Australia's immigration policies caused its diplomats. He pressed for a liberalisation of the policy and especially sought to improve the quality of Australia's immigration officials. Heydon's administration was consumed with the intricacies entailed in enforcing immigration laws, including problems associated with false statements, rackets and bogus marriages. He was equally apprehensive of ethnic conflicts emerging, notably among the Chinese communities in Melbourne and Sydney, and with certain 'Southern Italian and Sicilian newcomers' allegedly engaged in various illegal enterprises. Behind all this was the old fear that the immigrants would introduce their own internecine conflicts into the Australian community and the equal apprehension that some kinds of immigration were tending to '[build] into our population a few relatively big national minorities'. The latter consideration was an argument for further diversification of sources, which was indeed reflected in the opening of Australian offices in Rome, Athens, Lisbon, Madrid, Belgrade, Cairo, Ankara, Beirut and the United States. Despite the scepticism of the Department of External Affairs, Heydon was aware that the old policy was founded on 'racial superiority'. Looking back he identified 1966 as the key year in the erosion of White Australia.

Already in 1964 Heydon had proposed a policy for allowing non-Europeans into Australia based on criteria regarding suitability, integration and qualification and without specific quotas, but without jeopardising 'the essential homogeneity of the population'. Menzies remained resistant, indeed continued to believe in positive discrimination: as Heydon remarked of the prime minister: 'as a Conservative, he is finding this change hard to take, especially as he realizes it is symbolic of great changes [to come] everywhere'.[78] Nevertheless the experiment was begun in the form of a very gradual and tentative relaxation, barely perceptible: the possibility of the demission of White Australia had been established.[79] In the first instance the changes related to visa requirements and the waiting periods for naturalisation: these were small alterations in procedure usually associated with emphatic reassurances that the Department of Immigration was 'not departing from the fundamental principles of our immigration policy'. Already there were more than 12 000 Asian students in Australia, much facilitated by the Colombo Plan which was designed to sweeten relations with Asian countries. Some of these students were stranded in Australia, being unable to return to Communist China and elsewhere.[80] There was a growing feeling, even in conservative quarters, to accept certain Asian migrants, 'well qualified people wishing to settle in Australia ... on the basis of their suitability as settlers, their ability to integrate readily, and their possession of qualifications which are in fact positively useful to Australia'. This marginal liberalisation under Menzies was heavily underscored by the repeated guarantee that the 'primary aim in immigration is a generally integrated and predominantly homogeneous population'. Harold Holt, as prime minister (1966–67), introduced measures to allow non-Europeans to become Australian citizens. He began the formal dismantling of the White Australia system.

The road towards liberalisation was paved with minor obstacles including considerable resistance within the ranks of the government. John Gorton, for example, was an unreconstructed member of Old Australia, wanting to preserve the old certainties. He loathed the lectures he received from Commonwealth leaders, especially Lee Kwan Yew of Singapore who delighted in provoking White Australia.[81] Gorton, like many of his generation, was unable to understand the fuss and the distinction made between the idea of 'assimilation' and 'integration', whether for Aborigines or immigrants. They should all be absorbed into the Australian community without delay and the government should 'avoid measures' which 'set them permanently apart from other Australians' and cause their separate development. The aim was 'a single Australian community'.[82] Gorton staunchly rejected any radical shift away from the White Australia policy.

But international conditions were becoming more complicated, even for Britain, still the main supplier of Australia's migrants. In 1961 Britain was itself confronting the political repercussions of large immigrations flowing in from the Caribbean, Africa, Asia and the Mediterranean, and the government moved to restrict the intakes. Moreover Britain could no longer discriminate in favour of Australians, who were therefore now unprecedentedly required to carry entry permits and began to complain vehemently of obstructive treatment at British entry ports. Australians were being treated just like other nationals and the strength of the traditional relationship seemed to count for nothing. The issue was seriously divisive at a time when there were up to 50 000 Australians living in the United Kingdom.[83] It was not helped when Australia refused an assisted passage to a British resident of non-European descent who then complained to the United Kingdom Race Relations Board, which subjected the Chief Migration Office to a judicial interrogation. This goaded Gorton into a declaration that Australia's immigration policy was no business of the British and that it was Australia's sovereign right to determine its migrants.[84]

The old policy remained mainly intact until the end of the 1960s but there had been a quiet shifting of social attitudes and small adjustments which, in retrospect, seemed to auger larger changes for which the old school, represented by Gorton himself, was still unprepared. The creation of the Immigration Reform Group, begun among academics in Melbourne in 1962, heralded the 'first systematic critique of the White Australia policy on the basis of the offence it caused in Asia and the gains in "tolerance" that would follow a closely controlled system of Asian immigration'. Academics and journalists were beginning to break their long silence.[85] And already some Liberal politicians accepted that there was a place for Asians in Australia, notably 'distinguished and highly qualified' non-Europeans. The operation of the Colombo Plan had already positively conditioned Australians to Asian faces in their midst, creating a strong demonstration effect for a wider liberalisation. In 1958 all references to race and nationality were expunged from official policy. But discrimination continued as the true foundation of the policy.

Results

In June 1968 Peter Heydon gathered his thoughts on the 'Effects of Immigration on Australia's Growth', which offered a grand retrospect on the postwar years. He pointed out that Australia's commitment to immigration was 'the uncontested objective of all major political parties'. In 20 years the Commonwealth had spent $585 million on immigration including post-arrival services. In rough terms this had yielded a net population gain of 900 000 at an average cost of about $500 per head. 'Born here, they would have cost vastly more', he said. Between 1947 and 1961 immigrants provided 73 per cent of the increase in the workforce (comprising 82 per cent of the male workforce and 55 per cent of the female workforce). He made no bones about Australia's motivations – selection has been in

Australia's self interest; it had never been considered as altruistic. Instead Australia had become 'a social laboratory in migration for industrialized communities'.

Heydon was proud of the achievement: 'in general millions have been absorbed with remarkably little friction'. Worrying concentrations of certain national groups in Sydney and Melbourne had posed a possible danger to proper integration. But the anxiety had faded and the communities were now observably relaxed. Partly it was the result of very good planning. Moreover there had been an important social dividend for Australia. The much more diversified immigration had broken down parochialism and the intellectual life of Australia had benefited immeasurably. He pointed out that one-third of university appointments were overseas-born, and skill and professional gains were increasing. Future growth, he predicted, would continue to depend on immigrants, especially those with skills not supplied by Australia's own training systems. And Heydon also registered increasing difficulties in recruitment, declaring that 'The supply of suitable migrants is no longer assured'. Yet Australia was still a long way from reaching its optimal population size; to reap modern economies of scale Australia needed a still larger population and this would be enhanced by a greater proportion of skilled personnel among its immigrants in the future (38 per cent of its migrants in 1968 were 'skilled'). Looking forward to the 21st century Heydon expected current policies of population growth and economic development would be maintained, and he predicted that Australia would recruit between 8 and 10 million by the turn of the century. The momentum would be sustained; Australia would double its GNP and become much richer with a population of perhaps 28 million.[86]

The late 1960s were a high point in the great migration program and there were many positive indicators of its achievements. These indicated relatively high rates of intermarriage between immigrants and the host population.[87] A survey in the late 1950s showed that most assisted immigrants were young married couples or single persons, and only 8 per cent were over 45. More than half of those assisted between 1947 and 1958 had been nominated by persons already in Australia, and therefore chain migration was a large element in the system. Of a sample of 400 personally nominated families, 283 had been nominated by former migrants from the United Kingdom; 158 were immediate family members and 80 were cousins, nephews or uncles, and the remainder were friends and fiancées.[88] A survey in the early 1960s found that about two-thirds of husbands and wives were broadly satisfied with life in Australia.[89] This, of course, implied dissatisfaction (and considerable return migration) in the rest of the immigrant population.

Measuring the social and economic consequences of immigration was usually beyond the tools of the social scientists. Indeed most immigrants wended their way in Australia's suburbs and remained largely invisible. Perhaps this was the greatest achievement of their long-distance relocation in the Antipodes.

9 White Australia dismantled: the 1970s

Migrants and cohesion

By 1970 the flood of migrants from the postwar years had produced a kaleidoscope of diverse peoples. These European migrants had also engaged with the previous generations of Australian immigrants, mainly British in origin, which remained the largest single category throughout. The immigrant dramas, large and small, consolidated into modern Australian society, which began to preen itself on its multicultural credentials. During the 1970s there was a discontinuity in the annals of Australian immigration. Many of the conditions favouring the reception of mass immigration began to evaporate and now threatened the continued growth of the Australian population.

Australia had been carried forth on the crest of the postwar immigrant program: during this heroic phase Australian society had become a palimpsest of immigrants. They included Zelman Cowen's grandparents, who were Jews from Belorussia in tsarist Russia. One grandfather was Solomon Cohen, who settled in London before re–emigrating to Western Australia in 1908, accompanied by Zelman's father. The other grandfather's family were the Granats, relatively well-placed Jews from the Russian town of Mohilev, who arrived in Melbourne in 1891. The intermarrying families included a Jewish hawker from Ballarat and another who came to Melbourne as a draper. From similarly complicated Russian Jewish roots also emerged Isaac Isaacs who, from 1931 to 1936, was the first Australian-born governor-general and also the child of Russian Jewish immigrants.

These Jewish families had been on the move across Europe following the assassination of the tsar in 1881, which led to pogroms and the largest forced migration out of Europe since the Jews left Spain in the 15th century. Nearly 2 million Jews left Russia between 1880 and 1914, mainly heading towards Britain and then on to the United States, where they left an indelible mark on every aspect of 20th century American life. Their Australian-bound counterparts found it relatively easy to enter the country though there was no assistance. Zelman Cowen saw himself as part of that long tradition of migration and he later commented (in 2003):

> I appreciate our government's right to maintain
> control of the process of deciding who is allowed to
> settle in this country. Yet it is clear that aspects of
> our response to this difficult situation have caused
> concern ... My background gives me a sense of that
> powerful urge to find something better ... There
> is no doubt that the world is watching how we
> respond, and future generations will judge us.

In 1977–82, in the Australian era of European immigration, Sir Zelman Cowen was governor-general of Australia, and he declared that his appointment was like a miracle and 'proof that anyone in this country could aspire to its highest office'.[1]

The sheer variety and numbers of its postwar immigrants was

Australia's greatest challenge. The radio broadcaster Robyn Williams, himself a British immigrant, made several trips to and from England and Australia in the 1960s and 1970s and described some of the accompanying British emigrants. In 1964 he travelled on the *Castel Felice*: 'the ship was off-white and stank of stale fat. The other immigrants were little Englanders "one step ahead", as they put it, of all the "fuzzy-wuzzies" – who'd taken over in their home country'. He recollected that

> Everyone was running away from something, our
> families, failed love affaires, the End of England, the
> blacks. Apart from the oddballs I befriended, I found
> most of the immigrants offensive. They appeared
> to be in training for the Whingeing Pom Olympics.
> And the forced repatriation of nig nogs.[2]

Williams offered rare testimony: few migrants, British or otherwise, were so critical of their fellow migrants.

Racial attitudes remained surprisingly dormant throughout these decades, partly because few non-Europeans had entered Australia. But this changed in the 1970s when the first of the 'boat people' began to arrive out of the chaos of the Vietnam War. The Vietnamese experience in Australia was highly varied and inevitably those who succeeded were best documented and celebrated. One was Hieu Van Le, who arrived in 1977 in Darwin Harbour on a dilapidated old boat with 40 other Vietnamese. The fraught voyage, the end of a long prior saga, was assaulted by pirates, volcanic debris and monsoonal rains. On arrival Hieu Van Le had the wit to ask for the nearest police station and was received as one of the beneficiaries of Prime Minister Malcolm Fraser's more welcoming refugee policy. Le was born in Quang Tri in 1954; his father was killed during the French occupation and the surviving family was caught in the extreme turmoil of war, and they especially feared being drafted into the army. He and his new bride plotted for a

The last of the migrant liners: the *Australis* on the final voyage, arriving at Port Melbourne, December 1977. *Bureau of Immigration Research*, Bulletin, *August 1995*

year to escape by way of Malaysia to Australia, which meant leaving behind his mother and his brothers. After Darwin he was located at Pennington in Adelaide, the reception hostel which had been used for the earlier waves of postwar migrants. Within a fortnight he and his wife were picking fruit at Loxton on the Murray, then back in Adelaide for better work at the Actil factory. Subsequently Le went to university and became well qualified as a senior manager with ASCI for 15 years. He was one of the 150 000 Vietnamese in Australia by the turn of the century, together with 50 000 of the next generation. Hieu Van Le himself was the very model of the new racially diverse Australia. He served as the chair of the South Australian Multicultural and Ethnic Affairs Commission and in 2007 became deputy governor of the state.[3]

The tangle of emotions felt among the immigrants was a closed book to most of Australia – most immigrants remained invisible and inaudible. But by the 1970s Australia was receiving immigrants from

Britain, Europe and now from Asia: it had clearly shifted away from Arthur Calwell's adamant opposition to racial heterogeneity which underscored the first stage of the postwar policy. The racial issue, in the 1970s, was taken off the official agenda of government immigration policy. 'White Australia' was ostensibly consigned to the dustbin of history by both political parties. But its reverberations continued while at the same time migration became more complicated, not only in Australia but in the rest of the world too. Australia's relationship with its old partner in migration, Britain, was one such entanglement.

As Geoffrey Bolton pointed out, the 'British became a minority among Australia's intake of migrants, especially after the abandonment of the 10 pound migrant scheme in 1971'. At the same time Britain's own restrictions (which were primarily intended to limit the inflow from Pakistan, India and the Caribbean) were affecting the entry of Australians into Britain. Bolton remarked, 'It remains galling for Australians to stand in the foreigners queue at Heathrow while Germans and Italians who may have fought against Britain in wartime enter easily because of the European Community membership'. As Bolton pointed out:

> Australian governments retaliated so that British
> migrants found it increasingly difficult to bring
> out elderly family members to join them. These
> bureaucratic problems probably did as much
> as anything to loosen the ties between the two
> countries.[4]

The British in Australia had been overtaken by Europeans, especially by Italians (though their numbers were actually still less than the British).

Indeed by the 1970s Australia was openly celebrating the Europeanisation of its population, the success of the great experiment inaugurated by Arthur Calwell back in 1947. The whole project had been crucially facilitated in the context of full employment: there was indeed a parallel to the way that North America had been settled and Europeanised in the previous century under a similarly inexorable expansion of the great American economy.

The capacity of Australia to accommodate the great changes in its demographic and social composition was always a matter of political debate, especially when official discrimination was abolished in the early 1970s. The success of the European chapter of the story gave some confidence for the future and special credit was accorded to the Italian immigrants who had been the effective pioneers of the first diversification of British Australia. They had eroded the narrow Anglocentric monoculture of Australia, partly as a consequence of their refusal to assimilate totally to the host culture. They had retained much of their own ways of life even in suburban Australia. Italians found effective ways of Europeanising their version of 'the Australian dream' and the 'the lucky country', that is, a house with a garden, a car, outdoor life, good prospects for children and 'a place favoured by nature with a good climate and endless space, with a peaceful history, tolerant towards newcomers, and now offering an affluent, egalitarian, and classless society'. Indeed until the 1970s most Italian immigrants were from Abruzzi, Sicily, Calabria and Campania – they were mostly rural people with limited education (though this was less true of those from Veneto) and were clearly economic migrants. They were mainly engaged in manual industrial work on arrival, in the classic pattern of European migration over the previous century. Thus in Melbourne in the 1950s and 1960s 68 per cent of Italians were manual production workers, though this proportion declined in the next decade. The evolution of the Italian communities was a template for succeeding waves of migrants. Despite all the vicissitudes of adjustment by the migrants and the host nation, there had been little serious conflict. The Italian experience seemed emblematic of the Australian experience, and suggested that Australia might become more receptive to Asia and the rest of the world.[5]

In 1970 there was a sense of self-congratulation across Australia about the long migrant experiment since 1947. This vital outcome was demonstrated by the fact that the non-British immigrants did not coalesce into a block of resistance or antagonism to old British Australia. The immigrants did not become an oppositional force in society at large, nor even in Australian politics, even when the so-called 'ethnic vote' emerged in the coming decade. Conflict among the immigrants, so far, had not eventuated in any significant way despite earlier forebodings. Australia not only survived the great influx of aliens, it had thrived on their coming.

The new context

The framework of Australian immigration changed radically in the 1970s. The extraordinarily long postwar boom in the Western world, subsequently identified as the Golden Age, came to an end and levels of unemployment began to rise ominously.[6] In parallel were the repercussions of the great turmoil in South-East Asia associated with the Vietnam War. In this new phase the demand for labour in Australia increased much less automatically than in the previous three decades. It was the end of the certainties that had characterised the Menzies era. Policy towards immigration became equivocal and less predictable for the first time in 25 years.

The Vernon Report into the Australian economy in 1965 had advocated targets which entailed a steady 5 per cent annual growth rate without inflation, with induced savings, a maximum tariff, and steady net immigration of 100 000 per annum. Menzies was philosophically opposed to such a degree of governmental planning and rejected the report. But the expansion had continued and even as late as 1967 Arthur Calwell, the architect of the original expansion, continued to urge the rapid growth in population numbers. 'We still need a great inflow of migrants to build up our numbers', he declared, 'we cannot become the great independent thinking nation we wish to see established until we have a population of at least 50 million'. In the 1960s immigrants contributed 41 per cent of the growth of the population. It is clear that Australia had become dependent on immigrant workers; secondary industry now faced an actual decline in the number of native-born workers in its factories. A reigning assumption was that immigration was necessary for full employment: Calwell asserted that 'We cannot have full employment without immigration, just as we cannot have immigration without full employment'.[7] The economy had been running hot with high levels of migration and low levels of unemployment; at the same time arrivals and departures were rising very sharply. The system seemed to be less stable and showed signs of leakage.[8]

By 1971 the Australian economy slipped into much more difficult times and the 1974–75 crisis in the world economy was the worst since the 1930s. Unemployment in Western countries rose sharply and real growth declined; moreover the instability persisted for many years and the recession of 1980–83, though less severe, was more prolonged. Australia, therefore, entered a new 'age of uncertainty' and began to cut and adjust its immigration programs as the pulse of the economy weakened. Now immigration became a tool of policy to combat instability; it was no longer simply the engine of growth. Growth had actually been fuelled by immigration during the long boom.[9] The reduction of immigration at times seemed to cause sudden shortages in certain migrant-dependent industries – especially in the steel and motor industries – which was then connected with rapid wage increases in 1974/75. The Labor government stabilised immigrant intakes in 1972–74 and produced a slight rise – and then cut back severely in 1975, reducing the intake by 55 per cent, which produced the smallest total intake of immigrants since 1948.[10] Between 1970 and 1976 the number of settler migrants accepted declined dramatically – from 170 000 down to 52 748. Gough Whitlam in 1972 cut immigration to an average of 56 000 per annum (1971–76); under the Liberals the average intake between 1975 and 1980 was 70 000, rising to 100 000 in 1982/83.

During these years British immigration fell to one-fifth of the total and the balance with other European countries became negative. Most immigrants came from New Zealand, Asia and the Middle East.

The reduction in the number of immigrants was paralleled by the political renunciation of the White Australia policy. By 1973 the White Australia policy had been abandoned by both major parties. The selection of migrants became, in principle, non-discriminatory as to race, colour, ethnicity, country of birth and gender; moreover economic factors, including skill, were made less important than social factors such as family reunion. In the new context the prevailing origins of Australia's migrants changed rapidly. By 1975 Europeans fell from two-thirds to less than half and Asian numbers increased from 8 to 15 per cent. But since the total inflow was reduced the Asian numbers did not increase in absolute terms. Nevertheless the foundations of immigration policy shifted and many Australians (including some of the postwar migrants) became apprehensive about the consequences.

These changes in scale and composition made the 1970s a watershed in Australian immigration history. Meanwhile the relationship with Europe also altered, mostly because living standards in much of Europe were converging with Australian levels. The abolition of quota restrictions by the United States in 1965 and increasing freedom of movement in the widening European Common Market diminished the relative lure of Australia. It now became increasingly difficult to attract Europeans, and this was exacerbated by recession. In 1971 Minister Philip Lynch declared that 'Our traditional sources of immigrants are now so short of labour that they are competing with us in seeking "guest" workers from other countries'.[11] Moreover return migration to Europe was running high, rising from 6034 in 1959 to 18 300 in 1966. The reliable supply of European immigrants was evidently running down. Among immigration officials there was a feeling that the last great intake of 185 825 immigrants, in 1970, simply demonstrated that the average quality of the immigrants was being sacrificed. This was the time when Yugoslavia became a major source of Australian migrants (overtaking the Italians) and further recruitment was being extended eastwards to Turkey, Lebanon and Syria. There was little economic migration from Asia and little assistance was offered to prospective Asian immigrants. Over the following few years the traditional sources in Europe declined and there was a proportional rise of migration from the Asia-Pacific region. When Ian MacArthur went to recruit emigrants in Poland in 1977 he found that the Poles did not want to encourage emigration of skilled workers. In Bulgaria emigration was opposed and emigrants were almost regarded as criminals deserting the fatherland; Romania was a happier hunting ground.[12]

In his maiden speech in the House of Representatives, in 1956, Malcolm Fraser had announced his 'optimistic faith in immigration and development', but he later emphasised the view that the economic conditions required a careful balancing of the pattern of development. In the early 1970s he advocated a temporary slowing of the rate of immigration: 'The solution was to reduce the annual migrant intake to below 90 000 for the present while encouraging secondary industries to export'. Fraser was responding to the economic problems then facing his new government, but his usual stance was more expansionary and he regarded himself as a high immigration person.[13] Indeed, as early as 1968 Fraser had lectured in Adelaide about Australia becoming 'an Asian nation', and he declared enthusiastically for much more Asian language teaching. Even before the 1970s Fraser had been an advocate of multiculturalism and a critic of assimilationism.

Australia appeared to be moving towards a multicultural society, especially since immigrants were now intended to integrate rather than assimilate. As Peter Shergold, the economic historian turned public servant, put it:

> No longer was the central image that of a bubbling
> melting pot into which all newcomers were expected

to plunge, emerging after sufficient cooking as well-done Australians. Rather, the watchword was integration, a concept which saw a value in allowing Asian newcomers, like other ethnic groups, preserve and disseminate their ethnic heritage within the value-system and social customs built by tradition. To the extent that the need for assimilation was no longer an unargued assumption, non-Europeans could more readily be tolerated. Mental as well as administrative barriers were slowly being removed.[14]

Government passage assistance had been, for much more than a century, a crucial determinant of Australian immigration policy; the careful distribution of assistance (mainly to British migrants) had guaranteed that, until the 1970s, the size of the intake and its composition remained under firm control. Assistance, apart from refugees, was phased out in the early 1970s, and thus the traditional program came to an end. It was also the demise of one of Australia's key levers of discrimination – assisted immigration had always given the nation control over selection. In 1972 the new Whitlam government authorised recruitment of migrants in non-traditional sources for migrants, including South America. The military coup against Salvador Allende in Chile in 1976 soon yielded a new supply of refugees. As one of the Australian recruiting officers recollected:

Our government was keen on diversifying migration. The source in Europe was drying up. The push factors didn't exist in Europe any more and Australia's pull factors were diminishing. The inhabitants of South America were seen as being something between those in Europe and Asia, largely European. I think the decision was wrong, personally. We would have been better off to have made a commitment to Asia earlier than we did, but, I suppose, given the politics of the day and the public attitudes at the time, we may not have been successful if we'd concentrated on Asia.[15]

From 1973 the Immigration Office was being besieged by refugees and quasi-refugees. This widened the range of immigrant sources, eventually to bring 15,000 from Argentina, 10000 from Uruguay, and 10000–12,000 from Chile. In effect the old mould was broken in the early years of Labor. But the new mould was not fully tested until the primary flows of refugees emerged in large numbers in the aftermath of the Vietnam War.

The end of White Australia

One of the achievements of the post-1947 immigration policies was the manner in which the Australian population at large was coaxed into accepting great changes. As we have seen, the Europeanisation of the immigration sources was implemented incrementally, with assurances to calm the fears of the receiving society. It was accomplished by good and persuasive government, helped by lucky economic conditions. Calwell was especially effective in this crucial effort. He had made the policy palatable by insisting that it never jeopardise the foundations of White Australia, and indeed would strengthen the ramparts. The second, and more momentous, stage in Australia's immigration history was the actual demission of the policy based on racial discrimination in the 1970s. Subsequently a controversy arose among political commentators about the trajectory, tactics and wisdom of the change. In particular it was alleged that the White Australia policy was removed by stealth, if not by actual deceit. It was alleged that the Australian public was inadequately consulted about the political changes which demolished White Australia and introduced hundreds of thousands of non-Europeans into the country in the course of the following three decades.[16]

There had been a long succession of small erosions of the policy over the previous 20 years and the actual propulsion of the change came from several sources which had different political colourings. The final political ending of White Australia came relatively swiftly at a time when the population was still, in essence, racially unmixed. Though there had been prior changes, the end of the policy was nevertheless a clear shift and decisive in terms of Australia's reputation in the world at large. Most of the change happened within 10 years. The label 'White Australia' was removed from the main political platforms by 1965; by 1975 all manifestations of racial discrimination had been erased and outlawed. The White Australia policy was officially terminated in 1966 when the Liberal government announced that immigrants would be admitted on the basis of their 'suitability as settlers, their ability to integrate readily, and their possession of qualifications which are in fact positively useful to Australia'. In 1971 the Labor Party resolved that it would avoid discrimination on any grounds of race, colour of skin or nationality, though there was still much apprehension of opening flood gates to Asians. The number of non-Europeans entering the country had increased and many Colombo Plan students studying in Australia were staying on, without serious complaint within the host nation. But there was no actual promotion of non-white immigration. The country was still resolutely monocultural and the watchword remained that of assimilability. Resistance to the idea of 'Asianisaton' of Australia was substantial in its alleged threat to social cohesion.[17]

Meanwhile, through the 1960s there was a quiet shift in social attitudes which became cumulative though not well documented. Some of the attitudinal change was consolidated as substantial sections of Australia society became more tolerant of social and cultural differences in their midst, more cosmopolitan, better educated and less fearful of other cultures. But there was also a more positive response to foreign opinion and a greater sensitivity about Australia's international reputation. In some sense Australia began to adjust to, even to appease, the critics of its immigration policy both internally and externally.

Already by 1966 public opinion polls recorded 55 per cent of the public as favourable to a liberalisation of immigration policy. Only 34 per cent wanted a continuing outright ban on non-white immigration; 11 per cent were still undecided. As *Nation*, the independent political journal, said, 'There is already a disenfranchised majority opinion on the issue'.[18] For the time being the admission of 'coloured immigrants' was feared for its likely political unpopularity and the political parties remained decidedly wary of the question.[19] But by the 1970s there was a growing confidence that change was acceptable and that there was widespread and growing 'public acceptance of a substantial immigration from Asian countries'.[20] The writing had been on the wall for some years and powerfully underlined by changes in the United Nations and the British Commonwealth, both of which presented platforms on which new nations could openly berate Australia for its policy of racial exclusion.[21] In 1966 India and Malaysia were exerting direct pressure on Australia to change its policies.

Another consideration was the future of Australian trade with Asia, which was increasing in significance throughout: 'It was bad for business to assist migration from the other side of the world while proclaiming that traders from the neighbourhood were unfit to take up residence'.[22] In May 1971 *Nation* declared that 'In Australia the liberal has no party'. *Nation* challenged the policy, and by this stage 'both sides of politics agreed that the White Australia policy must go, or at least must appear to go'. In 1971 the Australian Workers Union at last lifted its ban on admitting Asians to its membership. Yet Arthur Calwell, at the federal Labor Party conference in Launceston in 1972, still warned that 'red-blooded Australians' were in danger of creating 'a chocolate-coloured nation'.[23] Calwell however had become isolated in his intransigence, a stranded relic of the 1940s in a country which he himself had done so much to transform. In 1973 the Whitlam government removed the last formal vestiges of the White Australia policy and its specific restrictions on non-white immigration.

As we have seen, the formal demolition of White Australia was the last step in a long chain of small adjustments which can be traced back at least to the Holt government. These changes had proceeded via bureaucratic shifts and alterations in emphasis in adjudicating particular cases. Not surprisingly there was subsequent dispute about to whom or to which party the credit or blame should be attributed.[24] In 1973, however, Australia reached the unambiguous position of effective, practical and bipartisan non-discrimination equal to that attained in Canada in 1967. Canada had also led the way in the promotion of multiculturalism both as an ideology and a practical policy, apparently originating in Banff in 1965 as a reaction among Slav Canadians against the bilingual and bi-cultural dominance of Anglo-French Canada.[25] The thinking and policy was subsequently translated to Australia, where it had gained substantial influence by 1970.

These changes, in reality, coincided with a marked reduction in normal immigration, which consequently delayed some of the immediate effects of the change. Indeed the highest point of postwar immigration was reached in 1970, followed by the lowest in 1975, a swift and sudden turnabout. The net intake of migrants in 1975–76 was a mere 20 259.[26] At the time it seemed that Australia had passed beyond its heroic phase of immigration. This phase coincided with the two decades in which Europe had sought to drain its population, a process which proceeded eastwards in Europe through the period. This came to an end by the late 1960s, and Australia reduced its intakes and Europe fell away as a supply centre. Within a decade Australia moved into a new refugee-receiving phase which was related to the end of empire and decolonisation. Many of the migrants in this later stage were people departing ex-colonial countries, especially out of India, Sri Lanka, Indonesia, South Africa, Zimbabwe and Chile. Overlapping this process was the trauma of the Vietnam War, which brought the refugee question towards the centre of Australian consciousness.

Australia's involvement in the Vietnam War generated a series of obligations and a thorough-going reconsideration of Australia's relationship with Asia which inevitably entailed confronting the racial issue. Maxwell Newton observed that in 1965

> We in Australia are coming to appear in Asian eyes
> as supporters of White imperialism, neo-colonialism
> and exclusiveness. We bow to a White British Queen
> over the seas, we have a racist immigration policy,
> we send troops to Asia to fight against brown men,
> we give little foreign aid outside New Guinea, we
> have commercial policies which hit the interests of
> Asian trade.[27]

The end of the Vietnam War and the fall of Saigon left a legacy of moral and political problems and debts with which the Australian government was now forced to grapple. Eventually it exerted a profound effect on its immigration program at the very moment when Australia had removed its policy of racial discrimination. The refugee crisis which followed the fall of Saigon coincided with the end of the traditional mass immigration program.

An inside view of the changes was later recorded by John Menadue, who served as a senior public servant to the governments of both Whitlam and Fraser. He located the end of White Australia in the earlier moves inaugurated by the Holt government and then consolidated under Labor which formally abolished all discrimination. Menadue pointed out that 'the immigration intake under Labor was so minimal that the new policy was never put to the test'. He also pointed out that Fraser was responsible for accepting a large number of Indo-Chinese refugees after the fall of Saigon in 1975. Those refugees, 'supported by a generous Australian community response, were the decisive turning point in moving Australia away from White Australia'. Menadue regarded

Fraser as the most full-blooded reformer of the time, an inspiration to work with in the field of immigration and multiculturalism: 'His commitment to non-discriminatory immigration was deep-seated. He buried White Australia as no other prime minister had'.[28] Fraser took the new policy much further than his predecessors. Unlike his successors Fraser was passionately committed to the reshaping of the nation's attitudes.

Refugee policy

Amid the political and economic turmoil in Australia in the early 1970s the great issue was not the reduced immigration program but the crises associated with the unpredictable refugee inflows and their political consequences. The refugee issue, as a central question of government policy, came hot on the heels of the abolition of White Australia. There had been refugee episodes ahead of the great Vietnamese humanitarian crisis. The Whitlam government had been extremely cautious of refugee intakes on both economic and political grounds. Its previous response to the needs of the Ugandan Indians was slight and it also showed reluctance in receiving refugees out of the Chilean crisis in 1973. Australia temporised over the humanitarian crisis in Timor in 1975, when Whitlam allowed 1700 boat refugees to land but refused to grant permanent status. When the Vietnamese question erupted the government was slow to respond. In the first stage 500 Vietnamese were accepted via Hong Kong and Singapore in addition to some orphaned children. But even the Vietnamese staff of the Australian Saigon embassy were refused asylum. Under Whitlam the policy towards the great refugee crisis flowing out of the Vietnam War was essentially restrictive and fully controlled. The stance and thinking of the Whitlam government to both the Timor and Vietnam refugee crises later became a source of great contention and a clash of memories.[29]

At the end of the Vietnam War there was confusion and chaos

across South-East Asia, with tens of thousands of refugees in a state of panic and desperation. Under Whitlam the response of Australia was generally unprepared and negative; Whitlam himself gave the impression that the Vietnamese refugees would not be welcome, partly because they would agitate in Australia for a free Vietnam. He wanted to restrict refugee intakes to small symbolic gestures at a time when there was a growing apprehension across Australia than large numbers of refugee boats were converging on Darwin. There was a general atmosphere of anxiety, especially when it was revealed that refugees were arriving in Malaysia at the rate of more than 10 000 a month. Out of this chaotic situation agreements were eventually engineered by which Australia would accept a quota of the refugees, a policy towards which Fraser demonstrated much more resolution and generosity than his predecessor.

Fraser's government introduced a full-scale refugee policy and explicitly accepted the full obligations out of what was interpreted as a combination of humanitarianism and guilt. In 8 years 78 000 Indo-Chinese were admitted to Australia, a figure which included boat people, the first of whom arrived in Darwin in April 1976. The percentage of Asians in Australian immigration increased from 14 per cent in 1974 to 36 per cent in 1979; the rising gradient was significantly affected by the relatively small conventional immigration occurring in these years. By 1986 some 100 000 Indo-Chinese refugees had entered Australia.

One of the officers responsible for these early intakes recollected assembling 1600 refugees in buses to be delivered to Bangkok: 'They had all gone through these extremities of torture, escape, and everything else, but when it came to settling in Australia, Vietnamese didn't want to travel with the Laotians. Laotians did not want to recognise the Cambodians'.[30] Some of the stories were recollected by the refugees themselves. One of them, Nguyen Hong Thi Thu, daughter of a general, remembered the small boat with 20 people from South Vietnam first getting to Malaysia, and hoping to go to America. They bribed local officials with gold, sailed for

Unofficial immigrants from Asia: Van Tha Chan and family, 'boat people', at Pennington Hostel, Adelaide, 1978. Advertiser, *7 June 1978*

7 days in horrifying conditions, expecting to die. They arrived at a camp in Malaysia where they stayed for 4 months before being sent to Kuala Lumpur and then on to Australia, by air, feeling extreme relief that their ordeal had ended.

Absorbing large numbers of Asian refugees was a new challenge for Australia. There was certainly opposition from the start, some of which revived simple racial prejudice but was always alloyed with other concerns. For instance, a group called People against Communism in Australia claimed that the refugees would include communists infiltrating the country. There were recurrent stories about the likelihood of such immigrants introducing brothels, lice and exotic diseases. There was a fear of that the boats arriving in northern Australia would carry foot-and-mouth disease to threaten the local cattle industry. When refugees were permitted to bring family members on the reunion policy, Dr Mick Ryan declared that 'We're getting a lot of aged people in, a lot of whom have cataracts, some of whom have had strokes. We are looking at people with disabilities coming into a country where there is probably a crisis in the hospital situation'. They would strain facilities and cause a backlash in the Australia community.[31]

These and other arguments were resisted by the government, which stayed firm in its refugee policy. Indeed, despite many doubters in its midst, Australia was relatively generous in its intake of refugees, taking proportionately more than the United States. It was a peaceable experiment and was surprisingly uncontroversial until the late 1970s when there was indeed a backlash against immigrants, fuelled by recurring and rising levels of unemployment, a combination causing members of the Labor government to doubt the wisdom of its continuance. Robert Manne, writing in 1978, diagnosed the issue as 'our deepest collective neurosis' and took issue with Bob Hawke, president of the ACTU, who was chastising boat refugees for jumping the immigration queue.[32]

Costs and benefits

The end of White Australia was a seminal moment taken in a mood of confidence enhanced with a sense of growing liberality. This was tested by the great shifts in the context of international migration. Indeed the overseas reception of Australia's renunciation of racial discrimination was less rapturous than some had expected. There was widespread ignorance or scepticism about the end of White Australia. Thus in 1977 when John Menadue went as Ambassador to Japan he discovered that many of his

Japanese counterparts implicitly believed that White Australia was still official policy. Menadue was aware that this was a broad and damaging misunderstanding of Australia and he wanted 'permanently laid to rest the myth of White Australia ... Those that do not know us well have one basic unfavourable view of us, that we are racist'. He reported that the ghost of White Australia followed him all over Japan, which he found galling:

> I pointed out that, despite our history, Australia in
> the 1970s had the least discriminatory migration
> policies in the region. But they didn't believe me.
> Perhaps the intense feeling about White Australia
> in Japan arose because in the late 19th century
> Australia was closed to Japanese at the only time in
> their history when they were interested in migration.

Menadue said that the Japanese were only concerned about the idea of discrimination against themselves; in 1998 some Japanese businessmen told him that they thought that Australia was actually allowing too many Chinese into Australia.[33]

The termination of White Australia, in one influential view, was at the core of a more general transformation and liberalisation of the broad texture of Australian society. But there were sceptics who questioned the gravity of the other changes. Such critics believed that social attitudes in Australia had altered very little and that the changes in policy were essentially cosmetic, indeed superficial.[34] Lee Kuan Yew, the provocative Singaporean leader, decried the Whitlamite policies because they discriminated in new ways. He pointed out that Australia recruited only highly skilled migrants from Asia, while thousands of unskilled migrants were still coming from southern Europe. This made the policy a form of mere 'tokenism'.[35] In purely arithmetical terms the number of non-Europeans entering Australia clearly increased, while the total immigration numbers actually declined in the 1970s. Immigration in 1972 was 56 000; in

1975, 89 147; by 1976 immigrant intakes were cut to 52 748; then averaged 73 000 over the next three years.[36]

The increases in the proportion of Asians in the total immigration to Australia were, therefore, partly the coincidental product of a rise of refugee migration at a time of declining economic migration from traditional sources. It was equally clear that the end of White Australia had not been designed as a concerted and planned shift in the sources in a new phase of immigration. The refugee crisis, historically, obscured more structural tendencies at the end of the 20th century. In short, parts of Asia began rapid industrialisation, which soon reshaped patterns of labour migration, generating new and complicated flows into and out of Australia, the subject of later chapters.

One of the criteria of the entire immigration policy was the degree to which Australia had been able to accommodate radical changes in its composition, and large numbers of alien peoples. There was a fear that Old World animosities would be transplanted into Australia, which would exacerbate tensions with the host society and the imported ethnicities. Indeed spasms of internecine, inter-ethnic antagonism and even violence punctuated the history of postwar Australian immigration. Several imported long-standing grudges were certainly introduced and 'certain groups resorted to terrorist tactics'. Thus on 16 September 1972 Balkan extremists exploded two bombs in Sydney, both directed at Yugoslav travel agencies in the inner city. In fact it was one of a series of episodes dating back to the mid 1960s, apparently related to the execution of Croatians with Australian passports in Yugoslavia. The first bomb injured 16 people and the other exploded harmlessly.[37] There followed many police raids on Croatian homes in Sydney, after which the trouble subsided.

Generally, however, there was little friction against the immigrants. There were differential levels of assimilation. Occasionally there were small eruptions of anti-British sentiment related to their alleged prominence in the unions, troublemakers at large (some regarded them as representatives of the dreaded 'British disease' of wild-cat strikes); and there were other mild manifestations of anti-Pommie sentiment. But these antagonisms towards immigrants never reached enough mass to constitute a sustained political question, even in the 1970s.

When Andrew Fabinyi, a distinguished Melbourne publisher of Hungarian origin, reviewed the literature on migration in 1970 he came to the view that 'press comment on the social, cultural as well as political issues is abundant, uniformly pro-migration and pro-migrant in tone'. There seemed to be general agreement that the cultural and social doubts surrounding immigration had been resolved. In fact, in the coming decades the issue became an erratic political football, especially among conservative elements in the Australian political contest. Meanwhile, however, Fabinyi argued that before the European migrations, many people believed that Australia had possessed no authentic and recognisable culture of its own. By 1970 it had developed an identifiable persona; moreover, he added, 'most of us would agree that Australia is not a torn society ... it is no longer homogeneous and has never been classless'. He pointed out that most of the European migrants were in fact not from 'old and long-established cultural patterns who are coming to a new and younger culture'; they were not carriers of ancient traditions but people open minded to the new world. While Australia positively bore the marks of Shakespeare and Queen Victoria upon it, migrants such as the Turks were from 'brand new' places, such as Ankara. They had not yet exerted a profound influence on Australia and he noted that all federal and state parliamentarians, except for one, were British-Australian by birth or origin. He particularly detected serious delays in the integration of southern Europeans into the 'mainstream of Australian everyday life'. Indeed 'Prejudice, bigotry, taboos, everyday habits are still deeply entrenched when we come to the mixing of race, religion or language'.[38] Intermarriage was a litmus test of communal integration and 8 per cent of all marriages between 1947 and 1963 were contracted between non-British people marrying an Australian or a person from another national group. Here the southern Europeans still exhibited the lowest rate of intermarriage.

Despite his reservations, Fabinyi regarded the postwar program as an enormously successful public relations exercise 'which has made Australians accept, at worst with indifference, waves of Germans, Northern Europeans, Hungarians or more recently Spaniards, Lebanese, Egyptians or Turks who eschewed the ingrained self-perpetuating cohesion and isolation of Southern Europeans'. He noted that 'today we are combing Europe, the Americas, the Middle East in an attempt to entice people to come'. Indeed Fabinyi accurately sensed that the whole European experiment was running down:

> The economic rationale of high-level accelerated migration is under scrutiny ... There is a growing feeling, articulated by white-collar workers, that at least a portion of the immense resources devoted to migration should be diverted to the social, economic and cultural welfare of those who are already here. Targets of 25 million Australians by the end of the century, 50 million soon after, do not belong to today's Australian Utopia.[39]

The economic effect of immigration was always contentious in public debate, partly because it was extremely difficult to measure its impact in either the short or the long run. The National Population Inquiry in 1975 (with a supplement in 1978) recognised that the consequences of immigration were entwined with economic fluctuations; it also affirmed the idea that doubling the population was possible and even desirable; falling fertility levels had to be recognised in any consideration of future immigration levels. The inquiry calculated that a net annual intake of 50 000 migrants, including refugees, would yield a population of 17 million by 2000. The reduced target of 50 000 per annum was in operation in 1975, but Fraser raised intakes especially of refugees; and then moved to triennial intakes of about 270 000.

The refugee component in the total was rising in the late 1970s and certainly dominated public debate. In a sense it was a reprise of the White Australia debate in a proxy mode. But other issues were also emerging, including the notion that immigration exacerbated urbanisation, since 90 per cent of the immigrants congregated in the cities. Already there was talk of environmental degradation through excessive population in a country which was traditionally regarded as empty of people. Already the old Calwellian target of 2 per cent per annum population growth was jettisoned at a time when the basic arguments about the assumed economic benefits of immigration were increasingly questioned.

10 The end of the heroic days: the 1980s

Immigrants and the change

In the three decades after 1947 Australian immigration possessed a unity of national purpose and direction. In the 1980s immigration lost its bipartisan character and, for the first time since the Second World War, policy became a matter of division and controversy. Moreover the flows of migration became more confusing. Immigrants, especially Asians, became less welcome at a time when the country was jettisoning the legacies of White Australia. The old certainties had been lost. The Bicentenary in 1988 was a vantage point from which to observe the patterns of immigration, old and new, as well as the shape of the future.

The Bicentenary was a great stocktaking of two centuries of European occupation and settlement in Australia. But the symbolism of the Bicentennial was itself contested: Malcolm Fraser had wanted to celebrate not only the success story of immigration during the previous 30 years but also the place of multiculturalism in the new Australia. His successors were increasingly hesitant.[1] As we will see, the FitzGerald Report had already recognised national misgivings about the direction of Australian society and these apprehensions began to weigh more heavily on the national psyche.

The simplest statistic showed that in 1988 one in five Australians had been born overseas. This made Australia the most immigrant nation on earth, apart from Israel. It also showed that Australia had achieved Calwell's goal of 1 per cent per annum population growth from net immigration over the previous 30 years. Meanwhile Australia's population had risen to 15.7 million by 1985 and consequently the maintenance of Calwell's target of 2 per cent growth per annum required ever increasing numbers of immigrants. As many as 200000 per annum were needed to reach this number, which was entirely improbable by the end of the 1980s. Already, at the start of that decade, the target was being questioned from several directions and the planned immigrant intakes were recalibrated year by year.

The composition of the immigrant nation's new recruits was also clearer. Since 1959 there had been 3270690 arrivals. Of these Europe accounted for 2158760. The British Isles, despite the great shift, remained the greatest contributor with 1205570, followed in descending order by Italy, Greece, Yugoslavia, the Netherlands and Malta. Of the remainder, Asia provided 570130, Turkey 33620 and the Americas 160910. In addition there were substantial arrivals from Africa, 48670 of whom came from South Africa and 24340 from Egypt. Oceania provided 239760 (including 187650 from New Zealand and 123120 from Fiji).

Arrivals had to be set beside departures, which of course undermined the net gains of the migrant program and diminished the benefits of the nation's investment in immigration. Indeed, 467590 'settlers' had actually departed between 1959 and 1988, more than half of them British (whom Calwell had regarded as the most desirable immigrants). Return migration had always occurred but the rate in the late 20th century suggested that the actual character of immigration was itself changing. Many immigrants were now sojourners, short-stayers and the internationally mobile. They were administratively and statistically difficult to pin down. The numbers were insecure but the best estimate was that from 1947 to 1991 overall settler loss was 20.8 per cent, with a further loss of 7.4 per cent of Australian-born persons. Australia's retention rate was relatively good, but lower than Canada's. Between 1959 and 1965 more than 16 per cent of settler arrivals had returned home and this was regarded as a sign that the system was malfunctioning. By the mid 1980s the return figures rose further and were generally greater to traditional source countries and less among refugees.[2] Settler loss not only undermined the system of immigration; it also persuaded the government that the benefits of assisted immigration were increasingly dubious. In the Billy Snedden years, 1966–70, assisted immigration reached 537 000. Thereafter the numbers began to diminish: in 1971–73 there were 240 000 settler arrivals of which 54 per cent were assisted; at the end of the 1970s only a quarter of immigrants were assisted, and the total fell to 81 000 in 1980. By 1988 total immigration had declined and the government was less committed to cumulative population increase. Assistance was largely terminated, thereby ending a system that had operated for most of the previous 150 years.[3]

Economists' debates and immigration thinking

During the long postwar era immigration had proceeded helter-skelter because the economy was hungry for labour, the supply of which was generally more problematic than demand. This context had changed and now Australia reconsidered the notion of simply bolstering its population at almost any cost. The nation's debate turned to matters of identity, assimilation, the country's carrying capacity, its unity and economic efficacy. These issues were bound to be more divisive. The politics of Australian immigration were redefined and with it the essential question of the size of the population. Australia's expectations became less expansive and confident. Two questions now loomed: the first was how many immigrants did Australia want and what would be the optimal future size of the population? The second was where should the immigrants come from? The latter was a question which implied a need to reconcile the legacy of the White Australia policy with its aftermath.

This sea change in Australian immigration attitudes displaced the previously unassailable priorities of population growth and defence. Underlying currents were detected – thus changes in military technology now made battalions of humans less necessary for Australia's defence; meanwhile scientists had wakened the nation to environmental and other disamenities of population growth; and, most of all, the reappearance of relatively high unemployment rates revived the widespread notion that immigrants robbed jobs from residents.[4] Consequently the immigration debate became more political and also more technical. Economists battled with their unsatisfactory statistics and formulae to measure the impact of immigration on national growth and welfare. Their results were not definitive but generally veered towards the proposition that immigration normally gives a fillip to aggregate demand and to the derived demand for labour. Thus, despite higher unemployment in the 1980s, the Labor Party maintained a policy of positive immigration.[5] The same broad approach was adopted in New Zealand, Canada and the United States. But it was an uneasy policy full of questions and recurrent opposition.

The political commentator Paul Kelly charted the manner in which Australia had come to terms with the end of White Australia and also the end of expansion based on immigration and its strategic importance. Thus Fraser had led the Liberals into multiculturalism, which he declared to be his greatest achievement. The previous essential arguments about 'populate or perish', linked with that of national security, had evaporated. Immigration was 'the sleeping issue' in Australian politics. Much of the debate was a matter of balance and mix in the immigration intake, and there were divisions on both sides. Andrew Peacock in Opposition in 1984 had flirted with its political potential, pointing out that 'The Caucasian component has dropped and the proportion of Asian intake has risen ... the Minister has to explain why the imbalance has occurred and what he is prepared to do to correct it'. Hawke made his own defence of the policy, but even he was saying that it was essential 'to ensure that our migration program does not threaten the stability and fabric of Australia society'.[6]

The arguments about the economic consequences of immigration were equally perplexing and at best indeterminate. It was indisputable that since 1945 immigrants had accounted for half of Australia's population growth. But because they possessed a high participation rate, they made an even bigger contribution to the work force. On the other side of the equation the immigrants also boosted levels of demand in the economy and thereby the very demand for labour brought about by their presence.[7] This seemed to be generally true and denied the idea that immigration caused unemployment or fuelled inflationary tendencies. The problem was that the statistical verification of these propositions was weak, partly because the effects were in any case somewhat marginal, especially when the economy contracted as it had in the 1980s. This inexactitude gave little guidance to the sharp debates that developed in the 1980s about the general shape of Australia's policy governing immigration.

Consequently immigration policy could no longer be founded on the secure economic grounds that had prevailed since 1945; at the same time the social consequences of migration now emerged to haunt Australia more forcefully than at any time since the Depression. The bipartisan consensus about immigration was under pressure and serious discord broke out even within the main political parties. Some of the new bitterness and cynicism was exposed in the political memoirs of Peter Walsh, the iconoclastic self-educated Finance

Minister who served in the Hawke government in the 1980s. He recorded Cabinet discussion concerning immigration targets: Walsh argued for lower intakes but was opposed often 'because it would antagonize the ethnic lobby', and targets were characterised by 'blow-outs and cave-ins'. The effect was a loss of control over immigration numbers and an 'unplanned and unintended doubling in four years ... at the instigation of the ethnic mafia', a scathing term by which Walsh referred to the allegedly disproportionate leverage of lobby groups which had formed among immigrant communities in the large cities. Four rapid changes of immigration ministers created what Walsh regarded as chaos in the policy, exacerbated by the prevailing system of family reunion 'which debased migrant employability'.

Walsh indeed argued that the economists were wrong about the tendency of immigrants to generate economic growth, because migrants dampened average per capita income. He took the view that immigration depended on, rather than generated, a higher rate of economic growth. Immigrants needed large social infrastructure provision which then 'bleeds funds away from productive investment. In short, migration adds more to demand than it does to supply, ipso facto it blows out the current account deficit'. Immigrants damaged the trade balance and generally increased congestion and social problems in the cities. Walsh quoted evidence that unemployment among Turkish migrants, 10 to 22 months after their arrival, was as much as 87 per cent. He noted that Australian unemployment benefits were higher than average incomes in Turkey. He also cited examples of corrupt practice among immigrants and the abuse of social security provisions. The Hawke government, he asserted, was unable to rectify the system or control intakes because it was beholden to the 'professional ethnics' lobby who could deliver blocs of ethnic votes.[8] Walsh's recollections exposed the bitterness of the internal debates in the 1980s in Labor ranks, and even the less polemical account, by the pen of another minister, Neal Blewett, subsequently confirmed the disintegration of accord within the Labor government.

Policies in practice

By the 1980s Australia was operating a different form of immigration. It was no longer driven by assistance schemes or by targeted recruitment in favoured traditional locations, such as the United Kingdom. The old controls had ceased and in the new context preferential subsidisation and open discrimination no longer prevailed. The Australian government, nevertheless, now more than ever insisted on controlling the volume and composition of immigration. It therefore developed new and adjustable rules for entry. These were aligned with the economic and social priorities of Australia at large, and also in terms of its international obligations (notably for refugees) and its own much-vaunted recent rejection of discrimination. Both aspects were intensely political in their reverberations. In this tighter environment, with rising levels of public anxiety about the scale and composition of immigration, the government employed a range of levers to regulate the entry of immigrants.

The first lever operated by the government was its annual target figure for immigration, the national intake quantum set as appropriate to prevailing economic conditions. These targets were adjusted downwards in the recession of the early 1980s. The second lever of control related to the formulae which vetted prospective immigrants: the NUMAS (Numerical Multifactor Assessment System) requirements juggled the criteria of skills, language ability, capital and family connections – and gave the government considerable discretion.[9] The third lever concerned the intake of refugees and their acceptance in Australia. Each lever was worked in these years: the total intakes were reduced in 1980 and 1982 and kept at a relatively low level until 1989, when cautious increases were sanctioned. The NUMAS system was altered to give greater emphasis to skills and specific family connections, and eventually the entire intake was categorised into three streams – family, skilled and humanitarian. The general tightening was symbolised in 1981 by the new requirement that all persons arriving in Australia needed

Family reunited: Mrs Selladuray from Sri Lanka, aged 85 and suffering cataracts, joins her son in Adelaide in 1987, permitted on humanitarian grounds. *From Bureau of Immigration Research*, Immigration in Focus 1946–1990: A Photographic Archive, *1990*

passports, a regulation directed at the lax entry of migrants by way of New Zealand. In the same year all assisted immigration terminated, except for refugees.[10]

Policy regarding refugees, especially those reaching Australia in the aftermath of the Vietnam War, was the most testing issue of the day. For instance, in 1981 among 146 people aboard a fishing boat from Vietnam, there were found fee-paying passengers attempting to enter illegally. Such stories caused greater urgency in response to the refugee crisis and in 1982 an agreement was organised with the Vietnam government for an 'orderly Departure Program', which was another critical moment in Australia's immigration history. The immediate effect was to increase Asian immigration at a time of falling European migration. In 1983 refugees were also accepted from El Salvador, Sri Lanka and the Lebanon, whose arrivals added fuel to rising public concern about Asian immigration. The government reaffirmed its commitment to non-discriminatory policy. The events in Tiananmen Square in China in 1989 caused Prime Minister Hawke suddenly to pledge asylum for very large numbers of Chinese students currently in Australia.

The enhanced mobility of population across the world also created perplexing problems. The numbers and meaning of movement in every category were increasingly ambiguous and baffling. For instance, the extent of tourism, always a source of confusion in migration statistics, was rising in every direction and some of it was transmuted into temporary or permanent settlement among many who departed and many who arrived; counting them accurately was almost impossible. Studies in the 1980s demonstrated that the out-migration among Australian-born was running at about 28 000 per annum, rising to 143 000 within 3 years, yet though these were categorised as long-term departures, many eventually returned to Australia. There was also a considerable leakage of migrants: between a fifth and a quarter of all settlers left the country either temporarily or permanently. Something like 16 per cent of the entire population of Australians 'departed' in a single year, which reflected many simultaneous currents but most of all the sheer mobility of the modern world. And there were many unofficial immigrants: an amnesty in 1980 produced 15 000 illegal immigrants but there were probably twice as many across the country. Counting migrants was almost as difficult as herding cats, but with greater political reverberations.

The transition out of the traditional immigration policy led to no immediate political crisis but nevertheless caused accumulating tensions within the political firmament. An inside account of the operation of the policies in both Labor and Liberal coalition governments was charted by John Menadue. He had been head of the Department of Prime Minister and Cabinet (1974–76) and then Ambassador to Japan, and was appointed by Malcolm Fraser as head of the Department of Immigration and Ethnic Affairs, working with Minister Ian Macphee. Menadue saw his mission to 'do my bit to end White Australia forever', to which purpose both Fraser and Macphee were evidently both fully committed.[11]

Menadue discovered that the old immigration bureaucracy was set in its ways and still selecting immigrants in a discriminatory fashion. He noticed that the British still received the lion's share of assisted passages. Thus in September 1980 there was an advertising campaign in Manchester and soon 11 000 people were queuing up with inquiries. Menadue determined that 'We had to advertise on a non-discriminatory basis and where the most skilled applicants could be found. For the first time we commenced advertising the business migrant scheme in the *Far Eastern Economic Review* in Hong Kong'.[12] Labor had already in 1979 said that assistance should be means tested and 'should not favour citizens of any particular country', that is, it should stop favouring the British.[13] The previous Liberal government had baulked at the idea, saying that 'there would be an outcry from the Government's pro-British supporters if we did so'.[14] Macphee and Menadue quickly moved to abolish all assisted passages in April 1981 without any outcry, and some of the savings were used to help non-English speaking migrants learn their new language. The hostels were thenceforward reserved for refugees and other humanitarian cases.

Adopting a muscular, even provocative, reforming stance, Menadue declared that a 90 per cent Asian intake was perfectly acceptable, and Macphee apparently agreed with him. When Menadue announced that it was immaterial whether immigrants came from the United Kingdom or Malaysia he was roundly criticised by the Returned Servicemen's League, and also faced graffiti which read 'Menadue = mongrelisation'. The *Australian* accused him of having too much initiative and not leaving policy to Cabinet nor ensuring the support of the great bulk of the Australian people. Menadue implicitly conceded that he and the Department of Immigration were proceeding ahead of public opinion.[15] He was determined to bring British Australia to an end and did so with some relish. When he and Macphee toured Europe in 1981 it was reported that they had announced

> that Australia does not want British migrants unless
> they are skilled tradesmen or businessmen. Those
> offended are British Government officials and those
> who see migration to Australia as an alternative for
> the under privileged ... hopeful that Australia might
> draw off some of their army of unemployed. The
> British are getting no joy from the visit.[16]

But, in fact, Lord Carrington told them that Australia should indeed look to Asia just as the United Kingdom was looking to Europe.

Menadue was also instrumental in removing the automatic citizen rights which had always been accorded to the British in Australia.[17] He tried to introduce ways of determining whether immigrants were sympathetic to racial tolerance, prompted by the fear that white migrants entering from Southern Rhodesia were fomenting trouble in Western Australia. Nor did the Fraser government accept sectarian imports from Britain itself. The question arose when the British government asked Australia to take in a number of 'supergrass' informers against the IRA, under cover and with aliases. This was vetoed by Macphee, who wanted to keep out the violence that had 'bedevilled Northern Ireland', and wanted no part of such contagion. According to Menadue, the prime minister, being of Scottish descent, 'probably didn't feel inclined to help the English anyway. Macphee ... stuck to his decision. Australia had ceased being a British penal colony. Why should we start again?'[18]

The Fraser government, clearly egged on by Menadue, drove

more nails into the coffin of White Australia. The much-vaunted non-discriminatory policy was now greatly reinforced by a rigorously non-discriminatory administration. This philosophy, together with the refugee situation, rapidly increased the level and ratio of Asian immigration. In 1976/77 only 15 per cent of immigrants were from Asia; by 1980/81 it was up to 24 per cent, and by 1983/84 it was 38 per cent, helped by the first official influx of Indo-Chinese refugees. Immigration Department resources were switched to the Asia-Pacific region.

Menadue also became exercised by the question of the so-called 'illegals', who were, he maintained, not being treated in an even-handed fashion: 'Illegals were people staying in Australia without proper papers'. The boat people constituted a minuscule proportion of these so-called 'queue-jumpers'. In reality most 'illegals' in Australia were British tourists, who came legally and then stayed illegally after their entry permits expired. As Menadue put it, 'The assumption was that if you were white you were probably legal'. There was no simple solution to this problem even though it dominated public opinion and policy. At the same time the policy was rigorously applied to bogus immigrants and such were sent back to Taiwan and Hong Kong; and in 1981 a Romanian soccer player seeking asylum was also dispatched from Australia. Such rigor was prompted by the understanding of the minister and his public servant that

> an important reason why Australians supported
> immigration was confidence that the Australian
> government controlled the program. If the
> Australian community, then or now, believed that
> there was no real control at our borders, that people
> entered and stayed illegally, there would be a
> serious loss of confidence in the program. There is a
> harshness about a strong enforcement policy, but I
> felt that a liberal policy had to be firmly enforced.[19]

Menadue favoured substantial population growth for Australia, a target closer to 50 million than 18 million, and he became disenchanted with the apparent timidity of the governments of the 1980s. But his insistence on the equal treatment of all immigrants was the source of much wider dispute.

Towards the end of the 1980s the immigration debate became increasingly divisive. Menadue recalled the idea of 'the Asian priority', which eventually met its demise in 1988 when John Howard, then leader of the Opposition, attacked the immigration program. According to Menadue 'It was a subliminal call to revert to the discrimination and anti-Asian immigration of the past. He [Howard] spoke in code of the need to slow down migration and to alter the migration mix to preserve social cohesion'. This was a dramatic moment within the Liberal Party: Philip Ruddock, in response to a motion about racism, resigned as shadow minister and Macphee crossed the floor to vote with the Labor government.[20] By then the question of Asian immigration had become inflammable in Australian politics. The origins of the fiery debate were located in the last days of White Australia and in the reverberations of the war in Vietnam.

Asian immigration

The first real test of the removal of White Australia came at an awkward time: in the early 1980s Australia had entered a period of recession in which all immigration was under a cloud; and the intake of large numbers of Asians began in the moment of crisis at the end of the Vietnam War. The region was inundated with the human wreckage of the conflict and this found its expression in the refugee crisis.[21] Various dangers associated with open access to Australia were publicised, including the sordid traffic in refugees in which the Vietnamese government seemed to be complicit. As Paul Kelly remarked, the 'nation faced the consequences of abolition of White Australia, an event that had taken place less than two decades earlier'. The mass arrival of Asian refugees soon began to 'transform the social and ethnic nature of whole suburbs in Sydney and Melbourne'.[22]

The Australian government had been unprepared when the first boat loads of refugees appeared in April 1976; by late 1977 about 2000 refugees from a total of 5000 had arrived by boat and there was evidence of a rising traffic in immigrants. Lee Kuan Yew, always ready to provoke, mocked Australia's mean-spirited and hysterical response, which he said was a true measure of the legacy of racism in Australia. Australia was urged to be part of the cooperative effort to solve the refugee crisis and take its fair share. Eventually Australia girded itself to receive a substantial number of refugees, and by 1985 tens of thousands had been accepted from Indo-China for permanent settlement. This, on a per capita basis, substantially outranked most, if not all, other countries. Moreover the Indo-Chinese refugees inevitably constituted a growing proportion of the intake because total Australian immigration was diminishing in these years. This concentrated the entire question of Asian immigration in the minds of the Australian public.

To begin with, the refugee policy attracted bipartisan support. Within the subsequent public debate there quickly emerged a controversy about the definition of 'refugee', which had never been an issue with European refugees (apart from allegations of fascist contamination). The 'boat people' were no more than a small fraction of total immigration yet monopolised anxiety in Australia, which continued over the following two decades. They were always perceived as a direct challenge to the almost sacred principle that Australia would control its population intakes. The boat people were represented as an anarchic and sinister threat to Australian security, a fear enhanced by the residual alarm relating to racial assimilation. Meanwhile 150000 Vietnamese arrived in Australia between 1975 and the early 1980s. By the late 1980s Asia had replaced the United Kingdom and Europe as the main source of immigrants and was the fastest growing part of the immigrant population.

The Asian immigrants arrived at a more difficult time in the economy than had the earlier European immigrants. They too found themselves in camps in the suburbs, and were generally regarded as homogeneously 'Asian' despite many diverse origins and divisions among them, especially between the ethnic Chinese and the rest. Many had few if any skills and little English language. Where they obtained employment they were in low-skill jobs, especially the women. The experiences of the Vietnamese, en route and then within the receiving country, were more dramatic and disturbing than any since the 1950s and were subsequently documented in powerful detail.[23]

Among the tens of thousands of refugees in South-East Asia at the end of the war were the two Tran brothers from South Vietnam. Their lives were overturned after the communist victory in April 1975: their father was taken off to re-education camps; the family's land was confiscated, their savings eliminated in the currency chaos that followed. Aged 15 and 11, the brothers worked frenetically to support their devastated family; the elder brother became involved in political resistance, which landed him in prison. On his release he escaped first to Thailand and then to Malaysia, whence he was accepted as a refugee to Perth and Melbourne. He had been as flotsam in the vast sea of refugees, passing through hostels and migrant services. Against the odds he reunited with his brother and began to find the basis on which to reconstruct his life out of the total chaos from which he had escaped. As his oral biographer put it:

Ten years of transition have seen Huong metamorphose from a boy distraught at the loss of his family to the man who completely provides for them. By the late 1980s he was sending substantial remittances home from Melbourne and nurtured the belief that Vietnam would soon rise against its communist masters and allow him to return.[24]

In the host society there were clear signs of apprehension and growing resistance to the idea of substantial Asian immigration. The case was most dramatically voiced by the historian Geoffrey Blainey, who persuaded many fellow Australians that the country was losing control over its own destiny. This alarum was delivered out of the blue in a speech made by Blainey at a Rotary Club in Warrnambool in early 1984. Blainey was no extremist, at least at this stage: he had supported the end of White Australia and extolled the contribution of immigrants to modern Australia. He said that Australia's story was 'one of the most successful migrations in the history of the world', precisely because it had absorbed so many aliens.[25] But he lamented the loss of the Australian/British identity in the flood of unassimilated immigrants. Blainey wanted to preserve British Australia, which he believed was under threat from excessive Asian immigration. He believed that the government had lost touch with public opinion, especially at a time of rising unemployment (which had reached a postwar peak of 9.8 per cent in 1983). He said that the Vietnamese and other South-East Asian immigrants were falling into dependency and living on the taxpayer, through no fault of their own: 'The present [policy] is arrogant and insensitive to a large section of the Australian population', he declared.[26]

Looking over the apparent creation of ghettos of Asian immigrants in certain poor locations in Australia's cities, Blainey argued that the new immigrants were putting too much strain on the poor parts of society. Many years before, the sociologist Jean Martin had analysed systematically the difficulties encountered by recently arrived European immigrants in the community at large. They were faced with basic disadvantages; often they were from peasant backgrounds and experienced mounting family problems on arrival in urban Australia. They needed special community services and a sensitive understanding of the cultural and social adjustments forced on them in the new society.[27] The Vietnamese were not categorically different when Blainey made his impassioned speech in 1984. He claimed that Asian immigrants were creating congestion, depressing house prices and even endangering public health in the suburbs. As the debate became more heated Blainey, a polemicist by nature, began using stronger language. He particularly conjured up ominous portents of racial conflict (Manning Clark, another historian, had also predicted political violence in 1975). Blainey spoke of the dangers of ethnic enclaves causing deep resentment. It was easy to extrapolate his influential views to the notion that Australia was being threatened by 'Asianisation', though Blainey denied that he said this. Soon, however, he was warning of the danger of race riots, and the shadow minister for immigration and ethnic affairs called for a review of immigration. Blainey drew attention to the virtues of the Old Australia, which he thought was being endangered by an elitist government out of touch with the people of Australia. Meanwhile Phillip Adams scornfully satirised prewar Australia as 'the most remote, ethnocentric, inward-looking and changeless society on earth'.[28]

Blainey's language sharpened and he began to speak of a 'myriad of small things' that contributed to growing resentment.[29] Though he claimed to support Asian immigration he talked of Asians as invading the suburbs – which, according to a Sydney suburban resident, had become the front line, with 'pavements now spotted with phlegm and spit' and the skies 'filled with greasy smoke and the smell of goat's meat', and Old Australians being frightened to say what they think. Despite his denials, Blainey had obviously reintroduced race into the politics of immigration. He said 'He did not propose exclusion on grounds of race but, rather he was concerned with the incorporation of immigrants into the host society'.[30] He now claimed that Asians were being given favour in the selection of immigrants and in August 1984 advocated a ceiling be placed on Asian immigration, 'placed openly and honestly'.[31] Blainey said he did not believe a slow Asian takeover of Australia was inevitable; 'we can control our destiny'. An Asian Australia was not the alternative to White Australia. And 'at present the Government is shunning a vital section of public opinion'. Asian immigration should be much slower. Otherwise the nation was adopting a 'a surrender Australia' stance and the entire capitulation was driven by misplaced guilt.[32] According to one commentator, Blainey lit ' a fuse which burned with spasmodic fury during the eighties'.

Blainey's views showed no mellowing and he began to question the very bases of multicultural policy. He wanted to speak for 'the battlers', the 'everyday Australians', and declared that ' It's easy for me in my secure job to say I welcome Asian immigrations ... I do welcome them, but they do not compete with me for work and they do not alter the way of life where I live'.[33] In highly charged language, reminiscent of the inflammatory words of Enoch Powell in United Kingdom in the 1960s, Blainey argued that Australia had become too fearful of international opinion to the neglect of ordinary Australians whose anxieties were being ignored. The government had shunned public opinion; there was now a danger that Australia would replicate the racial conflicts common in the United States and South Africa. Australia was accepting too many immigrants and too many refugees and the tolerance of ordinary Australians was being stretched to an impossible degree. Blainey suffered considerable vilification for his views and debate lasted through most of 1984.[34]

Blainey's intervention was not completely out of tune with broad attitudes even within the Labor government, part of which was seriously uncomfortable with the scale and disarray of the refugee intakes. An official of the Immigration Department had told Blainey that 'increasing Asianisation was inevitable', and it was predicted that by 2000, 4 per cent of Australia's population would be Asian. Nevertheless, for the moment the refugee policy was retained on its bipartisan foundations, the policy inherited from Fraser which had welcomed refugees from South-East Asia. This, of course, was totally at odds with Blainey's position which, if taken into effect, would have entailed a reactivation of discrimination on a racial basis in the immigration program. Hawke talked about 'enmeshing' Australia with Asia, while Blainey's arguments were about social stabil-

Professor Geoffrey Blainey in the 1980s, caught by Rennie Ellis.
© Rennie Ellis, *National Library of Australia, vn4083655*

ity. His opponents said it was all exaggerated, but the rift had been opened wide.

Public reaction to the refugees, and the ensuing debate, undoubtedly rattled the Labor government and its ministers became much alarmed. The old bipartisan policy was under siege and there were obvious electoral gains in the offing for someone prepared to break ranks. This was heightened by Blainey's claim that immigration policy was being conducted by government in 'a secret room', driven by an elite without regard for the feeling of 'the Australian people'.

In opposition to Blainey's claims, it was pointed out by Shergold that the total intake of immigrants had actually been reduced since the start of the recession; moreover all applicants were sorted by the same criteria, and a much higher proportion of British and Irish applicants were successful than those from Asia. Asians indeed would account for only 4 per cent of the Australian population in the new century: 'They made up some small enclaves, as earlier groups of migrants had done in the past, but were just as likely to dissipate. Recent public opinion polls revealed no greater antagonism than before'.[35] Blainey was simply tapping the inarticulate anxiety of the community at large, concerned at the apparently uncontrolled and unsanctioned shift in the character of the nation.[36]

To the national identity question Blainey seemed to be reactivating the race issue. Andrew Peacock was already warning that 'the size and composition of the immigrant intake should not jeopardize social cohesiveness and harmony'. This remained a mild flirtation with racial policies and the Liberals kept pulling back, reflecting the fact that 'the majority sentiment within the Liberal Party [was] for bipartisanship on a non-discriminatory policy'. But Blainey had certainly touched 'a nerve-centre of discontent'.[37]

The impact of the debate seemed to be cumulative though it was not until 1988 that the traditional political consensus began to break up. In Opposition the shadow leader, John Howard, gained temporary political leverage by promising to reduce Asian immigration and abandon multiculturalism. Howard asserted that multiculturalism was turning Australia into a 'cluster of tribes' and he specifically argued that the Asian influx should be reduced in order to preserve social cohesion. This was regarded as a severe break with accepted principles and caused a split in his own party when, as we have seen, four senior Liberals crossed the floor against Howard, who seemed at the time to misjudge the issue.[38]

Australia had kept company with Canada and the United States as countries which accepted significant numbers of refugees over a long period for permanent settlement. All three countries faced political repercussions and implemented new legislation at the end of the 1970s, followed by 'great immigration debates' in the 1980s. Canada won a fine reputation for its generosity towards refugees but when, in July 1987, 174 Sikhs landed on a secluded beach near Charlesville, Nova Scotia, there was a national furore.[39] Each of the countries continued to agonise over the obligations and costs of refugees and informal immigration into the next century. Australia, despite its island status and distance from most sources, was now drawn into the global quandary regarding not only refugees but many other sorts of migrants from Third World conditions.

The 1988 perspective

Prime Minister Hawke was keenly aware of this corrosive dissension and attempted to identify a new sense of direction on the migrant issue when, in 1988, he commissioned a Committee to Advise on Australia's Immigration Policies with the sinologist, Stephen Fitz-Gerald, as chair. Recession, unemployment and a collapse of terms of trade in the late 1980s had set the context for a much greater scrutiny of immigration as a national issue. The FitzGerald Committee recommended that immigration should be geared to long-term economic goals, and particularly measured by the net benefits expected to accrue to the nation as a whole. It recommended a steady increase in immigration, to 150000 per annum, but now with more emphasis on skills and education. The committee also advised new selection criteria which gave priority to economic benefits rather than family reunion. The policy, as it emerged, still reflected Hawke's commitment to the ethnic community, but was openly cautious about the nation's capacity to receive immigrants, and the administrative and legislative processes were strengthened. But behind the apparently cool rationalism of the committee's recommendations was a rising apprehension about social cohesion, an issue which had been dormant throughout most of the previous four decades, characterised by a much expanded and highly diversified immigration. It also recommended the creation of a 'systematic and well-resourced independent research' Bureau, which indeed began its work in May 1989.

The FitzGerald Committee was set up by the Hawke government and designed to clarify the economic and demographic issues surrounding immigration and to reassure the nation about the place of ethnicity in Australia. It was keen to re-establish a community of interest and the principle of non-discrimination. Thus it noted that the Asian-born population would be about 7 per cent by 2025 if such immigration continued and it acknowledged that immigration almost always caused transitional concentrations. But it noted also that there had been no race riots in Australia and that it possessed a successful story of highly diversified immigration. The committee suggested that previous governments had been precipitate both in the ending of the old policy of assimilation and the imposition of the new policy of multiculturalism. It recommended that the ideal of becoming 'Australian' should now be given greater centrality. The FitzGerald Report heralded a more guarded approach to immigration and pushed for a greater commitment to Australia over multiculturalism.

The remarkably independent FitzGerald Committee threaded its way between the pressures of rising nationalism, the needs of the government and the inclinations of the Department of Immigration, and was not nervous of offending the ethnic communities. It spoke in the ambiguous terms of its day, expressing caution over the levels of immigration on both economic and social grounds. Most controversially, for the times, it expressed doubts about the wisdom of multiculturalism when Australia was uncertain whether it could cope with more immigrants and more diversified immigration. In the outcome, capturing the mood of the day, the committee argued for a more careful expansion of immigration but emphasised the need for national solidarity as opposed to ethnic diversity. It suggested that family reunion was not the most efficient method of expanding immigration numbers. Its anticipations of future population growth were somewhat vague, reaching towards the higher range (that is, from 30 to 50 million), which was out of tune with the rising chorus of environmental pessimists. One committee member, the Czech-born economist Helen Hughes, calculated that Australia would need to take in 125 000 immigrants a year to reach a population of 26 million by 2030; to reach 35 million it would require 280 000 per annum and for 50 million it needed 540 000, which was beyond any serious contemplation.[40]

The FitzGerald Committee Report was a statement of the national interest and tried to locate a consensus in which immigration would be defused as a divisive issue by establishing clearer targets which would attract public support. The committee favoured a relatively high overall migrant intake of 150 000 per annum and attempted to place the whole question in the middle ground of public opinion. It sought to balance three national objectives, economic, humanitarian and compassionate, which would then be connected with general immigration, refugee intakes and family reunion. It had blazoned its pride in the achievement of Australia to cope with diversity of immigrants; it was 'a cause for self-congratulation', it said. But it also recognised that the 'voice of opposition to multiculturalism [had] to be taken seriously'[41] and that the question of 'Australian identity' was a central consideration.

If the purpose of the FitzGerald Committee had been to return Australia to a national unanimity, it had the opposite effect. Its proposal to expand immigration numbers was soon abandoned in favour of very cautious growth. The ethnic communities were suspicious that the committee had sacrificed multiculturalism to economic considerations; it seemed to veer towards old-fashioned assimilationism. Another critic believed the recommendations were too far oriented towards business priorities and, indeed, one of the members thought that Asian immigration would be most likely to provide the entrepreneurial and competitive types needed to 'jolt a sleepy, union regulation-bound economy out of its lethargy'.[42]

The committee also gave prominence to the matter of 'Australian identity', thereby chiming in with, and encouraging, current pre-occupations at the time of the Bicentennial. FitzGerald may have underestimated the strength of feeling about Asian immigration and the strength of the European elements who felt undermined by the report and did not want Asian immigration to be favoured. In effect the FitzGerald Report stirred up passions not anticipated by the Hawke government, which swiftly distanced itself from the findings. The reaction to the report, on the other side, persuaded some Liberals to reconsider the political potential of the immigration issue in electoral terms and to chance their arm with anti-immigration ideas.[43]

The FitzGerald Report therefore yielded considerable fuel to the Opposition since it provided a comprehensive critique of current policy. It included a repudiation of the ethnic lobby and argued that community support for immigration had faltered and that some new national concept of immigration was required which entailed a new rationale and justification. The report certainly reaffirmed non-discrimination; but it also recommended that the immigration program should be returned to the middle path, which gave emphasis to Australia's own needs and was decidedly not driven by multiculturalism. The committee pointed out that 43 per cent of immigrants had chosen not to take citizenship and said that 'It is the Australian identity that matters most in Australia. And if the government will affirm that strongly, multiculturalism might seem less divisive or threatening'. It was by implication severely critical of the government and left Hawke displeased and the Opposition divided as how best to make political capital.

The FitzGerald Committee was meant to put the cat back in the bag; that is, the cat that had been released by Blainey's outburst in 1984. The outcome mocked these intentions. The public debate was now revived and the polls showed that two-thirds of Australians favoured reduced immigration and especially a reduction of Asian immigration; and a majority was opposed to multiculturalism. The question of national identity began to emerge as a central issue. It also seemed to expose 'the clear cleavage' in the community – based on education. People with higher education favoured Asian immigration, and vice versa'.[44] This was rich soil for political opportunism and the Report coincided with a broader stocktaking at the time of the Bicentennial in 1988.

Political scientists, drawing upon opinion polls, equally identified shifting currents in social attitudes at large which related especially to national identity and ethnicity. The broad context was one in which 4 million new settlers had reached Australia since the war, less than half of them British. Until the 1970s the primary public question was how the immigrants should adjust to Australian conditions, symbolised by the Good Neighbour movement created in the 1950s. Changing attitudes were symbolised by the decision in 1958 to give consideration to the immigration of 'well-qualified people wishing to settle in Australia', which was a 'euphemism for non-whites' and, in retrospect, regarded as a preliminary breach in the old principle of racial discrimination.[45]

In 1968 the sociologist Jerzy Zubrzycki had called for modest commitment to cultural diversity through the maintenance of immigrant languages and the development of studies in European culture. Immediately there were critics who believed that such 'multiculturalism' might jeopardise consensus and legitimacy in Australia society at large. Frank Knopfelmacher argued that it could lead to ethnic turbulence and civil strife, and break up 'the Anglomorph character of Australia'. The term 'multiculturalism' had already been in common usage in Canada from October 1971; it was established in principle by the Galbally Report in 1978 and sustained as bipartisan policy until the mid 1980s.[46] But, in the 1983 election the issue of Asian immigration emerged, and was kept bubbling thereafter. Blainey's assertion that the government had been moving too far ahead of public opinion seemed to be confirmed by the FitzGerald Report and by the opinion polls which demonstrated a general conservatism.

Latin-American recruits: Chilean-Australians welcome new Chileans to the Westbridge Migrant Centre in Sydney, 1987. *From Bureau of Immigration Research*, Immigration in Focus 1946–1990: A Photographic Archive, *1990*

The debate slewed into broad questions of national identity and the essential character and composition of Australia – and its compatibility with alien newcomers. A school of thinking claimed that current immigration threatened Australians' sense of themselves.[47] Moreover by the late 1980s vociferous groups emerged to advocate the necessity of limiting Australia's population growth, which revived the debate about the population limits of Australia.[48] All this debate seemed to prepare the way for the disjunction inaugurated by John Howard in 1988 when he broke the bipartisan approach by questioning the community's ability to absorb Asian immigration.

In essence he revived the spectre of racial discrimination and questioned the entire concept of multiculturalism, and now sought to curb Asian immigration. At the time he garnered little support and his initiative seemed to backfire and damage his political career.[49]

Prime Minster Hawke's recollections of immigration policy in the 1980s skirted around the divisions in his own ranks. He was inordinately proud of Australia's immigration history but was particular to assert unambiguously that 'It is the sovereign right of the Australian government to determine the size and composition of our immigration program'.[50] Looking back on his record Hawke claimed that 'we saw our future as inextricably linked' with that of Asia. Out of 143 000 settler arrivals in 1987/88, one-third were Asians – and more if Lebanon, Cyprus, Turkey and Israel were included. He claimed also that Asia now recognised that Australia had totally repudiated racial discrimination.[51] He took credit for the radical realignment of Australia towards Asia, which he had intended as a turning point in the nation's evolution. Hawke continued the strong immigration policy of his predecessors and believed that northeast Asia would be the ascendant force in the coming years.[52] In his mood of self-congratulation, Hawke asserted that his government had balanced economic reform and social progress, and claimed that without it there would have been retrogression – indeed he had always been a believer in the efficacy of high immigration.[53] He testified to the fact that the decision regarding 30 000 Chinese students at the time of the Tiananmen Square massacre was as much driven by sentiment as calculation.

The rift

In retrospect, it is clear that the end of White Australia eventually stirred up considerable tensions in the public mind and changed the agenda of politics. While it was common to castigate Blainey and Howard (and later Pauline Hanson) for agitating racial demons in the population, it is also clear that the Labor Party itself was nervous of the actual consequences of administering the non-discriminatory policy when large numbers of Asian migrants were entering the country. The retrospective gloss which Hawke placed on the narrative was not consistent with the internal evidence of the ALP in these years. Contemporary accounts of Labor's reaction to the refugee phenomenon were not so calm. Thus when Whitlam as prime minister at the end of the Vietnam War responded to a request for the admission of 'certain categories of refugees', he reportedly told his colleagues Willesee and Cameron, in private, that he was 'not having hundreds of fucking Vietnamese Balts coming into this country with their religious and political hatreds against us!' His subsequent public utterances, indeed welcoming 3000 refugees, indicated a change of mind. In similar vein, Hawke later regarded some Cambodian boat people as queue jumpers and threats to the immigration policy. 'Let no one think we are going to stand idly by and allow others, by their autonomous action which reflects perhaps some unhappiness with the circumstances in which they find themselves in their own country ... to determine our immigration policy', he declared. Hawke's government indeed began the system of mandatory, indefinite incarceration of boat people, without trial, in the early 1990s. That this flouted all international conventions was, apparently, a secondary matter.[54]

11 Whither immigrant Australia?

Migrant Australia in the 1990s

Since its colonial beginnings Australia has always adjusted its immigration levels to meet the state of the labour market. Whenever the economy ran into recession the flow of immigrants was stemmed and even reversed. Sometimes it seemed that immigration would never again revive, and it was not difficult to reach this conclusion in the 1990s. Several negative factors, including the fluctuating economy, created a sense of finality. The traditional stream of settler migration, not only those from Britain but also from Europe, seemed to be in terminal decline. The rising chorus of environmentalists' rhetoric, with increasing volume and conviction, asserted that Australia had now reached the limits of its population capacity. They said that Australia was already overstocked with people: there was no place for further immigration.

More certainly, Australia was no longer guided by a grand plan of immigration which had united the nation since 1947. Immigration was now a matter of management, of responding to the immediate needs of the economy and Australia's humanitarian obligations. Both issues were now politically charged for the electorate and therefore also for the managers of migration. Moreover the inflows of migrants had become less predictable, in part because Australia was no longer financing immigration, except for its refugees. It now relied on quotas to determine levels of immigration, but there were many other inflows of people whose status and intentions were unpredictable. The impact of succeeding international crises was brought to Australia by its commitment to humanitarian relief obligations. These episodes punctuated the story of immigration and created their own tensions for each successive government.[1]

By the 1990s many of the earlier immigrants had emerged prominently in Australian society and sometimes they were given special publicity to set beside the adverse reaction to immigrants in the narrowed economy of the early 1990s. Some of Australia's wealthiest and most outspoken figures were immigrants, a few of them products of the most recent intakes of migrants. An arbitrary index of success was the list called 'The Rich 200 in Australia'. In 1991 it showed that one in three were immigrants, which suggested disproportionate ambition and success compared with the home-grown population. Twenty-seven of them had come from Eastern Europe, many of them previously refugees, for example Chaim Liberman and his brother Jack, who had spent time in the Soviet gulag.[2]

Richard Pratt, the Polish-born head of Visy Industries, was one of six billionaires listed. He recollected, 'I came here as a child aged three, literally tucked under my mother's arm as she fled the gathering storm in Europe' before the Second World War. Pratt believed that Australia's interests were not being well served by the current anti-immigration climate: he pointed out that the United States celebrated its immigrants and that half of the engineers in California's Silicon Valley were immigrants. Henry Korngold was another great Australian plutocrat, the creator of Capital Carpets, who had served in the Polish army before it was crushed by the

Germans; he had fled first to Lithuania and then into Russia, on to Vladivostok and then took a boat to Japan at Tsuruga. He was lucky to get to Australia. Of Jewish roots, Korngold was a supreme individualist who had little affection for Europe and was critical of those who stayed in their own communities after arrival in Australia. Similarly, Ervin Graf was born in Hungary and became a refugee after 1945: he too managed to get to Australia. He recollected, 'I told them I was a bricklayer, although I had never laid a brick in my life ... I was young, ambitious, and willing to work – seven days a week, 52 weeks a year ... for the first six and a half years I was here'. He succeeded, and later ascended into great wealth as the owner of Stockland Company.

The immigrant success stories of the 1990s now included some of the former 'boat people' who had made spectacular progress, and their stories rivalled even those of the survivors of Hitler's death camps and purges. For instance, Huy Truong had founded his own Internet company employing 80 people: his family had a long story of migration, a grandfather having left China at the turn of the century, later acquiring a Vietnamese family name. Truong's own father had been close to death in the war, his son recalling an incident in which he had an AK-47 at his head. The families fled Vietnam and were 2 months at sea in a stinking fishing boat, followed by 4 months in a refugee camp near Jakarta. In October 1978 he was officially admitted to Australia with his two sisters and parents. They had no English and went to a hostel at Nunawading in Melbourne. In the year 2000 they had four children with degrees and Huy Truong had acquired an MBA from Harvard. Australia was accommodating itself to these people and their cohorts; as always, each new phase was a test of its toleration and the resolution of the migrants.

In 1966 there had been about 2500 Turkish-born people recorded in the Australian census and only a minority of them were Muslim. Their numbers increased in the 1970s as a result of bilateral agreements between Turkey and Australia (starting in 1967). By 1996 they numbered 28 869. They settled mainly in Melbourne,

The most positive version of the new Australian future, 1995. *Fairfax Group Ltd*

were now predominantly Muslim and faced 'many barriers and challenges' in Australia.[3]

One of them was Mustafa, who had left difficult economic conditions in Izmir where he had sold fruit and vegetables from a push cart. With his reluctant wife and their young sons, they emigrated in the late 1960s, extremely suspicious of the food supplied by Qantas on the flight from Ankara to Melbourne. Typically they struggled to find accommodation, to learn English, both eventually finding factory employment. They began to save and raised a mortgage, discovered a few fellow Muslims and ensured their sons were fully educated. After 7 years they were prosperous and their relatives were joining them from Turkey. Revisiting their homeland they were appalled by its mixture of poverty and political turmoil. In Melbourne they arranged marriages for their children and set up several small businesses. They invested most of their energies in creating their own economic security, especially by way of education; at the same time they reinforced the rigour of their religious faith which, they believed, was more feasible in Australia than in secularising Turkey. In effect, they adjusted to Australia which itself adjusted to their differences, guardedly on both sides. As Mustafa said, 'Although I have rarely visited Australians in their homes, I like them and I have not been subjected to bad behaviour by them'.[4]

By 2008 there were more than 350 000 Muslims in Australia, originating from many different countries and increasingly home grown and representing close to 2 per cent of the population.[5] Muslims as migrants, in Australia, as elsewhere, encountered greater tensions in the new century: not only were they culturally more distant from the host society than most other migrants, they also found it difficult to avoid association with international extremism from which many were specifically escaping.

Parametric shifts and economists' calculations

Immigration in the 1990s was tightly controlled, constrained by the lacklustre performance of the economy and the transition of political power from the ALP to the Liberals in 1996. A great boom had begun in 1985, reaching its peak in 1989 when, it was claimed, 'Never before in Australian history had so much money been channelled by so many people incompetent to lend into the hands of so many people incompetent to manage it'.[6] Credit grew at 15 per cent per annum, concentrated in the corporate sector and associated with a frenetic building boom and a growth in spending power leading to a massive increase of imports. Rising interest rates on home loans (up to 18 per cent) were accompanied by a worrying inflation rate. The subsequent recession of 1990, presided over by Paul Keating, was a local variant on the much larger international deterioration. It was no more severe than in the rest of the OECD countries but was a shocking turnabout for Australians. The inflation rate fell to 2 per cent and by 1992 recovery was sighted, leading to a very long non-inflationary economic expansion through into the next century during which time Australia experienced a higher growth rate than many of the OECD countries. It was punctuated by the Asian crises of 1997 and 1998, which Australia easily weathered, guided firmly by a more independent Central Bank.[7]

For much of the 1990s the prevailing political psychology was cautious and was reflected in the migrant program, which gauged the level of confidence of the government in the idea of economic and social expansion. The program was set at 126 000 in 1990, reduced to 110 000 in 1991 and then to 80 000 in 1992. Within these targets the government made minor concessions; for instance, entrants from Sri Lanka, Iraq and Kuwait were given extension of stays in 1990, and student entry arrangements were eased to assist the export education industry (a growing factor in the national economy). Special assistance visas were given to 4000 applicants from the former USSR, Yugoslavia, Croatia, East Timor and Lebanon. In 1996 the migrant program was further reduced from 82 500 to 74 000 (excluding refugees) and continued at relatively low levels into the new century.

But these data masked important ongoing changes: thus the number of short-term stayers was increasing and many temporary visitors converted informally to permanency. It became increasingly difficult to distinguish bona fide visitors from authentic migrants. The rapid growth of business and tourist traffic, together with people on working holidays, was phenomenal and soon outstripped actual identifiable migrant movements. By 1995 New Zealand-born migrants had become the largest category of 'settler' arrivals, now greater than British-born entrants. Business skills entry applications increased greatly.

Meanwhile the government adjusted its regulations each year, mostly to dissuade certain sorts of migrants – notably 'boat people' and those likely to become dependent on the State. In 1997 the State determined that 2 years must elapse before social security income could be paid. Yet the humanitarian refugee intakes continued to be honoured. And the ratios of skilled to humanitarian intakes were adjusted, while considerable effort was invested in reducing the number of unauthorised 'boat arrivals'. At the same time, in 1999, 'permanent departures' were at their highest level since 1973/74. Mobility of all sorts was ratchetted upwards in many different ways.

Evidently migration had become more complicated, more confusing and increasingly political, all at the same time. The word on everyone's lips was 'globalisation'; the demographer Graeme Hugo declared that the world immigration situation of the 1990s was 'a totally new one', and he gave emphasis to three burgeoning categories in the Australian story, viz. return migration, second generation migration, and the emigration of Australian-born people. Indeed in the 1990s the gap between long-term arrivals and departures was decisively narrowed; there was an overall net loss of Australian-born, usually young professional people leaving Australia.[8] Hugo identified what he termed 'parametric shifts' in the course of recent Australian immigration: these comprised, first, the ending of 'White Australia'; second, the context of relatively high unemployment levels; third, the introduction of skill tests; fourth, the failure of reunion and special lobbying groups; fifth, the substitution of multiculturalism for assimilationism; and, finally, the growth of refugee intakes and business immigration.[9]

Divining the direction and consequences of immigration had become powerfully political issues which no amount of analysis was able to resolve, least of all by social scientists. One of the first acts of the newly elected Liberal government was to abolish the Bureau of Immigration, Population and Multicultural Research in 1996, an institution which was meant to supply independent and 'high quality research work' for the nation at large. This was a symbolic act and a clear gesture against the idea of expert opinion leading and informing Australia's immigration policy. Nevertheless most social scientists seemed to agree that immigration had not caused any net increase in the unemployment rate in Australia.[10] But there was an accumulation of evidence that some migrant groups had very high rates of unemployment and others very low. Economists did complicated sums to show that immigration affected both the demand and supply sides of the public purse. More significantly it was clear that for many immigrants the U-shaped curve applied as it had done for centuries, i.e. recently arrived immigrants were rarely able to rise in the host society until they had time to find their feet, which depended on many circumstances including the prevailing levels of employment.[11] They were at the bottom of the heap when they arrived. Success required time and adjustment and in the interim they were easy targets of manifold criticism from their adversaries. A journalist noted that

> A family that arranges to be smuggled out of
> depressed and oppressed Iraq, with the courage,
> skill and energy to get half way across the world, is
> unlikely to be on welfare for long. The likelihood
> is that the country welcoming such a family will
> be rewarded. The history of the past 55 years is
> evidence of that.[12]

There were other questions at issue. Humanitarian immigration was accepted as a national priority, but it had to be explained to the Australian public that it was controlled and consistent with social and economic conditions, all of which were in question throughout the 1990s. The spectacle of illegal immigrants arriving by boat in obviously uncontrolled ways alarmed the population at large and jeopardised the humanitarian project to which the nation subscribed. Nor was the case for their free entry made in any convincing way which demonstrated clear benefits to Australia.

Policy became harder nosed – based on the assumption that some immigrants were more valuable than others and that their selection should be fully coordinated. Added to the debate were two other issues which affected attitudes to immigration, though from opposite directions. One was the environmentalists' claim that Australia's population was already large enough; the other was the realisation that a static population would become an ageing population.[13]

The new politics of immigration

The immigration controversy swirled through the Australian press and reverberated within the inner recesses of government. The inside story later seeped into political memoirs, which made it abundantly clear that the government was increasingly jittery about the immigration issue. Opposition spokesmen discovered new opportunities for electoral gain.

The last years of the Hawke government were electorally precarious. At the time of the Tiananmen Square massacre (1989) the prime minister had responded with an immediate and large-hearted gesture to Chinese students in Australia, who were offered asylum on their graduation. His immigration minister, Gerry Hand, was extremely doubtful about the wisdom of this pledge and tried to rein in the scale of the commitment. Meantime the Opposition became highly critical of refugee policy and their vehemence grew with each further landing of 'boat people' along the northern coasts of Australia. Soon the issue was overwhelmed by the economic recession, described as the worst downturn since the Great Depression. The government felt weak and embattled on the immigration issue; and the Opposition broke ranks over the bipartisan concord which had held since the war.[14] The government made a principled commitment to pay 'benefits to people seeking political asylum in Australia', and this seemed to inflame public opinion against the policy at large. It was part of a general psychology which believed that refugees would become destitute in Australia and create a substantial burden on the taxpayer.[15] This, of course, was a common refrain over 200 years of immigration.

Within the government there were open divisions. Neal Blewett emphasised the uncontained anger expressed by Minister Hand towards the generosity Hawke had pledged to students who, Hand asserted, should not be allowed to stay because they would ultimately produce a million more Chinese immigrants. As for the boat people, they were 'not a pretty mob, mostly gangsters and madams'. The Labor Cabinet was at odds and Treasurer John Dawkins wanted to send all the students home. This suggestion was rejected, primarily because it would have severely negative international consequences. Hand's anger was undiminished, and he believed that refugee immigration was extremely dangerous for the future of the government; and he especially railed against the 'meddling lawyers' whom he regarded as the 'worst kind of human beings'. Blewett himself thought that the benefits available to refugees should be set at a level which avoided destitution but offered no incentive to further arrivals. Hand favoured a policy of locking up all 'illegals'. In May 1992 Hand became tougher still and was empowered to keep the refugees interned for 9 months. Blewett remarked in his diary that

> Immigration remains a disaster area, with hasty
> *ad hoc* expedients cobbled together to stem the tide.
> Hand supported his proposals with his usual blend
> of vivid anecdotes on the wickedness of the boat
> people and their sinister manipulators (Chinese
> tongs this time) and attacks on the self-righteous
> attitude of the churches and the do-gooders.[16]

Much of the Cabinet disputation was connected with the cost of supporting immigrants at a time of budgetary stringency: Hand soon realised that interning refugees on a grand scale would be very expensive indeed. He led the push to reduce immigrant intakes from 110 000 to 80 000 and recrimination mounted that the government was opposed to southern Europeans; others said the policies were anti-Asian; and there was a rising perception that Labor policy was indistinguishable from that of the Liberals. A damaging article in the ethnic newspapers reported that one in four immigrants was still on social security benefits 2 years after arrival. Hand, in late 1992, introduced still more rigorous plans for monitoring 'illegal' immigrants by way of tax file numbers. Blewett's insider story gave the impression of a government utterly perplexed by the immigration issue, and rent with divisions which were never resolved. Senator John Button had pointed out that the shrunken immigration policy was antipathetic to the idea of economic growth, against which argument Treasurer Ralph Willis reminded him of the 900 000 unemployed. The actual impact of immigrants on the economy remained as indeterminate as ever.[17]

The interior story of the subsequent Keating years revealed equal confusion between ideals and realities. Keating's biographer and advisor, Don Watson, recollected that Keating wanted to recast and realign Australia's place in the world. He particularly sought to modify the traditional allegiances to Britain and America and to bring Australia towards much closer ties with Asia. This meant an end to old fears of Asia and movement towards much closer associations with Asian countries. He wanted to stop being 'what Manning Clark called Austral-Britons'. At the same time Keating rhapsodised about multiculturalism and 'the contribution of European and other migrants ... the entrepreneurial spirit, their loyalty, the flesh-and-blood drama of capital accumulation'. When Keating visited Asia he experienced the legacy of the Old Australia, which strengthened his resolve to change Australian's policies. In South Korea, for instance, Watson was bearded by a Korean who asked him why Australia prohibited the entry of Asian migrants. It continued to be foreign affairs department policy not to mention White Australia, but on tours of Asia one found oneself sitting with officials and businessmen who regularly raised it. The middle-aged in Asian countries remember what they were taught at school. Keating answered the questions as directly as he could at each occasion the subject was raised'.[18]

Keating believed that he was orchestrating an 'unprecedented cultural shift' (on, for example, Aboriginal land rights, industrial relations, the idea of an Australian republic, and military cooperation with Indonesia), but the immigration issue remained intractable. His government interned 'illegal immigrants', and Keating was aware of the poor conditions imposed on refugees in the new detention centre at Port Hedland, and insisted that the department speed up the processing of applications. Misunderstandings were rife, and when Keating met the German Chancellor, Helmut Schmidt, he was told that Australia was fortunate compared with Germany with regard to immigrants. Schmidt pointed out that Australia had no neighbours except New Zealand and that while Germany attracted too many undistinguished immigrants from all around it, Australia was 'wisely choosing the cleverest races in Asia – the Chinese and the Vietnamese'.[19]

This was not the view of Graeme Campbell, the maverick ALP representative for Kalgoorlie, who railed against immigration and said that the 'Asianisation of Australia' was a betrayal of the nation. His reaction was described as part of 'the disaffected responding to the ancient call of race and xenophobia, the ethnic idea of the nation which, though dormant for long periods, has coexisted with the political conception since the Australian Commonwealth was born'. It was totally at odds with Keating's vision and represented a continuing current of hostility amid both Liberal and Labor sides of politics in the 1990s.[20]

The political turmoil and apprehension about immigration spilled over into a debate about which side of Australian politics had been responsible for the hardening attitudes in the treatment of refugees. It was generally agreed that Whitlam had been negative and had opposed Asian refugee immigration, concerned not to alienate the semi-xenophobic blue-collar vote or the unions. Paul Kelly's political commentary *The End of Certainty* remarked that: 'Whitlam believed that the Vietnamese would provide the right wing with another influx of rabid anti-Communist recruits to torment another generation of Labor just as the postwar Eastern European immigrants [had become] a constituency for the right wing'. Malcolm Fraser had reversed the policy and accepted more than 50 000 refugees between 1976 and 1982, of whom 2000 came by boat and others were taken from islands off Malaysia where they had been stranded. Cameron Stewart pointed out that it was Labor in late 1991 that first impounded children and set up the internment system. The Hawke government was not faced with boat people crises until 1989, when the first Cambodians arrived. Many of these were suspected of being economic migrants and their arrivals created great alarm even though it was a trickle compared to the Fraser years. In 17 months only 381 arrived – but Minister Gerry Hand announced in 1991 'the establishment of the first detention centre for illegal boat arrivals' at Port Hedland.

Thus the policy had moved from the provision of asylum for prospective refugees towards their automatic detention and the lengthy scrutiny of incoming boat people behind barbed wire. The policy was instituted without division in the Labor government, though the understanding was that the determination of refugee legality would be swift. In reality the detention system kept people penned up for very long periods, creating great controversy in the general community and attracting adverse attention beyond Australia.

Keating maintained the policy even though it was at odds with his pro-Asia stance. The minister, Gerry Hand, continued to be tough and stuck by the rigorous process. While the policy and its administration were highly controversial, Australia's record as an asylum for legal and official refugees was exemplary, especially on international comparisons. As Atchison pointed out, in the years 1975–79 Australia had a record of 'considerable international generosity': Australia was close to the top of the table for refugee resettlement, second only to Canada in the ratio of refugees to population.[21] Thirty years later Australia's generosity settled at lower levels (6000 per annum by 2007).

Migrant behaviour and experience

Immigrants in most societies almost always encounter some form of resistance: rarely are they positively welcome, more often they are treated with indifference or, at worst, hostility and loathing. Australia actively sought immigrants for much of its modern history and sustained one of the highest proportions of immigrants of any modern nation. But Australia's response to its immigrants has varied over time and was certainly less welcoming in periods of high unemployment. The reception and accommodation of immigrants was a recurrent source of contention, especially at the end of the 20th century.

As soon as they arrived most immigrants entered working-class Australia, usually in suburbia. Here they faced communities which retained traditions of an 'old working class communal culture' which often resented change, especially the intrusion of alien newcomers. Local histories sometimes exposed the 'ugly xenophobic side, all too apparent to the new immigrants who endured the locals' taunts of 'Go home to your own country, wog'. This was the finding of a Commonwealth Youth Employment Grant oral history of Richmond, *Copping it Sweet* (1988). Nevertheless the Richmond survey also identified the emergence of a new sense of community among the Vietnamese newcomers.[22] The immigrants, of course, had their own problems, which were mainly invisible – though the status of their health was not easily concealed since they were subjected to compulsory examination before they arrived in Australia. The rates of tuberculosis among the Vietnamese migrants were very high and even after 2 years in Australia they exhibited a rate of 120 per 100 000 compared with less than 3 for the Australian-born.[23]

Australia's generalised dismay about Asian immigration mounted during the recession in the 1990s. The fear of being overwhelmed by Asians, or refugees of any stripe, was widespread and the new Liberal government of 1996 was wary of its electoral consequences. Opponents of immigration, as we have already seen, had been alleging since the 1980s that politicians had conspired by means of a bipartisan conclave to defeat the will of the people at large. Remarkable success stories among the immigrant population did little to disperse such negativity. Each new intake of refugees was greeted with alarm. The Kosovar crisis of 1990 persuaded the government to accept only a hundred or so refugees, and they were subject to strictly limited terms which required their return to Kosovo at the end of hostilities – which, as in Britain, generated further controversy.[24] Similarly the arrival of a few thousand boat people created 'public hysteria' and refuelled the arguments against refugees. Civil disruption and resistance in the detention camps carried all the marks of protest movements.[25] Yet Australia was largely beyond reach of the refugee outflows associated with the turmoil in post-communist Eastern Europe and the conflicts in the Middle East.

Australia's policy to accept a substantial number of Asian immigrants and refugees from many different countries had occurred in a context of rising public debate. One recurrent allegation was that the government and intellectuals at large had suppressed and ignored the true opinions of the majority of the public. Katharine Betts, in her book The *Great Divide* (1999), claimed that 'a cultural gap' separated the business and intellectual elites from the masses, who were misled about the consequences of multiculturalism: 'the elites have an interest in changing society while the masses have an interest in preserving it'. This was a clear echo of current allegations voiced in North America that 'multiculturalism was weakening the solidarity of western societies'. As one of the more forthright spokesmen put it, 'Australia like the USA is fast becoming a conglomerate of warring tribes, not a nation'.[26] Asian immigrants were greater in number than British and Irish in most of the 1990s, and they returned home less. This caused the demographer Charles Price to express concern about excessively rapid changes in the composition of the population which, he pointed out, gave Pauline Hanson et al. too much easy ammunition.[27] Such views fuelled growing opposition to the family reunion programs on the grounds that incoming immigrant parents 'cost the Australian community a great deal of money'. The parent quota was tightened to such an extent that the waiting period for entry was 40 years by 1999.[28] This was a measure of the influence wielded by the increasingly vocal conservative school of thought.

The controversy came to a sharp point, and attracted international attention, when Pauline Hanson, a perfectly ordinary Australian, won a parliamentary seat in Canberra in 1996 and voiced all the fears of the allegedly neglected and alarmed public. She became the populist mouthpiece of the counter reaction to the changes that had happened since the 1970s. Her rhetoric reached a wide public but was not, in the event, matched by overt public demonstration; nevertheless her eruption on the airwaves and in parliament was clearly manifested in the opinion polls and the elections. Her comet-like blaze across the political skies was effective in reinforcing the breakdown of the Australian bilateral consensus on immigration that had prevailed since 1947. The new Howard government did little to combat the impact of Hanson's maiden speech in 1996. Even the conservative commentator Gerard Henderson felt impelled to declare that Australians were not intrinsically racist, and called for political leaders to promote the acceptance of refugees. Hanson's intervention produced angry reactions in leftist circles and James Jupp, doyen of immigration commentators, declared that 'By any standards Australia is one of the most harmonious societies in the world and has had a democracy for 140 years, universal suffrage for a century. Its non-European element in immigration is still well below the United States or Canada'. The opponents of multicultural Australia were, he implied, merely fearmongers of the worst sort.[29]

The refugee question remained high on the national political agenda through into the new millennium. Public attitudes and votes were at stake and some commentators asserted that the heavily politicised opposition to refugees was a recrudescence of White Australia in a new guise. In some ways it was surprising that the issue erupted so vociferously. After all, Australia had resettled almost 600 000 refugees and displaced persons in the previous 50 years and was generally pleased with, and proud of, this achievement. Moreover there was considerable public sympathy for refugees fleeing Chile, Kosovo and East Timor. On the other hand the arrival of an unprecedented number of asylum seekers, especially those in boats, without official sanction aroused collective anxiety, which was not allayed until the government introduced increasingly rigorous methods to control the influx at the end of the 1990s. In general terms Australia exhibited all the symptoms of apprehension and resistance seen in each of the affluent countries of the OECD, which inevitably attracted migrants of all sorts from poor countries. It was not only a matter of defining and regulating 'refugees' and distinguishing them from 'economic migrants'. It was also a question of controlling the inflows and calming public opinion. Control was the critical issue, even though the actual numbers of illegal immigrants were small compared with other, much larger, streams of people entering Australia in no less unregulated form. The political psychology of the debate was inflamed since the fugitives were described as 'illegal migrants' and 'queue jumpers' who were leapfrogging 'genuine refugees'.

The government treated the arrival of various refugee groups, notably the inflow from the conflicts in the region of Iraq, as a national emergency. Immigration Minister Philip Ruddock warned that 'whole villages' in the Middle East were on their way to Australia, and stressed the need to guard against terrorists in each cohort of asylum seekers. It was a late revival of the old Yellow Peril fears.[30] With each succeeding episode, the response of the government became increasingly stringent, its laws strengthened.

Thus 'illegal' refugees were now to be confined in detention centres which were designed not only to 'process' (that is, to determine the legal basis of the refugees' claims for asylum) but also to deter further incursions by such refugees. In 1998/99, 45 per cent of all detainees had been held in detention for more than 3 months. Practical questions of incarcerating such people inevitably increased. Most detainees expected their refugee claim in Australia to be determined immediately their story was heard. Yet many of them possessed little or no checkable identification. Tensions developed in the detention centres, usually located in the most remote and unprepossessing places in Australia, associated with hunger strikes, breakouts and full-scale riots. The sudden influx of boat people at the end of 1999 led to the commissioning of new detention facilities at Woomera in South Australia and elsewhere. Conditions were far from luxurious and led to allegations of harshness and brutality. Australia was finding it increasingly difficult to conform with its international obligations towards refugees, the definition of whom was itself becoming highly contested.

After terrorist atrocities in New York in 2001 and, more directly, in Bali in October 2002, a new dimension was added to official vigilance governing aliens entering Australia; refugees from the Middle East came under even greater scrutiny. New powers of surveillance, apprehension and imprisonment were introduced to safeguard Australia from terrorism. Inevitably these extra precautions overlapped with the general control over immigrants at large and especially over applicants for refugee status, who were subjected to even greater scrutiny and suspicion. Consequently another shadow fell over the system and further tension was created between those who favoured a humanitarian and liberal administration of the immigration system and those who wanted more stringent control. Inevitably resources were diverted away from the reception of immigrants and their future welfare towards their incarceration and control.[31]

The British relationship

Meanwhile the long tradition of British immigration had shrivelled in a general context in which all forms of migration were in flux. Graeme Hugo pointed out that modern immigration has 'gradually become more complex with a movement away from simple demographic and economically driven recruitment of workers and their families to include refugees and humanitarian, family reunion and business elements'. The British immigrant became a lesser player in this new context. As we have seen, British emigration was sustained for 25 years after the Second World War by Australia's extraordinarily generous assisted passages, which were virtually free in the 1960s. But by the 1970s the flow was greatly diminished, and assistance was discontinued in 1983.[32] Irish migration to Australia had long been in decline; thereafter the British figures declined also. In 1993/94 there were only 9500 British immigrants which, in proportional terms, was vastly less in intensity than it had been a hundred years before.

The change in the British connection was marked by a shift towards much larger short-term transfers of people: there were now far more visitors than migrants from Britain. By the early 1990s the flows between Australia and the United Kingdom operated in both directions and in some years the balance was reversed. Over the years from 1947 to 1994 the United Kingdom component of Australian immigration fell from 78 per cent to 14 per cent. New permanent British immigration in the mid 1990s was primarily in the form of family reunion. With diminished immigration, and the ageing factor, it was not surprising that the proportion of the British-born in the Australian population was falling rapidly by the end of the century, partly by the return of British people retiring homewards.[33] At the same time, however, the traffic between the two countries continued to grow, though its balance was reversed. The number of British visitors travelling to Australia in 1999 was 568 900, which was substantially greater than the flow in the opposite direction.[34]

The decline of immigration from Britain was a factor in the changing relationship between Britain and Australia, as was the growth of republican sentiment in Australia. Inevitably both affected the strength of the idea of British Australia. The push for an Australian republic emerged as an issue in the debate about national identity – which was characteristic of the mood of the 1990s, had been 'a thriving industry since the early 1980s'[35] and related to the nature of Australia nationalism. A school of thought, associated particularly with Geoffrey Blainey, was opposed to the dilution of Anglo-Australia and became vociferous about the danger of a hybrid nation and the 'Asianisation of Australia'.[36] The extent to which immigration had increased or diminished inequality and tolerance were great questions within the debate.[37] In the outcome Australia voted against the progression to a republic, a clear manifestation of the conservatism of the times.

The long view

New perspectives on the Australia experience became evident in the 1990s. For instance it was now clear that immigration was no longer the prevailing priority and automatic assumption for Australia's future development. It had been displaced by matters of stability, the sustainable environment and international obligations. Partly, as we have emphasised, this was determined by short-term demands in a less buoyant economic context. But there was a transition – immigration was now a matter of short-term modification, no longer integral to an unquestioned expansion of numbers. Each year produced marginal adjustments, a touch on the tiller, as though immigration would henceforward become a small element in the life of the nation. Immigration, both refugee and normal intakes, were matters of sensitive management with a keen eye to public opinion and diplomacy, rather than a grand design in national life. In the 1950s and 1960s immigration had been widely regarded as economically positive; this was no longer the reigning assumption.

Thus, in the recession year 1995 the stream of traditional economic migrants was no more than 23 000 in a total of 83 000 arrivals in Australia. It seems that more than 60 per cent were accounted
by family categories (and the high proportion of spouse migration
produced great scepticism among critics who thought that many
immigrants' marriages were shams). Since 1947 more than 5 million
immigrants had arrived in Australia, but by 1995 natural increase
had easily overtaken immigration as the main demographic force in
Australia. Immigration had become much more a matter of fulfilling
humanitarian responsibilities than simply following economic imper-
atives. The numbers of refugees changed from year to year and the
government varied the total intakes of immigrants to take account
of these variations. In the 1990s Australia effectively ran two modes
of immigration – the Migration Program and the Humanitarian Program. Immigrants came as family, skilled or humanitarian but the
categories were fluid and even the totals were difficult to measure,
still less their consequences for the community at large.

A rough snapshot of the Australian population at the end of the
old century was offered by the official statistics. The population
had reached 18.94 million, a little short of Calwell's dream. Live
births were in the last year about 250 000, while deaths amounted
to 128 300, yielding a natural increase of 121 700 to which was
added 85 100 by net overseas immigration. Of the overseas-born
living in Australia the top country was still the United Kingdom
with 1 227 000, followed by New Zealanders at 361 000 and Italians
at 244 600. This, of course, was the legacy of the mid century and
Australia was living off its effects. The total overseas-born was 4.48
million and this was 23.6 per cent of the total population, which
kept Australia near the head of immigrants countries. But immigration was at a fairly low ebb in 1999/2000 with only 92 272 permanent arrivals (Oceania most with 26 039, mainly New Zealanders;
only 9949 from the United Kingdom, 4865 from Southern Europe,
6809 from China, 5691 from South Africa and 4631 from India)

and 41 078 permanent departures. Among the permanent arrivals were 19 896 in the 'family' category, together with 32 350 'skilled immigrants' and 7267 'humanitarian' migrants. These figures were dwarfed by the visitors, students, temporary residents and others who totalled 513 879.[38]

At the same time the context of immigration was now much more perplexing. Australia was still one of the three or four countries which had a positive immigration policy. While immigration had dwindled to less that 100 000 per annum there was a vast growth in other sorts of international mobility, so that 2.5 million visitors arrived in Australia, including 77 000 temporary migrants and 51 000 overseas students. The tourist trade was growing mightily and it rose towards 8 million at the time of the Sydney Olympic

The widening catchment: Mrs Consuela Salinas, a refugee from El Salvador, 1991. Severely damaged by torture in her homeland, she settled with her family in Sydney: 'I didn't want to come to paradise. I just wanted to live and not be murdered'. Dilgea Review, *Canberra, 1991*

Games in 2000. Amid such astonishing mobility it was not surprising that categorisation should be ambiguous and variable in the extreme. The statistics of migration, never an exact science, became not only confusing but politically volatile. The sensitive categories included 'special humanitarian', 'special assistance', 'family reunion', 'refugee', 'skills' and then various groups of 'asylum seeker'. The longstanding Australian priority of control was increasingly difficult to sustain because the categories dissolved: thus refugees could be controlled and selected at the points of origins, but 'refugees' also arrived by informal means; some were not refugees in the normal sense but had bought their way to Australia for one reason or another; some immigrants arrived as visitors but stayed on without official sanction. The work of the gatekeepers was extremely difficult and the more so because it was the focus of intense media scrutiny. This was further heightened in the new context in which the world was becoming globalised, with a tendency to increasing liberalisation of trade and capital markets. Australia possessed a bureaucratised immigration system heavily monitored by the Department of Immigration. The less immigration became a national priority the greater it loomed as a political issue, and this was a paradox of the post mass-immigration phase in Australia's history.

Australia's population growth targets were now lower and were satisfied by reproduction and certain modes of immigration. Immigration seemed unlikely to be a major variable in the future development of Australia. This was reflected in the technical debates about the impact of changes in immigration on various aspects of Australia's economic performance and on the state of public opinion. In general, the social scientists concluded that immigration was either neutral or benign in its effects on savings, expenditure and balance of payments. Most of the arguments were about allegations that the system was being manipulated by interest groups, especially in terms of family reunion and education requirements. There was also a rising argument that the interests of the resident home population rather than humanitarianism should be the main factor.

There was another mantra – that the Left had been too influential in the course of making immigration policy and that the public was not being consulted properly. The standard answer to this was that Australia was a democracy and that parliament was the true guardian of democracy.

Beyond all the professional and careful exercises to measure the economic impact of immigration there was little consideration of the larger question. Australia had engineered a colossal augmentation of its population by immigration since 1945. This great national mission had been achieved with remarkably little calculation of its larger impact. In the 1990s the main questions related to the short run – namely small-scale changes in the equations, which generally produced small results. In terms of Australia's long-term destiny there was a paralysis of political thinking. It was remarkable that so little was said about the larger sum, namely whether immigration actually benefited the nation, more particularly in the long term.[39] The heroic experiment of the 1940s was long gone.

12 The new century

Generations of names

By the new century many of the European people who had emigrated to Australia in great waves after the Second World War were beginning to return 'home', usually to retire. But most stayed on in their adopted land and they had higher rates of citizenship than the British immigrants of the same era. Now their generation was beginning to pass away. Many of their stories were poignantly encapsulated in simple obituaries in the Australian press. Thus Antonio Russo, who had been born in 1929 in Zolli Roccabascerana, Avellino in Italy, died at the beginning of 2004 in Adelaide. He was survived by his wife Elena. And the names of his grieving family charted the following generations – his children Guiliano, Flavia and Carmelina and his children-in-law Attilio, Michelle and Sue. And then came their grandchildren – Chris, Steven, Peter and Madison. But Antonio Russo's memory was in both Italy and Australia. It was a generational declension repeated in a thousand columns across the country.[1] The names were testimony to the transitions of migrants into the new Australia that they had created.

Economics and morality

Migrants of all sorts continued to flow into Australia but the categories became ever more rubbery. 'Refugees' captured public attention because there was a prevailing fear (which had been in the background for a century, though rarely articulated) that these aliens would eventually swamp the country; the fact that refugees were difficult to define added to the apprehension. 'Refugee' was a category which threatened Australia's careful control over the character and volume of its immigration. It was not difficult to believe that the anxiety was a reprise of older racial attitudes under a different guise.[2]

Determining the total number of immigrants had become even more problematic. Government targets were clear enough. In 2001, for instance, the official migrant intake was set at 93 000 and in May 2002 the Howard government announced that the intake for 2003 would be 105 000. It also declared that it would maintain immigration at above 100 000 for the following 4 years.[3] The Department of Immigration and the Australian public at large welcomed such clarity. In March 2002 Australia welcomed its 6 millionth postwar immigrant, a Filipina information technologist.[4]

The problem was that migration was much more difficult not only to control but even to define and measure. Migration numbers have always been notoriously flexible. In Australia the government set immigration targets each year and reported on the levels of immigration which, for more than a quarter of a century, had carried electoral implications which no political party could ignore. The data, even in a regulated world, were highly malleable: it was increasingly difficult to record and categorise the greatly heightened flows of people in and out of any Western country at this time. While the nation argued vociferously about the issue of immigration there was no agreed formula by which to calculate actual net migration. This was not by any means peculiar to Australia: the same confusions reigned in Britain and elsewhere.

The official numbers were far from definitive. Thus in 2003 the Australian Bureau of Statistics registered a total immigrant intake into Australia of 154 000 for the previous year, which was a new record. This figure created immediate controversy and Peter McDonald, Professor of Demography at the Australian National University, claimed that it was 'grossly misleading' and had 'created a myth of rapidly rising migration levels' over the previous 5 years. McDonald said that the 154 000 contained much double counting, including those 'people who were in Australia on long term visas and had left for an overseas holiday and then returned, as if they had migrated multiple times'.[5] The bureau acknowledged much of the problem but was not able to correct the figure. McDonald questioned its reliance on air travellers' in-flight information cards. Many entrants to Australia changed their plans and their categories, jumping from one to another to create a statisticians' nightmare. The bureau conceded that it was a 'complex area of demographic statistics'. And McDonald, employing a different system, produced statistics of net immigration which were almost a third lower.[6] The opponents of immigration had already used the bureau's data to raise anxieties about the integrity of the Australian population composition.

The political implications of this confusion were significant: at the time of the arithmetical controversy Australian banks were citing high immigration as a contributory cause of soaring house prices and high levels of lending. The numbers were evidently wobbly. The consequences of immigration were equally difficult to calculate yet politically sensitive.

At the start of the new century planning was made within a more constrained environment, reflected in the higher levels of normal unemployment established during the previous two decades and which now appeared to be a new fact of life for Australia (and indeed higher now than appeared to be the case in the places traditionally the suppliers of immigrants to Australia). War and recession were always enemies of immigration (apart from the new flows of refugees created by the former). Australia had already decided to reduce its role as a people importer. It had certainly stopped paying ordinary economic migrants to come to this continent – and this was the reversal of a century or more of assistance. By the start of the 21st century the grand visions of immigration had dissolved or dwindled into a much more pedestrian and calculating philosophy.

As in most other OECD countries Australia now had a level of fertility that would not sustain even demographic replacement. The fact that it is a shade higher than other places in this bracket was a legacy of the extraordinary immigration program of the mid century. In a sense, therefore, Australia was living off the demographic investment of a previous generation. Eventually this would curb its growth and create an increasingly unbalanced population. The enemies of growth captured the debate and 'Fortress Australia' now prevailed. The experience of the past half-century had however demonstrated that in an environment of economic growth, Australia could accommodate immigrants easily. It is clear that Australia could also recruit immigrants relatively quickly. The tap could be turned on and off without much delay and the conveyance of people was much easier and prompter than before.

International migration occupied a paradoxical position. The regrowth of free market ideology was widely extolled, as was the liberalisation of world trade, encompassing capital and technology, and globalisation was on every tongue. But the glaring exception was the movement of labour across frontiers, which was less and less allowed in this free trading climate. The exception seemed to be skilled labour, which was crossing frontiers with greater ease than before (often in the sojourner mode), and Australia was no exception to this new trend in brain migration.[7]

Migration has always been unpredictable and difficult to control except by way of prohibitions and generous subsidies. Even the British flows were difficult to predict. For more than half a century commentators announced the imminent end of British emigration, and in the 1990s there were indeed signs of serious decline in the British flows to Australia. Yet in the middle of the first decade of the new century more British than ever were reported as leaving Britain on a permanent basis, and their favourite destination appeared to be Australia.[8] Measuring any of these flows was extremely problematic as we have seen, but the British were again on the move; moreover Britain itself was, more than ever, a sorting house for humanity, absorbing larger numbers of newcomers than ever before. Among them of course were large numbers of Australian-born migrants of every sort.[9]

A new cycle

The debate about the economics of immigration was more technical, less passionate, and no more decisive, than the headline-seeking controversy about refugees. Social scientists were unable to resolve the question; they were not able to demonstrate that immigration was a decisive benefit in terms of either growth or employment. At best, immigration did not steal jobs from residents, and did not impede the growth of living standards. But it could not be shown, categorically, to significantly boost the economy.[10] This was lukewarm stuff for any government, especially when the political climate cooled against immigrants. A proposed federal regional program designed to boost growth in struggling country areas was advocated and it entailed channelling visaed migrants to settle beyond the cities. But the academic analyst Robert Birrell showed that 4 out of 5 of them ended up in the cities, and that they failed to have any lasting impact on the rural areas they were intended to help.[11]

Although the economy continued to grow, the unemployment problem seemed intractable. Australia experienced a 12-year period of uninterrupted economic growth, and the average income per capita had grown at an extraordinary rate – reportedly by 85 per cent to $40 000 per annum – and unemployment was reckoned to be down to 5.7 per cent. But the proportion of the population dependent on government support had remained static. Moreover, about

20 per cent of the population were thought to be living on less than $12 000 per capita, described as subsistence level.

The reality was that the unemployment level, though reduced in official reporting, was actually higher than 5.7 per cent because so many people had simply stopped looking for work. Almost every policy had been tried and the problem seemed no longer to respond and, as one prominent economist, Bob Gregory, declared despairingly in April 2004:

> We are doing more of everything we have done
> before, but it is not having much impact ... Nobody
> knows where to go. Deregulation of the labour
> market had done its bit, but we haven't got much
> out of that for jobs ... It is all much more intractable
> than people have imagined ... All the tax and
> unemployment policies seem to have no impact.
> Here or elsewhere.

He warned that the last time this combination of problems had beset the Australian economy was in the 1930s, which only the onset of the Second World War had solved. He suggested that an intake of more skilled immigrants would push up the growth rate and draw more of the unskilled into the labour market.[12]

The idea that a new round of immigration could lead the economy into greater development was not politically persuasive. In the past, grand national schemes of immigration, such as those of EG Wakefield and of Calwell, had galvanised Australia's destiny. In reality they had been essentially intuitive in their inspiration, leaps in the dark. It was always extremely difficult to calculate, still less predict, the consequences of immigration. In the new century, the nation equivocated.

The longstanding bipartisan policy had certainly crumbled to dust. Moreover the environmentalists now argued vociferously that Australia already accommodated too many people, who were damaging the delicate ecology of the 'last continent'. By 2000 the great Australian clock had turned 180 degrees: the national mission to swell the people, to defend the shores and create a United States of Australia had dissolved into pessimism. The population was still a little less than 20 million (which had been Calwell's target 50 years before); it was widely predicted that eventually it would be a continent of the geriatric. The birth rate was now below replacement level and the population expected to stagnate for the next 50 years. Demographer Bernard Salt predicted that over that period the population would increase by only 6 million.[13] Already living standards had been overtaken by most European and OECD countries – most remarkably even by Ireland, which had once supplied so much of Australia's bone and sinew. It was inevitable that many people of European background were leaving Australia in numbers greater than those entering.

Dealing with refugees

Ministers of immigration until the 1980s were largely uncontroversial figures who orchestrated bipartisan policies to general approbation. At the end of the century this had changed. The longest serving and most divisive figure was Minister Philip Ruddock. While a backbencher in the Liberal government he had been critical of the resurgence of discrimination in his own party and in 1988 he had famously crossed the floor of the House to support the non-discriminatory policy of the Hawke government. He had also condemned Hanson's advocacy of temporary migrant status – saying in 1998 that the refugee immigrants would never know where they stood and that it would be an unconscionable addition to the trauma and terror of their escape to Australia.[14]

In 1996 Ruddock became minister and subsequently attorney-general, and thus responsible for the determination and execution of immigration policy. He was soon accused of further dismantling the bipartisan accord and encouraging xenophobia. Ruddock eventually introduced in 1999 legislation governing Temporary Protection Visas (TPVs), which prevented spouses and children joining their refugee families in Australia. He refused to allow refugees re-entry into Australia if they went to visit their family abroad. 'All up, the policy is harsher than that implemented by any other Western country', said one commentator, Mike Steketee. In essence, Ruddock was using the policy as a deterrent to unofficial asylum seekers and it gave him great discretion over the lives of the refugees. Almost half of the 8589 people on TPVs were Iraqis, most of whom the government wanted to repatriate at the very time when Australian tourists were being warned away from Iraq. Similarly many Afghans were kept in indefinite limbo: 'What earthly reason could there be for incoming immigration minister Amanda Vanstone to deny such people the opportunity to rebuild their lives?' asked Steketee.[15] Many among the Liberals believed that the government overreacted to the problem of asylum seekers and had failed to show sensible flexibility. Instead the government had fanned fear and bigotry in the community at the expense of very small numbers of pathetic boat people. Liberals declared that the government's energy should be diverted to immigrants who entered the airports under false documents and with criminal intent.[16] In Australia at the end of 2002 there were reportedly 14 000 asylum seekers whose applications for refugee status had been rejected. They were virtually fugitives. There were also an estimated 60 000 tourists who had overstayed their visas – demonstrating the porous character of Australia's borders.[17]

In Ruddock's defence it was pointed out that by 2003 the Islamic population of Australia had increased by 40 per cent since 1996, largely by the introduction of immigrants and refugees. Immigration was also higher, as far as could be measured, than in the time of Keating, at 108 070 in the previous financial year, which was 46 per cent greater than in 1996/97. 'Ruddock has the numbers', as one less than neutral journalist said. Between times Ruddock had also cracked down on family reunion frauds and boosted skilled immigration from 37 per cent in 1996/97 to 61 per cent of total immigration in 2002/03. The number of illegal incursions by boats diminished and, it was claimed, 'The government's tough stance on illegal immigration has meant that, since 2001, only one boat has arrived in Australia'.

Ruddock's review system dealing with boat people from Afghanistan and Iraq appeared severe but in the outcome about 85 per cent of them were granted protection visas, which was the primary stage in the process. His administration gave priority to 'those who languish in appalling conditions in refugee camps around the world', and Australia had one of the largest per capita refugee and humanitarian programs and 'a record intake last year from these camps'.[18] The curious matter was that the asylum issue related to only 5 per cent of the Australian immigration intake, yet this question occupied at least 95 per cent of media and political attention.

These policies were popular in the electorate and followed literally the resounding declaration of Prime Minister Howard that 'we will decide who comes to this country'. Ruddock stood for mandatory detention of asylum seekers, border control and remotely located detention centres. But he also stood for a rigorous, generous and well-financed legal refugee programme, for which he received less credit. Opposition was vociferous. Part of the controversy was related to the delays regarding the 'processing' of the asylum seekers and their legal status. The minister seemed to hold discretionary powers which enabled him to make decisions over visa appeals and thereby circumvent the courts – and he usually gave quick and positive responses. He was the gatekeeper.[19]

The opposition to the rigorous policies of the government was on parade in the daily letters columns of the newspapers. The critics would not accept the notion that refugees should enter the country only in the official mode. There were 3.4 million Afghan refugees in Iran and Pakistan and very big numbers spilling out of the Iraq war. Australia took few of them – and these people indeed bought their desperate way to Australia by selling their businesses, borrowing and paying very dearly to get out of the war-torn regions of the Middle East. Migration agents made fat gains at the expense of many of these people needing assistance.

By 2003, 8000 people from Afghanistan and Iraq had been recognised as refugees by Australia – but only on temporary visas which produced great suffering. 'Their anxiety is extreme and unnecessary', said one observer.[20] The rancorous national debate continued, yet many of the central propositions were barely knowable. As we have seen, the actual number of immigrants was a matter of great speculation since the statistics were extremely hazy; nor were the economic consequences of immigration established with any certainty; and the social and cultural consequences were simply matters for bar-room disputation.

The government regarded boat-people asylum seekers as queue jumpers who used their money to take advantage over poor people in the official camps. At the same time, however, it was granting visas to most of these people – 8200 were successful between 1999 and 2002, that is 90 per cent of boat arrivals according to Minister Amanda Vanstone. But these were temporary visas which required the asylum-seekers to prove their credentials.[21] Deterrence remained the main purpose of the policy of detention and some commentators regarded the policy as harsher than was implemented by any other Western country.[22]

Tampa

The fear of inundation by unwanted alien immigrants in overwhelming numbers was not easily allayed. The White Australia policy had long been sanitised, but the old anxieties, deep in the Australian psyche, stirred once again in the new century. The political debate was couched in nationalistic language even though the issue was by no means unique to Australia.

Australia's reaction to the refugee problem reached a new pitch (and attracted attention across the Western world) during the *Tampa* crisis in 2004. The *Tampa* was a Norwegian container ship which picked up a sinking boatload of stricken asylum seekers off northern Australia, and then sought to land them on Australian territory. The Australian government adamantly refused the request and thereby aroused extreme emotions on all sides. These events coincided with a federal election campaign in which the crisis itself became a decisive matter for both political parties. At the time of the *Tampa* episode Australia suddenly halved its contribution to UNHCR, the UN refugee agency, down to $7 million.

The crisis had been building for several years. Thus 86 unofficial refugee boats had arrived in late 1999 carrying people from Afghanistan, Iran and Iraq: Australia was being reached via Malaysia and Indonesia. By mid-2001, 8300 such people had arrived and the numbers now began to exceed unauthorised air arrivals; the total of boat arrivals was rising towards 2000 a year. Within 2 years there were more than 4000 arriving annually and no sign of letting up. The growing perception was that Australia was being besieged by an avalanche of boat people and that 'a line had to be drawn'.[23] Deterrence became the primary focus of policy, and this entailed the dispatch of boat people to detention centres in the desert and, subsequently, to off-shore islands. Australia also entered a tacit understanding with Indonesia that police would scuttle prospective refugee boats.

In October 2001 confused reports circulated about the catastrophic fate of a refugee vessel code-named SIEV-X (that is, suspected illegal entry vessel X) which had sunk between Java and northwestern Australia. The SIEV-X had left Bandar Lampung in southern Sumatra on 18 October, heading for Christmas Island (2700 kilometres west of Darwin). It was a decrepit 30-metre wooden fishing boat 'whose three decks had a combined area smaller than a standard tennis court', carrying 421 passengers who had paid as much as $US1000 each for the passage. They included 23 Afghan

Hazara who were so alarmed at the state of the vessel that they got off in the Sunda Strait. The SIEV-X sank in a storm 110 kilometres south of Java and 146 men, 142 women and 65 children were lost. Australian intelligence apparently knew the boat was dangerously overloaded but no rescue mission was sent out. In April 2004 there was a trial in Indonesia of a man accused of organising the people-smuggling operation. Australian authorities admitted that the tragedy helped to discourage the departure of asylum boats in the last few months of 2001.[24]

In August 2004 the *Tampa* picked up people from a similarly sinking vessel off the north coast of Australia. On board were 433 people and 27 crew, and the ship's predicament immediately became the centre of an international incident. The Australian government was already aware that another 2500 people were waiting in Indonesia to embark on the same journey. The boat people aboard the *Tampa* apparently threatened its crew with violence and suicide if not taken to Christmas Island. The Norwegian captain, Arne Rinnan, had been asked by Australian authorities to pick up the boatload of persons in distress. He was then denied permission to land them in Australia or to enter Australian territorial waters. The government in essence simply refused humanitarian aid to a boatload of asylum seekers. The Australian government of John Howard dug in its heels and refused to land the refugees. After much delay and rising hysteria, some of the refugees were accepted by New Zealand and the rest were deposited on Nauru, as part of the so-called Pacific Solution which enabled Australia to assess their claims without incurring legal responsibility. The entire operation was designed to transmit a message to Asia that Australia was not an easy destination for 'illegal' refugees. It was also meant to persuade the voters in Australia that the government was steadfastly protecting their shores.[25]

The *Tampa* episode occurred in a blaze of publicity and brought Australian immigration policy into world spotlight for a short period. Previous asylum seekers, including many Afghans, were already being detained behind razor wire at the Immigration Reception and

Prelude to controversy: the disabled KM *Palapa*, with 433 asylum seekers, pulls alongside MV *Tampa*, 2004. © *Agence France-Presse*

Processing Centres at Woomera, Port Hedland and Baxter. Senator Bill Heffernan explained to the Jesuit lawyer, Frank Brennan, that the system was like a firebreak against a bushfire: it was like destroying property to save the larger community. 'Its not pretty', he said, 'These are hard moral decisions. But you have to do it'. The government boasted that the firebreak was working: 'The borders were secure and Australia could choose those refugees whom it wished to offer places, under its generous offshore refugee selection program'.[26]

Brennan summarised the problem with which the boat people

confronted the Australian government. They arrived without sanction, usually having already passed through several other countries. Most often they had destroyed all their travel documents and other forms of identification. In the post-September 11 environment (that is, following the terrorist attacks in the United States) their claims for asylum were bound to be treated with suspicion if not with fear. Once released into the Australian community they were unlikely to return for their claims to be examined. As Brennan noted, 'Governments running an orderly migration program are entitled to insist on measures to facilitate their removal'.[27]

In practice most of the boat people were found to be genuine asylum seekers, many indeed fleeing the Taliban. The minister himself emphasised that 84 per cent of the boat people were found to be refugees, which was a much higher ratio than the claimants who entered Australia by air.

But the critics of the government were nevertheless eloquent in their fury.[28] Brennan himself declared that Australia had not found the balance in its immigration policies between protection of its borders and the protection of refugees: 'We need to be more neighbourly, generous and collaborative ... we need to pull our weight internationally, rather than exporting our problems or keeping them off shore out of sight, out of mind'.[29] Similarly John Menadue poured scorn on the Howard government, asserting that there was no refugee crisis and that Australia was probably taking about 4000 refugees a year out of the 20 million around the world. He claimed that 'we're tying ourselves in knots over this trivial flow when in fact, in Australia, we have about 60 or 70,000 illegals'. This statistic referred to the legal United Kingdom and United States visitors (among others) who illegally overstayed their visas and were rarely tracked down and deported. Instead Howard was demonising and punishing some of the most 'vulnerable people on earth'. Howard, it was alleged, had conducted a race election and was appealing to the parochialism and, in some degree, the racism of this Australian community. But now 'the Australian debate is ... debauched', fulminated Menadue.[30]

Most Australians supported the government policy, but many were queasy about keeping children in detention in remote places for long periods. Brennan said that the 'firebreak policy' demanded 'ongoing, excessively brutal treatment of those who turn up on our shores without a visa. It is important that the key components of any permanent firebreak are decent, workable and affordable'.[31] Australia's solution to illegal immigration divided the country, but Howard won the election and enhanced his political standing.

Wider opinion

The *Tampa* episode consolidated public opinion to the advantage of the Howard government, which was returned with a handsome majority in 2004. Opinion in other quarters was more critical. Particularly objectionable was the policy which, by means of financial inducements, diverted refugees to poor nearby countries where they were held for assessment, the 'Pacific Solution'. The retired diplomat Richard Woolcott chastised the immigration policy, which he believed had turned its back on Asia and damaged Australia's reputation in the world beyond. Immigration and refugee issues had darkened the mood and the future character of the country: 'the handling by the government of refugees, boat people and asylum seekers has been widely criticised as inhumane; in particular the government's rigid determination to ensure that those coming by sea, often risking their lives, would not land on Australian soil'. This attitude may have caused the avoidable drowning of hundreds of boat people; it had also imposed severe political pressure on aid-dependent states such as Nauru and Papua New Guinea. The Pacific Solution, rooted in a mixture of costly chequebook diplomacy and official pressure, had damaged Australia's reputation in the South-West Pacific and beyond.[32] Woolcott declared that Australia's treatment of its asylum seekers (as well as its indigenous inhabitants) was, in the eyes of its neighbours, a test of its good faith. It also tested the true demise of the White Australia policy. He asserted that Australia was failing both tests. But it was equally clear that the Australian government was adamantly following its own priorities and was prepared to ignore overseas opinion for the sake of it sim- migration policy.

Another influential Australian internationalist was James Wolfen- sohn, president of the World Bank at the turn of the century. Wolfen- sohn was deeply concerned about the problems of poverty across the world and his official role, in principle, made him responsible for lift- ing the living conditions of 5 billion people. He urged much greater spending by the rich countries on programmes of development aid, which currently received less than they spent on agricultural pro- tection and on military infrastructure. Poverty bred terrorism and he believed that free trade arrangements between, for instance, Aus- tralia and the United States were probably damaging to the interests of underdeveloped countries. But Wolfensohn was equally alarming about the more distant future of Australia and he sounded warning bells which seemed to echo the fears of a century earlier. He pre- dicted that the world's population in poorer countries would grow from 5 billion to 7 billion in the next 25 years, and that most of this growth would be in Asia. For Australia there would be an extra 1.5 billion people to the north, in Asia, within 30 years. His views were reported under the headline, 'World Bank warns on Asian migrant influx'. Wolfensohn said the question was inevitable: 'Because if you have another billion and half people to the north of you, that's a lot of people, and so the question has to be asked. But what the answer is, I don't know'.[33] He pointed out that legal and illegal migration in Europe and the United States was already changing the nature of their societies: 'If you fast-forward in Australia you have to ask the question: What sort of Australia is it going to be in 30 years time? … Is it going to be the ethnic mix of the scale that it now is, or is there a challenge of something different?' Wolfensohn knew as much as anyone about the real distribution of wealth and poverty in the world, but he had no answer to his own questions.

When the United Nations High Commissioner for Refugees, Rudolphus Lubbers, visited Australia in March 2004 he was keenly aware of the 'Pacific Solution', the uses of detention camps and the *Tampa* affair. He sensed the generalised attitude that refugees represented a threat, which he effectively placed in perspective for his hosts. He pointed out the extraordinarily wasteful uses of taxpayers' revenues. Border protection had cost Australia $2.8 billion in 2002/03 to keep at bay a few thousand boat people: 'That is 150 times more than the $18.4m that Australia contributed in that year to the UNHCR'. The first priority and purpose of UNHCR was to improve conditions that 'lead people to flee in the first place'. In the previous year Australia had received 4260 applications, the United Kingdom 61 050, and 50 000 in France and Germany. Moreover the pressure seemed to be easing in Australia.[34] Lubbers remarked, 'I don't think Australia is flooded with refugees'. He was, in effect, saying that political leadership should be able to convince Australian voters that they had little to fear. He was especially repelled by the notion of children in detention, but he chose also to notice Australia's generally pro-refugee attitude and the practical aspects of the policy which tended to be obscured by the recent *Tampa* crisis.

As the economy gathered more vigorous pace by 2004 labour shortages began to emerge. Already it was clear that there was a rising international demand for skilled immigrants and that Australia was 'in danger of being left behind as a savage new competition for migrants begins'.[35] There was growing support for TPV holders, especially in country areas which were short of fruit pickers and meat workers, a classic symptom that the tide was turning in the immigration context. Minister Vanstone indeed announced that Australia's refugee quota for the next financial year would increase from 4000 to 6000. She told Lubbers it was to 'make it clear that Australia is more refugee friendly than one says normally these days'. She wanted to shift the perception that the government was inhuman, 'without offending the still strong sentiment for border protection'. This was, of course, the central tension within the policy: at the very time that Australia increased its intake of refugees it was turning away 14 Kurdish asylum seekers and excising another 4000 islands from Australian's migration zone. The minister argued that the more it was able to restrict the illegal intake of boat people the more it would be able to take genuine and properly administered refugees. The greater the border controls, the more refugees Australia would be able to accept. The gospel of control remained paramount, even though it was pregnant with mis-understandings. But the publicity attending many shocking stories of detention in 2002 caused even conservatives to reckon that the moral and financial cost was too great to stomach.[36]

There were, therefore, two essential issues. First, how many and what sort of immigrants Australia needed and wanted (and on what terms it was prepared to recruit them). And second, how generous Australia wanted to be, and should be, in terms of taking refugees who, in ordinary circumstances, it would not seek to recruit. How was need to be measured and how was generosity to be evaluated? These had become political issues and were unresolved, and were certainly not unique to Australia.

Refugee intake was an aspect of the general question of assist-ance by the rich to the less rich countries of the world, which has entered the international culture in the postwar years. The United Nations urged a target of 0.7 per cent of GNP on Overseas Devel-opment Assistance. In 1998 Denmark gave 0.99, Norway 0.91, Hol-land, 0.80, Ireland 0.31, Canada 0.29, Australia and Japan 0.28, New Zealand 0.27, the United Kingdom 0.26 and the United States 0.10.[37] This was a significant measure of comparative generosity and political maturity.

By 2007 the Australian economy was running hot and, true to its form, it was becoming hungry for immigrants.[38] This was channelled into a burgeoning intake of skilled migrants at a time of record low unemployment. The government quietly expanded the migration levels – incrementally, in small increases, 'to avoid risk-ing a backlash against massive migration growth in an election year'. But the intake had grown to 102 5000 in the year 2007/08, which

Protest among asylum seekers: Woomera Detention Centre, 2002. *Peter Mathew*

Asylum-seeker children in detention on Nauru. *Andrew Bartlett*

dwarfed the boat people issue which still took up much more attention. In fact Australian business wanted a much bigger increase. The Department of Immigration granted 148 200 permanent visas of which 50 079 were in the 'family' stream. Among the 'skilled immigrants' were 24 800 from Hong Kong, 15 865 from India, 14 688 from China, 4293 from South Africa and 3838 from Malaysia. The refugees came mainly from Sudan, Burma, Iraq, Afghanistan and Burundi, in that order (and included 'white settlers' fleeing Zimbabwe).[39] This bipartisan immigration policy was closely articulated and based on the calculation that skilled migrants were much better for the economy and cheaper than family migrants.[40]

At the same time the new minister was cracking down on the exploitation of immigrants by employers. The humanitarian program was held at 13 000 places – the expectation was that the intake would be a total of 166 000 in 2007/08, which was described as a record. In the federal election of November 2007, which installed the new Rudd Labor government, the immigration issue was relatively dormant, the competing parties choosing to minimise their differences on policy towards refugees in particular.[41]

A new revival

Public attention and controversy oscillated between, on the one side, anxiety about the small numbers of asylum seekers and, on the other, the much bigger issue of an Australian population policy and sustainable growth strategy. The Business Council of Australia in 2004, in an echo of the Calwell postwar equation, called for an annual 1.25 per cent growth rate via natural increase and net immigration, to yield a population of 30 million by 2050.[42] This was symptomatic of a quiet shift in the national and government mood, associated with continuing economic growth, on the broad immigration issue. Migration programs were expanding, increasingly geared to skilled immigration and a stream of fee-paying overseas students who were likely to convert into permanent migrants. In effect the appetite for immigrants was reviving in the Australian labour market and the anti-growth protagonists were receiving a deaf ear.

This delayed revival of immigration was mainly a response to the realisation that otherwise Australia was, in the middle future, almost certain to confront a declining population. Estimates predicted that by 2025 new workers would enter the Australian labour market at the rate of a mere 14 000 a year, compared to 180 000 new entrants in 2005. As the influential economist Glenn Withers said, Australia depended on 'Skilled and lively people living in growing and vibrant population centres', and they would be 'the best revenge against the tyranny of distance. Our national sovereignty is highly dependent on our population growth in that sense'.[43] Otherwise Australia would fall behind the dynamic economies of Europe and Asia. There was considerable division in the ranks of the state Labor governments about the levels of immigration: Steve Bracks wanted much increase, to raise the Victorian population to 6 million by 2025; Bob Carr in New South Wales wanted reduced levels to avoid the greater growth of Sydney.[44]

Actual immigration quietly increased after 1997/98, rising from a planned 67 100 to 120 000 in 2005. Skilled immigration increased by 122 per cent to 77 100 and Asians made up the largest contingent of the skilled element. In 2003/04, 17 per cent of the immigrants came from the United Kingdom, 32 per cent from China, Hong Kong, Indonesia, Malaysia and Singapore and 17 per cent from India. It was observed that 'These figures tell a simple but clear story: contrary to popular perception, Howard has not in any way sought to curb immigration – Asian or otherwise – to this country.' But the program has been re-weighted – 'family migration' has fallen from 47 per cent of the total to 35 per cent.[45]

Specific labour shortages were exposed as the economy reached towards full employment. Some employers recruited groups of skilled immigrants from entirely new sources. Thus meat workers from very remote parts of rural China were introduced into the abattoir industry in such places as Murray Bridge and other regional centres across Australia. Similarly 'backpacker' labour became a major element in Australia's use of temporary migrants – instead of using a formal system of 'guest workers', Australia was using itinerant labour whose numbers grew to substantial proportions in the new century. As early as 1996 the government moved in favour of more flexible attitudes towards temporary skilled migrants who could fill gaps in the labour force. They were called 'working holiday makers' and increased to 134 6000 in 2006/07, having risen by 18 per cent from the previous year. They were vital, for instance, in the fruit-picking industry and elsewhere in the Australian economy. Mango growers in Carnarvon said they were a godsend. They were from many countries including Taiwan and Japan. They were in effect a small segment of the global mobility of the new century and Minister Ruddock declared that they were part of 'the new dotcom world'.[46]

Measuring the success of Australia as an immigrant nation was more difficult to determine, and a source of endless debate among the disputants. Objective measures were scarce but one central index was the degree of intermarriage between migrants and the host society (which included, naturally, many immigrants). 'Marrying out' was an indicator of the degree of melting in the multicultural pot. By the third generation about 70 per cent of Chinese, Indian and Lebanese in Australia were 'marrying out', not much less that the 80 per cent among southern and northern Europeans. This was a greater degree of admixture than in the United States where, for instance, the Chinese still tended to marry fellow Chinese. Intermarriage in the second generation was considerably less evident, but significant ethnic intermixing and upward mobility was undoubtedly happening. Pauline Hanson's nightmare of a 'nation of tribes' was not being realised. In 2000 the demographer Charles Price announced that 'the typical Australian' was now an offspring of a mixed ethnic partnership, 60 per cent of the population being now ethnically mixed. He calculated that while 90 per cent of the

The convergence of immigrants: Turks and Greeks in Australia. Mustafa and Ümran with Orania and Erdal on their wedding day, March 1990. *HH and V Baçarin, The Turks in Australia, 1993*

population had been Anglo-Celtic in 1947, their proportion had fallen to 74.5 per cent in 1988, and to 70 per cent by 1999.[47]

The debate about immigration had begun to return to some of the issues that propelled the great postwar programme, reflecting the cumulative growth of the economy that had set in before the turn of the century. Paul Kelly offered a longer view when he claimed that 'over that past 40 years, half of Australia's GDP growth has been driven by population growth'. He argued that a rejection of this long-standing policy would represent a fundamental reversal of Australia's direction and destiny and would lead to economic stagnation. It was, in effect, a plea for a return to the grand immigration strategy that had guided the nation over the previous half century.

Optimistic opinion declared that migrants added significantly to Australia's human capital, extended its markets, produced a more cosmopolitan and flexible labour force; moreover migrants tended to avoid the under-employed sectors of the economy. The main problem was that refugees are not given enough official support and training on arrival. And there were economists who were perfectly clear that immigration was still a force for national development. For instance, in 2000 Glenn Withers pointed out that the tax revenues derived from ordinary migrants paid fully for the services they required; moreover their crime rates tended to be lower than those of Australian-born citizens. Immigrants, he said, created at least as many jobs as they took and they tended, if anything, to reduce unemployment. Indeed, said Withers, migrants in Australia tend to disperse and have high tertiary education rates in the second generation; they were necessary for vigorous population growth even in the great cities. He pointed out that dynamic Singapore received more migrants annually than Australia.[48] Withers, an optimist like most economists, declared that economic development could solve most problems in the environment. Similarly positive and robust arguments in favour of population growth were advocated by the economist Max Corden in October 2003. Dismissing arguments about ageing and water requirements, he averred that a larger population would allow Australia to achieve more in the world; but he conceded that the benefits could not be precisely quantified.[49]

The future population

These larger perspectives were consolidated by a group of Australian demographers in 2003. They confirmed that the regime of low fertility was likely to become permanent in Australia, in tune with the rest of the affluent industrial countries of the world. McDonald showed that the record of migration between 1950 and 2000 had fluctuated roughly around a mean of 85 000 per annum: it had always been above 40 000, rarely above 120 000. Since 1995 it had remained at about 85 000 per annum but since 2003 had begun to rise again. United Nations data showed that in 2000 the stock of immigrants in Australia was 24.6 per cent, while in Canada it was 18.9 per cent, in the United States 12.4 per cent and in the United Kingdom 6.8 per cent. The rate in the Western European countries was rising faster.[50] McDonald also pointed out that the Calwellian figure of 1 per cent per annum population growth by net immigration had actually fallen to 0.43 per cent in recent years, though this was still one of the highest rates in the world. Indeed to achieve the Calwellian target in the new century would have required immigration to run at 200000 per annum, which was much higher than ever previously achieved. There was a paradox in the fact that Australia had 'one of the highest rates of net migration of any country in the world', but had become a small player in the market for international migration. It was extremely difficult to calculate and monitor the actual level of net permanent migration, and this added to the confusion and the paradoxes.

The impact of immigration on the age structure of the Australian population was a central issue: the net migrant inflow over many years has been younger than the average resident population and 'this has slowed population ageing'.[51] But the demographers were adamant that immigration had only a small role to play in retarding the ageing of the Australian population. With a net intake of about 80000 a year it would have 'a worthwhile and efficient contribution to the retardation of population ageing. After that it is increasingly ineffective ... The effects upon ageing of a younger immigrant intake or high migrant fertility are very small ... They are not realistic options'.[52] In this analysis, ageing was virtually inevitable and irresistible.

Two other large perspectives concerned the perceptions of Australia's demographic capacity and, secondly, the likely size of its future population.[53] The reality was that 70 per cent of the land was empty and another 8 per cent settled at a very modest level of 1–10 people per square kilometre; in fact, 76 per cent of the population lived at densities of over 100 per square kilometre and occupied only 3 per cent of the land. This was not surprising, nor was it much different from the United States and even China. Yet, remarked Geoffrey McNicoll,

> We retain the strange idea that empty spaces must
> be filled, like nature abhorring a vacuum ... There is
> a common feeling that settlement should be spread
> out, that the bush deserves support just for being
> there, as if to make up for being so far from the
> beach. This was once manifested in organised rural
> resettlement schemes, with their ideology of yeoman
> farmers (typically to be created out of demobilized
> soldiers) as the salt of the earth. The schemes failed
> fairly abysmally, from western Victoria to the Ord
> River.[54]

It was part of a long tradition which recurrently resurfaced in public debate.

Population predictions also had a long and inglorious history in 20th century Australia, and the story was no more persuasive or concordant in the new century. In the so-called Great Australian Population Debate in 2004, the businessman Richard Pratt asserted that 50 million should be the target, supported by expansionists (like Malcolm Fraser) who wanted to achieve this total within the next 50 years; environmentalists, such as Tim Flannery, wanted the population reduced to between 6 and 12 million in the coming century, as its sustainable total.[55] It was not difficult to prove that, with the likely birth and death rates, neither was feasible with any acceptable immigration program.[56] A net immigration policy of 150 000 per annum seemed well 'beyond our present absorptive capacities but if fertility were to fall to 1.4 births per woman, a net migration level of 150,000 would merely lead to zero population growth, the lower end of our acceptable range'.[57]

The future population of Australia was essentially a balance between the fertility rate (over which the government seemed to have only slight influence) and the rate of net migration. At the turn of the century the fertility level was 1.78 births per woman and looked likely to fall to 1.65. In such circumstances Australia would require a net immigration of 80000 simply to avoid long-term population decline. To achieve a population of 25 million would require a substantially higher migration rate, or a recovery of fertility rates. By 2006 the government and business were becoming visibly more responsive to both considerations. Diplomat Rawdon Dalrymple said that many people in South-East Asia continued to believe that Australia was under-populated 'and that we must avoid a shrinking population if we are to deter external threats'. Frank Fenner countered with the view that it was nonsense to think that Indonesia should be feared as the source of a likely deluge of population. A few extra million people in Australia 'would be little deterrent'. Yet in 1997 the occasionally provocative Malaysian prime minister, Dr Mahathir Mohamad, warned that Asian and African countries might swamp Europe and America with migrants if the developing nations were not allowed to prosper: he remarked that 'Masses of Asians and Africans should inundate Europe and America' as their response to the new imperialism of Globalisation.[58]

Thus, in the background there were a number of even larger long-term questions which were by no means exclusive to Australia. The American political theorist Samuel F Huntingdon drew attention to the long-term impact of massive Hispanic and other immigration on the United States (which had taken in 30 million migrants in the past three decades). Huntingdon described his country as 'the old Anglo-Saxon fortress' which was in danger of being overwhelmed by immigrants from Mexico. Huntingdon's nightmare was of a 'bilingual, bicultural society' where the Latinos would take over certain states and United States foreign policy would be dictated from Mexico City. This was one of the subtexts in the parallel Australian debates of the time. The opposing view pointed out that 'Study after study shows that virtually everyone in the second generation grows up proficient in English, and by the third generation, two-thirds speak only English'. In Australia the threat is much slighter, and United States immigrant numbers were vastly greater.[59]

Australia certainly faced a problem common to all affluent nations at the turn of the new millennium. This was the generic phenomenon of 'clandestine migration' propelled by the magnetic attraction of refugees and economic migrants towards the rich countries. People were crossing the Sahara from West Africa to reach the southern shores of affluent Europe; the people of Latin America were moving to the north and even eastward across the Atlantic to the former colonial powers; the flows out of the old Soviet bloc and the Balkans were heading towards the European Union. There was fear of inundation among all the affluent countries. According to one commentator it was 'a record of a morbid reluctance on the part of the rich world to come to an accommodation with people in distress'.[60]

Australia was largely insulated by distance from most of these massive flows of humanity, but its response to the boat people exposed its deep anxieties, reminiscent of the time when the Yellow Peril was feared. One academic commentator mocked these fears, suggesting that Anglo-Australia had always attempted to defy geography and build a British enclave in the Pacific. The Fall of Singapore in 1941 had been a dire shock, but Australia had kept Asia 'at bay' by mass European immigration, expecting them to convert into Anglo-Australians. In the outcome the Italians in particular had resisted assimilation and instead helped to transmogrify Australia. Eventually multiculturalism had emerged and Australia became broadly more open to alien cultures and then to Asian immigration also. Out of this unplanned mélange a new mentality had arisen in this new 'post-European society' on the Pacific Rim. Australia had become 'a society which is learning how to slough off its defensive

European identity and is developing a vision of what this part of the world can become in the 21st century'. This was perhaps the most optimistic and liberal vision of Australia's future after two centuries of immigration.[6]

13 Retrospect

The long view

History as a perspective-seeking activity often claims to identify long-run tendencies that are hidden from contemporaries. Indeed some historians think it is impossible to write anything reliable about contemporary Australian history.[1] Nevertheless the 20th century is now emerging in a clearer historical silhouette, to the broad features of which this final chapter turns.

In the 1920s the Australian statistician CH Wickens memorably likened the course of Australian immigration to the feeding habits of a snake, the boa constrictor.[2] Australia's appetite for immigrants was indulged in concentrated bouts of engorgement. Having satiated itself, the country fell asleep for a long period of demographic digestion. When it eventually awakened it found its appetite again ravenous and engaged in a further furious feeding frenzy before once more relapsing into sleepy recession. This, of course, usually coincided with economic downturns.

This perennial and powerful metaphor applies to the entire

course of the modern re-peopling of Australia and probably also to its future. The cycles of immigration stand out in the story, as do the periods of recessive digestion. But it is also clear that Australia's appetite was not the only determinant – the conditions of recruitment were also decisive. As Australia became increasingly engaged with the outside world it was subjected to much wider forces than the state of its stomach for migrants. The story of 20th century immigration is largely cast in Australia's shifting alignment with global changes often outside its own control.

The foundations of Australia's distinctive immigration career were established in the colonial era, which set the context for the modern experience. In brief, Australia belonged in a broad category of new societies which included the United States, Canada, South Africa, Cuba, Argentina and Brazil. Their settlement in the 19th century depended on transfusions of people from the Old World, mainly from Europe and Africa. Australia was far from unique, but exhibited important differences from these other 'countries of recent settlement'.

What were these defining differences?

First, and most famously, Australia had begun its European history with a convict population which comprised most of its immigrants until 1840, and continued to receive criminals until 1868. In the colonial era, to 1900, about a tenth of its immigrants had arrived as convicts.

Second, the great distance of Australia from Europe placed it beyond the range of most ordinary emigrants from that continent, even from the emerging and widening diasporas issuing out of Europe and Asia by the end of the 19th century.

Third, Australia found it feasible to assist a high proportion of its immigrants – about half of all those who arrived before 1900. These were usually carefully selected and served most of the labouring needs of the emergent economy. Because it was so distant a destination, and because it funded a large proportion of its immigrants' passages, Australia had a long tradition of determining the selection of its incoming people; it was in the special position of being able to design its population. This, of course, was the sine qua non of White Australia. These special conditions gave Australia almost unprecedented control over the composition of its introduced population. The Immigration Restriction Act of 1901 enabled Australia to restrict non-European immigration and gave total authority over entry into the country.

Fourth, colonial Australia chose to take virtually all its migrants from the British Isles and this entailed a special reliance on Irish immigrants, so that Australia became significantly more Irish than other places in the British diaspora. Australia had been able to induce immigration in accordance with its economic needs and the pattern of its development. Thus in the 1890s when the economy was slack it simply turned off the immigration tap (as also in 1906/07 and again in the 1930s). When the economy stirred, Australia reverted to assistance programs. But, unlike other countries which subsidised immigration, Australia insisted on total freedom of movement and contract for its incoming immigrants. This contrasted with countries such as Brazil which linked assistance schemes with indentures and tight contract conditions. Labour was a powerful and democratic force in all Australian colonies and continued to exert its influence into the newly federated Australia. The labour movement was a prime influence in the history of Australian immigration.

Fifth, the equal bifurcation of immigration between the assisted and the unassisted sectors registered an important distinction in the incoming peoples. The unassisted were not only self-financing but held larger resources and higher social status. Nevertheless the two groups were absorbed into the receiving society without perpetrating any marked social rift in the general firmament.

Sixth, the flows of migrants were also subject to occasional, unpredicted and almost random factors. In the 19th century the most significant was the spectacular effect of the gold rushes in the 1850s, which produced a sudden flood of immigrants remarkably heterogeneous in character and from many quarters of the globe, though still mainly from the British Isles. This brought to southeastern Australia a spectacular increase of population of the unassisted sort – but it quickly diminished after 1856. The gold rushes were an anarchic moment in the evolution of Australian colonisation, breaking out of the orderly development of its population and society. More than half of the unassisted immigrants to reach Australia in the 19th century arrived in the 1850s.

Seventh, there were a few other small channels which brought other kinds of immigrant to colonial Australia. The most important had been the spontaneous development of contract Chinese immigration during the gold rushes – overwhelmingly male, with very high rates of return to their origins. A small number of Germans and Swedes arrived under private initiatives. The only other substantial groups were the Pacific Islanders – Kanakas – brought into Queensland to service the sugar industry, and a smaller flow of Italians who also made their way to Australia. Each of these non-British groups faced varying degrees of hostility in the receiving society and the issue of their exclusion united the colonies more than any other single question.

Eighth, Australia was in little danger of any other sort of immigration so long as the unions opposed, and as long as more attractive destinations were cheaper. So far as immigration was concerned colonial Australia was a peripheral player in the international system: its position gave Australia special control over its inflows but it also left it out of many of the primary supplies of potential migrants. Unlike the United States and Canada in the late 19th century, Australia was not reached by the great new diasporas pouring out of continental Europe – from Spain, Russia, Italy, Germany and the Balkans after 1880 – and it effectively blocked those from China, Japan and India, all on the move before 1900.

The decade before the First World War was the last great expression of the Great Age of European Emigration. This was the climax of the surges of people out of Europe, and the United States stole the vast majority of them. Australia, when it was lucky (or determined) enough, attracted up to 10 per cent of the emigrants, but it continued to restrict itself almost exclusively to British migrants, even though the main supply of migrants had shifted to other parts of Europe. Consequently (and unlike Canada, Argentina, Brazil and the United States) Australia received very few from the new sources in its own population expansion. The White Australia policy was primarily a product of the original assisted immigration system, which gave the colonies control over the selection of a large proportion of their immigrants. It had been breached only in the special circumstances of gold and sugar, which brought in Chinese and Pacific Island labour, and these generated union resistance which combined with general sentiment to terminate and erase these exceptions from the policy of white British exclusivity.

The culture of control

Similar long historical perspectives are also becoming visible for the 20th century. The past 100 years has seen a quintupling of the total population of Australia and also several radical swings in the catchments of its migrants. The first 50 years of the century saw Australia competing for immigrants through the broken decades of prosperity, war and depression, without altering its objectives or the sources of its immigrants. In general, from 1913 to 1947 Australia's efforts were poorly rewarded in terms of net migration. Australia continued to seek rural immigrants and remained almost exclusively dependent on the British Isles. This was a time of ultra-British immigration adhering to the rigorous requirements of White Australia, which had been emphatically demanded in the founding precepts of the Commonwealth in 1901.

After 1945 the story of immigration passed through three major transitions. The first was the end of exclusively White British Australia, which was engineered in 1947–51 with the recruitment of a great new diversity of European immigrants. This was, in Australian terms, a revolutionary change which rapidly created a much more variegated European population. It remained, however, decidedly White in complexion and, indeed, reasserted the White Australia policy which was its central rationale.

Much more gradual and evolutionary was the subsequent liberalisation of White Australia, which ended with the declaration of non-discriminatory immigration by Whitlam in the early 1970s. Under the new policy the immigration intakes were more diverse and were subject to new circumstances which affected the flows of people – especially the emergent waves of refugees and the increasingly globalised character of migration.

At the end of the 20th century Australia had a much reduced appetite for immigrants of any sort; there seemed to be signs that Australia had ceased to be a people-seeking country, an impression reinforced by its determination to rigorously control illegal immigration. Yet, perplexingly, the movement of humanity into and out of Australia was greater than ever; moreover by 2000 the old demographic anxieties about the vitality of the home population were beginning to revive in the minds of the planners, and the business world was worried about the capacity of the home work force to meet its future labour needs. It was clearly premature to claim that this was 'the end of history' as far as Australian immigration was concerned.[3]

Twentieth-century Australia thus passed through two revolutions in its peopling – the end of British White Australia, and then the end of White Australia, which subsequently became embroiled with a succession of refugee crises which tested the strength of the new political compact and the resolve to end discrimination. These changes also coincided with serious fluctuations in the Australian economy. In retrospect it is surprising that the political consequences were not much greater.

The critical historical question was how Australia managed these great shifts.[4] Australia always regarded immigration as a source of labour and the essential requirement for the development of the continent and the economy: immigration became a planning tool in a planned society. But immigration has also been a defence strategy and a way of consolidating the nation's grip on the continent, most belligerently in the context of White Australia. When Australia moved away from racial discrimination, a largely moral decision, it changed the composition of the country, a process which was reinforced by its recognition of the obligation to receive refugees in its role within the international community. Immigration was therefore part of a reciprocating relationship with the changing external world.

Australian immigration was a product, on the one hand, of its fluctuating need for labour expressed in its migration programs and, on the other hand, the conditions which generated mobile populations in the rest of the globe. Australia remained the most distant receiving zone at the very edge of that world but, in 1900, it believed that it could determine its future peopling. This remained a central objective, which was well sustained in the years of White Australia but came under increasing pressure in the later years of the century, though was never completely displaced.

Australia (like Canada and a few other nations of 'recent settlement') self-consciously designed its population in terms of size and composition. But immigration was also the most significant connection between Australia and the rest of the world. Much of Australia's reputation in the 20th century related to the character of its immigration policies. For most of the time it was branded, almost indelibly, with the label 'White Australia', from which, even 40 years after its official termination, it was still unable fully to dissociate itself. More directly, however, the millions of individual migrants were the umbilical cord with the rest of the world, the carriers of many of the dramas and global changes that marked the 20th century. The migrants themselves therefore earn the centre stage in the greater narrative. Sometimes the origins of migrants were so painful that their memories were self-suppressed;

sometimes the pathways to Australia were so mundane that they were barely mentioned. Between the two, much of the history of modern Australia was contained. The transit of millions of people to Australia was a vast enterprise in the wider history of human migration in the modern era.

Control remained the spinal column of Australia's immigration history. It was an assumption then built into the country's psyche and became part of its culture of control. It was not so much a matter of exclusion but of determining who came, their being selected and designed for Australia's needs. There was always resistance to the idea that migration was a solution to other people's problems. Australian mainly paid for and orchestrated its own population: it was crucial to its sense of sovereignty and political direction. This was an abiding bipartisan principle in Australian life, pursued with disregard for the odium it brought upon Australia in the wider world.

This indelible tradition of control allowed Australia to develop a distinctive social psychology which governed its expectations. Australia was especially jealous of its 'hard-won cohesion' and even its most liberal-minded intellectuals, including HC Coombs, regarded unregulated immigration as a potential threat to the nation's equilibrium.[5] Such suspicion, however, did little to staunch the great inflows of immigrants after 1947. Another habitual pattern of thinking in Australia was the belief that immigration was manipulable to its needs. Australia worked on the assumption that, when its labour market tightened, it could always rely on immigrant labour to feed its demands, especially for targeted groups such as doctors, academics, geologists etc. When the labour market became generally undersupplied, the floodgates were opened. This was a recurring cycle: thus in 2005, at the height of another surge in economic activity, South Australia imported dozens of British 'bobbies' to fill vacancies in its own police force. There was a rising fear that skills were in poor supply and that the education system should be redeployed in their training. There was a claim that scientists were in severe potential shortage – that by 2010 Australia would be short of 85 000 scientists unless moves were made to avert the result.[6] Australia lived by its historical tradition that immigration was always an available resort.

In 1996 the Minister of Immigration encapsulated the commonsensical and pragmatic philosophy that guided his policies: he declared that 'the success of the program depends on a question of balance. In a globalised, high-tech, highly competitive world, this balance is more important than ever to ensure that immigration, both short and long term, continues to be a coordinated, integral part of Australia's future development'.[7] His balance was not easily maintained in the following decade. James Jupp pointed out that freedom of movement in the world is much less than it was in the 19th century and that 'Australia, with a visa system for all entrants except New Zealanders, had very tight control' by these international standards. He put the matter in further perspective by pointing out that most of the Asian migration was east to west and not north to south: Australia was essentially a 'branch line' in all of this. He predicted that most Australian immigration would become increasingly middle class, English-speaking and readily employable; the humanitarian stream would remain relatively small in these flows into Australia.[8]

Continuities and change

The rural obsession

Australian immigration began as a way of colonising the land; at the beginning it sought agricultural people for rural development. This complemented British propensities and assisted in the drift from the land within the British Isles. Eventually, by the start of the 20th century, the transfer changed once and for all. Rural labour supplies in the British Isles ran down as industrialisation became virtually comprehensive. Simultaneously Australia itself became a highly urbanising country, even before it industrialised after 1945. Consequently migration became an exchange of urban people to an urban destination and mirrored changes at both ends of the chain of Anglo-Australian migration. It was a structural change which Australians were slow to acknowledge and slower to assimilate. Such was the strength of the 'rural myth' which long continued to promote rural settlement as the best form of development.

The anxiety about the differential growth of the cities and their undesirable effects on Australian life was pervasive. Thus in 1893 William Affleck (himself an old immigrant born in Fife in Scotland in 1845, son of a paper maker and one of 13 children, who was assisted to New South Wales in 1854) advocated a special plan to settle the land for the specific purpose of relieving the pressure on the cities. He thought that cities, among other things, encouraged corruption and alcoholism, which combined to undermine the good society. He wanted the government to establish a central loan fund of £3 million to resettle people in model rural settlements with amenities which would compete with those of the city but in a more wholesome context and scale.[9] Affleck gave voice to the commonest Australian response to the perplexing matter of the growth of cities: it was a mentality that was unable to imagine that the future of Australia would be overwhelmingly urban. He realised that the cities had extraordinary magnetism and the only way to counter their attraction was to ensure that rural settlements could offer countervailing facilities. This, in reality, was a contradiction in terms, but captured the essence of the dilemma for those who could see nothing but corruption in the endless expansion of the cities. This psychology influenced immigration policy for more than half a century and certainly remained central in the thinking of Arthur Calwell in 1947.

Australia, well into the 20th century, continued to regard itself as an agricultural country which sought rural settlers to intensify its use of the land. Michael Roe called it 'the yeoman ideal', which was pitted against 'the disposition of an average citizen, recent migrants most of all, to live in cities'.[10] Even at the end of the 20th century there continued to be resistance to the idea that most people would inevitably locate themselves in the mega-cities, notably Sydney and Melbourne, especially newly arrived immigrants. Sending immigrants to the country remained a recurrent theme, a recrudescence of thinking derived from the previous century. Yet trends towards unstoppable urbanisation were becoming the dominant tendency across the entire world in the new millennium.[11]

The British component

The foundation population of colonised Australia was British and Irish, and no other immigrant country relied for so long on such a single source for its population. The British Isles supplied more than 90 per cent of its immigrants until the great change in the post-1947 years and, even then, the British retained majority status for most of the succeeding decades. They were basically ordinary people moving from one suburb to another within the British world. This was indeed the essential attraction for many British migrants and the way it was sold to them – it seemed to be hardly migration at all.[12] These British people melded into Australian society so smoothly that they became almost invisible, barely rising to the condition of distinguishable ethnicity. This is unfortunate because it robbed them of their individuality, even in sociological terms. They were extraordinarily difficult to categorise.[13]

When Mark Twain visited Australia in 1895–96 he said that it was 'an entire continent peopled by the lower orders'.[14] He was referring to a people derived from the British Isles, many of them specially chosen as labourers and domestic servants, which gave some credence to his description. In reality Australia had attracted migrants from every stratum of British society, the good, the bad and the indifferent. There were intellectuals and poets, bourgeois and aristocrats: Lord Salisbury's nephew, Cecil Balfour, disappeared to Australia over an affair of a forged cheque and died here, it is said, of drink.[15] Most British immigrants were less colourful but more useful and longer lived. They were generally more literate than the people left behind in Britain.

In the Australia of 1861, British-born people still outnumbered the Australian-born. A further million came between 1861 and 1900 but internal population growth began to outnumber the immigrants long before the end of that century, thereby replicating the British-American experience of the 18th century. Australian living standards were higher than those in Britain and British emigrants departed the relatively poor conditions generated in, and left over by, industrialisation. When Rudyard Kipling urged his gardener to emigrate after the First World War it was an echo of this mentality. Forty years later the story of the migration of the Liverani family from Glasgow in 1952 was a further symptom of the pinched character of urban life in late industrial Scotland, and the dream of better lives in the Antipodes. The outward impulse from Britain had been wavering in the 1920s, but the incentives were eroded only slowly. It was in this context that Australia continued to recruit its British migrants into the middle decades of the century, the flow resuscitated by its passage scheme, the most generous in the history of international migration. A recurrent theme was that the British immigrants were somehow lost in the crowd.

British dominance among its immigrants may have imposed the British character on Australia. But there was a reverse interpretation (advanced by CWE Bean, himself an immigrant): that Australia exerted a transforming effect on 'the British race' in this distant place. The 'Australian race' was allegedly different from, and an improved version of, the British immigrant. In Bean's hands, and then in the local patriotic model, this idea was the Antipodean variant of the Turner frontier thesis in North America. It reconciled Australian identity with the imperial connection, manifested in Bean's own life. Britain had been settled long before; its own pioneering was long finished and the Briton was 'inclined to settle on his oars', quite different from the Australian spirit. Indeed the Australian 'was becoming to some extent distinguishable from the Englishman in bodily appearance, in face, and in voice. He also displayed certain markedly divergent qualities of mind and character'. These evolved differences between Australians and the English became sharply comparable when they converged on the battlefields of the First World War. 'Men passed in Australia for what in themselves they were worth' – and into one class. They were bigger than the pink-cheeked lads from the Manchester cotton mills. They had become a different people.[16]

There was a serious racial element in Bean's contemplation of the British in Australia. He considered that the Australian's determination to keep his country racially pure was part of the struggle between East and West which went back to the beginnings of history and was deep in the nature of man: thus Britons 'must be encouraged to settle, so that the right people may be got in as well as the wrong people kept out'. Bean remarked that 'the Australian from the country … was a Briton with the stamina and freshness of the 16th century living among the material advantages of the 20th century'. The Bush made men into natural warriors. Military preparedness was vital, otherwise 'life would have to be lived not as you think right, but as some Asiatic might think right, as not worth living at all'.[17]

The incoming British migrants at the start of the 20th century sensed the need to toe the Australians' line: the colonial son felt 'independent and cocky', and they spoke of 'an Australian race to distinguish themselves from Englishmen'. At the same time they also felt 'imperiled and needed Imperial Britain to safeguard their independence'. 'They would never yield up their White Australia, yet alone they could not defend it. The Empire had power to shield them, but neither British protection nor British commitment to a white Australia seemed certain'.[18] Behind this broad Australian psychology there lurked a notion that Australia was coveted by alien forces who would appropriate the country they possessed only tenuously.

Australian immigration persisted as a dominantly British story until the 1970s and the relationship with Britain was central until after Menzies. Moreover Australia continued to recruit the majority of its immigrant people from the British Isles even when Britain began to decline as a great people exporter. The success of Australia in maintaining the flow (now against the odds) was demonstrated in the distribution of the British diaspora in 1985. At that time Australia had more British-born people than any other destination of the overseas British. In Canada they numbered 793 000, in New Zealand 235 000 and a similar number in South Africa. The United States, once the most favoured destination, was home to 584 000, which was little more than half the number of British-born in Australia, at 1 030 000.

This was a measure of the success of Australia's recruitment schemes in Britain after the Second World War. Australia did remarkably well among the dwindling emigration of the British, during the last throes of the British diaspora. This was surprising because, from 1947 onwards, Britain itself experienced serious labour shortages, and it was a time when Britain actually recruited and paid for immigrants for its own needs.[19] By the end of the 20th century Britain (and even Ireland) had become a country of substantial net immigration and more people emigrated from Australia to Britain than in the opposite direction. The Empire was migrating back home by this time.

Within this British story there had been a radical decline in the Irish component. In the 19th century the Irish comprised about 25 per cent of Australia's immigrants and reached its maximum accumulation of 228 232 in 1891. By 1947 the Irish-born in Australia had dwindled to 44 813. Partly it was the result of the declining Irish exodus, but it was also a consequence of the restriction of assisted passages to the Ulster Irish (and to people born in Ireland before 1949). In the years 1947–98 about 115 200 settlers arrived from all Ireland, which was 2.4 per cent of immigrants. In the late 1990s less than a thousand Irish emigrated to Australian per annum.[20] The Celtic fringe was much frayed by 2000.

In 1971 there were more than 1 million British-born in the Australian population. In terms of their concentrations there were higher proportions in Adelaide and Perth than in Sydney, and there were a few places with particularly high percentages of British, most notably the towns of Rockingham (Western Australia) and Elizabeth (South Australia). But it was difficult to find a wider phenomenon of British 'clustering', and still less ghettos. British emigrants were primarily suburbanites who easily blended into Australian suburbia in the postwar decades. Their generally relaxed mentality in Australia was associated with a relatively low rate of naturalisation among the British compared with other migrants. British immigrants on average possessed better educational qualifications, lower unemployment rates and higher incomes than the average of the Australian population at large. Moreover they were little inclined to express any militant sense of separate identity in the host society. They, like their predecessors, had migrated in large majorities into a staunch zone of the 'Anglo-sphere', little threatened by their hosts or the non-British migrants of the postwar years.

In the long run the predominance of the British was eroded by their own falling numbers and the rise of other sources of immigration. Nevertheless 29.6 per cent of all new settlers in Australia between 1947 and 1998 came from the United Kingdom and Ireland, compared with 29.1 per cent from the rest of Europe and 24.35 per cent from Asia. With the simultaneous expansion of the Australian population and the relative decline of British immigration, Australia became a demonstrably less British country. In 1986, 7 per cent of the total Australian population had been born in United Kingdom, 7 per cent in other European countries, 1 per cent in the Middle East, nearly 3 per cent in Asia. Clearly the British- and European-born population of Australia was declining while the Asian share was increasing.[21]

The relative decline of the British component of the Australia population had two elements. First, total new immigration from Britain declined in the 1990s: for instance, in the 3 years 1996–99 there were only 27 652 'permanent' arrivals and 11 195 departures,[22] minute numbers compared with the great days of 1910–13 and the early 1960s. Second, the cohorts of British immigrants of the early postwar years were beginning to die off, and the absolute numbers of British-born were falling in total. The British connection seemed to reach a terminus.

Al Grassby, Minister for Immigration, was born in Brisbane in 1926, British in origin but his identity was elastic. His mother was Irish but had a strong Scottish accent. Grassby himself had been a 'gypsy wanderer' and was abroad for many years, and served in the British Army. Oddly enough he seemed to embody continental Europe in all its colour and exoticism, a living paradox of multiculturalism, the personification of Australia's native cosmopolitanism. By contrast, the British immigrant seemed pale and barely visible, especially in comparison with the Europeans and the boat people. Displaced Persons and boat people often carried marks of their tragic circumstances, refugees out of some of the world's nastiest conflicts and circumstance. This was in raw contrast with the privileged emigration of the British, passing quietly and economically between indistinguishable parts of the 'Anglo-sphere'.

In Australia there were very small groups representing great conflicts on the other side of the world, remnants of far distant traumas. The story of the Copts in Australia was a microcosm. They had fled the convulsions of Upper Egypt, very late examples of the flight of the last remnants of a long-lost Christian empire. These people were described as 'the last stalks in the process of being uprooted', following the 'hot winds of change that scoured the Levant' 1400 years ago. Indeed Australia has been a refuge, often reluctant, for a wide array of the flotsam released by such eruptions across the world. In the main Australians have been blithely unaware of the dramas that have produced many of their new citizens. Australia's main concern is that these exotic people from alien places fully discard their enmities as they enter their new country.[23]

Australian immigration gathered into its story many of the common mobilities of the modern world and the transit of working people from one part of the globe to another. It was the most distant destination and remote from many of the currents of the modern world. Yet its immigrants, often in significant numbers, also provide immediate links with some of the most central shifts in the world. In Australia arrived representatives of these distant dramas, mostly living in suburban homogenised calm on the edge of the Pacific, and usually well insulated from the circumstances that precipitated their extraordinary emigrations in the first place. They and the British majority merged into the new society.

Immigration, defence and development

Australian immigration was generally governed by two national priorities: first was the defence of the realm, and second the development of the economy. By the time of the new millennium the priority of development began to revive, and labour shortages were anticipated in the near future. Defence was less straightforward because it was now less connected with the sheer size of the population, less dependent on numbers available for the armed forces, more contingent on capital equipment. The revival of immigration still caused anxieties about cheap labour undercutting established wage-rates and creating uncontainable strains in the social fabric.

Defence and development were sometimes in tension. In February 1885 Sir Henry Parkes had written that the colony (New South Wales), with a population of 900 000, could not be involved in Empire military conflicts because every man was wanted 'in colonizing work': 'With the right hand we are expending our revenues to import able-bodied men to subjugate the soil, while with the left hand we propose to squander our revenues to deport men to subjugate Sir Edward Strickland's "Saracens"'. He opposed involvement in distant imperial military action.

Nevertheless the defence of the Australian continent was crucial and in February 1890 Parkes openly declared that the threat was not from Europe or Russia but from 'the countless millions of inferior members of the human family who are within easy sail of these shores'. He said that all the colonial forces should be amalgamated into a federal force for defence. This became a uniting banner of the new Commonwealth. In 1891 Parkes said that the threat facing the Empire was greater than at any time in the past 500 years:

> I think it is more than likely, more than probable,
> that forms of aggression will appear in these seas
> which are entirely new to the world … We have
> evidence abundant on all hands that the Chinese
> nation and other Asiatic nations – especially the
> Chinese – are awakening to all the powers which
> their immense population gives them in the art of
> war, in the art of acquisition and all the other arts
> known to European civilization, and it seems to
> me … [that] it will be by stealthily … effecting a
> lodgment in some thinly-peopled portion of the
> country where it would take immense loss of life and
> immense loss of wealth to dislodge the invader.[24]

The fear was persistent and CWE Bean told the *Spectator* in 1907 that Australia was likely to be under siege:

> There are some three million odd whites in Australia
> inhabiting three million square miles. To the North
> at its very gates, up to within a day's sail, are eight
> hundred million Orientals … Three men to hold
> Australia against every eight hundred – that is the
> quality of the danger.

Prime Minister Alfred Deakin observed in 1908 that the visit of the United States fleet to Australia was 'universally popular here ... because of our distrust of the Yellow Race in the North Pacific ... the Yellow Peril to Caucasian civilization, creeds and politics'.[25]

At the start of the 20th century population increase, and therefore immigration, was regarded as the sine qua non of the nation's future. As David Pope remarked, it was 'a kind of cure-all, a panacea, for problems of defence and development in all but the years of deepest recession'. In 1920 Billy Hughes put it squarely: 'Population is the golden key which will unlock all doors, sweep aside all obstacles'.[26] The defence argument remained paramount, enhanced immeasurably by the two world wars and the perennial background fear of invasion. It was always difficult to defend an entire island continent and the existence of a larger home population was the most credible way to maintain long-term security. But, by the end of the 20th century the defence argument was overtaken by changing technology which reduced emphasis on sheer numbers and gave much more emphasis to military capability measured in weaponry and communications systems.

Similarly the character of economic development also altered Australia's population needs. In effect Australia shifted its category during the 20th century. It had started as a 'country of recent settlement' – an immigrant-seeking, primary-producing country desperate to increase its population but still rural-centred in its economy and ideology. This remained the case for much of the next half century. But by the mid 20th century Australia was becoming an industrial country and was still seeking population and immigrants. By the end of the century it was part of the OECD countries, one of the advanced industrial countries, and no longer sought the relatively unskilled immigrants who had been the main elements of its earlier history (though there were shortages of low-skilled labour in the domestic sector and in seasonal demands on the land).

'White Australia' was the most distinctive and contentious element in the entire history of Australian immigration. Even after its demise all the old issues of 'exclusion' repeatedly threatened to reactivate in the national debate. In the long run Australia had difficulty shaking off its reputation for racial discrimination, primarily because discrimination resided deep within the national psyche. White Australia, as we have seen, was widely regarded as 'The foundation idea of the Australian Settlement'. As Paul Kelly said, it was 'the mark of national individuality in an Empire of coloured races. White Australia was not just a policy, it was a creed which became the essence of Australian nationalism and, more importantly, the basis of national unity. It was endorsed by Labour and Conservatives, employers and unions, workers and housewives'. Deakin had been its clarion:

> The unity of Australia is nothing if that does not
> imply a united race. A united race means not only
> that its members can intermix, intermarry and
> associate ... but implies one inspired by the same
> ideas ... of a people possessing the same general
> cast of character, tone of thought, the same
> constitutional training and traditions ... Unity of
> race is an absolute to the unity of Australia.[27]

The policy was defended, even in its unequivocal form, by a broad spectrum of leading Australians for three-quarters of the forthcoming century and they included, for example, Henry Lawson, Frederic Eggleston, Vance Palmer, RG Menzies and, most volubly, Arthur Calwell.

The racial element in the programs was prominent and derived from racial theories combined with expectations of assimilation, fears of discord and racial turmoil, and the undercutting of wage-rates. It was translated into discriminatory policies of recruitment by the mid 19th century. There had been colonial disquiet about disproportionate Irish and 'Celtic' immigration, but this paled in comparison with the adamant opposition to coloured immigration, even to peoples from southern Europe. As late as the 1940s and

1950s Australians remained apprehensive of such newcomers, but economic considerations prevailed and the immigration policy widened without serious social repercussions.[28]

A broader perspective would acknowledge that discrimination against non-white immigration was far from unique to Australia. For instance, by 1920, across the Tasman Sea, parliament and people were united in the creation of a 'White New Zealand' and legislation was enacted to prevent the settlement of 'Asiatics'. In New Zealand at the end of the 19th century 'The most unrelenting racial hatred [was] directed against "Asiatic" especially Chinese people' and there was great fear of 'the Yellow Peril'.[29] The prospect of miscegenation was regarded with 'irrational horror'. The New Zealand Act of 1920 gave discretion to the minister to keep out immigrants and was highly flexible, and did not entail dictation tests. It was used in the 1920s to keep out Yugoslavs, Italians, Indians and Chinese. There was virtual unanimity on the question of staying white. Nevertheless New Zealand managed to avoid the degree of opprobrium directed at Australia, partly because of the bi-racial character of New Zealand society and its generally 'moderately good' Maori–Pakeha relations. Moreover New Zealand was more generous to non-Maori Polynesian immigration than Australia.[30]

In the British Empire at large there were counter currents in operation long before 'White Australia' was institutionalised. Much imperial idealism was devoted to 'fair play' and the fundamental equality of humanity. The imperial ideal was 'of a universal monarch whose subjects, regardless of religion, colour, or ethnic origin were equal before the law', which became 'the basis of an imperial philosophy of sorts'. Yet, in reality, racial discrimination was rife in many parts of the Empire. As Huttenback noted, 'In the minds of many of the settlers, *Niggers* really did begin at Calais'. The liberal rhetoric of empire could not hide the realties in the white man's colonies nor the implicit claims on behalf of the 'manifest destiny of the British race'. In truth there was increasing animosity, especially regarding Indians in South Africa and Canada; yet Indians were British subjects.[31] In 1899 British Columbia passed laws prohibiting Chinese or Japanese from working below ground. Many efforts were made to restrict employment opportunities on racial grounds employing the so-called 'Natal formula', which cloaked racial discrimination behind a literacy test.

The legacy of Federation and the White Australia policy became the way most foreigners saw the nation, even long after the official demise of White Australia. Given this total commitment to the policy until the late 1950s, the serious historical question was the 'demission' of White Australia and the fact that the opposition was relatively slight. It was a tribute to the political skills of its

A satirical perspective: invasions, 1788 and 2001. *Tamara Asmar*

undertakers; it also reflected the weakness of the opposition and the bipartisan element in the account. The consensus began to unravel in the 1980s, but it was difficult to prevent the continuation of the non-discriminatory policy without curtailing all immigration.

The new context: the 1990s and beyond

From 1947 to the 1990s Australia engineered relatively large population transfusions out of the theatres of postwar emigration – people from the aftermath of the Second World War in Europe and, three decades later, more dislocated people out of the ravaged landscapes of South-East Asia, the Balkans and the Middle East. It was a long remove from the certitudes of British White Australia, but the receiving country retained its social equilibrium, even while its politicians fretted.

By the start of the new century the context became yet more perplexing. Globalisation was the new mantra and there was great pressure towards the liberalisation of world trade. Human mobility in scale and velocity were greater than ever. Yet Australia appeared to have reached the end of its history of re-peopling. Moreover, despite the philosophy of globalisation, many of the advanced countries were erecting new barriers to the flow of labour. It seemed like a new age of mercantilism. In North America the doors are ostensibly closed, yet the numbers of its immigrants were colossal. Australia's place in this global scheme of things was paradoxical. The end of Empire and the rise of great prosperity in western and southern Europe had, by the 1980s, reversed the flow of migrants from the traditional supply regions. Meanwhile the rise of massive urbanisation and industrialisation in Asia had created an entirely new context – which, on historical precedent, might have been expected to induce great out-migration to mega-cities. The mystery was that Australia, on the doorstep of developing countries, did not receive the flows which elsewhere were virtually unstoppable.

As we have emphasised throughout, Australia always insisted on great control over its immigration. Its response to relatively small numbers of refugees was disproportionate in comparative terms. Though still protected by its insular and remote location, it remained anxious about the possibility of large-scale incursions of uncontrolled immigration.

There were other changes in the structure of migration which affected Australia. From 1945 to 1991 about 4.8 million people from 100 countries had settled in Australia and by the end of the century two-fifths of the population was born overseas or the children of immigrants. Among them was a 'sense of Australia as a refuge ... well understood by those working class immigrants who have come from southern Europe, Asia, the Middle East, India, Chile and elsewhere, who have transformed this society into one of the most culturally diverse on earth'.[32] But by 2000 the context had changed in many of Australia's old source countries. In the OECD countries, including Britain, Germany, Italy and Japan, there were serious concerns about the long-term slow down or decline of population. Although the population of the world was likely to increase by 50 per cent by 2050, the number of Russians, for instance, was expected to fall by 17 per cent, and the German population by 9 per cent. Some of the European countries were loosening their controls over some forms of immigration to help fill the shortages of skilled workers and to counter the ageing problem. The demographic declension was broadly attributed to the forces of 'modernisation', which caused young adults to avoid the burdens of large families and especially the costs of education. It also expressed the widening independence of young women. Australia, by 2005, quietly followed all these tendencies, which worked to revive the case for selective immigration once more. The United States was on a different track, expecting its population to rise by 43 per cent to 420 million by 2050, largely propelled by the effects of immigration and rising birth rates. According to Bernard Salt this demographic dynamism would guarantee the United States's continued economic growth and prosperity. To achieve similar growth in Australia would require net immigration of at least 310 000 per annum.[33]

In Australia the public debate about immigration had continued cacophonously for 20 years. John Howard presided over the policy for more than a decade and the swings in his own utterances suggest that the policy was improvised along short-term lines. Thus in August 1988 he said, 'I wouldn't like to see it [the rate of Asian immigration] greater'. Though he explicitly warned against any reversion to 'a White Australian policy', he emphasised the fragility of the nation's social cohesion and its capacity to absorb certain sorts of immigrants. As Opposition leader Howard attacked Asian immigration but faced a backlash from within his own ranks, and he later apologised for his comments and conceded that his stand had cost him his job at the time. Yet when Howard achieved government, after first slashing immigration in his first term between 1996 and 1998, he steadily ratcheted up the intake levels until they exceeded those under Labor in the 1980s. Thus in 2003/04 the Bureau of Statistics announced that Australia had crossed two thresholds: the overseas-born proportion of the population was 24 per cent, which was the highest since the 1890s, and the Europeans' share was below 50 per cent for the first time. Now Howard seemed genuinely pleased when the numbers were read out to him – 'Really? I think it demonstrates that we have run a truly non-discriminatory policy', he remarked.[34]

Australia's relationship with the immigrant world

Until the 1970s Australia was generally not a humanitarian haven for refugees; thereafter its attachment to international conventions and its involvement in wars eventually caused it to take more refugees than it had in the past. Yet even before this change Australia had been the last resort for a miscellany of immigrants fleeing adversity and ejected from the other side of the world, even though Australia was the least likely destination for many of them. Imperialism, modernisation, war, revolution, famine, all generated migration which reached Australia and these people represented some of the greatest historical movements of the 20th century. Their stories gathered many of the critical currents in the evolution of the 20th century, as we have seen in the previous chapters. Australia's immigrants were drawn from several primary categories which reflected their connections with the world beyond.

Most of Australia's 20th century immigrants derived, in reality, from late industrial Britain, a country which had passed through cyclical and structural shifts with a population long-educated in the ways of emigration. Some of the British postwar emigrants claimed they were fleeing the Welfare State and all its associations; some of them sought refuge in 'White Australia', insulated from the sort of coloured immigration entering Britain itself. Most of the British migrants were not politically propelled: they were classic economic migrants within the 'Anglo-sphere'.

Second were the large cohorts of dislocated peoples, victims of wars and their subsequent turmoil, including representatives of the Second World War, the Vietnam War, the communist repressions in Eastern Europe, the Chilean turmoil, and escapees from the conflicts in the Balkans and the Middle East at the end of the 20th century.

Third, were many people from southern and Eastern Europe in the 1950s and 1960s, who were often recruited straight out of semi-rural contexts, only recently touched by the spreading influence of industrialisation. As James Jupp noted in 1965, 'the bulk of migrants now come from Mediterranean peasant societies whose customs and habits are difficult to accommodate into the Australian way of life'.[35] They were especially prominent in the 1970s. In historical terms they were representatives at a particular moment in the postwar evolution of continental Europe, its recovery from war and its transformation into a fully articulated industrial economy with a shrinking rural base. But there was virtually no recourse to *gastarbeiter* (guest worker) immigration in Australia because it set its face against such forms of labour, which may have reduced Australia's flexibility and delayed the diversification of its population pool. It is clear, for instance, that the non-English speaking immigrants did not become 'a disadvantaged reserve army of labour at the behest of the capitalist employers' and, as Robert Birrell pointed out, they generally achieved a remarkable level of educational and occupational mobility in Australia.[36]

Fourth, Australia attracted some of the people dislodged, or sent packing, at the End of Empire in many parts of the world – essentially later intra-imperial movements out of South Africa, Sri Lanka, India, Hong Kong and Rhodesia. The large movements from New Zealand to Australia were more strictly economic migration, part of the traditional reciprocating mechanism between the two countries.[37]

Fifth, were the rising categories of sojourners and other 'ambiguous' migrants, the skilled mobile elements of the global world who were part of the growing interchange within the new international aristocracy of labour. They were often jetted into and out of many countries including Australia, unpredictable in their final resting places, part of the frenetic global movements of the new age.[38] They included technicians, medical personnel, business leaders and others – from Canada, India and Singapore, for instance, whose inflows and outflows included many Australian-born in the astonishing new mobility of so-called 'parachutists' of the global economy.[39] Much less well rewarded were the increasing legions of young backpackers and working holiday-makers who traversed the world, adding flexibility to many economies including Australia's.[40]

Twentieth-century migrants to Australia therefore came out of radically different circumstances. Some were from pre-industrial rural communities in remote parts of central and Eastern Europe. Others were suburban migrants of a certain economic sort. Some were refugees born in wartime camps, entirely deracinated and lacking any kind of settled background. Some arrived in liners of the most modern construction; others came by intercontinental jet aircraft; others in pathetic boats; some travelled overland to Singapore and then threaded their way into Australia; many were accidental immigrants, tourists and travellers who did not move on; many were escapees from crime, military service, divorces and racial intolerance. Their variety was astonishing yet their intermingling in a society which generally had set its face against diversity is one of the marvels of this story.

The history of Australian immigration has not attracted the massive scholarship, nor the deep debates, which have been invested in the epic story of peoples uprooted and transplanted to North America. A classic American lament is that too much emphasis was devoted to the destination in the migration story, elevating the receiving over the sending countries and thereby erecting a 'salt-water curtain' inhibiting the understanding of their European origins.[41] Even where historians overcame this bias they tended to provide only a condescending account of the original contexts of emigration, dealing essentially in stereotypes. The same deficiencies infect the Australian account, which similarly gives little attention to the heroic and often tragic qualities of the emigrant experience. Australia also tends to represent the immigrant story as a matter of assimilation and successful adaptation to Australian needs rather than the sum of the extraordinary lives which began in forgotten places among people whose extraordinary migrant stories long preceded their landfall in Australia.

Clearly not all Australian immigrants were either traumatised peasants or bland British suburbanites. Many emigrants had 'acquired momentum in Europe itself'. The postwar Latvians, for instance, who were conscripted into Russian then German armies, and then shunted into concentration camps, and Displaced Persons camps, entered Australia with psychological burdens which few in Australian ever understood. The early postwar migrants carried memories, some of childhoods spent in concentration camps including Belsen, unreleased till much later.[42] Some of the migrants' trails were even longer. Thus, in his account of the decline of Christianity in the Middle East, the modern writer William Dalrymple recounted the story of the last remnants of the great Armenian and Greek communities which once flourished in Constantinople and Antioch as well as in many sites in Turkey. They suffered systemic persecution, ejection and massacre in one of the appalling ethnic and religious horrors of the 20th century. There was, pari passu, a diaspora of the Armenians and others. Small numbers of them came to Australia. These immigrants were part of that remote drama connecting Australia with grand and tragic currents of the distant world. There had once been 15 000 Christians in Antioch, of the Greek Orthodox Church: in 1996 there were a mere 200 families amid the rubble of their churches. They left for 'new lives in Syria, Brazil, Germany and Australia', in parallel with many Istanbul Greeks, many of them now found in Melbourne and elsewhere.[43] These casual references connect Australia with the world beyond in vivid terms of which Australia was little aware.

Australia's immigration policies were not designed to relieve British social and economic problems; nor were they designed to provide humanitarian assistance to postwar refugees from Europe. These were essentially incidental consequences of a much more pragmatic and Australia-centred purpose; similarly policy in the past two decades has been, in the first instance, directed to the needs of the Australian economy and its demographic aspirations. This nevertheless should not obscure the humanitarian element in its policies – clearly Australia meets a large part of its international obligations towards humanitarian relief even as it jealously guards its frontiers.

It was only in the last third of the 20th century that Australia confronted the problem of refugees en masse and its own obligations under the UN Universal Declaration of Human Rights of 1948. Australia's gyrations upon this issue revolved about the common political determination that every state has an unrestricted right to determine whom it shall admit within it frontiers. The exception is the international law to which they subscribed, the duty to admit refugees.[44] Refugees and economic migrants from poor countries constituted a generic problem for all countries with high living standards. Such countries were like magnets to less affluent people, who behaved in perfectly rational ways by attempting to emigrate. In the United States opinion ran higher than in Australia, some regarding illegal immigration as a cancer ruining the State and the country, and liberals were denounced as promoting 'these invaders'.[45] In the United Kingdom in 2005 there were moves which explicitly followed the Australian system towards a 'points formula' for evaluating the eligibility of all applicants for immigration; it was designed to exclude those 'illegals' regarded as 'abusing British hospitality'. The United Kingdom wanted people who would make a contribution to the country with skills and talents and not become a burden. British polls showed the immigration issue as one of the few areas where the conservative Opposition was making headway against the Labour government. Meanwhile in Denmark a centre-right party was making good political advances on anti-immigration policies by promising to cut immigration by 90 per cent.[46] In the greatest of emigrant nations, that is in Ireland, resistance to immigrants had become vociferous.[47] In Europe a prominent German commentator referred to the 'popular alarmism, dramatization and scandalization of migration issues', to the widespread creation of 'the enemy image of "illegal immigration", and "the negative coalition against unwelcome immigration"'.[48] There was a widening anxiety about asylum seekers in Europe.[49]

Australia conducted its own political debate about immigration, but most of the issues were already canvassed in each of the other OECD countries, none with any final resolution. Moreover, as Australia's economic performance improved after 2000, the appetite for immigrants was again resurgent and once again the policy was made anew.

The final account: the impact of immigration

In the wide perspective of modern history Australia was clearly a far distant and small player in the story of international migration. In the great era of the diasporas, from about 1840 to 1940, roughly 160 million people were engaged in long-distance migration – about 60 million from Europe to the Americas, 50 million from India and southern China to South-East Asia and the Pacific Rim, and 47 million from North-East Asia and Russia to Manchuria and Siberia. In that period the flow to Australia was about 2.3 million.[50] Australia was a relatively late participant in some of these flows – indeed more than half of Australia's immigration occurred in the years 1947–70, when it drew on people from the southern and eastern zones of continental Europe, 80 years after similar flows of people had transformed migration to the United States and Canada.[51] In the postwar years Australia notably followed the road already travelled by Canada and created more open access to different racial and ethnic groups, which meshed in with changing labour requirements and a diminished availability from traditional source countries. The criteria for the selection of immigrants were liberalised in both countries, ending discrimination and White Australia towards the end of the 1960s.

The later resurgence of anxiety about immigration was striking in the Australian political debates, but was echoed in many other countries. The British general election of 2005 was shadowed by the issue of illegal immigration and the Opposition declared that British immigration controls were a shambles and that the statistical record of such 'illegals' was a total fiction. The British debate (in parallel with controversies in most other European countries and the United Stases) demonstrated than the Australian anxiety was generic rather than exceptional.[52]

Measuring the success or failure of immigration in the life of modern Australia is exceedingly difficult since so many competing criteria were involved, surrounded too by incalculable counterfactuals.[53] It was however incontestable that the population growth of Australia was greatly boosted by immigrants and their offspring. By 2005 the population was 20 million but growing at a very slow rate (though faster than most other OECD countries), yet some regarded it as already too large for the continent. Of the population, 51 per cent was female and they were living longer: life expectancy was more than 77 for boys born in the new century, and 83 for girls. The respective figures for Aborigines were 60 and 65. Half the population was over 36 and by 2020 the under-15s together with the over-65s were predicted to account for 17 per cent of population. The fertility rate had been falling since the beginning of the 20th century but was raised to 3.5 in 1961 by the effects of recent immigration; it subsequently declined continuously down to 1.75 at the turn of the century. Half the women who gave birth in Australia in 2004 were over 31. The Bureau of Statistics warned that in 2011 the most common family type would be couples without children, and this was related to the ageing question. Real income had risen, but unequally: since 1994-95 there has been a 12 per cent increase for low-income people, but 16 per cent for the higher income people. About 80 per cent of the population lived within 50 kilometres of the sea and 70 per cent were in cities of more that 100 000. It was clear that Australia was already closely aligned to global trends.

Australia's most influential commentator on demographic trends forecast, in 1999, that the proportion of the world's population living in towns and cities would rise from one-third in 1960 to one-half by 2000 and to two-thirds by 2050. By then life expectancy in the Third World would be 76 years, converging with the First World. Moreover population growth, after centuries of increase, would draw to a halt. This would derive from rising incomes, technology, and globalisation.[54] For Australia, further immigration offered partial solutions to ageing, population decline and economic stagnation. In the past it was an option which Australia had taken up, but always with doubts, and this remained a constant factor in the prevailing mentality.

Australia was still not convinced that immigration had fulfilled the Calwellian dream of the late 1940s. Yet in terms of living standards, health, economic growth and peaceability the Australian story, in 2005, was unambiguous.[55] Immigration had clearly generated no revolution, little internecine conflict, no riots in the streets of any significance, little communal turmoil and no permanent ghettos. Since the 1980s Australia had become one of the most culturally diverse societies in the world and half of the intake of immigrants has been Asian. This was no guarantee for the future, but the record was undoubtedly positive over 50 years of radical transformation.[56]

Political divisiveness on the issue had also been slight, and the main complaint was that a bipartisan gag had been placed on public discussion. Even when the muzzle was removed in the 1980s, the political consequences were relatively mild in terms of the general condition of the body politic of Australia. Any calculation of Australia's record in receiving millions of migrants must give weight to the intensity of the intakes (which were proportionally greater that in other countries) and the diversity factor. In 1998 overseas-born people accounted for 22.3 per cent of the population but were only 12.5 per cent of parliamentary representatives; 14 per cent of the Australian population were from non-English speaking backgrounds but only 4 per cent of federal parliamentarians were of these origins. Absorbing a homogeneous body of immigrants was less a test of success than containing a very diverse set of peoples, which of course Australia experienced after 1947 and more especially after 1970. It also depended on the size of the intakes and the ratio of immigrants to the home population. On this scale Australia competed well in the international record. Other indicators, such as rates of inter-marriage and return migration, also suggest that the consequences were positive. Most of all it is clear that, despite such palpable success in social engineering by immigration, Australia remained no less nervous of the subject than in its past.

For half a century the vision of 1900 was remarkably well sustained. The British transplantation had created one of the most uniform and introverted societies in the world. Australia had indeed continued its essential relationship with Britain and maintained the defining exclusivity of its peopling. After 1947 change came in accelerated form – most notably the sudden widening of its range of immigration. But for another 20 years the rapid recruitment of European migrants was essentially the next best compromise to preserve the essence of the old exclusionist society. Even after the formal end of White Australia, continuities remained: thus in 1900 and 2000 there were atavistic fears in some parts of Australian society that immigration would increase miscegenation and disease. On the other hand, by 2000 immigrants were no longer regarded as essential for the future defence of the country; nor were they regarded as necessary for the occupation of the land, as required for closer settlement. The transition of Australia into a variegated and heterogeneous society was a social revolution which affected the very foundations of Australian life and altered its relations with the rest of world. It was a continuing transition and one with which Australia wrestled into the 21st century. Indeed in 2000 there was no agreement that immigration was even a positive benefit to the country – and one school believed that immigration added to the nation's problems by way of its pressure on resources. That was the problem with migration: it was a great but incalculable factor in the life and history of the nation.

Beyond the politics and demography of immigration, of course, was the experience of the immigrants themselves. Most were undoubtedly beneficiaries of the long boom of rising living standards in Australia after 1947 and resumed at the end of the century. Most of these people were economic migrants and experienced great material success in Australia. The greater the gap from their origins the greater the material benefit. Their remittances home were often vital in the foreign earnings of some of the original countries, for instance in the case of many Pacific Islands. Emigrants in the first generation often remitted large sums of money back home, helping development in such places. Emigration levelled off as soon as the home standards of living began to reach those of the destination country. This happened in the case of migrants from southern Europe and later among those from Eastern Europe. Emigration to Australia enabled these people to experience better living standards than those they would have had at home. When this ceased to apply, emigration ceased and some returned home to retire.[57]

Finally, among all the uncertainties of historical causation, it seems most likely that immigration was a grand positive propellent of economic, social and political growth and maturity in Australia. It is often said of the parallel case that the economic growth in the United States in the past four centuries could only be explained by its extraordinarily expansive attitude to immigration.[58] Australia has equally been a great beneficiary of international migration, despite the perennial anxieties that have dogged its story.

Statistics

The measurement of migration is often insecure and subject to definitional difficulties. There are significant discrepancies between various estimates, especially for the most recent decades. These tables are drawn from 'official' data and offer merely a generalised version of the story. Only the total population figures are unambiguous. Some critical discussion of Australian migration statistics is found in the official source (Australian Bureau of Statistics, *Australian Demographic Trends 1997*, Appendices 10, 11, 12) and in Katharine Betts, *The Great Divide*, Duffy & Snellgrove, Sydney, 1999, Appendix 1, and SE Khoo and P McDonald (eds), *The Transformation of Australia's Population*, UNSW Press, Sydney, 2003.

TABLE 1: Australia: components of population increase, 1901–2005

sources TJ Skinner, *Australian Demographic Trends* 1997, Australian Bureau of Statistics,1997; *Year Book Australia*.
note Statistics for 1901–95 are for calendar years; those for 1996–2005 are for financial years.

Year	Total population	Natural increase	Net migration	Year	Total population	Natural increase	Net migration
1901	3 824 913	56 615		1931	6 552 606	61 949	-10 094
1902	3 875 318	54 698	-4 293	1932	6 603 785	54 176	-2 997
1903	3 916 592	51 150	-9 876	1933	6 656 695	52 152	758
1904	3 974 150	60 541	-2 983	1934	6 707 247	47 246	3 306
1905	4 032 977	61 427	-2 600	1935	6 755 662	47 726	689
1906	4 091 485	63 557	-5 049	1936	6 810 413	52 141	2 610
1907	4 161 722	65 042	5 195	1937	6 871 492	54 635	6 444
1908	4 232 278	65 119	5 437	1938	6 935 909	53 964	10 453
1909	4 323 960	69 899	21 783	1939	7 004 912	53 744	15 290
1910	4 425 083	71 211	29 912	1940	7 077 586	57 963	15 142
1911	4 573 786	74 324	74 379	1941	7 143 598	63 349	6 936
1912	4 746 589	80 911	91 892	1942	7 201 096	61 517	7 311
1913	4 893 741	83 925	63 277	1943	7 269 658	74 809	2 653
1914	4 971 778	86 263	-8 226	1944	7 347 024	83 748	-615
1915	4 969 457	82 089	-84 410	1945	7 430 197	90 329	-934
1916	4 917 949	77 229	-128 737	1946	7 517 981	101 718	-13 344
1917	4 982 063	81 936	-17 822	1947	7 637 963	108 916	11 205
1918	5 080 912	75 490	23 359	1948	7 792 465	101 137	53 365
1919	5 303 574	56 360	166 303	1949	8 045 570	106 001	147 104
1920	5 411 297	80 117	27 606	1950	8 307 481	112 404	149 507
1921	5 510 944	82 122	17 525	1951	8 527 907	111 510	108 916
1922	5 637 286	86 185	40 157	1952	8 739 569	120 053	91 609
1923	5 755 986	78 986	39 714	1953	8 902 686	122 047	41 070
1924	5 882 002	79 947	46 069	1954	9 089 936	120 451	66 799
1925	6 003 027	81 224	39 801	1955	9 311 825	125 641	96 248
1926	6 124 020	76 210	44 783	1956	9 530 871	126 045	93 001
1927	6 251 016	75 416	51 580	1957	9 744 087	135 405	77 811
1928	6 355 770	74 700	30 054	1958	9 947 358	138 781	64 490
1929	6 436 213	68 623	11 820	1959	10 160 968	137 764	75 846
1930	6 500 751	73 068	-8 530	1960	10 391 920	141 862	89 090

Year	Total population	Natural increase	Net migration	Year	Total population	Natural increase	Net migration
1961	10 642 654	151 025	58 658	1991	17 384 470	138 101	81 877
1962	10 846 059	143 918	58 992	1992	17 573 218	140 491	51 774
1963	11 055 482	140 795	68 117	1993	17 746 629	138 630	35 243
1964	11 280 429	128 555	95 816	1994	17 932 079	131 359	55 506
1965	11 505 408	123 139	101 329	1995	18 168 599	131 057	108 028
1966	11 704 843	119 210	80 225	1996	18 310 700	124 000	109 661
1967	11 912 253	126 593	80 817	1997	18 524 200	126 400	87 079
1968	12 145 582	131 359	101 970	1998	18 751 000	120 600	106 223
1969	12 407 217	143 679	117 955	1999	18 966 790	121 700	96 500
1970	12 663 469	144 468	111 784	2000	19 157 000	120 900	107 300
1971	13 198 380	165 711	79 060	2001	19 413 200	118 600	135 700
1972	13 409 288	155 209	56 320	2002	19 641 000	117 200	110 600
1973	13 614 344	136 848	67 494	2003	19 872 600	114 300	116 500
1974	13 831 978	129 344	87 248	2004	20 111 300	121 000	117 600
1975	13 968 881	123 991	13 513	2005	20 328 609	127 010	110 095
1976	14 110 107	115 148	34 030				
1977	14 281 533	117 501	68 027				
1978	14 430 830	115 756	47 397				
1979	14 602 481	116 561	68 611				
1980	14 807 370	116 832	100 940				
1981	15 054 117	126 839	123 076				
1982	15 288 891	125 132	102 708				
1983	15 483 496	132 486	54 995				
1984	15 677 282	124 120	59 823				
1985	15 900 566	128 540	89 321				
1986	16 138 769	128 427	110 663				
1987	16 394 641	126 638	136 060				
1988	16 687 082	126 327	172 794				
1989	16 936 723	126 621	129 478				
1990	17 169 768	142 586	97 131				

TABLE 2a
Main countries of birth of the Australian population, census years

SOURCES FOR TABLES 2A AND 2B *Year Book Australia*, which derives statistics from *Migration, Australia* and ABS data available on request, *Estimated Resident Population*; Wray Vamplew (ed.), *Australians: Historical Statistics*, Sydney, 1987.

NOTE China excludes Special Administrative Regions and Taiwan.

	1901	1911	1921	1933	1947	1954
British Isles	679 200	601 753	681 674	716 769	541 300	664 200
New Zealand	25 800	32 130	38 757	45 983	43 600	43 400
Italy	5 700	6 773	8 164	26 760	33 600	119 900
Indochina/Vietnam	na	4	25	30	28	200
China	29 900	20 918	15 265	8 579	6 400	10 300
Greece	900	1 883	3 664	8 338	12 300	25 900
Germany	38 400	33 296	22 522	16 875	14 600	65 400
Philippines	700	453	330	234	100	200
India	7 600	6915	7 072	7 070	8 200	12 000
Netherlands	600	751	1 397	1 275	2 200	52 000
Malaysia	932	914	703	1 266	1 000	2 300
South Africa	500	3 919	5 430	6 183	5 900	6 000
Lebanon	1 645	1 542	1 817	2 024	1 900	3 900
Hong Kong	200	418	339	237	800	1 600
Poland	na	na	1 787	3 241	6 600	56 600
Former Yugoslavia	na	na	831	3 971	5 900	22 900
United States	7 400	6 703	6 642	6 068	6 200	8 300
Sri Lanka	600	616	640	638	694	2 000
Australia	2 908 300	3 692 825	4 593 931	5 726 566	6 835 200	7 700 100
Total population	3 773 800	4 455 005	5 435 734	6 629 839	7 579 400	8 986 500

TABLE 2b
Main countries of birth of
the Australian population,
2004

	1961	1971	1981	1991	2001
	755 400	1 081 300	1 120 900	1 244 300	1 182 800
	47 000	74 100	160 700	286 400	394 100
	228 300	288 300	275 000	272 000	238 500
	320	717	52 299	124 800	169 500
	14 500	17 100	25 200	84 600	157 000
	77 300	159 000	145 800	147 400	132 500
	109 300	110 000	109 300	120 400	117 500
	400	2 300	14 800	79 100	112 200
	14 200	28 700	41 000	66 200	103 600
	102 100	98 600	95 100	100 900	91 200
	5 800	14 400	30 500	79 900	87 200
	7 900	12 200	26 500	55 800	86 900
	7 300	23 900	49 400	78 500	80 000
	3 500	5 400	15 300	62 400	75 200
	60 000	59 500	59 000	69 500	67 500
	49 800	128 200	148 600	168 000	64 000
	10 800	26 800	28 900	49 500	59 000
	3 400	9 000	16 800	40 400	58 600
	8 729 400	10 173 100	11 388 800	13 318 800	14 931 200
	10 508 200	12 719 500	14 516 900	17 284 000	19 413 200

	2004
UK	1 190 900
New Zealand	442 200
Italy	227 900
China	182 000
Vietnam	176 600
Greece	128 700
India	128 600
Philippines	125 100
Germany	116 100
South Africa	109 200
Malaysia	97 800
Netherlands	88 700
Lebanon	84 300
Hong Kong	76 500
Australia	15 360 400
Total population	20 111 300

TABLE 3
Settler arrivals in Australia by nationality / country of birth

The countries selected are the highest ranked source countries in each of the 5-year periods.

SOURCES *Official Year Books of the Commonwealth*;
Bureau of Immigration Research, *Australian
Immigration: Consolidated Statistics*, Canberra.
NOTES
a) The category 'British' includes Irish, Maltese and
Cypriots; see *Official Year Book of the Commonwealth*,
no. 37, 1946–47, p. 732.

b) Excludes Danes.
c) Excludes prisoners of war (1915).
d) Excludes returned troops and nurses.
e) Excludes Ireland.
Re Nationality/birthplace: we have followed the
designations in the Year Books, where there is a
clear change of terminology.

Period	Nationality	Number	% of total intake
1902–05	British (a)	149 392	80.4
	French	5 879	3.2
	Chinese	4 439	2.4
	German	3 939	2.1
	Italian	3 522	1.9
	Pacific Islander	2 566	1.4
1906–10	British	324 600	84.7
	German	9 717	2.5
	Chinese	7 875	2.1
	French	7 604	2.0
	Scandinavian (b)	4 875	1.3
1911–15	British	546 747	87.6
	German (c)	12 558	2.0
	Chinese	10 807	1.7
	Scandinavian	6 663	1.0
	North American	5 708	0.9
1916–20	British (d)	261 705	87.5
	Chinese	9 276	3.0
	North American	5 469	1.8
	French	3 363	1.1
	Japanese	3 274	1.0
1921–25	British	404 792	84.7
	Chinese	17 133	3.6
	Italian	17 092	3.5
	United States	6 875	1.4
	Greek	4 247	0.9
1926–30	British	386 669	82.2
	Italian	19 170	4.1
	Chinese	15 649	3.3
	United States	8 916	1.9
	Yugoslav	4 426	0.9

Period	Nationality	Number	% of total intake
1931–35	British	200 159	83.6
	Chinese	8 709	3.6
	Italian	7 234	3.0
	United States	5 065	2.1
	French	3 090	1.3
1936–40	British	254 803	79.3
	United States	10 671	3.3
	Italian	10 520	3.3
	German	9 514	3.0
	Chinese	7 804	2.4
1941–45	British	48 086	66.9
	United States	4 799	6.7
	Indonesian/ Javanese	4 288	6.0
	Chinese	3 975	5.5
	Dutch	1 859	2.6
1946–50	British	437 856	62.4
	Polish	66 572	9.5
	Latvian	48 803	7.0
	Italian	26 532	3.8
	Yugoslav	20 201	2.9
1951–55	British	683 875	66.5
	Italian	102 700	10.0
	Dutch	69 936	6.8
	German	43 718	4.3
	Greek	29 298	2.9
1956–60	British	845 748	66.9
	Italian	97 943	7.7
	Dutch	57 250	4.5
	United States	47 080	3.7
	Greek	40 373	3.2

Period	Birthplace	Number	% of total intake
1961–65	UK & Ireland	303 750	42.5
	Italy	92 749	13.0
	Greece	70 710	9.9
	Germany	35 010	4.9
	Yugoslavia	33 870	4.7
	Netherlands	28 010	3.9
	Malta	19 800	2.8
1966–70	UK & Ireland	371 500	46.2
	Yugoslavia	73 700	9.2
	Italy	61 900	7.7
	Greece	53 100	6.6
	New Zealand	22 800	2.8
	Germany	19 000	2.4
1971–75	UK & Ireland	252 810	41.3
	Yugoslavia	53 120	8.7
	Greece	25 040	4.1
	Italy	22 190	3.6
	United States	21 620	3.5
	New Zealand	18 320	3.0
	Lebanon	13 850	2.3
1976–80	UK (e)	86 200	25.0
	New Zealand	39 800	11.6
	Vietnam	30 600	8.9
	Lebanon	18 400	5.3
	South Africa	10 200	3.0
1981–85	UK (e)	119.500	25.5
	New Zealand	50.700	10.8
	Vietnam	49.900	10.7
	Poland	15.500	3.3
	Philippines	14.800	3.2

Period	Birthplace	Number	% of total intake
1986–90	UK (e)	107.000	17.4
	New Zealand	82.500	13.4
	Vietnam	38.900	6.3
	Philippines	36.200	5.9
	Hong Kong	27.500	4.5
	Malaysia	26.600	4.3
1991–95	UK (e)	64.300	13.9
	Hong Kong	40.300	8.7
	New Zealand	39.700	8.6
	Vietnam	39.000	8.4
	Philippines	24.300	5.2
	India	20.800	4.5
	Former Yugoslavia	20.100	4.4
	China	16.100	3.5
1996–2000	New Zealand	80.600	18.4
	UK (e)	48.100	11.0
	China	36.300	8.3
	Former Yugoslavia	28.300	6.5
	South Africa	21.400	4.9
	India	16.400	3.7
2001–05	New Zealand	84 959	16.2
	UK (e)	66 786	12.7
	China	42 013	8.0
	India	34 759	6.6
	South Africa	26 514	5.0

Notes

Preface

1   This was accomplished splendidly in Kate Walsh, *The Changing Face of Australia: A Century of Immigration, 1901–2000*, Allen & Unwin, Sydney, 2001.

1 The new century: 1900 and 2000

1   Small clusters of Afghans, Italians, Chinese and Germans persisted for many decades, long before the flood of change in the 1950s and after.

2   See VG Kiernan, 'Britons old and new', in Colin Holmes (ed.), *Immigrants and Minorities in British Society*, Allen & Unwin, London, 1978, pp. 23–59.

3   See Eric Richards, 'Immigrant lives', in Eric Richards (ed.), *The Flinders History of South Australia: Social History*, Wakefield Press, Adelaide, 1986, pp. 143–70; Reminiscences of William Clayton, c.1833–1912, State Library of South Australia, D6424(L).

4   DE Darbyshire, *In Time for Lunch: The Personal Diary and the Official Journal of Douglas E. Darbyshire*, Fremantle Arts Centre Press, Perth, 1991, pp. 15, 44, 91, 95.

5   Jared Diamond, *Guns, Germs and Steel: The Fate of Human Societies*, Jonathon Cape, London, 1997, ch. 15.

6   See David Pope, 'Population and Australian economic development, 1900–1930', in Maddock & McLean (eds), *The Australian Economy in the Long Run*, p. 46.

7   Michael Davie, 'The fraying of the rope', *Daedalus*, no. 114, 1985, p. 372.

8   Estimates by Charles Price, cited in Markus, *Australian Race Relations*, p. 152. In 1947, 90 per cent were 'Anglo-Celtic' in origin, 2.4 per cent were from eastern and southern Europe, 1.1 per cent Asians and Aborigines.

9   John C Caldwell, *Pushing Back the Frontiers of Death*, Cunningham Lecture, Academy of the Social Sciences in Australia, Canberra, 1999.

10 See A Maddison, *Monitoring the World Economy, 1820–1992*, Development Centre of the Organisation for Economic Cooperation and Development, Paris, 1995.

11 *Official Year Book of the Commonwealth of Australia*, no. 1, 1908, p. 211; no. 5, 1912, pp. 151, 207. There seemed to be a direct link between drought and departures from Australia – the 1902/03 drought was associated with a net outflow of 10 000 people. Moreover, as if to emphasise the connection between harvests and demography, the natural increase of births over deaths was abnormally low in the year of drought.

12 Caldwell, *Pushing Back the Frontiers of Death*, p. 1.

13 Hugh Stretton, obituary of John Tregenza, *The Australian*, 8 June 1999, p. 17.

14 See Eric Richards, 'The limits of the Australian immigrant letter', in Bruce Elliott, David A Gerber & Suzanne M Sinke (eds), *Letters across Borders*, Palgrave, New York, 2006, pp. 56–75.

15 See TA Coghlan, *The Wealth and Progress of New South Wales 1900–1901*, Government Printer, Sydney, 1902, pp. 944–51.

16 Quoted in LL Robson, *The First AIF: A Study of its Recruitment*, Melbourne University Press, Melbourne, 1970, p. 6.

17 John Bannon, 'Birth of a nation', *The Australian*, 'Review', February 1998, pp. 10–11; Helen Irving, *To Constitute Australia: A Cultural History of Australia's Constitution*, Cambridge University Press, Cambridge, 1997, p. 61.

18 EM Andrews, *The Anzac Illusion*, Cambridge University Press, Melbourne, 1993, pp. 12–13.

19 Charles A Price, *The Great White Walls Are Built*, Australian National University Press, Canberra, 1974, p. 40.

20 See Eric Richards, 'Migrations: the career of British White Australia', in Deryck Schreuder & Stuart Ward (eds), *Australia's Empire: Oxford History of the British Empire: Companion Series, Australia*, Oxford University Press, Oxford, 2008, pp. 150–75.

21 Bannon, 'Birth of a nation', p. 10.

22 G Blainey, 'Australia: a bird's eye view', *Daedalus*, no. 114, 1985, p. 12.

23 Coghlan, *The Wealth and Progress of New South Wales*, p. 953.

24 Bannon, 'Birth of a nation', p. 10.

25 Kelly, *The End of Certainty*, pp. 1–2.

26 'Traders of the Orient', in *Memento* (Australian Archives), May 2004, pp. 16–17.

27 Nicolas Rothwell, review of Henry Reynolds, *North of Capricorn: The Untold Story of Australia's North*, in *The Australian*, 11/12 October 2003.

28 *Manchester Guardian* and *Spectator*, late December 1899, quoted in Michael Harrington, 'The present century in the past', *Spectator*, 3 February 1996, p. 8.

29 See WW Rostow, *The Stages of Economic Growth*, 2nd edn, Cambridge University Press, Cambridge, 1971.

30 G Jackson, 'The Australian economy', *Daedalus*, no. 114, 1985, pp. 231–58.

31 *OECD in Figures: Statistics on Member Countries*, 2001.

32 *OECD in Figures*, 2001.

33 See Bell & Hugo, *Internal Migration in Australia, 1991–1996*, p. xiii.

34 Bernard Bailyn, *Context in History*, La Trobe University, Melbourne, 1995, p. 8.

2 The slow awakening: 1901–14

1. New South Wales Bicentennial Oral History Collection, MSS 5163, Mitchell Library, State Library of New South Wales. On return migration, see DC Baines, *Migration in a Mature Economy: Emigration and Internal Migration in England and Wales*, Cambridge University Press, Cambridge, 1985; Richards, *Britannia's Children*, pp. 214–15.

2 Diary of Annie Amelia Duckles, MS 644, National Library of Australia. See also Penelope Layton, 'All at sea', *National Library of Australia News*, August 1997, pp. 10–14.

3   G Blainey, *The New Federalist*, no. 4, 1999, p. 96.

4   See TJ Hatton & JG Williamson, *Migration and the International Labor Market, 1850–1939*, Routledge, London, 1994, p. 5 (figure); Roger Daniels, *Coming to America: A History of Immigration and Ethnicity in American Life*, HarperCollins, New York, 1990, pp. 124–25; Baines, *Emigration from Europe*, pp. 10–11; Richards, *Britannia's Children*, ch. 10.

5   See especially Baines, *Emigration from Europe*.

6   *Australian Immigration Consolidated Statistics*, AGPS, Canberra, quoted in Jupp, *Immigration and Multiculturalism*, p. 126.

7   See Gigi Santow, WD Borrie & Lado Ruzicka (eds), *Landmarks in Australian Population History*, Australian Population Association, Melbourne, 1988, p. 137.

8   Neville Hicks, *'This Sin and Scandal': Australia's Population Debate 1891–1911*, Australian National University Press, Canberra, 1978, Introduction.

9   Quoted in Alison Mackinnon, 'Bringing the unclothed immigrant into the world': population policies and gender in twentieth century Australia', *Journal of Population Research*, vol. 17, no. 2, 2000, p. 19.

10 Peter McDonald, 'Demographic history', in G Davison et al. (eds), *Oxford Companion to Australian History*, Oxford University Press, Melbourne, 2001, pp. 181–83.

11 Powell, *An Historical Geography of Modern Australia*, Cambridge University Press, Cambridge, 1988, p. 28, quoting *Daily Telegraph*, 5 March 1904.

12 Australia was not exceptional in its unwelcoming attitude to immigrants, nor to racial prejudices. It was only different in the way it institutionalised its policy and made a clarion call of its whiteness. It was not even exceptional in the British world. See TC Smout, *A Century of the Scottish People, 1830–1950*, Collins, London, 1986, pp. 22, 248.

13 See Robin Gollan, *Radical and Working Class Politics: A Study of Eastern Australia, 1850–1910*, Melbourne University Press, Melbourne, 1960, p. 8.

14 *Boomerang*, 21 January 1888, quoted in Gollan, *Radical and Working Class Politics*, p. 116.

15 D Walker 'Climate, civilization and character in Australia', in Michael Bennett & David Walker (eds), *Intellect and Emotion*, Faculty of Arts, Deakin University, Geelong, 1998, pp. 77–78. See M Roe, *Nine Australian Progressives*, University of Queensland Press, Brisbane, 1984, p. 131.

16 KS Inglis, 'C.E.W. Bean, Australian historian', in J Lack (ed.), *Anzac Remembered*, Department of History, University of Melbourne, Melbourne, 1998, pp. 69–70.

17 AM Taylor, 'Mass migration to distant southern shores: Argentina and Australia, 1870–1939', in Hatton & Williamson, *Migration and the International Labour Market*, p. 111.

18 BR Wise, 'Australia and its critics', in *The Empire and the Century*, John Murray, London, 1905, p. 443.

19 Quoted in David Pope & Glenn Withers, 'Do migrants rob jobs?: lessons of Australian history, 1861–1991', *Journal of Economic History*, vol. 53, December 1993, p. 720. The unanimity of these attitudes is attested in Stuart Macintyre, *The Succeeding Age*, Oxford History of Australia, vol. 4, Oxford University Press, Melbourne, 1986, pp. 123–24. In New South Wales in 1909 a Labor premier was sanctioning immigration, but as soon as the labour market slackened there were protest meetings. 'Generally the intensity of Labor's disapproval varied with the labour market'. This was an iron law of immigration in Australia as elsewhere.

20 WK Hancock, in J Holland Rose et al. (eds), *Cambridge History of the British Empire*, vol. 7, part 1, Cambridge, 1933, p. 503.

21 Hancock, in *Cambridge History of the British Empire*, vol. 7, part 1, p. 503. See also Wise, *The Empire and the Century*, p. 444.

22 In 1909 George Knibbs, the Commonwealth Statistician, calculated that the population of Australia would be only 8.167 million by 1950, which he regarded as totally unsatisfactory.

23 *Argus*, 14 January 1905, quoted in Langfield, '"Fit for the Elect of the World"'. More comparable were Canada which had attracted 244 000 immigrants and Argentina 62 000 in only 2 years.

24 Compare HC Allen, *Bush and Backwoods: A Comparison of the Frontier in Australia and the United States*, Angus and Robertson, Sydney, 1959 and Jared Diamond, *Guns, Germs and Steel: The Fate of Human Societies*, Jonathon Cape, London, 1997.

25 Quoted in Langfield, '"Fit for the Elect of the World"', p. 112.

26 Smout, *A Century of the Scottish People*, p. 261.

27 Immigration League of Australia, first Annual Report, Sydney, 1906. See Jupp (ed.), *The Australian People*, p. 52.

28 Quoted in Macintyre, *The Succeeding Age*, p. 35.

29 Quoted in Sydney Labor Council, Report on Immigration, 1907.

30 See Richards, *Britannia's Children*, p. 226.

31 See Langfield, '"Fit for the Elect of the World"', pp. 82–85. *The Times* was cited in the *Argus*, 6 July 1910: 'The overseas dominions must not expect the very classes needed for the homeland but must be content with a good average. The best means of obtaining it is to attract immigrants while they are still young'.

32 Langfield, '"Fit for the Elect of the World"', pp. 54, 65.

33 Langfield, '"Fit for the Elect of the World"', pp. 72–75, 108–14, 121. See also 'Imperial emigration and its problems', *Proceedings of the Royal Colonial Institute*, vol 40, 1908–09), pp. 313–40.

34 Langfield, '"Fit for the Elect of the World"', pp. 75–76. A premiers' agreement in 1911 set uniform rates of £6 for males under 45 and £3 for females under 35.

35 The Dreadnought Scheme began as an effort in New South Wales to raise funds for a battleship as a gift to Great Britain. But some was eventually used as a fund to assist British boys to emigrate. The trustees found £8 towards the fare and the Commonwealth the other £12. There was a 3-month training at Scheyville or a 12-month apprenticeship. Eventually half its funds were used to carry 1787 immigrants (1911–14) between the ages of 15 and 18. Victorian received 4116 boys from the West Ham Distress Committee in 1914; South Australia and New Zealand also had boy schemes, and the Fairbridge Scheme operated in Western Australia.

36 Langfield, *More People Imperative*, p. 134.

37 See Roe, *Australia, Britain and Migration*, pp. 6–7, 22; Roe, 'Richard Arthur', *Australian Dictionary of Biography*, vol. 7; Walker, 'Climate, Civilization and Character in Australia', pp. 77–95.

38 Wray Vamplew (ed.), *Australians: Historical Statistics*, Fairfax, Syme and Weldon, Sydney, 1987, pp. 5–7. Most of the statistics of the period are discrepant and much confused with ordinary passenger movements, which were ambiguous as to migration, business and pleasure.

39 ET McPhee, 'Australia: its immigrant population', in WF Willcox (ed.), *International Migrations*, vol. 2, New York, 1931, pp. 176–77; David Pope, 'Australia's development strategy in the early twentieth century: semantics and politics', *Australian Journal of Politics and History*, vol. 31, 1985, pp. 218–29; Langfield, '"Fit for the Elect of the World"', p. 118. See also James Jupp, *The English in Australia*, Cambridge University Press, Melbourne, 2004.

40 See Marjory Harper, *Emigration from Scotland between the Wars*, Manchester University Press, Manchester, 1998, p. 47.

41 Langfield, '"Fit for the Elect of the World"', pp. 83–85, 90–93.

42 See K Windschuttle, *The White Australia Policy*, Macleay Press, Sydney, 2004. He asserts that the White Australia policy was not about 'Whiteness' as such, but about protecting wage levels for the Australian labour force: 'White' was merely a synonym for 'cheap labour'.

43 Barry York, 'The dictation test: White Australia's tangled web', *Canberra Historical Journal*, vol. 27, 1991, pp. 33–39.

44 See John Reynolds, *Edmund Barton*, Angus and Robertson, Sydney, 1948, pp. 177–80; Paul Jones & Vera Mackie (eds), *Relationships: Japan and Australia, 1870s–1950s*, History Department, University of Melbourne, Melbourne, 2001. See also TE Smith (ed.), *Commonwealth and Migration*, Macmillan, London, 1981, pp. 2–3.

45 Geoffrey Bolton, *Edmund Barton*, Allen & Unwin, Sydney, 2000, pp. 243–48.

46 Clive Moore, 'The South Sea Islander community and deportation', *The New Federalist*, no. 4, 1999, pp. 22–29. See also P Corris, 'White Australia in action: the repatriation of Pacific Islanders from Queensland', *Historical Studies*, vol. 15, 1972, pp. 237–50. In 1906 only 1654 were allowed to stay out of 9324: Markus, *Australian Race Relations*, pp. 142–44.

47 Printed in full in Raymond Evans, Clive Moore, Kay Saunders & Bryan Jamison, *1901: Our Future's Past: Documenting Australia's Federation*, Macmillan, Sydney, 1997, pp. 217–24.

48 See Ganter, *The Pearl-Shellers of the Torres Strait*, p. 105 and chs 3, 4.

49 Quoted in D Pope, 'Population and Australian economic development 1900–1930', in Maddock & Maclean (eds), *Australian Economy in the Long Run*, pp. 47, 58.

50 Quoted in Harry Martin, *Angels and Arrogant Gods*, p. 1.

51 BR Wise, 'Australia and its critics', pp. 424–25.

52 See Denis Judd, *Balfour and the British Empire*, St Martin's Press, New York, 1968, pp. 305–306.

53 Papers of Dr Richard Arthur, c.1883–1932, MSS 473, Box 3, Newspaper clippings on immigration, Mitchell Library, State Library of New South Wales.

54 MS 5163, Mitchell Library, State Library of New South Wales. This splendid body of evidence provides the cases that follow.

55 See Richards, *Britannia's Children*, pp. 209–10.

56 Gollan, *Radical and Working Class Politics*, p. 163.

3 Migrants and the Great War: 1914–18

1 CEW Bean, *The Story of ANZAC*, vol. 1, Angus & Robertson, Sydney, 1937, p. 43.

2 JNI Dawes & LL Robson, *Citizen to Soldier*, Melbourne University Press, Melbourne, 1977, p. 68.

3 EM Andrews, *The Anzac Illusion*, Cambridge University Press, Melbourne, 1993, p. 185.

4 This and the following stories are from Dawes & Robson, *Citizen to Soldier*, pp. 62–63, 70, 72, 75, 77, 83.

5 Langfield, 'Recruiting immigrants', pp. 55–65.

6 Bill Gammage, *The Broken Years*, Penguin, Melbourne, p. 312.

7 See James Jupp, 'Migration from the north of England', in Jupp (ed.), *The Australian People*, p. 303.

8 See Langfield, *More People Imperative*, p. 11.

9 Andrews, *The Anzac Illusion*, pp. 44–46.

10 See LL Robson, *The First AIF: A Study of its Recruitment*, Melbourne University Press, Melbourne, 1970, pp. 1–2; Robson, 'The origin and character of the First AIF, 1914–18: some statistical evidence', *Historical Studies*, vol. 15, 1973, pp. 737–49.

11 Andrews, *The Anzac Illusion*, p. 183.

12 Walsh, *The Changing Face of Australia*, p. 64.

13 See Gerhard Fischer, *Enemy Aliens: Internment and the Homefront Experience in Australia 1914–1920*, University of Queensland Press, Brisbane, 1989.

14 See J Perkins, 'Germans in Australia during the First World War', in Jupp (ed.), *The Australian People*, p. 372; I Harmsdorf, 'Guests or Fellow-countrymen: A Study in Assimilation', PhD thesis, Flinders University, 1989.

15 Fischer, *Enemy Aliens*, p. 128; Markus, *Australian Race Relations*, p. 146.

16 LF Fitzhardinge, *The Little Digger*, Angus & Robertson, Sydney, 1979, p. 199.

17 Walter A Ebsworth, *Archbishop Mannix*, H.H. Stephenson, Melbourne, 1977, p. 194. My thanks to Neville Meaney for this reference.

18 Markus, *Australian Race Relations*, p. 146–47.

19 Fitzhardinge, *The Little Digger*, p. 200.

20 M Langfield & P Roberts, *Welsh Patagonians*, Crossing Press, Sydney, 2005, pp. 144–49, 215–32.

21 See Karen Agutter, 'The Enforced Repatriation of Italian "Reservists" from Australia during the First World War', BA(hons) thesis, Flinders University, 2002; Agutter, 'National identity explored: emigrant Italians in Australia and British Canada in World War I', *Flinders Journal of History and Politics*, vol. 23, 2006, pp. 84–99.

22 Quoted in Tom Pocock, *Rider Haggard and the Lost Empire*, Weidenfeld and Nicolson, London, 1993, pp. 166, 173.

23 Pocock, *Rider Haggard and the Lost Empire*, pp. 141–43; N Etherington, *Rider Haggard*, Twayne, Boston, 1984, pp. 15–16, 18.

24 Pocock, *Rider Haggard and the Lost Empire*, pp. 172, 199, 205, 226.

25 *The Private Diaries of Sir Rider Haggard, 1914–1925*, edited by DS Higgins, Cassell, London, 1980, pp. 53, 61, 63.

26 Roe, *Australia, Britain and Migration*, p. 9.

27 Roe, *Australia, Britain and Migration*, p. 13.

28 This section derives from Fitzhardinge, *The Little Digger*, pp. 147ff, 166–68, 400–402, 507 (quoting VSS Sastri).

29 Mitchison, cited in Richards, *Britannia's Children*, p. 235. In 1914– 21 there were 41 824 marriages in Australia per annum, compared with 41 594 in 1913 and 44 731 in 1922.

30 Langfield, 'Recruiting immigrants', p. 64. Parliamentary debates spoke of 20 to 50 million as the population needed to maintain Australia's independence.

31 Langfield, 'Recruiting immigrants', p. 60.

32 Fitzhardinge, *The Little Digger*, p. 353.

33 Langfield, 'Recruiting immigrants', pp. 63–64; Richards, *Britannia's Children*, ch. 11.

4 White British Australia resuscitated: the 1920s

1 See Joanna Bourke, 'The battle of the limbs', *Australian Historical Studies*, no. 110, 1998, p. 59.

2 Roger Daniels, *Coming to America*, Harper Collins, New York, 1990, pp 278–84.

3 Quoted in Brown, *Governing Prosperity*, p. 8.

4 GRG7/24, 103/1925, State Records of South Australia; Correspondence between Acting PM and Premier of South Australia (Barlow), May 1921, GRG 7/23, 150/1921, CSO 128/24, State Records of South Australia. My thanks to Margrette Kleinig for this reference. Note particularly that statistics relating to arrivals, immigrants and net migration are extremely inconsistent and confusing in these years. See especially Roe, *Australia, Britain and Migration*, pp. 2–5.

5 Quoted in LL Robson, *Australia in the Nineteen Twenties*, Thomas Nelson, Melbourne, 1980, p. 72.

6 Letter of Arthur Hackett, 30 June 1960, MS 644, National Library of Australia.

7 Letter of Edward Miles of Huddersfield, 29 June 1960, MS 1767, National Library of Australia.

8 Letters of Robert Keen, MS 1767, National Library of Australia. His book was Robert C Keen, *Big Men, Little Men and Men in Between*, self-published, Tebworth UK, 1965.

9 Kipling to Munro Hull (a Queensland farmer) 29 Nov 1911, MS 4565, National Library of Australia.

10   Lord Birkenhead, *Rudyard Kipling*, Weidenfeld and Nicolson, London, 1978, p. 302.

11   Quoted in York, *Speaking of Us*, p. 111.

12   This testimony is derived from the *NSW Bicentennial Oral History Project*, which ultimately entailed recordings of 200 men and women born before 1907 who lived in New South Wales between 1900 and 1930; mainly recorded in 1986 and 1987.

13   David Pope, 'Empire migration to Canada, Australia, and New Zealand, 1910–1929', *Australian Economic Papers*, no. 7, 1968.

14   Bobbie Oliver, review of Kent Fedorowich, *Unfit for Heroes: Reconstruction and Soldier Settlement in the Empire between the Wars*, in *Australian Historical Studies*, no. 108, 1997, pp. 137–38.

15   Langfield, '"Fit for the Elect of the World"', pp. 51, 174.

16   Langfield, '"Fit for the Elect of the World", p. 6.

17   Mackinder, in a House of Commons debate, August 1916, quoted in Powell, *An Historical Geography of Modern Australia*, p. 74.

18   Introduction to L St Clare Grondona, *The Kangaroo Keeps on Talking*, London, 1924.

19   Tom Pocock, *Rider Haggard and the Lost Empire*, Weidenfeld and Nicolson, London, 1993, p. 228.

20   H Rider Haggard, *The Days of my Life: An Autobiography*, vol. 2, edited by CJ Longman, Longmans, London, 1926, pp. 202–203.

21   Quoted in Powell, *An Historical Geography of Modern Australia*, p. 75.

22   LS Amery, *The Leo Amery Diaries 1896–1929*, edited by J Barnes and D Nicholson, Hutchinson, London, 1980, p. 268.

23   Roe, *Australia, Britain and Migration*, pp. 51–57.

24   Quoted in C Edwards, *Bruce of Melbourne: Man of Two Worlds*, Heinemann, London, 1965, p. 103. See also Kosmas Tsokhas, *Making a Nation State: Cultural Identity, Economic Nationalism and Sexuality in Australian History*, Melbourne University Press, Melbourne, 2001.

25   JM Powell sees it as a 20th century elaboration of Wakefieldianism. See Powell, *An Historical Geography of Modern Australia*, pp. 72, 79.

26   *Argus*, 9 April 1925, quoted in Robson, *Australia in the Nineteen Twenties*, p. 76.

27   CD Kemp, *Big Businessmen: Four Biographical Essays*, Institute of Public Affairs, Melbourne, 1964, p. 30.

28   HW Gepp, *The Functions of the Developments and Migration Commission*, Commonwealth Club, Adelaide, 1929.

29   Langfield, '"Fit for the Elect of the World"', p. 6.

30   On the Round Table, see JE Kendle, *The Round Table Movement and Imperial Union*, University of Toronto Press, Toronto, 1975.

31   WA Sinclair, *The Process of Economic Development in Australia*, Cheshire, Melbourne, 1976, p. 205 n12; Pope, 'Empire migration to Canada, Australia, and New Zealand', pp. 171–72; CB Schedvin, *Australia and the Great Depression*, Sydney University Press, Sydney, 1970, pp. 59–67.

32   Amery, *The Leo Amery Diaries*, vol 1, 1896–1929, pp. 573–74.

33   Quoted in Powell, *An Historical Geography of Modern Australia*, p. 75.

34   Langfield, *More People Imperative*, pp. 64, 66.

35   HS Gullett, quoted in Powell, *An Historical Geography of Modern Australia*, p. 76.

36   Marjory Harper, *Emigration from Scotland between the Wars*, Manchester University Press, Manchester, 1998, pp. 49, 53.

37   Here again 'the scheme was not a success, as most persons availing themselves of the loans were unable to repay the Government'. It was suspended in 1933. See Ian Pearce & Clare Cowling, *Guide to the Public Records of Tasmania, Section Four, Records Relating to Free Immigration*, Hobart, 1975.

38   Quoted in Pope, 'Empire migration to Canada, Australia, and New Zealand', p. 167.

39 Langfield, *More People Imperative*, p. 12.
40 Second Progress Report on National Insurance, 1927, pp. 13–14.
41 Quoted in David Pope, 'Contours of Australian Immigration, 1901–1930', *Australian Economic History Review*, vol. 21, 1981, p. 42.
42 Pope, 'Contours of Australian Immigration'.
43 In the 1920s the fare to Australia was about £33, of which £11 was funded by the government for suitably nominated migrants.
44 Pope, 'Contours of Australian Immigration', p. 61.
45 Paula Hamilton & Barry Higman, 'Servant of Empire: the British training of domestics for Australia, 1926–31', *Social History*, vol. 28, no. 1, 2003, pp. 67–82.
46 Pope, 'Contours of Australian Immigration', pp. 40, 42.
47 See Correspondence between Acting Prime Minister and the Premier of South Australia, Barwell, May 1921, GRG7/23, 150/1921, CSO 128/24, State Records of South Australia. For this reference I am grateful to Margrette Kleinig.
48 See Langfield, '"Fit for the Elect of the World"', ch. 5.
49 Based on Kent Fedorowich, 'The problems of disbandment: the Royal Irish Constabulary and imperial migration, 1919–29', *Irish Historical Studies*, vol. 30, 1996, pp. 88–110, esp. p. 106.
50 Pope, 'Contours of Australian Immigration', p. 37; Cecil Edwards, *Bruce of Melbourne: Man of Two Worlds*, Heinemann, London, 1965, p. 103.
51 M Roe, '"We can die just as easy out here": Australian and British migration, 1916–1939', in S Constantine (ed.), *Emigrants and Empire: British Settlement in the Dominions between the Wars*, Manchester University Press, Manchester, 1990, p. 98.
52 G Sherington, in Jupp (ed.), *The Australian People* [1988], pp. 92–96, 105.
53 See Roe, '"We can die just as easy out here"', p. 105, citing *Report on Boy Migrants*, South Australian Parliamentary Papers, 1924, and pp. 110, 112.
54 Michele Langfield, 'Voluntarism, salvation and rescue: British juvenile migration to Australia and Canada, 1890–1939', *Journal of Imperial and Commonwealth History*, vol. 32, 2004, pp. 86–114.
55 *The Call of Empire*, Migration Department, Scouts Association, London, nd [1939], p. 3.
56 Sherington, in Jupp (ed.), *The Australian People* [1988], p. 94. See also Sherington, '"A better class of boy": the Big Brother movement, youth migration and citizenship of empire', *Australian Historical Studies*, no. 120, 2002, pp. 267–85.
57 For the charitable levels of migration in this period, see Michele Langfield, '"A chance to bloom": female migration and Salvationists in Australia and Canada, 1890s to 1939', *Australian Feminist Studies*, vol. 17, no. 39, 2002.
58 Roe, '"We can die just as easy out here"', p. 103.
59 There were subsequent lawsuits regarding child migrants, in both Australia and Canada. See G Sherington & C Jeffery, *Fairbridge: Empire and Child*, University of Western Australia Press, Perth, 1998; David Hill, *Forgotten Children*, Random House, Sydney, 2007.
60 Bolton, *A Fine Country to Starve In*, p. 37.
61 See, for example, John Selwood & Mark Brayshaw, '"From one room to another in the great house of the Empire": Devon and Cornwall Group Settlement in Western Australia', *Early Days*, vol. 11, 1998, pp. 477–95.
62 See Bolton, *A Fine Country to Starve In*, p. 37.
63 Bolton, *A Fine Country to Starve In*, pp. 46, 41.
64 Lamidey, *Partial Success*, p. 10. My thanks to James Jupp for bringing this to my attention. See also LS Amery, *My Political Life*, 3 vols, Hutchinson, London, 1953–55; Amery, *The Leo Amery Diaries*, vol. 1.
65 John Robertson, *J.H. Scullin: A Political Biography*, University of Western Australia Press, Perth, 1974, pp. 101–103.

66 See Langfield, '"Fit for the Elect of the World"'.

67 For America quota arrangements, see Pope, 'Contours of Australian Immigration', p. 35 n7.

68 See J Gentilli et al., *Italian Roots in Australian Soil: Italian Migration to Western Australia 1829–1946*, Italo-Australian Welfare Centre, Perth, 1983, p. 10.

69 Pope, 'Contours of Australian Immigration', pp. 34, 36.

70 Quoted in David Day, *Chifley*, Harper Collins, Sydney, 2001, p. 228.

71 Day, *Chifley*, p. 231.

72 See Langfield, *More People Imperative*, p. 28.

73 LF Fitzhardinge, *The Little Digger*, Angus & Robertson, Sydney, 1979, p. 559.

74 Kylie Tennant, *Evatt: Politics and Justice*, Angus & Robertson, Sydney, 1970, p. 60.

75 Markus, *Australian Race Relations*, p. 145.

76 Brown, *Governing Prosperity*, p. 18.

77 Robertson, *J.H. Scullin*, pp. 111, 212–13.

78 [John Davidson], *Scottish Delegation: Objects: To Advertise Australia, Its Products and Possibilities, To Stimulate Migration of Scottish People to Australia*, The Delegation, Melbourne, 1927. See more generally, Marjory Harper, '"Personal contact is worth a ton of textbooks": educational tours of the Empire, 1926–39', *Journal of Imperial and Commonwealth History*, vol. 32, 2004, pp. 48–76.

5 Malaise, recrimination and demographic pessimism: the 1930s

1   Letters of Robert Keen, MS 1767, National Library of Australia. He later collected his memories in Robert C Keen, *Big Men, Little Men and Men in Between*, self-published, Tebworth UK, 1965, pp. 37, 44–45.

2   York, *Speaking of Us*, p. 110.

3   See G Sherington, 'Immigration between the wars', in Jupp (ed.), *The Australian People* [1988], p. 93.

4   Sherington, 'Immigration between the wars', p. 94; Powell, *An Historical Geography of Modern Australia*, p. 105.

5   Petition of the British Migrants' Association of Australia, *Parliamentary Debates (Commons)*, 5th series, vol. 264, Session 1931–32, 14 April 1932, p. 967.

6   *Parliamentary Debates (Commons)*, 5th series, vol. 245, session 1930–31, 18 November 1930, p. 2225; Sherington, 'Immigration between the wars', pp. 93–94. See also Bolton, *A Fine Country to Starve In*.

7   See Charles Fahey, review of Marilyn Lake, *The Limits of Hope*, in *Australian Historical Studies*, vol. 23, no. 90, 1988, pp. 140–41.

8   CD Kemp, *Big Businessmen: Four Biographical Essays*, Institute of Public Affairs, Melbourne, 1964, p. 30. See also Roe, *Australia, Britain, and Migration*, p. 108; Lamidey, *Partial Success*.

9   Some parts of Canada laboured under similar influences; see John H Atchison, 'Immigration in two federations', in Bruce W Hodgins et al. (eds), *Federalism in Canada and Australia: Historical Perspectives*, Trent University, Peterborough, Canada, 1989, p. 203.

10 WA Sinclair, *The Process of Economic Development in Australia*, Cheshire, Melbourne, 1976, p. 172. See also David Pope, 'Australia's development strategy in the early twentieth century: semantics and politics', *Australian Journal of Politics and History*, vol. 31, 1985, pp. 218–29.

11 Dyster & Meredith, *Australia in the International Economy*, p. 124.

12 Carl Strikwerda, 'Tides of migration, currents of history', *International Review of Social History*, vol. 44, 1999, p. 388.

13 LF Giblin, *Australia: An Inaugural Lecture*, Melbourne University Press, Melbourne, 1930, p. 31. An amaranth is an unfading flower.

14   Barry Smith, 'Australian public health during the Depression of the 1930s', in MJ Bennett & D Walker (eds), *Intellect and Emotion: Essays in Honour of Michael Roe*, Deakin University, Geelong, 1998, pp. 96–106.

15   Dyster & Meredith, *Australia in the International Economy*, pp. 145–46.

16   CB Schedvin, *Australia and the Great Depression*, Sydney University Press, Sydney, 1970, p. 290, quoted in Dyster & Meredith, *Australia in the International Economy*, p. 147.

17   Dyster & Meredith, *Australia in the International Economy*, p. 151.

18   Dyster & Meredith, *Australia in the International Economy*, p. 239.

19   HV Wilson, 'Our Trip of Australia' (1936–37), MS 3450, National Library of Australia.

20   Walter A Ebsworth, *Archbishop Mannix*, H.H. Stephenson, Melbourne, 1977, p. 310.

21   CW14, 15, Archives Office of Tasmania, Hobart.

22   Langfield, '"Fit for the Elect of the World"', p. 271.

23   See Sherington, *Australia's Immigrants* [1988], p. 119. On return rates in general, see TJ Archdeacon, *Becoming American*, Free Press, New York, 1983, pp. 139–41.

24   See Brawley, *The White Peril*, passim.

25   AT Yarwood, *Australian Quarterly*, June 1958. K Tennant, *Evatt: Politics and Justice*, Angus & Robertson, Sydney, 1970, pp. 88–90.

26   See LJ Louis, 'The Victorian Council against war and fascism: a rejoinder', *Labour History*, vol. 44, 1983, p. 44. Barry York, 'The dictation test: White Australia's tangled web', *Canberra Historical Journal*, ns no. 27, 1991, pp. 33–39.

27   Langfield, *More People Imperative*, pp. 29, 34.

28   AC Palfreeman, 'The end of the dictation test', *Australian Quarterly*, March 1958, pp 43–50.

29   Langfield, *More People Imperative*, pp. 38, 39.

30   See Russel Ward, *Australia*, Ure Smith, Sydney, 1969, p. 146.

31   R Jay, 'Immigration into Australia', in Australian Institute of International Affairs, *Australian Foreign Policy 1935–6*, Brisbane, 1936, pp. 44–45.

32   David Pope, 'Population and Australian economic development 1900–1930', in Maddock & McLean, *The Australian Economy in the Long Run*, p. 45.

33   See Langfield, '"Fit for the Elect of the World"', pp. 41, 45.

34   CH Wickens, 'Australian population: its nature and growth', *Economic Record*, vol. 1, 1925, p. 5.

35   Langfield, '"Fit for the Elect of the World"', p. 44.

36   Those involved in the debate were PD Phillips, H Burton, A Lodewyckx, Gordon Taylor, KH Bailey, DB Copland, SM Wadham, RB Madgwick, WD Borrie, Griffith Taylor, FC Benham, AM Carr-Saunders.

37   Giblin, *Australia*, pp. 29–30.

38   See Langfield, '"Fit for the Elect of the World"', p. 48.

39   See Roger Schofield & David Coleman, 'Introduction: the state of population theory', in David Coleman & Roger Schofield (eds), *The State of Population Theory: Forward from Malthus*, Blackwell, Oxford, 1986, p. 5.

40   Quoted in Ian Castles, 'Vice-president's note', *Dialogue*, vol. 17, no. 4, 1998, p. 5. Castles presents a highly critical evaluation of Taylor's reputation.

41   See Griffith Taylor, *Environment and Race*, Oxford University Press, London [Humphrey Milford], 1927; JM Powell, *Griffith Taylor and Australia Unlimited*, University of Queensland Press, Brisbane, 1993. More generally, see Jupp, *From White Australia to Woomera*, pp. 164ff. See also Griffith Taylor, 'Possibilities of settlement in Australia', in I Bowman (ed.), *Limits of Land Settlement*, Council on Foreign Relations, New York, 1937, pp. 195–227.

42   See DN Livingston, *The Geographical Tradition*, Blackwell, Oxford, 1993, p. 277. See also JM Powell, 'Griffith Taylor emigrates from Australia', *Geography Bulletin*, vol. 10, 1978, pp. 5–13; Maire Sanderson, *Griffith Taylor*, Carleton University Press, Ottawa, 1988.

43 *Bulletin*, 20 October 1937, p. 107; Griffith Taylor, *European Migration: Past Present and Future*, Livingston Lecture, 1928, p. 6; Bowman, *Limits of Land Settlement*, pp 195, 227.
44 LC Wilcher, review of J Lyng, *Non-Britishers in Australia*, in *Australian Quarterly*, vol. 29, 1936, pp. 95–98.
45 See Langfield. "'Fit for the Elect of the World'".
46 Jay, 'Immigration into Australia', p. 47.
47 Langfield, *More People Imperative*, p. 79.
48 Sherington, 'Immigration between the wars', p. 96.
49 Neville Cardus, *Australian Summer*, Cape, London, 1937, pp. 13, 14, 243.
50 Richards, *Britannia's Children*, pp. 248–50.
51 Letters of Mr Albert Pace, MS 644, National Library of Australia.
52 Langfield, *More People Imperative*, p. 79.
53 Michael Roe, "'We can die just as easy here'": Australia and British migration, 1916–1939', in Stephen Constantine (ed.), *Emigrants and Empire*, Manchester University Press, Manchester, 1990, pp. 96–120, esp. 98.
54 SWB McGregor, quoted in David Pope, 'Australia's development strategy in the early twentieth century: semantics and politics', *Australian Journal of Politics and History*, vol. 31, 1985, p. 226.
55 Barry Higman, 'Testing the boundaries of White Australia: domestic servants and immigration policy, 1901–45', *Immigrants and Minorities*, vol. 22, 2003, p. 16. See also Ganter, *The Pearl-Shellers of Torres Strait*.
56 See Peter Read in Martin Crotty & David Andrew Roberts (eds), *The Great Mistakes of Australian History*, UNSW Press, Sydney, 2006, p. 41.
57 Barry Higman, *Domestic Service in Australia*, Melbourne University Press, Melbourne, 2002, pp. 95–96.
58 Higman, 'Testing the boundaries of White Australia', pp. 1–21.
59 Langfield, "'Fit for the Elect of the World'", p. 282.
60 Quoted in Ebsworth, *Archbishop Mannix*, p. 334.
61 Peter Scott, 'The State, internal migration and the growth of new industrial communities in inter-war Britain', *English Historical Review*, vol. 115, no. 461, 2000, pp. 329–53; Stephen Constantine, 'Introduction: Empire migration and imperial harmony', in Constantine (ed.), *Emigrants and Empire*. A very young first-year economics student, TW Swan, at the University of Sydney, wrote a remarkable essay on 'Migration' in 1936 which predicted the end of the 'free trade in humanity' and was pessimistic about any future revival of immigration (MSS 2180, Mitchell Library, State Library of New South Wales, p. 30).
62 AM Carr-Saunders, 'Migration movements to and from the British Isles', *Sociological Review*, vol. 29, 1937, pp. 232–42.
63 Jay, 'Immigration into Australia', p. 48.
64 Lack & Templeton (eds), *Sources of Australian Immigration History 1901–1945*, History Department, University of Melbourne, Melbourne, 1988, pp. 115–22, 171–74.
65 Based on Michele Langfield, 'To restore British migration: Australian population debates in the 1930s', *Australian Journal of Politics and History*, vol. 41, 1995, pp. 408–19.
66 See David Remnick, 'The spirit level', *New Yorker*, 8 November 2004, p. 85.
67 Quoted in Brennan, *Tampering with Asylum*, p. 1. Cf. Jupp, *From White Australia to Woomera*, p. 9.
68 See Markus, *Australian Race Relations*, pp. 131–32.
69 Langfield, *More People Imperative*, pp. 192–93.

6 Race, refugees, war and the future: 1939–45

1 HG Wells, *Travels of a Republican Radical in Search of Hot Water*, Penguin, Harmondsworth UK, 1939, pp. 48–52.

2   See Michele Langfield & Pam Maclean, 'But pineapple I'm still a bit wary of': sensory memories of Jewish women who migrated to Australia as children, 1938–39', in A James Hammerton and Eric Richards (eds), *Speaking to Immigrants: Oral Testimony and the History of Australian Migration. Visible Immigrants Six*, Research School of Social Sciences, Australian National University, Canberra, 2002, p. 83.

3   Ilma O'Brien, 'The enemy within: wartime internment of enemy aliens', in Martin Crotty & David Andrew Roberts (eds), *The Great Mistakes of Australian History*, UNSW Press, Sydney, 2006, p. 139. See Lamidey, *Alien Control in Australia 1939–46*. Lamidey, as secretary of the Aliens Classification and Advisory Committee of the Commonwealth government, authored the report to Minister Calwell (1947) printed in this volume.

4   'Who was Wolf Klaphake?', *Memento*, September 2003, p. 15.

5   Alrene Sykes, *Three Australian Plays*, Melbourne, Penguin, 1985, Introduction.

6   Jeffrey Grey, review of Peter Grose, *A Very Rude Awakening*, in *Australian Literary Review*, 2 May 2007, p. 18.

7   Phillip Knightley, review of David Day, *The Great Betrayal: Britain, Australia, and the Pacific War, 1939–42*, in *Sunday Times*, 17 July 1988.

8   Quoted in Geoffrey Serle, 'John Curtin', *Australian Dictionary of Biography*, vol. 13, p. 553.

9   Serle, 'John Curtin', p. 554.

10 See Ganter, *The Pearl-Shellers*.

11 See DCS Sissons, in Jupp (ed.), *The Australian People*, p. 523.

12 See Markus, *Australian Race Relations*, pp. 131–32.

13 See Paul R Bartrop, 'Before the refugees: foreign immigration policy and Australia in the 1920s', *Australian Jewish Historical Society*, vol. 15, 2000, pp. 382, 386–98.

14 See Langfield, *More People Imperative*, pp. 192–93.

15 Margot Melia, 'The Zunini Scheme: a plan for Italian Group Settlement in Western Australia, 1906–18', in Richard Bosworth & Margot Melia (eds), *Aspects of Ethnicity in Western Australia*, Department of History, University of Western Australia, Perth, 1991, pp. 17–27.

16 Langfield, '"Fit for the Elect of the World"', pp. 155–56.

17 David Day in Crotty & Roberts (eds), *The Great Mistakes of Australian History*, p. 127.

18 See Pearl, *The Dunera Scandal;* a retrospect was offered by DD McNicoll, 'Boatpeople who thrived', *The Australian*, 8 September 2000.

19 From WJ Hudson & HJW Stokes (eds), *Documents on Australian Foreign Policy 1937–49*, vol. 5, *July 1941–June 1942*, AGPS, Canberra, 1982, pp. 427, 431, 458. Cf. the reception of United States forces in Britain, R Winder, *Bloody Foreigners: The Story of Immigration to Britain*, Little, Brown, London, 2004, p. 328.

20 See also WD Forsyth', 'British migration to Australia: demographic and social aspects', *Economic Record*, 14 June 1938, pp. 39–47.

21 WD Forsyth, *The Myth of Open Spaces: Australia, British and World Trends of Population and Migration*, Melbourne University Press / Oxford University Press, Melbourne, 1942, p. 3.

22 John Andrews, review in *Historical Studies, Australia and New Zealand*, vol. 2, 1943, pp. 207–208.

23 Forsyth, *The Myth of the Open Spaces*, pp. 202–205.

24 Butlin & Schedvin, *War Economy 1942–1945*, p. 6.

25 Butlin & Schedvin, *War Economy 1942–1945*, pp. 6, 340–42.

26 Butlin & Schedvin, *War Economy 1942–1945*, pp. 378, 379.

27 Butlin & Schedvin, *War Economy 1942–1945*, p. 702, quoted in John H Atchison, 'Immigration in two federations', in Bruce W Hodgins et al. (eds), *Federalism in Canada and Australia: Historical Perspectives*, Trent University, Peterborough, Canada, 1989, p. 205.

28 Butlin & Schedvin, *War Economy 1942–1945*, pp. 627–29.

29 Butlin &Schedvin, *War Economy 1942–45*, p. 628.

30 Atchison, 'Immigration in two federations', p. 205; Butlin & Schedvin, *War Economy 1942–1945*, p. 702.

31 N Cain, 'LF Giblin', *Australian Dictionary of Biography*, vol. 8, p. 648.

32 Butlin & Schedvin, *War Economy 1942–45*, pp. 680, 683.

33 Butlin & Schedvin, *War Economy 1942–1945*, p. 703.

34 Butlin & Schedvin, *War Economy 1942–1945*, p. 704.

35 Butlin & Schedvin, *War Economy 1942–1945*, p. 706.

36 Serle, 'John Curtin', p. 556; LF Giblin, *The Problem of Maintaining Full Employment*, Oxford University Press, Melbourne, 1943.

37 Quoted at length in *In His Own Words: John Curtin's Speeches and Writings*, edited by David Black, Paradigm Books, Curtin University, Perth, 1995, pp. 237–38.

38 Cited in a review by HL Harris in *Australian Quarterly*, vol. 18, March 1946, p. 119.

7 Arthur Calwell and the new Australia: 1945–51

1 Petronella Wensing, Southern Stitches: A Story of European Resettlement and Growth in Australia, MS 1580, 1987, National Library of Australia; Wensing, 'Southern stitches', *Canberra Historical Journal*, ns no. 23, 1989, pp. 28–34.

2 Raimond Gaita, *Romulus, My Father*, Text Publishing, Melbourne, 1999.

3 A Rudzinski, 'Uprooted by the Nazis: Polish/Australian memories of wartime displacement', *Australian History Teacher*, no. 21, 1994, pp. 59–65.

4 R Keen, *Big Men, Little Men and Men in Between*, self-published, Tebworth UK, 1965, pp. 191, 207.

5 Powell, *An Historical Geography of Australia*, p. 206.

6 *Economist*, 1 June 1940, 7 July 1945.

7 IA Butler in *Australian Quarterly*, September 1947, pp. 122–23.

8 *Australian Quarterly*, September 1948, p. 114.

9 Frank Clune, *Land of Hope and Glory*, Angus & Robertson, Sydney, 1949.

10 Lamidey, *Partial Success*, pp. 30–31. See also LS Amery, *My Political Life*, Hutchinson, London, 1953–55; Amery, *The Leo Amery Diaries*, edited by J Barnes and D Nicholson, Hutchinson, London, 1980.

11 Roy Lewis, *Shall I Emigrate?: A Practical Guide*, Phoenix House, London, 1948, p. 15.

12 Stephen Constantine, 'Introduction: Empire migration and imperial harmony', in Constantine (ed.), *Emigrants and Empire*, p. 2.

13 Quoted in Michael Blakeney, 'The Australian Jewish community and postwar mass immigration from Europe', in Rubinstein (ed.), *Jews in the Sixth Continent*, p. 323.

14 AW Martin, *Robert Menzies: A Life*, vol. 2, Melbourne University Press, Melbourne, 1999, p. 100.

15 Cecil Edwards, *Bruce of Melbourne: Man of Two Worlds*, Heinemann, London, 1965, p. 438.

16 HB Gullett, letter to the *Argus*, 12 February 1947, quoted in Lack & Templeton (eds), *Bold Experiment*, p. 24.

17 See WD Rubinstein, *The Jews in Australia*, vol. 2, *1945 to the Present*, Heinemann, Melbourne, 1991, pp. 57–58, 67, 77. See also Peter Coleman, 'Books extra', *Weekend Australian*, 31 August / 1 September 2002, p. 8.

18 Colm Kiernan, *Calwell: A Personal and Political Biography*, Thomas Nelson, Melbourne, 1978, p. 14.

19 Kiernan, *Calwell*, pp. 55, 79.

20 Kiernan, *Calwell*, pp. 80, 81. Calwell remained tentative in 1945. In his *How Many Australians Tomorrow?* (1945) he remarked that 'Britain can ill afford to lose emigrants and will make every attempt to keep her people at home' (cited in HL Harris, review, *Australian Quarterly*, vol. 18, 1946, pp. 118–19).

21 Kiernan, *Calwell*, pp. 82, 83.
22 Dyster & Meredith, *Australia in the International Economy*, p. 190.
23 Commonwealth Immigration Advisory Committee, Report, February 1946, quoted in Lack & Templeton (eds), *Bold Experiment* pp. 21–23. See also Parliamentary Debates (Representatives), 5 April 1946; Leslie Haylen, *Twenty Years' Hard Labor*, Macmillan, Melbourne, 1969, pp. 94–103.
24 Meredith & Dyster, *Australia in the International Economy*, p. 193.
25 Walter A Ebsworth, *Archbishop Mannix*, H.H. Stephenson, Melbourne, 1977, p. 370.
26 Brown, *Governing Prosperity*, p. 25.
27 Brown, *Governing Prosperity*, p. 199.
28 Harry Martin, *Angels and Arrogant Gods*, p. 1.
29 Lamidey, *Partial Success*, p. 29.
30 Lack & Templeton (eds), *Bold Experiment*, p. 20.
31 R Hawke, *The Hawke Memoirs*, Heinemann, Melbourne, 1994, p. 46.
32 Phillip Knightley, *A Hack's Progress*, Jonathon Cape, London, 1997, p. 29.
33 Between 1948 and 1957, 33.95 per cent of immigrants were British.
34 Kiernan, *Calwell*, p. 125. Calwell on 30 June 1947 told Chifley in a cable after visiting the camps in Germany that 'this is by far most speedy and economical method of securing best type of migrants required for Australia's economic rehabilitation from non-British sources in the shortest possible time'. Quoted in Brennan, *Tampering with Asylum*, p. 3.
35 Dyster & Meredith, *Australia in the International Economy*, p. 192.
36 G Freudenberg, 'Arthur Calwell', *Australian Dictionary of Biography*, vol. 13.
37 Kiernan, *Calwell*, p. 133.
38 On the general context of refugee movements, see MR Marrus, *The Unwanted: European Refugees in the Twentieth Century*, Oxford University Press, New York, 1985.
39 *Australian Immigration: Consolidated Statistics*, no. 10, 1978.
40 Collected in Harry Martin, *Angels and Arrogant Gods*, which provides the detail in the following paragraphs, esp. pp. 2, 7, 10, 13, 19, 22.
41 Eva Maria Chapman, *Sasha and Olga: A True Story of Survival*, Lothian Books, Melbourne, 2006.
42 Harry Martin, *Angels and Arrogant Gods*, pp. 23, 24.
43 See Jan Schmortte, 'Attitudes towards German Immigrants in South Australia in the Post-World War Two Period, 1947–1960', MA thesis, Flinders University, 2000.
44 Lack & Templeton (eds), *Bold Experiment*; see also Blainey, 'Australia: a bird's eye view', p. 318.
45 Lack & Templeton (eds), *Bold Experiment*, pp. xiii–xvi, 2–3.
46 Lack & Templeton (eds), *Bold Experiment*, p. 12.
47 Mary Elizabeth Calwell, in Jupp, *The Australian People*, pp. 71–72.
48 Quoted in Lack & Templeton (eds), *Bold Experiment*, p. 45.
49 Lack & Templeton (eds), *Bold Experiment*, p. 43.
50 Lack & Templeton (eds), *Bold Experiment*, pp. 39–42.
51 See Sean Brawley, 'Mrs O'Keefe and the battle for White Australia', *Memento*, Winter 2007, pp. 6–8.
52 Quoted in Brennan, *Tampering with Asylum*, p. 201.
53 Phillip Knightley, *Australia: Biography of a Nation*, Jonathon Cape, London, 2000, p. 217; AC Palfreeman, 'The end of the dictation test', *Australian Quarterly*, March 1958, pp 43–50.
54 Harry Martin, *Angels and Arrogant Gods*, p. 15.
55 Harry Martin, *Angels and Arrogant Gods*, p. 15.
56 Stan Arneil, *Black Jack: The Life and Times of Brigadier Sir Frederick Galleghan*, Macmillan, Melbourne, 1983, pp. 133, 144; Knightley, *A Hack's Progress*, p. 134.

57   Julius Stone, Professor of Law at Sydney University, was highly critical of Germans and of the screening process. See J Stone, 'Mass German immigration in Australia's future', *Australian Quarterly*, vol. 23, June 1951, pp. 18–28.

58   Kathy Laster, 'Crime and punishment', *Meanjin*, vol. 54, 1995, pp. 627–29; Nazi hunters were still at work in 1999 when Konrad Kalejs aged 86 was pursued to England after a long stint in Australia, which he reached at the end of the war as a DP; he was allegedly a mass murderer. See *The Australian*, 29 December 1999. More generally, see Mark Aarons, *Sanctuary: Nazi Fugitives in Australia*, Heinemann, Melbourne, 1989.

59   Roy Lewis, *Shall I Emigrate?: A Practical Guide*, Phoenix House, London, 1948, Foreword.

60   See Glenda Sluga, *Bonegilla: A Place of No Hope*, History Department, University of Melbourne, Melbourne, 1988.

61   Lack & Templeton (eds), *Bold Experiment*, p. 11.

62   Harry Martin, Angels and Arrogant Gods, p. 37.

63   See Richards, *Britannia's Children*, ch. 12.

64   Quoted in Brennan, *Tampering with Asylum*, p. 201.

65   Alfred Benedict Kuen, 'The Disowned Revolution: The Reconstruction of Australian Immigration, 1945–52', PhD thesis, Monash University, Melbourne, 1997, p. 283. See also Jupp, *From White Australia to Woomera*; AM Jordens, *Alien to Citizen: Settling Migrants in Australia 1945–75*, Allen & Unwin, Sydney, 1997; Jordens, *Redefining Australians*.

66   Kathleen Paul, *Whitewashing Britain: Race and Citizenship in the Postwar Era*, Cornell University Press, Ithaca NY, 1997. See also Stephen Constantine, 'The British government, child welfare, and child migration to Australia after 1945', *Journal of Imperial and Commonwealth History*, vol. 30, 2002, pp. 99–132.

67   David Esdaile Walker, *We Went to Australia*, Chapman and Hall, London, 1949, pp. vii, 77, 248.

68   Walker, *We Went to Australia*, pp. 81, 248.

69   Walker, *We Went to Australia*, pp. 77, 81–82, 220.

70   Walker, *We Went to Australia*, pp. 18, 30–31, 69, 77, 78.

71   Walker, *We Went to Australia*, p. 130. See also WD Borrie, *Italians and Germans in Australia*, Cheshire, Melbourne, 1954.

72   The program was vigorously reinforced by Harold Holt, Immigration Minister in the coalition government of Menzies and Fadden, which took office in December 1949. Holt held the portfolio until October 1956. His aim was to increase the target immigrant intake to 200 000 per year. He encouraged non-British immigration. During his years as minister the net population increase resulting from immigration was approximately 640 000. See Tom Frame, *The Life and Death of Harold Holt*, Allen & Unwin / National Archives of Australia, Sydney, 2005, pp. 64–75.

8 The great diversification: the 1950s and 1960s

1   Ian Warden, *Do Polar Bears Experience Religious Ecstasy?*, Queensland University Press, Brisbane, 1980, cover notes and p. 20.

2   Elizabeth Jolley, 'Who would throw streamers and sing to a container?', in *Central Mischief*, Viking, Melbourne, 1992, pp. 60–65. See also Roslyn Russell, *Literary Links*, Allen & Unwin, Sydney, 1997, ch. 11. Of British recollections, see especially Mary Rose Liverani, *The Winter Sparrows*, Michael Joseph, London, 1976, about her migration from Glasgow to Sydney in 1952, which captures the great gains that urban Scots could make by coming to Australia even in the confusion of the postwar world.

3   Mark Peel, *Good Times, Hard Times*, Melbourne University Press, Melbourne, 1995, pp. 10, 88, 114–15. Another important effort to rescue the British migrant from invisibility and the condescension of posterity is Hammerton & Thomson, *The Ten Pound Poms*.

For some contemporary British responses to the emigration experience, see Elizabeth & Derek Tribe, *Postmark Australia: The Land and its People through English Eyes*, Cheshire, Melbourne, 1964.

4   'Magazine', *The Australian*, 23/24 March 1996; see also Humphrey McQueen, 'Laying our cultural foundations', *The Age*, 17 November 2007, p. 19.

5   Judah Waten, 'In other tongues', *Nation*, 27 June 1970, reprinted in KS Inglis (ed.), *Nation: The Life of an Independent Journal of Opinion 1958–1972*, Melbourne University Press, Melbourne, 1989, pp. 248–50.

6   See Jamie Grant, review of Raimond Gaita, *Romulus, My Father*, in *Quadrant*, June 1998, pp. 77–78.

7   Andrew Riemer, *Inside Outside: Life between Two Worlds*, Angus & Robertson, Sydney, 1992. See also Patricia Donnelly, *Migrant Journeys or 'What the hell have we done?'*, Adelaide, 1999; Emery Bares, *Backyard of Mars: Memoirs of the 'Reffo' Period in Australia*, Wildcat Press, Sydney, 1980; Egon Kunz's scholarly study, *Displaced Persons*, Australian National University Press, Canberra, 1988; Paul Kraus, *A New-Australian: A New Australia*, Federation Press, Sydney, 1995.

8   *The Australian*, 15 July 2000.

9   Rose Lucas and Lyn McCredden, *Bridgings: Readings in Australian Women's Poetry*, Oxford University Press, Melbourne, 1996.

10   Brown, *Governing Prosperity*, p. 7.

11   PR Heydon, 'The effects of immigration on Australia's growth', Wagga Wagga Teachers College, 1968, p. 4.

12   Brown, *Governing Prosperity*, pp. 24–25.

13   Dyster & Meredith, *Australia in the International Economy*, ch. 10.

14   Brown, *Governing Prosperity*, p. 112.

15   AW Martin, *Robert Menzies: A Life*, vol. 2, Melbourne University Press, Melbourne, 1999, p. 155.

16   'Athol Townley', *Australian Dictionary of Biography*, vol. 16, p. 322.

17   AW Martin, *Robert Menzies*, vol. 2, pp. 296, 306–307.

18   Dyster & Meredith, *Australia in the International Economy*, p. 217.

19   Quoted in 'Arthur Calwell', *Australian Dictionary of Biography*, vol. 13.

20   A Townley, '"Bring out a Briton" will help thousands', *Digest: Report of the Proceedings of the Australian Citizenship Convention*, Canberra, 1957, pp. 7–10.

21   Townley, '"Bring out a Briton" will help thousands', pp. 7–10.

22   *The Age*, 28 January 1957.

23   On housing and the government policy, see especially Ann-Mari Jordens, *Redefining Australians: Immigration, Citizenship, and National Identity*, Hale & Iremonger, Sydney, 1995, p. 43.

24   A Downer, *Six Prime Ministers*, Hill of Content, Melbourne, 1982, pp. 66–67. Holt acknowledged that his 'greatest success' as minister was resisting pressure from members of his own party to wind back the immigration program; Tom Frame, *The Life and Death of Harold Holt*, Allen & Unwin / National Archives of Australia, Sydney, 2005, p. 74.

25   Downer, *Six Prime Ministers*, p. 61.

26   Bob Willoughby, federal director of the Liberal Party, quoted in I Hancock, *John Gorton: He Did It His Way*, Hodder Headline, Sydney, 2002, p. 82.

27   See Sara Wills, 'When good neighbours became good friends: the Australian embrace of the millionth migrant', *Australian Historical Studies*, no. 124, 2004, pp. 332–54.

28   The variations were considerable: 150 000 per annum 1949–50, then 43 000 in 1953; 70–100 000 per annum 1954–60, then 129 000 in 1969.

29   There is a good summary in AW Martin, *Robert Menzies*, vol. 2, p. 476.

30 Hancock, *John Gorton*, pp. 151–52.

31 AW Martin, *Robert Menzies*, vol. 2, p. 531; Lack & Templeton, *Bold Experiment*, p. 212.

32 Nonja Peters, *Milk and Honey – but No Gold*, University of Western Australia Press, Perth, 2001, p. 18.

33 See Richards, *Britannia's Children*, pp. 260–64.

34 George Gallup (ed.), *The Gallup International Public Opinion Polls*, 2 vols, New York, 1976.

35 British as percentage of all immigrants: 1947–51, 41 per cent; 1951–61, 33 per cent; 1962–66, 55 per cent; 1966–71, 54 per cent; 1971–73, 65 per cent.

36 Lack & Templeton, *Bold Experiment*, pp. 76ff.

37 From 1947 to 1970, 18 per cent of Italian migrants were assisted; 85 per cent from UK and Ireland; 74 per cent of northern Europeans; 60 per cent of Yugoslavs; 33 per cent of Greeks.

38 Jupp, *Arrivals and Departures*, p. 159.

39 See Jupp, *The Australian People*, pp. 16, 423, 251.

40 For a critical view of the historical treatment of European migration to Australia, see R Bosworth & J Wilton, 'A lost history?: the study of European migration to Australia', *Australian Journal of Politics and History*, vol. 27, 1981, pp. 221–31.

41 A Markus, 'Tasman Heyes', *Australian Dictionary of Biography*, vol. 14, pp. 446–47.

42 JR Nethercote, 'Peter Heydon', *Australian Dictionary of Biography*, vol. 14, pp. 445–46; John H Atchison, 'Immigration in two federations', in Bruce W Hodgins et al. (eds), *Federalism in Canada and Australia: Historical Perspectives*, Trent University, Peterborough, Canada, 1989, pp. 209–10.

43 PR Heydon, 'Co-operative administration in immigration', *Public Administration*, vol. 24, March 1965, pp, 47–59.

44 Dyster & Meredith, *Australia in the International Economy*, p. 210; see also Jan Schmortte, 'Attitudes towards German immigration in South Australia in the post Second World War period, 1947–60', *Australian Journal of Politics and History*, vol. 51, 2005, pp. 530–44.

45 For the emigrants' ships, see Anthony Cooke, *Emigrant Ships: The Vessels which Carried Migrants across the World, 1946–72*, London, nd [c1950].

46 Harry Martin, *Angels and Arrogant Gods*, p. 47.

47 Harry Martin, *Angels and Arrogant Gods*, p. 59.

48 The general issue of women immigrants is dealt with briefly and incisively in Sevgi Kilic, 'Australia's immigrant women', *Without Prejudice*, no. 9, 1996, pp. 14–20.

49 Harry Martin, *Angels and Arrogant Gods*, p. 29, 58.

50 Harry Martin, *Angels and Arrogant Gods*, pp. 66, 67, 92–93.

51 See Lamidey, *Partial Success*, p. 32.

52 See especially Peters, *Milk and Honey – but No Gold*.

53 Harry Martin, *Angels and Arrogant Gods*, pp. 31, 35.

54 Harry Martin, *Angels and Arrogant Gods*, p. 40.

55 Harry Martin, *Angels and Arrogant Gods*, pp. 73, 77.

56 Harry Martin, *Angels and Arrogant Gods*, pp. 81, 82.

57 Heydon, 'Co-operative administration in immigration', p. 56.

58 Australian Institute of Political Science, *Australia and the Migrant*, Sydney, 1953.

59 Life in the migrant camps often looks dreary and monochromatic in the photographs of the time. Some of its texture is more effectively evoked in later oral testimonies; see, for instance, Victor Thomas Turner (ed.), *Tin Huts and Memories: We Got our Ten Pounds Worth*, Adelaide, 2006.

60 Glenda Sluga, 'Bonegilla and migrant dreaming', in Kate Darian-Smith & Paula Hamilton (eds), *Memory and History in Twentieth Century Australia*, Oxford University Press, Melbourne, 1994, pp. 195–209; Sluga, *Bonegilla: A Place of No Hope*, History Department, University

of Melbourne, Melbourne, 1988. For another Bonegilla retrospect, see York, *Michael Cigler* and, more generally, the testimonies in Peters, *Milk and Honey – but No Gold*.

61 Harry Martin, *Angels and Arrogant Gods*, p. 37.
62 Sluga, 'Bonegilla and migrant dreaming', p. 199.
63 Richard Bosworth, 'Conspiracy of the consuls?: official Italy and the Bonegilla riot of 1952', *Historical Studies*, vol. 22, 1987, pp. 547–67.
64 Bosworth, 'Conspiracy of the consuls?', p. 567.
65 Geoffrey Blainey, quoted in Bosworth, 'Conspiracy of the consuls?', p. 547. See also Jupp, *From White Australia to Woomera*, pp. 24–25.
66 Warwick Eather, 'A human commodity: post-war immigration, employment and Ford Geelong, 1945–60', *Occasional Papers*, Centre for Australian Studies, Deakin University, Geelong, no. 1, 1990, p. 25.
67 Eather, 'A human commodity', p. 14.
68 I am grateful to my colleagues David Hilliard and Robert Fitzsimons for guidance in these issues. On religion and postwar circumstances see, for example, Joseph Takchi, 'The Maronite Catholic Church in Australia', *Australasian Catholic Record*, vol. 73, 1996, p. 13; Kathleen McCarthy, 'Problems encountered by the Ukrainian Catholic Church in Australia', *Australasian Catholic Record*, vol. 73, 1996, p. 42.
69 See *Justice Now*, which reprints some social justice statements by Catholic bishops. See also Frank Lewins, *The Myth of the Universal Church*, Canberra, 1978.
70 For a defence of the Catholic record in Australia, see A Pittarello, *Soup without Salt*.
71 Pittarello, *Soup without Salt*, pp. 22, 23.
72 Dyster & Meredith, *Australia in the International Economy*, p. 210.
73 AW Martin, *Robert Menzies*, vol. 2, p. 426.
74 AW Martin, *Robert Menzies*, vol. 2, p. 440, 492–93, 579.
75 See especially Richard Woolcott, *The Hot Seat*, HarperCollins, Sydney, 2003, p. 24.
76 AW Martin, *Robert Menzies*, p. 580. See also Ann-Mari Jordens, *Alien to Citizen: Settling Migrants in Australia, 1945–75*, Allen & Unwin / Australian Archives, Sydney, 1997, pp. 214–15.
77 Ian Hancock, *John Gorton*, Hodder, Sydney, 2002, pp. 203–204, 213.
78 Jordens, *Alien to Citizen*, p. 217.
79 LF Crisp, *Peter Richard Heydon*, privately published, Canberra, 1972.
80 H Opperman, *Immigration Policy Affecting Non-Europeans*, Commonwealth Government Publication, 9 March 1966.
81 Hancock, *John Gorton*, pp. 136, 304–308.
82 Hancock, *John Gorton*, p. 184.
83 Hancock, *John Gorton*, pp. 194–203.
84 Downer, *Six Prime Ministers*, p. 289.
85 Brown, *Governing Prosperity*, p. 44.
86 Heydon, 'The effects of immigration on Australia's growth'.
87 Appleyard, *The Ten Pound Immigrants*, p. 142.
88 Sherington, *Australia's Immigrants 1788–1978*, p. 131.
89 A Richardson, *British Immigrants and Australia*, Australian National University Press, Canberra, 1974, p. 169.

9 White Australia dismantled: the 1970s

1 Zelman Cowen, 'Where to?: questions for Australians', *Dialogue*, vol. 22, no. 2, 2003, pp. 4–5.
2 Robyn Williams, *And Now for Something Completely Different*, Viking, Melbourne, 1995, pp. 95, 98.
3 *Independent* (Adelaide), 17 February 2007, p. 8.

4   Geoffrey Bolton, 'Consigning the cringe', *The Australian*, 1 July 2000.
5   This section draws on Stephen Castles, 'Italians in Australia: building a multicultural society on the Pacific Rim', *Diaspora*, vol. 1, 1991, pp. 45–66.
6   Ian MacFarlane, *The Search for Stability*, ABC Books, Sydney, 2000, ch. 1.
7   A Calwell, 'Immigrants', *Quadrant*, vol. 11, 1967, pp. 93, 94.
8   Dyster & Meredith, *Australia in the International Economy*, p. 236.
9   MacFarlane, *The Search for Stability*, pp. 12–13.
10   Dyster & Meredith, *Australia in the International Economy*, p. 301.
11   Markus, *Australian Race Relations*, p. 193.
12   Harry Martin, *Angels and Arrogant Gods*, p. 86.
13   Philip Ayres, *Malcolm Fraser: A Biography*, Heinemann, Melbourne, 1987, pp. 69–70.
14   Shergold & Milne (eds), *The Great Immigration Debate*, p. 18, quoted in Dyster & Meredith, *Australia in the International Economy*, p. 301. Some of the cultural influences of early European immigration are charted in Butler, *The Europeans*.
15   Harry Martin, *Angels and Arrogant Gods*, p. 88.
16   See Betts, *The Great Divide*; Gwenda Tavan, 'The dismantling of the White Australia policy: elite conspiracy or will of the Australian people?', *Australian Journal of Politics and History*, vol. 39, 2004, pp. 109–25; more generally, Tavan, *The Long, Slow Death of White Australia*.
17   See Betts, *The Great Divide*.
18   Betts, *The Great Divide*.
19   On reform, see Brawley, *The White Peril*.
20   Frank Crowley, *Tough Times: Australia in the Seventies*, Heinemann, Melbourne, 1986, p. 6.
21   The political untenability of the policy grew each year. See Jupp, *From White Australia to Woomera*, pp. 10, 202; Richards, 'Migrations.
22   Dyster & Meredith, *Australia in the International Economy*, p. 260.
23   Crowley, *Tough Times*, p. 239.
24   See Peter Coleman, book review, *The Australian*, 6/7 September 2003. The transition to non White Australia was not without resistance, as Cabinet documents of 1971 showed when released 30 years later. See *The Australian*, 1 January 2002.
25   John H Atchison, 'Immigration in two federations', in Bruce W Hodgins et al. (eds), *Federalism in Canada and Australia: Historical Perspectives*, Trent University, Peterborough, Canada, 1989, p. 210.
26   Crowley, *Tough Times*, p. 239.
27   *Nation*, 15 May 1965, reprinted in KS Inglis (ed.), *Nation: The Life of an Independent Journal of Opinion, 1958–1972*, Melbourne University Press, Melbourne, 1989, p. 133.
28   Menadue, *Things You Learn along the Way*, p. 182.
29   See Viviani, *The IndoChinese in Australia*, p. 240; exchanges in *The Australian* October 2003, esp. 3 October, and in John Button, *As It Happened*, Text, Melbourne, 1998, pp. 167, 197.
30   Harry Martin, *Angels and Arrogant Gods*, p. 99.
31   Harry Martin, *Angels and Arrogant Gods*, p. 109.
32   Robert Manne, 'Indo-Chinese refugees and the Australian political culture', *Migration Action*, vol. 3, nos 2–4, 1976/78, pp. 11–13.
33   Menadue, *Things You Learn along the Way*, pp. 205, 206.
34   J Wilton & R Bosworth, *Old Worlds and New Australia*, Penguin, Australia, 1984; see also Castles, 'Italians in Australia'.
35   Crowley, *Tough Times*, p. 123.
36   See Jupp, *White Australia to Woomera*, p. 224.
37   Jupp, *White Australia to Woomera*, p. 83.
38   See John Curtain, 'Andrew Fabinyi', *Australian Dictionary of Biography*, vol. 14, pp. 121–22; Andrew Fabinyi, *Social and Cultural Issues of Migration*, Australian Citizenship Convention, Canberra, 1970, p. 13.

39   Andrew Fabinyi, 'Social and cultural issues of migration', *Australian Citizenship Convention: Background Papers and Addresses*, 1970, pp. 14, 20.

10 The end of the heroic days: the 1980s

1   See Macintyre, *The History Wars*, pp. 94, 100.
2   Hugo, *The Economic Implications of Emigration from Australia*.
3   Charles Price, 'Post-war immigration: 1947–98', *Journal of the Australian Population Association*, vol. 15, 1998.
4   David Pope & Glenn Withers, 'Do migrants rob jobs?: lessons of Australian history, 1861–1991', *Journal of Economic History*, vol. 53, 1993, pp. 719–42.
5   Pope & Withers, 'Do migrants rob jobs?', p. 720.
6   Kelly, *The End of Certainty*, pp. 128, 130, 131.
7   Kelly, *The End of Certainty*, p. 723.
8   P Walsh, *Confessions of a Failed Finance Minister*, Random House, Sydney, 1995, pp. 185–88. On the question of unemployment among first- and second-generation Turkish immigrants, see Jupp, *From White Australia to Woomera*. On comparative rates of unemployment among immigrants, see *The Australian*, 28 February 2008.
9   In 1982 a new immigration system was at work using a points system with five categories: family migration, labour requirements, independent immigration, refugee and special humanitarian program.
10.   Jupp pointed out that 'Essentially, assisted passages were a form of social engineering designed to keep Australia British … and to keep Australia white', Jupp, *From White Australia to Woomera*, p. 17.
11   Menadue, *Things You Learn along the Way*, p. 211.
12   Menadue, *Things You Learn along the Way*, pp. 211, 212.
13   Mick Young, *The Effects of the 'Razor Gang's Report' on Immigrants, Refugees and the Ethnic Communities in Australia*, Canberra, May 1981.
14   Menadue, *Things You Learn along the Way*, p. 214.
15   Young, *The Effects of the 'Razor Gang's Report'*, p. 22.
16   Greg Heywood in *Financial Review*, 2 July 1981, quoted in Menadue, *Things You Learn along the Way*, p. 214.
17   British people had full rights in Australia even without becoming citizens – a preferential treatment which was abolished in 1981.
18   Menadue, *Things You Learn along the Way*, p. 222.
19   Menadue, *Things You Learn along the Way*, p. 217.
20   Menadue, *Things You Learn along the Way*, p. 259.
21   See Lack & Templeton (eds), *Bold Experiment*, pp. 152–65.
22   Kelly, *The End of Certainty*, p. 124.
23   See Hawthorne, *Making It in Australia*. Vietnamese stories have been much gathered: see, for example, *The Age*, 4 November 2000.
24   Hawthorne, *Making It in Australia*, ch. 1; Hawthorne (ed.), *Refugee: The Vietnamese Experience*, Oxford University Press, Melbourne, 1982.
25   Quoted in Lack & Templeton, *Bold Experiment*, p. 235.
26   Macintyre, *The History Wars*, p. 114.
27   Jean Martin, *Refugee Settlers* and *Community and Identity*. See also *The Incidence of Mental Illness among Migrants*, Report of the Commonwealth Immigration Advisory Council, Canberra, 1961.
28   Quoted in Lack & Templeton, *Bold Experiment*, p. 230.
29   Summarised by Mary Kalantzis, 'Immigration, multiculturalism and racism', in Susan Ryan and Troy Bramston (eds), *The Hawke Government*, Pluto Press, Melbourne, 2003, p. 315.

30 Macintyre, The History Wars, pp. 82–83, 85.
31 Kelly, The End of Certainty, p. 126.
32 See especially Kelly, The End of Certainty, ch. 7.
33 Quoted in Kelly, The End of Certainty, p. 316.
34 Macintyre, The History Wars, pp. 72–75; see also A Markus and MC Ricklefs (eds), Surrender Australia?: Essays in the Study and Uses of History: Geoffrey Blainey and Asian Immigration, Allen & Unwin, Sydney, 1985.
35 Macintyre, The History Wars, p. 86.
36 See Kelly, The End of Certainty, p. 134.
37 Kelly, The End of Certainty, p. 134.
38 Jock Collins, 'Asian migration to Australia', in R Cohen (ed.), The Cambridge Survey of World Migration, Cambridge University Press, New York, 1995, pp. 37–39.
39 John H Atchison, 'Immigration in two federations', in Bruce W Hodgins et al. (eds), Federalism in Canada and Australia: Historical Perspectives, Trent University, Peterborough, Canada, 1989, pp. 218–19.
40 From Kalantzis, 'Immigration, multiculturalism and racism', pp. 317–19.
41 Kalantzis, 'Immigration, multiculturalism and racism', pp. 318–19.
42 R Birrell & K Betts, 'The FitzGerald Report on immigration policy: origins and implications', Australian Quarterly, vol. 60, no. 3, 1988, p. 264.
43 Brett, Australian Liberals and the Moral Middle Class, p. 186.
44 Birrell & Betts, 'The FitzGerald Report on immigration policy', p. 266.
45 Brett, Australian Liberals and the Moral Middle Class, p. 79.
46 Brian Graetz & Ian McAllister, Dimensions of Australian Society, Macmillan Education, Melbourne, 1994, pp. 76, 81.
47 Birrell & Betts, 'The FitzGerald Report on immigration policy', p. 265.
48 Kalantzis, 'Immigration, multiculturalism and racism'.
49 Howard never recovered, according to Kelly, p. 428; a misplaced judgment in this case.
50 Hawke in The Age, 9 September 1988, reprinted in Lack & Templeton, Bold Experiment, p. 245.
51 Hawke, 'Foreword', in Ryan and Bramston (eds), The Hawke Government.
52 Kalantzis, 'Immigration, multiculturalism and racism', pp. 312–13.
53 Kalantzis, 'Immigration, multiculturalism and racism', p. 313.
54 Clyde Cameron, China, Communism and Coco-Cola, Hill of Content, Melbourne, 1980, pp. 230, 233. Whitlam defended himself in The Australian, 4 October 2003. See also Kelly, The End of Certainty, p. 128. Hawke, reported in The Age 11 June 1990, quoted in David Marr & Marian Wilkinson, Dark Victory, Allen & Unwin, Sydney, 2003, p. 90.

11 Whither immigrant Australia?

1 See Peter Waxman, 'The shaping of Australia's immigration and refugee policy', Immigrants & Minorities, vol. 19, 2000, pp. 53–78.
2 This section draws on Nicholas Way, 'Riche nouveau Australians', Business Review Weekly, 26 May 2000.
3 Hurriyet Babacan in Jupp, The Australian People, p. 716.
4 Quoted in Hatice Hörmöz Baçarin and Vecihi Baçarin, The Turks in Australia: Celebrating Twenty-Five Years Down Under, Turquoise Publications, Melbourne, 1993, p. 75. On the typical devotion of new immigrants to education and security, cf. R Winder, Bloody Foreigners: The Story of Immigration to Britain, Little, Brown, London, 2004, p. 246.
5 Australian Bureau of Statistics, 2006 Census.
6 Trevor Sykes, quoted in Max Corden, review of Ian MacFarlane, The Search for Stability · (Boyer Lectures), The Australian, 7 March 2007.

7   *The Australian*, 7 March 2007, pp. 10–11.

8   Graeme Hugo, *The Economic Implications of Emigration from Australia*, AGPS, Canberra, 1994, p. 110; Department of Industry, Science and Tourism, *Australian Science and Technology at a Glance*, AGPS, Canberra, 1997, p. 10; Department of Education, Training and Youth Affairs, 'New Knowledge, New Opportunities', Discussion Paper on Higher Education Research and Training, June 1999, p. 4.

9   Graeme Hugo, 'Migration between Britain and Australia', in D Lowe (ed.), *Immigration and Integration: Australia and Britain*, Bureau of Immigration, Multicultural and Population Research, Melbourne, 1995, p. 19.

10   See, for instance, Glenn Withers, 'Immigration', in Ian McAllister, Steve Dowrick and Riaz Hassan (eds), *The Cambridge Handbook of Social Sciences in Australia*, Cambridge University Press, Melbourne, 2003, p. 76.

11   See Eric Richards, 'The limits of the Australian immigrant letter', in BS Elliott, DA Gerber and SM Sinke (eds), *Letters across Borders: The Epistolary Practices of International Migrants*, Palgrave Macmillan, New York, 2006.

12   Way, 'Riche nouveau Australians'.

13   See Withers, 'Immigration', p. 81.

14   See Neal Blewett, *A Cabinet Diary*, Wakefield Press, Adelaide, 1999, p. 16.

15   Blewett, *A Cabinet Diary*, pp. 16–17. Blewett made the point that the government had committed itself to benefits which now would cost $40 million per annum.

16   Blewett, *A Cabinet Diary*, pp. 43, 81, 106, 162. Some more insights into the immigration attitudes of the Whitlam regime are retailed lightly in James McClelland, *Stirring the Possum: A Political Autobiography*, Viking/Penguin, Melbourne, 1988, pp. 159–62. He was bored as the Minister of Immigration.

17   Blewett, *A Cabinet Diary*, pp. 114, 261.

18   Don Watson, *Recollections of a Bleeding Heart*, Knopf, Sydney, 2002, pp. 207, 390.

19   Watson, *Recollections of a Bleeding Heart*, pp. 229, 507, 559.

20   Watson, *Recollections of a Bleeding Heart*, pp. 665, 712. See also Jupp, *From White Australia to Woomera*, pp. 131–32.

21   Cameron Stewart, 'Past tense …' *The Australian*, 27 September 2003. Official data suggested that Australia's formal intake of refugees was one of the highest in the world and had 'operated for years … largely out of sight, out of mind of the media'. However, as Kelly pointed out, the cost of processing illegal immigrants was far greater than helping the refugees in the countries of origin. The number of boat people reaching Australia was very much smaller than the 59 000 people who, in 2001, had overstayed their visas. To the latter number should be added the unknown accumulated numbers of other illegal migrants who were occasionally offered amnesty. See Paul Kelly, *The Australian*, 16 July 2001; John H Atchison, 'Immigration in two federations', in Bruce W Hodgins et al. (eds), *Federalism in Canada and Australia: Historical Perspectives*, Trent University, Peterborough, Canada, 1989, pp. 219–20.

22   Cited in Graeme Davison, *The Use and Abuse of Australian History*, Allen & Unwin, Sydney, 2000, p. 211.

23   *IOM News* (Institute of Medicine), June/July 1996, p. 10.

24   *Guardian*, 20–26 April 2000; *The Australian*, 10 April 2000.

25   *Advertiser*, 10 June 2000.

26   Lionel Duncombe, *Immigration and the Decline of Democracy in Australia*, Canberra, 1992, Preface. One of the architects of Australian multiculturalism declared it 'a good idea that has gone wrong' and that 'Ethnicity has been cynically exploited for electoral and civic advantage'. Jerzy Zubrzycki, 'Cynics woo the ethnic vote', *The Australian*, 15 October 1996. On the breakdown of the bipartisan consensus and the consequences of economic rationalism, see Jupp, *From White Australia to Woomera*, passim.

27   *The Australian*, 8 January 1999.
28   Cope & Kalantzis, *A Place in the Sun*, p. 99.
29   See James Jupp, 'Noises off', *Meanjin*, no. 2, 1999, pp. 118–27. More generally, see Jupp, *From White Australia to Woomera*, ch. 7.
30   See Mary Cry Crock, in *ANU Reporter*, 6 October 2000.
31   See James Jupp, 'Terrorism, immigration and multiculturalism: the Australian experience', paper presented to a conference on immigration policies at the University of Texas at Austin, 2/3 March 2006. Cf. R Winder, *Bloody Foreigners: The Story of Immigration to Britain*, Little, Brown, London, 2004, pp. 436–37.
32   Hugo, 'Migration between Britain and Australia', p. 16.
33   David Lucas, in *ANU Reporter*, 1 September 2000. The distribution of expatriate British pension-holders in 1996 reflected earlier migration; the largest number were in Australia (245 311) followed by Canada (157 435) and the United States (132 083). See *Guardian*, 22 December 2006, p. 34.
34   *Year Book Australia*, 2001.
35   Ward, *Australia and the British Embrace*, p. 4.
36   Lack & Templeton, *Bold Experiment*, pp. 161–65. See also Jupp, *From White Australia to Woomera*, ch. 6.
37   John Hirst, in Lack & Templeton, *Bold Experiment*, pp. 250–57.
38   Department of Immigration and Multicultural Affairs, *Immigration in Brief*, 2000, statistics section with annual updates.
39   Many of these themes were nicely encapsulated in Peter Ryan, 'Immigration', *Quadrant*, May 1998.

12 The new century

1   *Advertiser*, 27 February 2004, p. 78.
2   See Glenn Nicholls, 'Unsettling admissions: asylum seekers in Australia', *Journal of Refugee Studies*, vol. 11, 1998, pp. 61–79.
3   John Hirst, correspondence in *Quarterly Essay*, no. 6, 2002, p. 91n.
4   See Jupp, *From White Australia to Woomera*, p. 1.
5   Net overseas migration is 'permanent and long-term arrivals' minus 'permanent and long-term departures' plus 'category jumpers'. On the problems of estimating net migration, see Peter McDonald, Siew-Ean Khoo & Rebecca Kippen, 'Alternative net migration estimates for Australia: exploding the myth of a rapid increase in numbers', *People and Place*, vol. 11, 2003, pp. 23–36.
6   Dennis Trewin, Australian Statistician, letter, *Sydney Morning Herald*, 15 September 2003; 'Migrant numbers wrong by 42,000', *The Australian*, 8 September 2003. See also Tim Colebatch, *The Age*, 8 September 2003, pp. 8–9.
7   On the implications of globalisation, see Jupp, *From White Australia to Woomera*, pp. 202–208. The minister was certainly conscious of the change in tendencies: see Philip Ruddock, 'Australia's immigration in a dot com world', *Options*, no. 11, 2000, pp. 4–5.
8   John Salt & Jane Millar, 'International migration in interesting times: the case of the UK', *People and Place*, vol. 14, 2006, pp. 14–25. Another factor was retirement migration: see Russell King, Tony Warnes & Allan Williams, *Sunset Lives: British Retirement Migration to the Mediterranean*, Berg, Oxford, 2000.
9   ABC Radio News, 23 August 2007. In 2006 (when the UK population exceeded 60 million) nearly 200 000 British-born moved overseas, the highest number since 1991, and mostly they went to Australia (71 000), Spain and France. Total emigration was 385 000, which included many foreigners returning home; the Office of National

Statistics remarked on the increasing transience of the population, both inwards and outwards. *Guardian Weekly*, 31 August 2007, p. 15; see also *Guardian Weekly*, 23 November 2007 on the continuing two-way mobility of the British population.

10   David Pope & Glenn Withers, 'Do migrants rob jobs?: lessons of Australian history', *Journal of Economic History*, vol. 53, 1993, pp. 719–42.

11   *The Australian*, 16 December 2003.

12   *The Australian*, 17/18 April 2004, p. 19.

13   *The Australian*, 18/19 October 2003, pp. 1, 4.

14   The recent political history of the immigration issue in Australia, and especially the refugee question, is particularly well surveyed in Jupp, *From White Australia to Woomera*. He supplies guides to the acronyms which have multiplied in the administration of immigrant policies as well as useful chronologies of ministers of immigration and their departmental secretaries, and the annual 'settler' intakes into Australia since 1973, pp. 222–25.

15   Mike Steketee, 'Parting blow to refugees', *The Australian*, 4/5 October 2003, p. 26.

16   See Ian Macphee, *The Australian*, 5 August 2002.

17   'Illegals make a joke of migration law' (editorial), *The Australian*, 17 December 2002, p. 8.

18   Janet Albrechtsen, 'Tribute to moralist under fire', *The Australian*, 17 September 2003.

19   *The Australian*, 23 September 2003.

20   Marc Purcell, Catholic Commission for Justice and Peace, letter, and Arnab Ghosh, *The Australian*, 23 September 2003.

21   'Refugee truth out of bag: Vanstone', *The Australian*, 30 October 2003, p. 4. For the experiences of the reception system by refugees in Tasmania, see Lyn Andersch, 'Tasmania: our most recent humanitarian arrivals', *Tasmanian Historical Studies*, vol. 10, 2005, pp. 27–30.

22   Mike Steketee, *The Australian*, 4/5 October 2003, p. 26. Deterrence was extremely expensive and diverted resources away from the provision of adequate services to newly arrived migrants. See Jupp, *From White Australia to Woomera*, p. 160 and ch. 10.

23   Brennan, *Tampering with Asylum*, p. 41.

24   *Guardian*, 8–14 April 2004.

25   Brennan, *Tampering with Asylum*, p. 43.

26   Brennan, *Tampering with Asylum*, pp. vii–viii.

27   Brennan, *Tampering with Asylum*, p. ix.

28   Some of the passions released by the asylum debate are gathered in Sara Wills, 'Un-stitching the lips of the migrants' nation', *Australian Historical Studies*, vol. 33, no. 118, 2002, pp. 71–89.

29   Brennan, *Tampering with Asylum*, p. 202.

30   Interview with John Menadue, ABC Radio website, 11 November 2001.

31   Brennan, *Tampering with Asylum*, p. x.

32   Richard Woolcott, *The Hot Seat*, Harper Collins, Sydney, pp. 291–92.

33   *The Australian*, 4 February 2004.

34   Mike Steketee, 'Ruud awakening', *The Australian*, 27/28 March 2004, p. 21.

35   Paul Kelly, *The Australian*, 30 March 2002.

36   See Greg Sheridan in *The Australian*, 18 May 2002; see also Neville J Roach, 'Show mercy', *Bulletin*, 12 February 2002.

37   Maggie Black, *The No-nonsense Guide to International Development*, New Internationalist Publications, London, 2002, pp. 30–31.

38   Since 1991 there had been no recessions and growth had been almost continuous for 16 years; unemployment was lower than for 30 years and immigration was higher than for 20 years. Australia's wealth had ostensibly trebled in 16 years. See John Edwards, 'The perils of prosperity', 'Review', *The Australian*, 5 September 2007, p. 8.

39　*The Australian*, 19 August 2007, 8 July 2000.

40　*The Australian*, 6 March 2000; by 2007, 70 per cent of the official immigrants were 'skilled': *The Australian*, 24 September 2007.

41　*Australian Financial Review*, 4 May 2007, p. 3; see also Alan Wood, 'Multiculturalism becomes poison for social capital', *The Australian*, 26 September 2007.

42　Paul Kelly, 'Nirvana in numbers', *The Australian*, 1/2 May 2004.

43　For a review of population debates, see Jupp, *From White Australia to Woomera*, ch. 9. Withers is quoted in Kelly, 'Nirvana in numbers'.

44　*The Australian*, 4 September 2007. Jupp, *From White Australia to Woomera*, pp. 169–71.

45　Hans van Leeuwen, 'Howard's clever manoeuvre on migrants', *The Australian*, 28 January 2005.

46　*The Australian*, 15 August 2007.

47　*The Australian*, 8 July 2004, 7 January 2000.

48　*The Australian*, 7 March 2000, p. 13.

49　See Paul Kelly, *The Australian*, 2 November 2003.

50　Khoo & McDonald, *The Transformation of Australia's Population*, pp. 7, 269–72; Peter McDonald in *The Australian*, 30 June 2000.

51　Budget Paper no. 5, Budget 2002/03, p. 2.

52　P McDonald & R Kippen, 'The impact of immigration on the ageing of Australia's population', DIMA Discussion Paper, Department of Immigration and Multicultural Affairs, Canberra, May 1999 http:Üadsri.anu.edu.au/pubs/

53　McDonald & Kippen, 'The impact of immigration on the ageing of Australia's population'. See also Ian Castles, 'Vice-president's note', *Dialogue*, vol. 17, no. 4, 1998, pp. 5–14.

54　McDonald & Kippen, 'The impact of immigration on the ageing of Australia's population', p. 5.

55　P McDonald & R Kippen, *Population Futures for Australia: The Policy Alternatives*, Parliamentary Library, Research Paper 5, 1999–2000, Canberra, 1999. See also 'Something's got to give', *The Australian*, 24 May 2004'; the title was Flannery's reference to the extra 3 billion people likely to exist in the next 70 years. See generally, Jupp, *From White Australia to Woomera*, ch. 9.

56　With current fertility and life expectancy, to achieve a population of 50 million by 2025 would require net migration of 463 000 per annum. Australia had managed 150 000 a year only three times in the past 50 years. Peter McDonald, quoted in Mike Steketee, 'The problem with people', *The Australian*, 6 April 2002.

57　McDonald & Kippen, *Population Futures for Australia*, p. 27.

58　*The Australian*, 7 May 1997.

59　Tamar Jacoby, review of Huntingdon, *Who Are We?: The Challenge to America's National Identity*, in *Guardian Weekly*, 27 July 2004.

60　Jeremy Harding, *The Uninvited: Refugees at the Rich Man's Gate*, Profile, London, 2000, p. 1.

61　S Castles, 'Italians in Australia: building a multicultural society on the Pacific Rim', *Diaspora*, vol. 1, 1991, p. 64; The global scope of migration was reviewed in *IOM News*, December 2002, pp. 2–3.

13 Retrospect

1　See Bob Reece, obituary of Don Baker, *The Australian*, 9 April 2007, p. 6.

2　CH Wickens, 'Australian population: its nature and growth', *Economic Record*, vol. 1, 1925, p. 5.

3　The spontaneous and vastly increased movement of people in and out of Australia greatly enhanced the problems of categorisation of the migrants. The sheer increase of scale and complexity inevitably weakened the ability of the government to regulate and measure the actual flows. As Peter McDonald remarked, 'Australian governments have control, via the migration program, of about 10 per cent of population movements in and out of Australia in any year'. Quoted in Alan Wood, 'Growth must depend on permanent settlers', *The Australian*, 27 February 2001. See McDonald, quoted in *The Australian*, 6 February 2008.

4   This was the 'bold experiment' examined in documentary detail in Lack & Templeton, *Bold Experiment*.

5   Tim Rowse, *Nugget Coombs*, Cambridge University Press, Cambridge, 2002, p. 5.

6   See Ian Lowe, 'The lure of Europe', *New Scientist*, 17 April 2004, p. 49.

7   P Ruddock, 'Immigration and Australia's population in the 21st century', opening speech at the Centre for Economic Policy Research workshop, Australian National University, May 1996, Discussion Papers, p. 9.

8   James Jupp, 'World migration trends', in Jupp (ed), *Immigration and Multiculturalism*, pp. 4, 11.

9   *Reminiscences of William Affleck from Infancy to the Present*, privately circulated, Sydney, 1916[?] (copy in Mitchell Library, State Library of New South Wales).

10   M Roe, in S Constantine (ed.), *Emigrants and Empire*, p. 98.

11   See, for example, 'Burgeoning cities', *Guardian*, 29 June 2007, p. 24; Graeme Davison & Marc Brodie, *Struggle Country: The Rural Ideal in Twentieth-Century Australia*, Monash University Press, Melbourne, 2005.

12   See Roy Lewis, *Shall I Emigrate?*, Phoenix, London, 1948.

13   See Hammerton & Thompson, *The Ten Pound Poms*; James Jupp, *The English in Australia*, Melbourne, Cambridge University Press, 2004.

14   Quoted in J Pilger, 'Swimming for home', *New Statesman and Society*, 15/29 December 1995, pp. 22–23.

15   Barbara Tuchman, *The Proud Tower*, Hamish Hamilton, London, 1966, p. 16.

16   K Inglis, 'C.E.W. Bean, Australian historian', in Jay Winter (ed.), *Anzac Remembered*, p. 83.

17   Inglis, 'C.E.W. Bean, Australian historian', pp. 70, 71.

18   Bill Gammage, *The Broken Years*, Penguin, Melbourne, 1975, pp. 1–2.

19   See David Coleman, 'The United Kingdom and international migration: a changing balance', in H Fassman and R Munz (eds), *European Migration in the Late Twentieth Century*, Elgar, Aldershot UK, 1994, p. 38.

20   David Lucas, *Community Profiles: 1996 Census: Ireland*, Department of Immigration and Multicultural Affairs, Canberra, 2000.

21   Stephen Castles, 'Italians in Australia: building a multicultural society on the Pacific Rim', *Diaspora*, vol. 1, 1991, pp. 52, 54.

22   Lucas, *Community Profiles*.

23   See William Dalrymple, *From the Holy Mountain: A Journey in the Shadow of Byzantium*, Harper Collins, London, 1997, pp. 411, 453.

24   Parkes, letter to *Sydney Morning Herald*, 18 February 1885; address to Federation Conference, Melbourne, 13 February 1890; address to National Australasian Convention, Sydney, 13 March 1891; reprinted in N Meaney, *Australia and the World*, Longman Cheshire, Melbourne, 1985, pp. 77, 105. Parkes, *The Federal Government of Australasia: Speeches Delivered on Various Occasions*, Turner & Henderson, Sydney, 1890, p. 127. Deakin quoted in Kelly, *The End of Certainty*, p. 3. See also Douglas Cole, '"The crimson thread of kinship": ethnic ideas in Australia, 1870–1914', *Historical Studies*, vol.14, 1971, pp. 511–25; Gavin Souter, *Acts of Parliament*, Melbourne University Press, Melbourne, 1988, pp. 57–65.

25   See CEW Bean, *Flagships Three*, Alston Rivers, London, 1913, pp. 209–10; Deakin to Richard Jebb, 4 June 1908, text in Meaney, *Australia and the World*.

26   D Pope, 'Population and Australian economic development, 1900–30', in Maddock & McLean, *The Australian Economy in the Long Run*, p. 33.

27   Kelly, *The End of Certainty*, pp. 2–3.

28   For a good summary of federal attitudes and politics regarding coloured immigration and its restriction, see Souter, *Acts of Parliament*, pp. 57–65.

29   PJ Gibbons in *The Oxford History of New Zealand*, edited by WH Oliver, Clarendon Press, Oxford, 1981, p. 304.

30   PS O'Connor, 'Keeping New Zealand white, 1908–1920', *New Zealand Journal of History*, no. 2, 1968, pp. 41–65.

31   Robert A Huttenback, 'No stranger within the gates: attitudes and policies towards the non-white residents of the British Empire of settlement', *Journal of Imperial and Commonwealth History*, no.1, 1971/72, pp. 271–302.

32   Pilger, 'Swimming for home'.

33   Genaro C Arman, 'Modern nations facing decline in population over the next 50 years', *The Plain Dealer*, 18 August 2004; Bernard Salt, 'Birth rate ensures US remains a superpower', *The Australian*, November 2007.

34   *The Australian*, 20 February 2006.

35   Jupp, *Arrivals and Departures*, p. 179.

36   Robert Birrell, in *Australian and New Zealand Journal of Statistics*, vol. 32, 1996, pp. 105–107.

37   Post-independence evacuation of white farmers from Zimbabwe to Australia was reported in 'Weekend Magazine', *The Australian*, 3 August 2002. See also David Lucas in Jupp (ed.), *The Australian People*. On movements from New Zealand to Australia, see, for instance, A Grimes, L Wevers and G Sullivan (eds), *States of Mind: Australia and New Zealand, 1901–2000*, Wellington, 2002, part 2.

38   Internal migration was no less frenetic. See 'Nomads?: on the move in Australia', *Dialogue*, vol. 24, no. 2 (special issue), 2006.

39   See the summary of recent movements in Stahl et al., *Global Population Movements and their Implications for Australia*, AGPS, Canberra, 1993.

40   On typical numbers of arrivals and departures in Australia in the new century, see Jupp, *From White Australia to Woomera*, pp. 197–202.

41   Frank Thistlethwaite, 'Migration from Europe overseas in the nineteenth and twentieth centuries', in *XIe Congres International des Sciences Historiques: Rapports*, vol. 5, Uppsala, 1960, reprinted in RJ Vercoli and SM Sinke (eds), *A Century of European Migrations, 1830–1930*, Illinois University Press, Urbana, 1991.

42   See Hetty Verolme, *The Children's House of Belsen*, Fremantle Arts Centre Press, Perth, 2000.

43   Dalrymple, *From the Holy Mountain*, pp. 61–62.

44   Michael Dummett, *On Migration and Refugees*, Routledge, London, 2001, p. 31.

45   *Los Angeles Times*, 9 November 2004.

46   *The Australian*, 9 February 2005.

47   *The Age*, 20 May 2000.

48   Klaus J Bade, *Legal and Illegal Immigration into Europe: Experiences and Challenges*, Institute of the Royal Netherlands Academy of Arts and Sciences, Wassenaar, 2003, pp. 11, 31.

49   See Natasha Bita in *The Australian*, 29 July 2002. The political and social problems relating to immigration were common to most OECD countries. The situation in the United Kingdom is superbly accounted in Robert Winder, *Bloody Foreigners: The Story of Immigration to Britain*, Little, Brown, London, 2005.

50   Adam McKeown, 'Global migration, 1846–1940', *Journal of World History*, vol. 15, 2004, pp. 156–57.

51   Michael James Kahan, 'Some Aspects of Immigration and Political Change in Australia since 1947', PhD thesis, University of Michigan, 1972 (xerox edition 1984).

52   'Australia by numbers', *The Independent Weekly*, 8–14 May 2005; *The Australian*, 18 April 2005.

53   Cf. the experience of Latin America since 1960, in Eric Hobsbawm, *Interesting Times*, Allen Lane, London, 2002, pp. 383–84.

54   JC Calwell, *Pushing Back the Frontiers of Death*, Cunningham Lecture, Canberra, 1999.

55   For an important weighing of subjective responses to immigration at the grass roots of Australian society, see Judith Brett & Anthony Moran, *Ordinary People's Politics*, Pluto Press, Melbourne, 2006.

56   Stephen Castles, review of Lack & Templeton, *Bold Experiment*, in *Ethnic and Racial Studies*, vol. 19, 1996, p. 950. See the sardonic and persuasive argument by J Hirst, 'More or less diverse', in Peter Beilharz & Robert Manne (eds), *Reflected Light: La Trobe Essays*, 2006, pp. 39–52. On social cohesion and the meaning of multiculturality, see J Jupp, J Nieuwenhuysen and E Dawson (eds), *Social Cohesion in Australia*, Cambridge University Press, Melbourne, 2007.

57   Cf. 'Slavery, migration and the Atlantic world' and interview with Piet Emmer in *Itinerario*, 30 March 2006, pp. 8–18.

58   See Dirk Hoerder, *Cultures in Contact: World Migrations in the Second Millennium*, Duke University Press, Durham NC, 2002, pp. 442–43.

Select bibliography

There is a growing and increasingly fragmented literature on Australian immigration history. It encompasses much official reportage of policies and statistics; there is also a large political chronicling of the subject. The newspapers and journals of the past century carry most of the basic story as well as the controversies that erupted recurrently. There is also a growing academic study of the subject which draws especially on demography, geography (transforming itself into environmental studies in recent times), sociology, economics, labour studies and, bringing up the rear so to speak, history itself. There is an expanding corpus of important theses, too often neglected in the vaults of university libraries. Running in parallel has been the emergence of a freer and more imaginative evocation of the immigrant experience in art, music, novels, plays and poetry, now a vibrant expression of the effort to understand what immigration has meant for Australian society and its culture. Added to this are the exploding fields of genealogy, oral history and family history, which often contain some of the most personal and penetrating chronicles of the Australian experience at large. Many national groups in Australia have produced their own histories of one sort or another. Finally there is an increasing accumulation of primary documentation in the widening range of archives across Australia and in the countries of the immigrants' origins. Of the archives, often the most exciting items are immigrants' letters and oral recollections, but the scope is much greater, partly because Australia's immigration system has been exceedingly bureaucratised since 1901. All the agencies of government have generated huge amounts of documentation and this is the contemporary historian's joy and burden – swimming or drowning in the ocean of detail.

Destination Australia draws on all these sources, which are far too voluminous to list in detail. There are good guides to be found in the admirable and encyclopaedic *The Australian People*, edited by James Jupp, and especially in the works of Michele Langfield. The National Library and other repositories all contain guides to their collections. Many individuals mentioned in the present account are covered concisely and expertly in the *Australian Dictionary of Biography*, whose volumes chart the passage of each new generation of migrants into the mainstream of Australian life.

The following is a brief list of the most accessible works in the field.

Aarons, Mark, *Sanctuary: Nazi Fugitives in Australia*, Heinemann, Melbourne, 1989.
Adelman, H, A Borowski, M Burstein & L Foster (eds), *Immigration and Refugee Policy: Australia and Canada Compared*, 2 vols, Melbourne University Press, Melbourne, 1994.
Appleyard, RT, *The Ten Pound Immigrants*, Boxtree, London, 1988.
—— *British Emigration to Australia*, Australian National University Press, Canberra, 1964.
Baines, DE, *Emigration from Europe, 1815–1930*, Macmillan, Basingstoke, 1991.
Bell, Martin & Graeme Hugo, *Internal Migration in Australia, 1991–1996*, AusInfo, Canberra, 2000.
Betts, Katharine, *The Great Divide: Immigration Politics in Australia*, Duffy and Snellgrove, Sydney, 1999.
—— *Ideology and Immigration*, Melbourne University Press, Melbourne, 1988.
Black, Peter, *Poms in the Sun*, Travel Book Club, London, 1965.
Bolton, Geoffrey, *A Fine Country to Starve in*, University of Western Australia Press, Perth, 1972.
Brawley, Sean, *The White Peril*, UNSW Press, Sydney, 1995.
Brennan, Frank, *Tampering with Asylum*, University of Queensland Press, Brisbane, 2003.
Brett, Judith, *Australian Liberals and the Moral Middle Class: From Alfred Deakin to John Howard*, Cambridge University Press, Melbourne, 2003.
Brown, Nicholas, *Governing Prosperity*, Cambridge University Press, Melbourne, 1995.

Butler, Roger, *The Europeans: Emigré Artists in Australia, 1930–1960*, National Gallery of Australia, Canberra, 1997.

Butlin, SJ & CB Schedvin, *War Economy 1942–45*, Australian War Memorial, Canberra, 1977.

Castles, Stephen & Mark Miller, *The Age of Migration*, 3rd edn, Palgrave Macmillan, Basingstoke, 2003.

Collins, Jock, 'Asian migration to Australia', in Robin Cohen (ed.), *The Cambridge Survey of World Migration*, Cambridge University Press, New York, 1995.

Constantine, S (ed.), *Emigrants and Empire: British Settlement in the Dominions between the Wars*, Manchester University Press, Manchester, 1990.

Cope, Bill & Mary Kalantzis, *A Place in the Sun: Re-creating the Australian Way of Life*, Harper Collins, Sydney, 2000.

DIMIA (Department of Immigration and Multicultural and Indigenous Affairs), *Immigration: Federation to Century's End, 1901–2000*, Canberra, 2001.

Dyster, B & D Meredith, *Australia in the International Economy in the Twentieth Century*, Cambridge University Press, Cambridge, 1990.

Ganter, Regina, *The Pearl-Shellers of the Torres Strait*, Melbourne University Press, Melbourne, 1994.

Hammerton, AJ & A Thomson, *The Ten Pound Poms: Australia's Invisible Migrants*, Manchester University Press, Manchester, 2005.

Harper, Marjory, *Emigration from Scotland between the Wars*, Manchester University Press, Manchester, 1998.

Hatton, TJ & JG Williamson, *Migration and the International Labour Market, 1850–1939*, Routledge, London, 1994.

Hawthorne, Lesleyanne, *Making It in Australia*, Edward Arnold, Melbourne, 1988.

Hodgins, BW et al. (eds), *Federalism in Canada and Australia: Historical Perspectives*, Trent University, Peterborough, Canada, 1989.

Hoerder, Dirk, *Cultures in Contact: World Migrations in the Second Millennium*, Duke University Press, Durham NC, 2002.

Hicks, Neville, *'This Sin and Scandal': Australia's Population Debate 1891–1911*, Australian National University Press, Canberra, 1978.

Hugo, Graeme, 'A century of population change in Australia', *Year Book Australia 2001*, pp. 169–210.

—— *The Economic Implications of Emigration from Australia*, AGPS, Canberra, 1994.

—— *Australia's Changing Population: Trends and Implications*, Oxford University Press, Melbourne, 1986.

Jayasriya, Laksiri, David Walker & J Gothard (eds), *Legacies of White Australia: Race, Culture and Nation*, University of Western Australia Press, Perth, 2003.

Johnson, JH & Colin Pooley, *The Structure of Nineteenth Century Cities*, Croom Helm, London, 1986.

Jordens, Ann-Mari, *Redefining Australians: Immigration, Citizenship, and National Identity*, Hale & Iremonger, Sydney, 1995.

Jupp, James, *From White Australia to Woomera*, 2nd edn, Cambridge University Press, Melbourne, 2007 [Angus & Robertson, 2002].

—— *Arrivals and Departures*, Cheshire-Lansdowne, Melbourne, 1966.

Jupp, James (ed.), *The Australian People*, revised edn, Cambridge University Press, Cambridge, 2001 [Angus & Robertson, 1988].

—— *Immigration and Multiculturalism: Global Perspectives*, Committee for Economic Development of Australia, Melbourne, 1999.

Kelly, Paul, *The End of Certainty: The Story of the 1980s*, revised edn, Allen & Unwin, Sydney, 1994.

Khoo, Siew-Ean & Peter McDonald, *The Transformation of Australia's Population, 1970–2030*, UNSW Press, Sydney, 2003.

Lack, John & Jacqueline Templeton (eds), *Bold Experiment: A Documentary History of Australian Immigration since 1945*, Oxford University Press, Melbourne, 1995.

Lamidey, Noel W, *Aliens Control in Australia 1939–46*, self-published, Sydney, 1974.

—— *Partial Success: My Years as a Public Servant*, self-published, Sydney, 1970.

Langfield, Michele, *More People Imperative: Immigration to Australia, 1901–39*, National Archives of Australia, Canberra, 1999.

—— 'Recruiting immigrants: the First World War and Australian immigration', *Journal of Australian Studies*, no. 60, 1999.

—— '"Fit for the Elect of the World", Government Policy and Contemporary Opinion about the Encouragement of Immigrants to Australia, 1901–1939', PhD thesis, Monash University, Melbourne, 1988.

Macintyre, Stuart, *The History Wars*, new edn, Melbourne University Press, Melbourne, 2004.

Maddock, R & IW McLean, *The Australian Economy in the Long Run*, Cambridge University Press, Cambridge, 1987.

Markus, Andrew, *Australian Race Relations*, Allen & Unwin, Sydney, 1994.

Martin, Harry, *Angels and Arrogant Gods: Migration Officers and Migrants Reminisce, 1945–85*, AGPS, Canberra, 1989.

Martin, Jean, *The Migrant Presence, Australian Responses 1947–1977*, Allen & Unwin, Sydney, 1978.

—— *Community and Identity: Refugee Groups in Adelaide*, Australian National University Press, Canberra, 1972.

—— *Refugee Settlers*, Australian National University Press, Canberra, 1965.

Menadue, John, *Things You Learn along the Way*, David Lovell, Melbourne, 1999.

Pearl, Cyril, *The Dunera Scandal: Deported by Mistake*, Angus & Robertson, Sydney, 1983.

Powell, JM, *An Historical Geography of Modern Australia*, Cambridge University Press, Cambridge, 1988.

Richards, Eric, 'Migrations: the career of British White Australia', in Deryck Schreuder and Stuart Ward (eds), *Australia's Empire: Oxford History of the British Empire: Companion Series, Australia*, Oxford University Press, Oxford, 2008, pp. 150–75.

—— *Britannia's Children: Emigration from England, Scotland, Wales and Ireland, 1600–2000*, Hambledon & London, London, 2004.

Roe, Michael, *Australia, Britain, and Migration, 1915–1940: A Study of Desperate Hopes*, Cambridge University Press, Cambridge, 1995.

Rubinstein, WD (ed.), *Jews in the Sixth Continent*, Allen & Unwin, Sydney, 1987.

Santow, Gigi, WD Borrie & Lado Ruzicka (eds), *Landmarks in Australian Population History*, Australian Population Association, Melbourne, 1988.

Shergold, PR & Frances Milne (eds), *The Great Immigration Debate*, Federation of Ethnic Communities' Councils of Australia, Sydney, 1984.

Sherington, G, *Australia's Immigrants, 1788–1988*, Allen & Unwin, Sydney, 1990.

Sluga, Glenda, *Bonegilla: A Place of No Hope*, History Department, University of Melbourne, Melbourne, 1988.

Tavan, Gwenda, *The Long, Slow Death of White Australia*, Scribe, Melbourne, 2005.

Viviani, Nancy, *The Indochinese in Australia, 1975–1995: From Burnt Boats to Barbecues*, Oxford University Press, Melbourne, 1996.

Walsh, Kate, *The Changing Face of Australia: A Century of Immigration 1901–2000*, Allen & Unwin, Sydney, 2001.

Ward, Stuart, *Australia and the British Embrace: The Demise of the Imperial Ideal*, Melbourne University Press, Melbourne, 2001.

York, Barry, *Speaking of Us*, National Library of Australia, Canberra, 1999.

—— *Michael Cigler: A Czech-Australian Story*, Centre for Immigration and Multicultural Studies, Australian National University, Canberra, 1995

Index

Aborigines 9, 18, 20, 24, 27, 50, 66, 135, 146, 238, 240
Adams, Grantley 237
advertising 48, 82, 94, 104, 112
Affleck, William 359
Afghan refugees 328–30
agreements (bilateral) 132, 160, 186, 190, 217–18, 229
Alexander, Albert Victor 130
Amery, Leopold Charles MS (Leo) 90, 93
Anti-German League 67
anti-immigrant feeling 105, 108, 124, 208
anti-Semitism 73, 139, 142, 148, 182
Argentina 44, 124, 149, 255
Argus 95, 97, 395
Arthur, Richard 44
Asian migration 18, 36, 54–5, 256, 260–62, 265, 269, 280, 281–96, 311
assimilation 151, 167, 189, 192, 206–9, 225, 234–41, 249
assisted migration 14, 20–1, 32, 43, 45, 82, 87–8, 93, 105, 131–32, 160, 164, 172, 182, 216–17, 220–21, 242–43, 248, 254, 271, 395, 408, 411
Assisted Passage Act (1938) 132
Atchison, John H 309
atomic warfare 171, 202

Attard, Emmanuel 116
attitudes of migrants 191, 200
Attlee, Clement Richard 174
Auschwitz 168
Australia: demographic capacity 53, 345–46
  economy 11, 12, 13, 17, 19, 20, 22–4, 85, 113–116, 127, 145, 156–57, 210, 242, 301, 325, 338, 343, 415
  empty spaces 92, 128, 138, 141, 151, 153, 155
  population: composition 12, 14, 25, 64, 81, 109, 110, 126, 213, 226, 270, 315, 317, 342, 364, 392
  population: predictions 73, 89, 90, 93, 106, 129, 154, 164, 169, 177, 180, 187, 201, 242, 267, 291, 346–47, 394, 416
  population: statistics 9, 14, 20, 22, 34, 45, 77, 97–8, 128, 159, 161, 204, 212, 226, 317
Australia House (London) 172, 187
Australian 278
Australian immigration: distinctive features 351–53
Australian Labor Party 37, 106, 164, 176, 179, 256–57

Australian Settlement 19, 369
Australian Worker 109
Austria 218
Austrians 220
Austro-Hungarians 67, 79
Ayr (Queensland) 51

backpackers 342, 376
Baldwin, Stanley 89
Balfour, Arthur 54
Balfour, Cecil 360
Bali 314
Baltic immigrants 183, 186
Bannon, John Charles 17
Barnardo scheme 103
Barton, Edmund 17, 49, 54
Barwell boys 103
Bathurst 61
Baxter Detention Centre 333
Beauchamp, Earl 11
Bean, Charles WE 36, 58, 66, 361–62, 367
Belgian immigrants 172
Belgium 58, 218
Belshaw, JP 171
Beograd (Belgrade) 225
Betts, Katharine 311
Bicester 61
birth rate 14, 34, 39, 72, 136-37, 154, 179,
    201, 324, 327
Birmingham 43
Birrell, Robert 325, 376
Blainey, Geoffrey 18, 25, 284–88, 292,
    293, 295, 316
Bland, HA 231
Blewett, Neal 274, 306-7
boat people 246, 260–61, 276, 280, 282,
    296, 299, 303, 305, 311, 331–32,
    413
Boer War 15, 59
Bolshevism 79
Bolton, Geoffrey 104, 248
Bonegilla 167, 195–98, 226–30
Booth, William 38
Borrie, WD 192, 210
Bosworth, Richard 229
Boxer rebellion 15
Bonython, Sir John Langdon 37
Boy Scouts 44, 103
Brennan, Father Frank 333–35
'Bring out a Briton' campaign 212, 216, 221,
    234

British Columbia 371
British Commonwealth 163, 202
British immigrants 77, 161, 191, 199–203,
    205, 208–9, 213, 215, 248, 279,
    315–16, 324, 360–66
Broome 135, 146
Brown, Nicholas 210
Bruce, Stanley Melbourne 91, 100, 106,
    108
Bulgarian immigrants 79, 253
Bulletin 37, 42
Burdekin (Qld) 52
Bureau of Immigration Research 303
Burke, Edmund 163
Burnside, Kennedy 29
Business Council of Australia 340

Cairo 49
California 44
Calwell, Arthur Augustus 143, 150, 176,
    210, 212, 218, 228, 248, 270, 326,
    345, 405
    and European migration 175–87
    Minister for Immigration 161, 164–65,
    175–87, 215
    opinions 177, 199–200, 202, 250–51,
    359
    and White Australia 178, 180, 191–93,
    248, 255, 257, 369
Cambodian immigrants 296, 309
Cambridgeshire 60
Cameron, Clyde Robert 296
Campbell, Graeme 308
camps and hostels 185, 195–98, 223, 226–
    30, 408
Canada 24, 33, 40, 57, 61, 94, 172, 258,
    289, 380, 395
Cantamessa, Joe 142
capital 112, 119, 120
Cardus, Neville 132–33
Carr, Robert John (Bob) 25
Carrington, Lord 279
Carr-Saunders, AM 129, 137
Casey, Richard Gavin Gardiner 153
Castrisson, James 55
Central Emigration Board 43
Central (Unemployed) Board 43
chain migration 30, 55–6, 248
Chang, Arthur Gar-Lock 193
Chapman, Eva-Maria 189
Charters Towers (Qld) 28

Chifley, Joseph Benedict (Ben) 108, 164, 179, 199
Child Emigration Society (Fairbridge Society) 44, 103, 395
child migration 95, 160–61, 180
Chile 254–55, 260, 313
Chinese 18, 20, 34, 35, 66, 192, 201, 277, 305–6, 342, 367
Chubut 69
Churchill, Winston Spencer 145
Citizens Conventions 230
citizenship 411
Clare, County 30–1
Clark, Colin 211
Clark, Charles Manning Hope 284, 307
Clarke, Sir Francis Grenville (Frank) 148
Clayton, William 3, 4, 5
climate 44
Clune, Frank 171
coal 129
Coghlan, Timothy A 10, 18, 21, 34, 40, 53
cohesion 244–50
Cold War 189
Colombo 110
Colombo Plan 239, 241, 256
Colonial Office 74
Communism 189–90, 225, 229-30, 262, 309
convicts 11, 35
conscription 67
Contarino, Sam 86–7
Coolidge, Calvin 81
Coombs, HC ('Nugget') 159, 180, 357
Copley, Samuel W 74
Coptic immigrants 365
Corden, Max 344
Cossack (WA) 20
cost of migration schemes 91, 107, 117, 131–32, 216, 241, 413
Cowen, Sir Zelman 244–45
crime 15, 107, 189
Cross, Sir Ronald 144
Culham (WA) 85
Culotta, Nino 206–7
Curtin, John 143–45, 151, 160, 163, 177, 180
Cuthbertson, Margaret 43
Czechoslovak immigrants 185–86
Czechoslovakia 219

Dachau 168

Dalrymple, Rawdon 347
Dalrymple, William 378
Danish immigrants 59, 172
Dantra, Colonel 39
Darbyshire, Douglas 5–7
Darwin 144
Darwin, Charles 18
Davis, Esther 56
Davis family 181
Dawkins, John 306
Deakin, Alfred 17, 38, 42, 48, 367, 369
defence 19, 21, 54, 90, 128, 141, 143–45, 157, 164, 176–77, 366-68
Denmark 218
Depression 28, 33, 102, 113–16, 119, 120–123, 166
Development and Migration Commission 92, 110
dictation test 19, 37, 39, 49, 50, 68, 107, 124–26, 193–94, 238
diseases 13, 29, 34, 66, 88, 310
Displaced Persons 185, 217, 405, 406
dissatisfaction of migrants 101, 105, 106, 117, 124, 198, 229
domestic servants 47, 48, 64, 105, 121, 123, 135
Dominions 33, 38, 172
Dominions Royal Commission 70, 79
Donnybrook (WA) 149
Dorman and Long 98,
Downer, Sir Alexander Russell 213
'Dreadnought' scheme 44, 103, 395
drought 10, 38, 146, 393
Dunera episode 151
Dutch immigrants 172, 182, 186, 191, 212, 217, 220, 222
Dyster, Barrie 221
Duckles family 29, 42
Durham 63, 65

Eastern Europe 220, 225
Economist 171
Edinburgh 221
education 34, 170, 192, 242
Edwards, Peter 223
Eggleston, Sir Frederic 93, 369
Egyptian immigrants 224
elections 107, 108
Elizabeth (SA) 205, 364
Ellis Island 56
El Salvador 277, 327

Empire (British) 33, 40, 70, 87–93, 103, 112, 119, 164, 203
Empire Emigration Development Conference 132
Empire Settlement Act (1925) 99, 118, 138, 160
Ener, Yalcin 224
environment 26
eugenics 36
European Economic Community 248
European immigration 138, 155, 161, 165, 178, 183, 186
Europeanisation 183, 191, 223
Evatt, Herbert Vere 109, 152–53, 236
Evian Conference 139
expenditure 118
ex-service personnel 172, 179, 187

Fabinyi, Andrew 266–67
Fadden, Arthur 212, 406
Fairbridge Society: see Child Emigration Society
fares 48, 61, 82, 83, 160, 399
farming 29, 85, 90, 113–17
Fascism 229
Federation 15–22, 39
Fenner, Frank 347
Ferry Commission 108
fertility 34, 156, 169, 346–47, 381
Fiji 194
FitzGerald Committee 289–93
FitzGerald, Stephen 289
Fitzhardinge, LF 76
Flannery, Tim 346
Ford Motor Works (Geelong) 231, 232
Forde, Francis Michael (Frank) 143, 179
foreign aid 336
Forest, Alexander 84
Forsyth, WD 153–56, 178
France 59, 61
Fraser, John Malcolm 246, 253, 259–61, 268, 269, 272, 278–79, 286, 309, 346
Freeland League 150–51, 154
Fremantle 5, 29
French immigrants 69, 172

Gaita, Raimond 167–68, 196, 207
Gaita, Romulus 167–68
Galbally Report (1978) 293
Galleghan, Sir Frederick 194–95

Gallipoli 60
Gamboa, Sergeant Lorenzo 193
Gepp, Sir Herbert 92, 118, 119
Gepps Cross Hostel 227
German immigrants 59, 67, 79, 143, 187, 188, 191–92, 202, 217, 220
Germany 21, 54, 139, 187–88, 190, 218
Giblin, LF 120–21, 128, 158, 160
Glasgow 41, 48, 85
Glyn, RGC 118
gold rushes 2, 20, 352
Goldfinch, Sir Philip 135–36
Goldhar, Pinchas 207
Gollan, Robin 57
Goodge, WT 55
Goodman, Benny 33
Gorton, Senator John 237
Graf, Ervin 299
Grassby, Albert Jaime (Al) 365
Great Britain: migration policy 87, 93, 137, 181, 216, 240, 248
Greece 218, 223
Greek immigrants 39, 55, 67, 69, 234
Gregory, JW 129
Gregory, Robert (Bob) 326
group settlement 104, 105, 149–50
Gruen, Fred 152
Gullett, Henry Baynton 175
Gullett, Sir Henry Somer 89, 94

Hackett, Arthur 83
Haggard, H Rider 48, 70–74, 89, 90,
Hamilton (Vic) 62
Hammerstein, Oscar 33
Hand, Gerard (Gerry) 305–7, 309
Hanson, Pauline 295, 312, 327, 342
Hawke, Robert James Lee (Bob) 181, 263, 273–74, 277, 286, 289, 292, 295–96, 305, 309
Hay (NSW) 152
Haylen Report (1946) 178
health 15, 224–25
Heffernan, Senator Bill 333
Henderson, Gerard 312
Herbert River (Qld) 108, 142
Herzfeld, Paul 142
Heydon, Sir Peter 219, 220, 225–26, 237, 239–42
Heyes, Sir Tasman 183, 200, 219
Hicks, Neville 34
Higman, BW 136

Hindoos 49
Holland 54, 132, 166, 189, 190, 222
Holman, William Arthur 74
Holocaust 175
Holt, Harold Edward 213, 217, 239, 258, 406, 407
Hong Kong 49
Hope, Alec Derwent 8
House of Commons 117
Howard, John Winston 281, 288, 294, 322, 329, 334–35, 341, 374
Hughes, Helen 291
Hughes, William Morris (Billy) 49, 53, 68, 74, 75, 76, 77, 88, 104, 109, 368
Hugo, Graeme 303
humanitarian concerns 298, 304, 309–10, 378
Humanitarian Program 317–18, 340
Hungarian immigrants 79, 185–86, 208, 218, 223, 235
Hunter Valley (NSW) 30
Huntington, Samuel F 347
Huttenback, Robert A 370

Immigration, Department of 161, 219–220, 227
immigration: planning 26–7, 36, 75, 76, 88, 91–3, 101–2, 119, 153–65, 170, 180, 187, 199, 210, 275, 305–10
immigration: points system (1982) 411
Immigration Reform Group 241
Immigration Restriction Act 21, 127, 352
immigration statistics 32–3, 45, 108, 119, 124, 219–21, 322–23, 341, 344–45, 395, 397, 408, 414, 416
immigrants illegal 108, 277, 280, 314, 334–35, 379, 413
indentured labour 37, 38
India 100, 222
Indonesia 179, 182
Indonesians 193, 222
industrialisation 81, 100, 129, 134, 145, 154–55, 157, 203, 211
Ingham (Qld) 131, 142
integration 254, 266
intermarriage 44, 81, 223, 242, 266–67, 342
IRO 182, 185
internment 67, 142–43, 147, 151–52, 296, 308–9, 314
Iraq 304, 313

Iraqi immigrants 329–30
Ireland 30, 43, 99, 218
Irish immigrants 8, 45, 79, 191, 352, 363
Irish Republican Army 279
Irving, Helen 17
Isaacs, Sir Isaac 245
Italian immigrants 37, 40, 69, 82, 87, 94, 106–9, 124, 127, 142–43, 149, 151, 157, 217, 221, 228–29, 249
Italy 32, 44, 70, 107, 190, 229

Janky, Peter 51
Japan 53, 75–6, 80, 122, 124, 142, 150, 179
Japanese 20, 34, 52, 143–46, 164, 183, 191, 201, 221, 264
Jardine, Douglas 118
Jarrett, Margaret 181
Jay, R 126–27
Jewish immigrants 25, 56, 59, 139–40, 142, 147–49, 150–51, 174–75, 185, 192, 207, 244–45
Jolley, Elizabeth 205
Jupp, James 218, 312, 358, 375, 415

Kalgoorlie (WA) 16, 39, 67, 124
Kamenka, Eugene 175
Kanakas see Pacific Islanders
Keating, Paul John 301, 307–09
Keen, Robert 85, 113–16, 169
Kelly, Paul 272, 281, 309, 343, 369
Kent Colonisation Society 43
Keynes, John Maynard 163
Kiddle, George 188
Kipling, Rudyard 44, 85, 86, 361
Kirkpatrick, John 'Simpson' 65
Kisch, Egon 125
Kitchener, Lord 74
Klaphake, Wolf 143
Knibbs, Sir George Handley 77, 394
Knightly, Phillip 181, 195
Knopfelmacher, Frank 293
Korngold, Henry 298
Kosovo 311, 313
Kurri-Kurri (NSW) 30

labour 35, 36, 98, 105, 106, 112, 297, 352, 394, 395
Labor Party 16, 394
Lamidey, Noel W 171, 180
Land 82

land settlement 26, 40, 41, 45, 71, 72, 74, 77, 82–3, 97, 101–4, 116–7, 178, 358–60
landing fees 124
Lane, William 35
Lang, John Thomas (Jack) 67
Langfield, Michele 138
Larwood, Harold 118
Latvian immigrants 185, 377
Laurier, Wilfrid 71
Lawson, Sir Harry Sutherland Wightman 126
Lawson, Henry 369
Le, Hieu Van 246–47
League of Nations 76
Lebanon 218, 277
Lee Kwan Yu 240, 264, 282
Lewis, Roy 196
Liberal governments 213, 278–79, 288, 327–28
Liberman, Chaim 298
literacy 14, 31
Lithuanian immigrants 185
Liverani family 361
living standards 23, 34, 37, 63, 83, 87, 106, 121, 384
Lloyd George, David 76, 87
Loan Plan (1924) 91–2
loans 91, 95, 101, 398
London 59, 60
Long Boom 210, 213, 250
Loveday (SA) 147
Lubbers, Rudolphus 337
Lucas, Lord 79
Lynge, J 130
Lynch, Phillip 252
Lynn, Elva 221
Lyons, Joseph Aloysius 130–32, 136

McArthur, Ian 253
McCallum, Senator JA 236
McDonald, Peter 323, 344–45
McEwen, Sir John (Jack) 236
Macedonia 225
Mackinder, Sir Halford 89
Macmillan, Harold 228
McNicoll, Geoffrey 346
Macphee, Ian 278–79
Maddison, Angus 12
Mahathir Mohamad 347
Maldon 167

Maltese 44, 68, 82, 106, 109, 116
Malthusianism 18
Manchester 278
mandatory detention 296
Manne, Robert 263
Manning, Frank 30
Mannix, Archbishop Daniel 68, 123, 137, 179
manpower see labour
manufacturing 123, 134, 157, 205
Market Harborough 98
Martin, Jean 198
Marx brothers 33
Massey, WH 39
Masters and Servants Act 50
Mayer, Henry 152
Melanesia 50–1,
Menadue, John 259, 263–64, 278–81
Menzies, Dame Pattie 211
Menzies, Sir Robert Gordon (Bob) 129, 172, 174, 192–93, 210–12, 214, 236–37, 239, 250 , 363, 369
Miles, Edward 83,
Mitchison, Rosalind 77
mobility 24, 26
Monash, Sir John 59
Mongolia 35
Monk, Albert 181
Moore, Clive 51
Morris, Dave 28
mortality rate 14
Moruya 98
motives for emigration 83, 86, 104, 375
multiculturalism 24, 253, 258, 272, 288, 307, 311, 348, 408
Muramatsu family 20
Murdoch, Sir Keith 89
Murdoch, Walter 150
Muslim immigrants 299, 301

Natal 19, 49, 371
Nation 257
National Health and Research Council 169
National Population Inquiry (1975) 267
nationalism 17
Nazis 139, 142–43, 151, 167–68, 189–90, 194–95
Nauru 335, 339
Negroes 49, 153
New Australia 182, 191

New Caledonia 68
New Guinea 51, 144–45,
New South Wales 101
New Zealand 29, 62, 82, 124, 172, 370
New Zealand immigrants 302
Newton, Maxwell 259
nomination schemes 42, 45, 97, 98, 99, 243
Northam (WA) 149
Northcote, Lord 54
Northern Australia 20, 130, 178
Northern Ireland 30
Northern Territory 52, 89, 110, 135
Norwegian immigrants 172
NUMAS 275

OECD countries 23–4, 302, 313, 368, 373,
        381, 418
O'Keefe case 193
O'Malley, King 37, 49
opinion polls 172, 190–91, 215
Opperman, Hubert Ferdinand 219
opposition to immigration 35–39, 67, 105,
        110
Orange (NSW) 143
Osborne (WA) 107
Oversea Settlement Board 133, 138

Pacific Islanders 37, 38, 48, 50–52,
Pacific Islands Labourers Act (1901) 51
'Pacific Solution' 335
Page, Sir Earle CG, 129
Palmer, Vance 369
Pan-Asian conference (1947) 236
Papua New Guinea 335
Parkes, Sir Henry 366–67
Patagonia 44
Pax Britannica 11, 89,
Peacock, Andrew Sharp 273, 288
Pearl Harbor 145, 163
pearling 20, 5, 135, 146–47
Peel, Mark 205
Pennington hostel 247, 262
petitions 117
Polish immigrants 168, 172, 183, 185, 189,
        209, 253
Pope, David 99, 100, 107
Port Hedland 333
post-European Australia 348–49
Prasad, Nancy 238
Pratt, Richard 298, 346
Prest, Wilfred 211

Price, Charles A 312, 342
protectionism 17, 19, 23, 31, 35, 37, 395
public health 121

quality of immigrants 91, 104, 176
Queensland 15, 37, 73, 74
quotas 106, 109, 138, 148, 302

racism 19, 35, 36, 39, 48, 80, 81, 89, 107,
        109, 123, 139–40, 246, 295, 370
Razak, Mohammed 193
recruitment of immigrants 39, 42, 43, 75,
        82, 88, 92, 94–100, 104, 111, 171,
        181, 187–91, 215–23, 225, 267, 405
refugees 139–40, 148, 150, 152, 168–75,
        182, 200, 245, 258–63, 276, 280–
        81, 296, 309, 311, 313, 319, 322,
        327–40, 378–79, 413
religion 97, 113, 232–34, 235, 378
Rendlesham, Lord 62
return migration 28, 30, 86, 103, 116–17,
        221, 228, 252, 271, 384
Rhodesia 237, 279
Richmond (Vic) 310
Riemer, Andrew 208
Riverina (NSW) 60
Roberts, Stephen 109
Rockhampton (Qld) 61
Rockingham (WA) 364
Roe, Michael 101, 103, 359
Romanian immigrants 167–68, 253
Roosevelt, Franklin Delano 225
Roosevelt, Theodore 71, 72
Rossen, Flora 56
Round Table 93
Round Table 37
Royal Colonial Institute 73, 74
royal commissions 34, 97
Royal Irish Constabulary 99
Rubery Owen 203
'rural myth' 92, 119
Ryan, Mick 263
Ruddock, Philip 281, 313, 327–29, 358
Russia 32, 54, 189, 244–45
Russian immigrants 69, 82
Russo, Antonio 321

Sadiq, Mohammed 193
Salt, Bernard 327, 373
Salvation Army 44, 73, 97, 102, 118, 133
Scandinavia 43, 191

Schutzstaffel (SS) 194–95
Scotland 44, 110
Scottish immigrants 56, 82, 98, 110
Scullin, James Henry 105–6, 110
selection criteria 275, 289
Serbian immigrants 70
Serle, Geoffrey 189, 244–45
Shaw, Artie 33
Shergold, Peter 253, 288
shipping 42, 182, 185, 221
ships:
    Arabia 68
    Australis 188, 247
    Castel Felice 221, 246
    Cornwall 5, 81
    Dunera 151
    Fairsea 221
    Flaminia 222
    Gange 68
    General Heintzelman 183
    Grand Trianon 3
    Hobson's Bay 110, 111
    Johan De Witt 175
    Largs Bay 181, 187
    Omar 86
    Orsova 29
    Ranchi 208–9
Sinclair, WA 119
Singapore 144
Sinn Fein 79
Six Hatters case 38–9
skilled immigrants 340–41, 376
Smith, FB 121
Smuts, Jan 76
Snedden, Sir Billy Mackie 271
Snowy Mountains Hydro-Electricity
    Scheme 189, 195–96, 199, 217
soldier settlement 73, 74, 75, 78, 88, 134
Solomon Islands 51
South Africa 124, 172, 190, 236–37
South America 220, 254–55
South Australia 102, 357
Spain 32, 218, 222
Spanish immigrants 69
Spectator 36
Sri Lanka 277
Steinberg, Isaac Nachman 150–51
Steketee, Mike 328
Stelling, Hans Max 39
Stephen, James 18
Stewart, Cameron 309

Stone, Jonathan 129
Stravinsky, Igor 33
Streaky Bay (SA) 62
Strikwerda, Carl 120
Suffolk 62
sugar industry 37, 50–1, 61, 70, 86, 130
suicide 117
Sweden 223
Switzerland 132
Sydney Harbour Bridge 98

Tampa episode 330–35
Tasmania 74, 95, 124, 183, 217
Tatura 143, 147, 152
Taylor, AM 37
Taylor, T. Griffith 129–30
Temporary Protection Visas 328, 337
terrorism 265
Theodore, Edward Granville (Ted) 73
Thursday Island 52
Timor 260, 313
Torrens Island 67, 78
Torrisi, Giuseppe 149
Townley, Athol Gordon 212
Townsville (Qld) 61
Tozer, Sir Horace 40
trade 89, 122, 131–32
trade unions 19, 35, 38, 98, 106, 107, 109,
    176, 181, 230–31
Tran brothers 283
Trecastagni 149
Truong, Huy 299
Trustees and Investors Review 40
Truth 193
Turkey 218, 220, 224
Turkish immigrants 67, 274, 299–301
Twain, Mark 360

Uganda 237
Ukrainian immigrants 185, 189
unemployment 11, 35, 42, 87, 106, 108, 117,
    120, 121, 123, 145, 151, 158, 176,
    179, 229, 250–51, 310, 325, 411
United Nations 219, 337–38, 378
United Nations Relief and Rehabilitation
    Administration 161
United States of America 32–3, 37, 38, 40,
    57, 80, 81, 90, 94–5, 106, 122, 124,
    144–45, 152–53, 163, 347, 373
  immigrants from 172
universities 16

urbanisation 13, 15, 42, 45, 77, 97, 99, 100, 154, 211
Uruguay 255

Vancouver 62
Vanstone, Senator Amanda 328, 330, 337
Vernon Report (1965) 214, 250
Versailles, Treaty 80
Victoria 100, 101, 102, 187
Victoria Creek (Williamstown) 4
Victorian Royal Commission 101, 118
Vietnam 250
Vietnam War 259–60, 296
Vietnamese immigrants 246, 276–77, 280, 282–84, 299, 309–10
voyages 5, 29, 246

wages 28, 36, 37, 60, 83, 85, 87, 103, 120, 123, 135
Wakefield, Edward Gibbon 326
Walker, David Esdaile 201–2
Walsh, Peter 273–74
Walwitz, Ania 209
war brides 66, 193
war: casualties 64, 76–7, 92,
War Crimes Amendment Act (1988) 195
Watson, Don 307
Webb, Sidney 16
Wells, HG 56–7, 90, 141–42
Welsh immigrants 50, 69
Wensing, Petronella 166–67
Western Australia 29, 59, 61, 85, 90, 102, 104, 113, 116–17, 133, 149
West Indians 49, 194
White Australia 10, 19, 34, 36, 40, 55, 57, 78, 82–112, 394
White Australia policy
  administration of 109, 152–53, 183
  and assimilation 234–41
  effects 32, 37, 66, 146
  end 244–68, 354–55
  and international relations 124, 152–53, 192, 307, 263–64, 356
  and planning 78–79, 135, 180, 183
  rationale 19, 36, 40, 48, 57, 67–68, 76, 142, 146, 174, 177–78, 192, 354, 356, 395
White, TW 139
Whitlam, E Gough 251, 254, 260–61, 296, 309, 355
Wickens, Charles Henry 81, 93, 128, 158
Willesee, Senator Donald 296
Williams, Robyn 246
Willis, Ralph 307
Wilson, HV 123
Windschuttle, Keith 395
Wise, Bernhard Ringrose 54
Withers, Glenn 341, 344
Wolfensohn, James 336
Wolfsohn, Henry 152
Wolverhampton 133
women 5, 34, 98, 183
Wood, GL 179
Woolcott, Richard 335
Woomera Detention Centre (SA) 314, 333, 339
Worker 42
working conditions 16, 19, 231
World Bank 336
Woy, Hedley Tong 66

xenophobia 67, 191

Yallourn (Vic) 187
Yalta Conference 189
'Yellow Peril' 71, 142, 144, 159, 169, 313, 348, 368
yeomen 40, 100, 359
YMCA 97,
Yorkshire 4, 29, 62
Yugoslavia 167, 218, 223, 253
  immigrants from: 185

Zubrzycki, Jerzy 293
Zunini, Leopoldo 149

FSC
Mixed Sources
Product group from well-managed forests and other controlled sources

Cert no. SGS-COC-004233
www.fsc.org
© 1996 Forest Stewardship Council

Text paper 70gsm Enso
Mixed sources product group from well-managed forests and other controlled sources. Forest Stewardship Council © 1996 FSC A.C. www.fsc.org promotes environmentally responsible, socially beneficial and economically viable management of the world's forests.

Coverboard 265gsm Candesce